久保帯人

recent photo of author

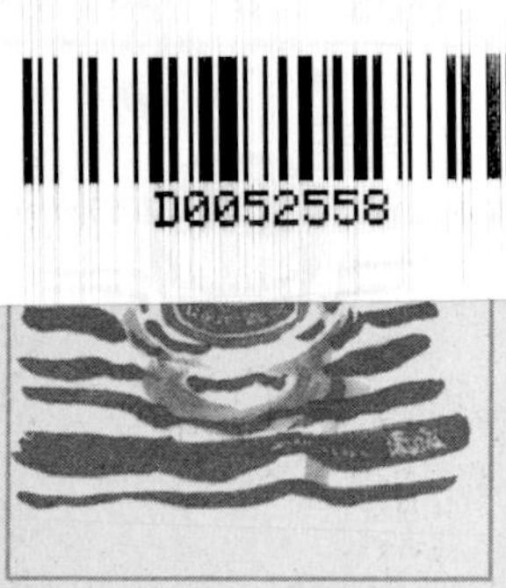

Since I moved here last year, my landlord next door has taken a real liking to me. His wife even cooks for me. The food's great and I'm thankful, but I feel bad because I've never told them that I can't eat onions.

Tite Kubo

BLEACH is author Tite Kubo's second title. Kubo made his debut with *ZOMBIE POWDER*, a four-volume series for *WEEKLY SHONEN JUMP*. To date, *BLEACH* has been translated into numerous languages and has also inspired an animated TV series that began airing in Japan in 2004. Beginning its serialization in 2001, *BLEACH* is still a mainstay in the pages of *WEEKLY SHONEN JUMP*.

BLEACH
Vol. 7: THE BROKEN CODA
The SHONEN JUMP Graphic Novel Edition

STORY AND ART BY
TITE KUBO

English Adaptation/Lance Caselman
Translation/Joe Yamazaki
Touch-Up Art & Lettering/Dave Lanphear
Design/Sean Lee
Editor/Kit Fox

Managing Editor/Elizabeth Kawasaki
Director of Production/Noboru Watanabe
Vice President of Publishing/Alvin Lu
Vice President & Editor in Chief/Yumi Hoashi
Sr. Director of Acquisitions/Rika Inouye
Vice President of Sales & Marketing/Liza Coppola
Publisher/Hyoe Narita

Printed in the U.S.A.

Published by VIZ, LLC
P.O. Box 77010
San Francisco, CA 94107

SHONEN JUMP Graphic Novel Edition
10 9 8 7 6 5 4 3 2 1
First printing, May 2005

We should not shed tears
That is a surrender of the body to the heart
It is only proof
That we are beings that do not know
What to do with our hearts

BLEACH 7 THE BROKEN CODA

Shonen Jump Graphic Novel

STARS AND

Rukia Kuchiki

Orihime Inoue

Ichigo Kurosaki

plot

Fifteen-year-old Ichigo "Strawberry" Kurosaki can see ghosts. Otherwise, he was a typical (?) high school student until the day a Hollow—a malevolent lost soul—came to eat him, and the Soul Reaper Rukia Kuchiki stepped into his life. To defeat the Hollow and save his family, Ichigo let Rukia transfer some of her Soul Reaper powers to him. But when Rukia was left powerless, she recruited Ichigo for her war against the murderous, soul-gobbling Hollows.

In mid-duel, Ichigo and Uryû Ishida, the Quincy, team up to fight the gigantic Menos Grande. In the process, Ichigo discovers latent power he was not aware of! In the aftermath of the battle, Rukia decides she has lingered in this world long enough. But things take a disturbing turn when she finds herself face to face with two hunters from the Soul Society!!

BLEACH ALL

柊木白哉
Byakuya Kuchiki

浦原喜助
Kisuke Urahara

Renji Abarai

阿散井恋次

STORIES

BLEACH 7
THE BROKEN CODA

Contents

53. Nice to meet you. (I will beat you.)

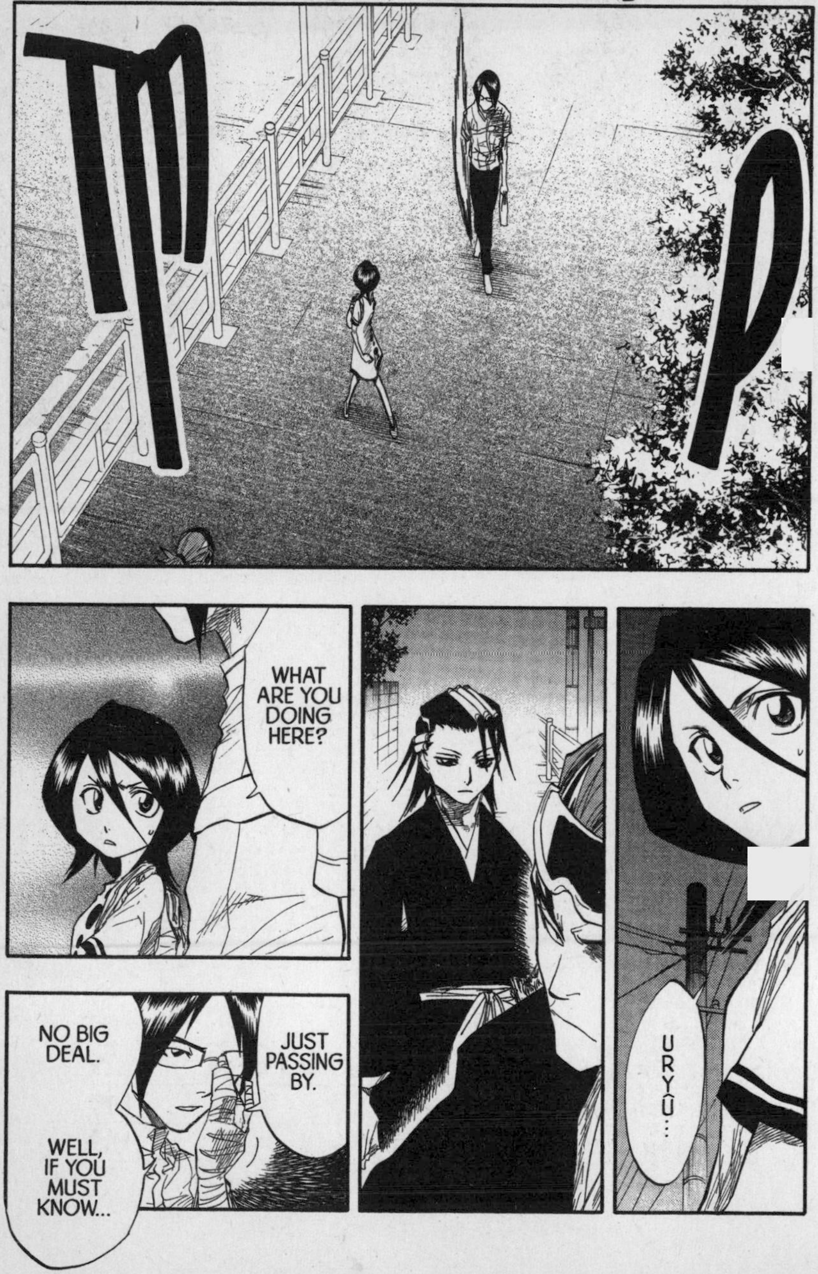
TMP
URYÛ...
WHAT ARE YOU DOING HERE?
JUST PASSING BY.
NO BIG DEAL.
WELL, IF YOU MUST KNOW...

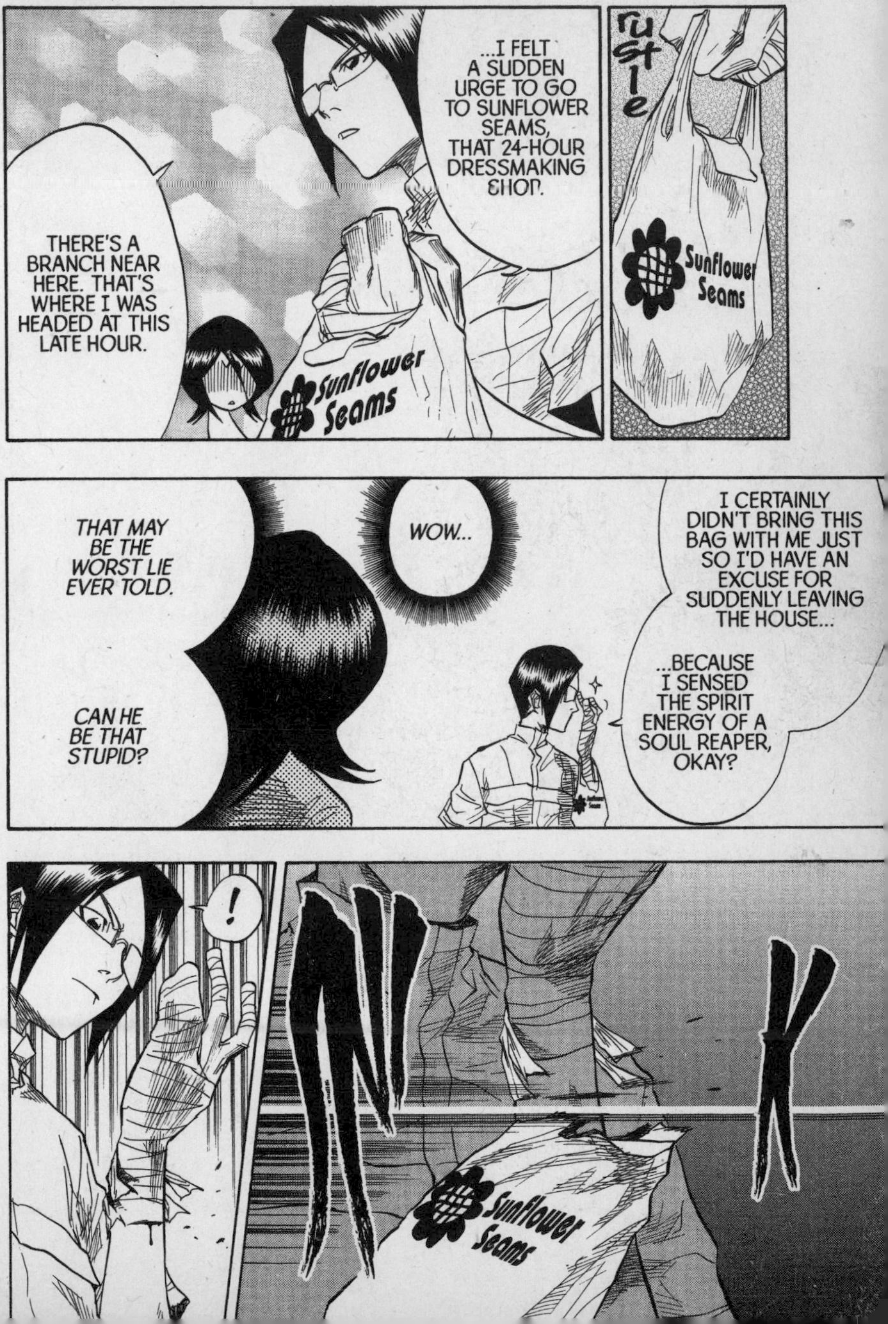
rustle
Sunflower Seams
...I FELT A SUDDEN URGE TO GO TO SUNFLOWER SEAMS, THAT 24-HOUR DRESSMAKING SHOP.
THERE'S A BRANCH NEAR HERE. THAT'S WHERE I WAS HEADED AT THIS LATE HOUR.
Sunflower Seams
I CERTAINLY DIDN'T BRING THIS BAG WITH ME JUST SO I'D HAVE AN EXCUSE FOR SUDDENLY LEAVING THE HOUSE...
...BECAUSE I SENSED THE SPIRIT ENERGY OF A SOUL REAPER, OKAY?
WOW...
THAT MAY BE THE WORST LIE EVER TOLD.
CAN HE BE THAT STUPID?
Sunflower Seams
!

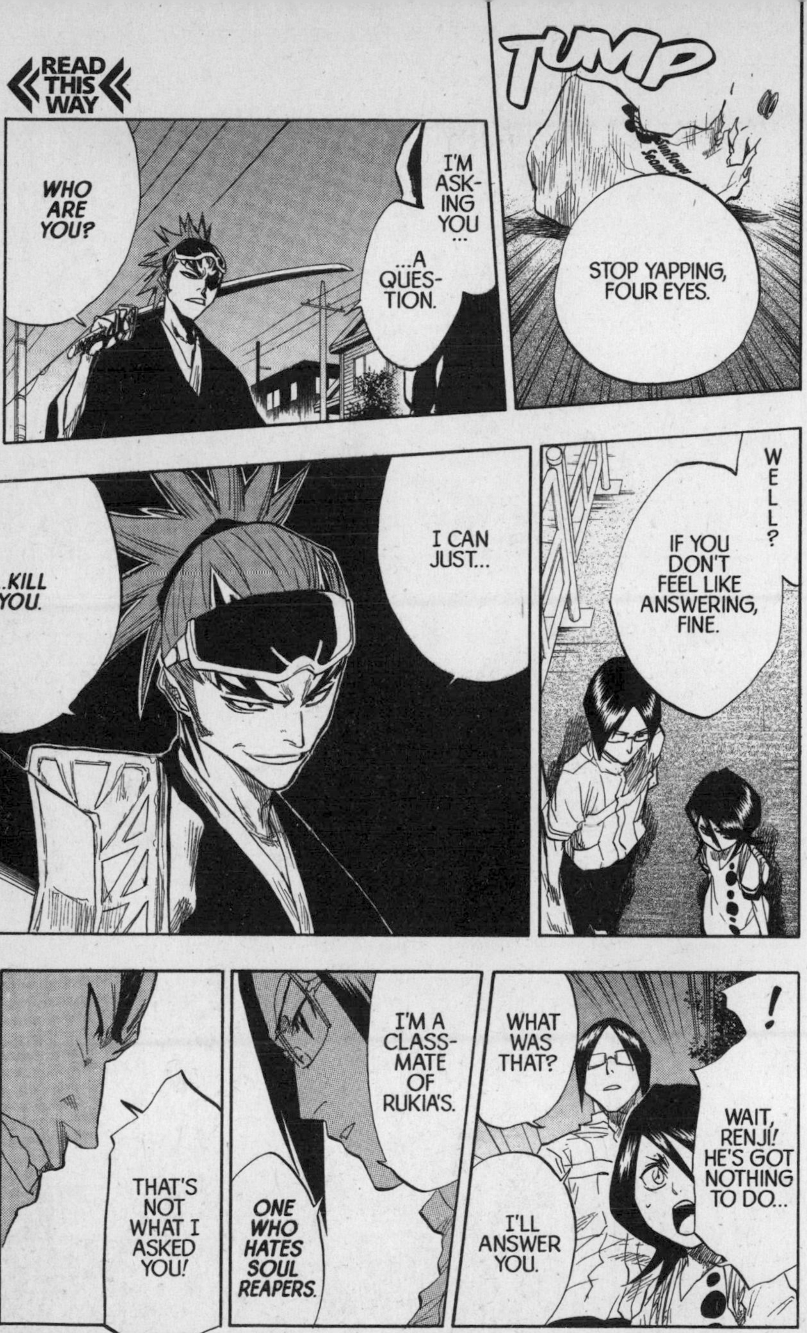
READ THIS WAY
TUMP
STOP YAPPING, FOUR EYES.
I'M ASKING YOU ...
...A QUESTION.
WHO ARE YOU?
WELL?
IF YOU DON'T FEEL LIKE ANSWERING, FINE.
I CAN JUST...
...KILL YOU.
!
WAIT, RENJI! HE'S GOT NOTHING TO DO...
WHAT WAS THAT?
I'LL ANSWER YOU.
I'M A CLASSMATE OF RUKIA'S.
ONE WHO HATES SOUL REAPERS.
THAT'S NOT WHAT I ASKED YOU!

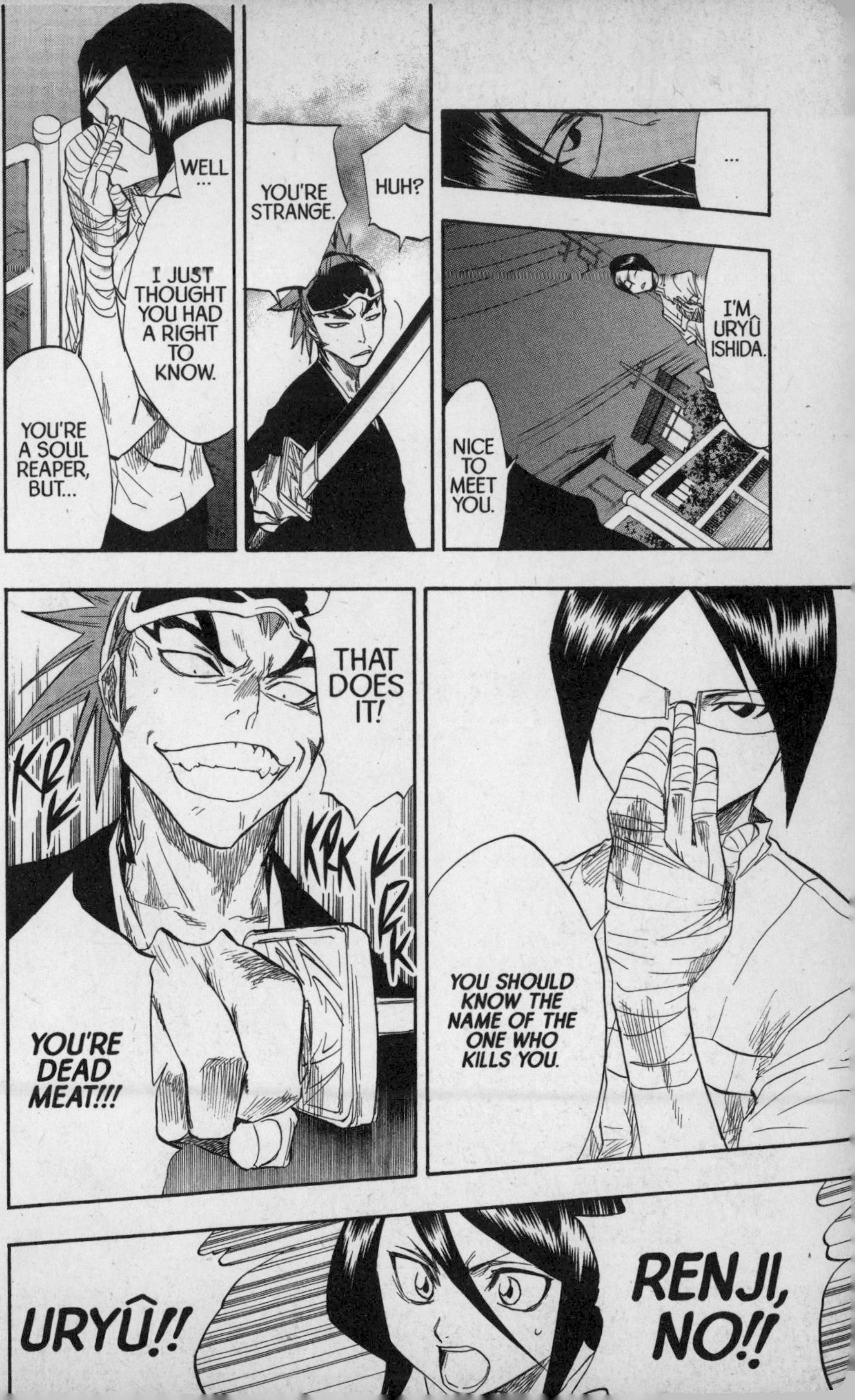
...
I'M URYÛ ISHIDA.
NICE TO MEET YOU.
HUH?
YOU'RE STRANGE.
WELL ...
I JUST THOUGHT YOU HAD A RIGHT TO KNOW.
YOU'RE A SOUL REAPER, BUT...
YOU SHOULD KNOW THE NAME OF THE ONE WHO KILLS YOU.
THAT DOES IT!
KRK
KRKK
KRK
KRK
YOU'RE DEAD MEAT!!!
RENJI, NO!!
URYÛ!!

53. Nice to meet you. (I will beat you.)

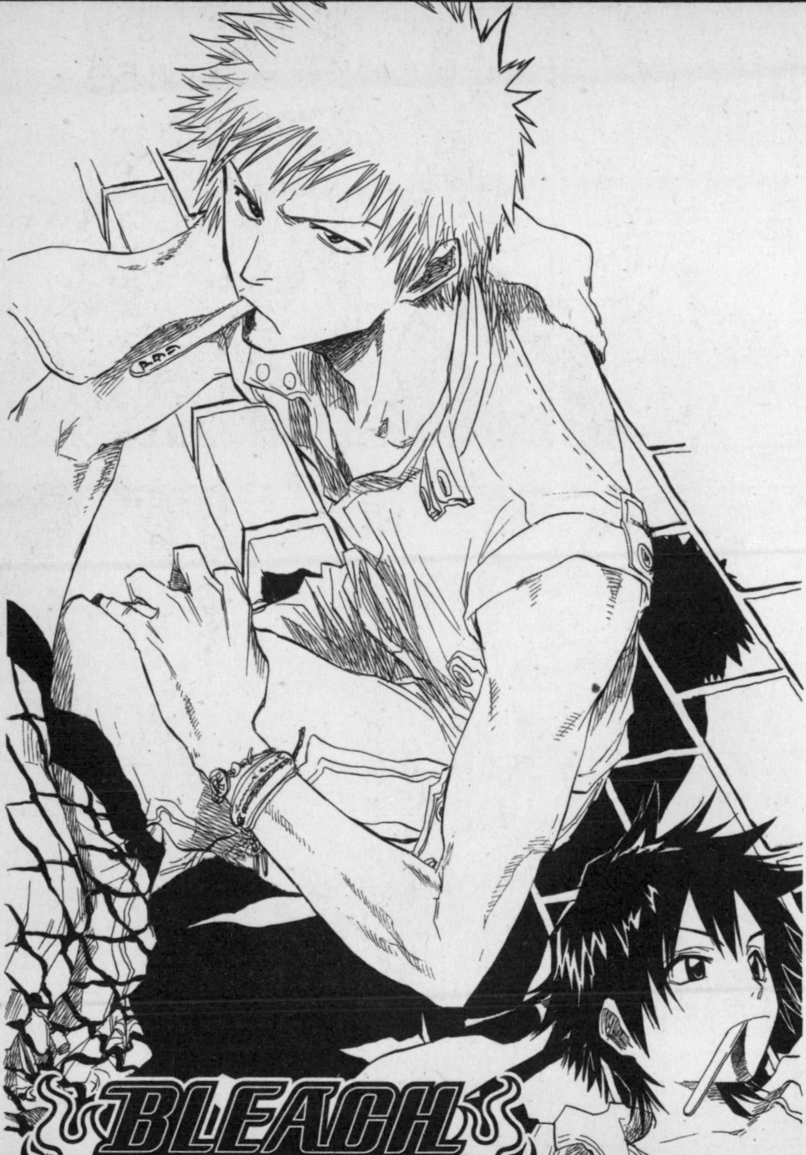
BLEACH
ブリーチ

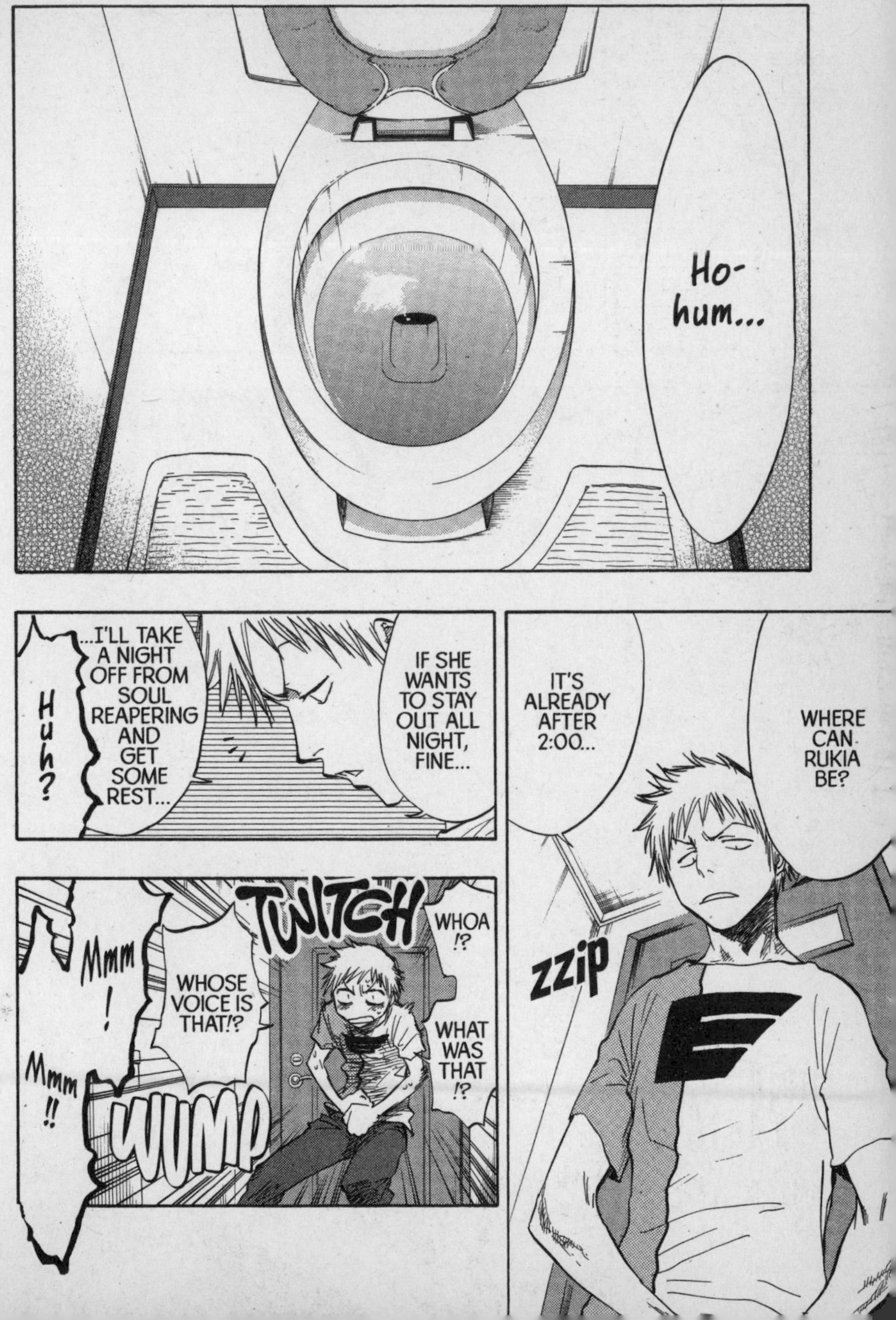

Ho-hum...
WHERE CAN RUKIA BE?
IT'S ALREADY AFTER 2:00...
zzip
IF SHE WANTS TO STAY OUT ALL NIGHT, FINE...
...I'LL TAKE A NIGHT OFF FROM SOUL REAPERING AND GET SOME REST...
Huh?
TWITCH
WHOA!?
WHAT WAS THAT!?
WHOSE VOICE IS THAT!?
Mmm!
Mmm!!
WUMP

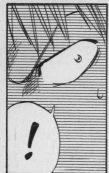

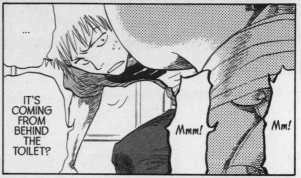

READ THIS WAY
Mm!
Mmm!
...
IT'S COMING FROM BEHIND THE TOILET?
!
YOU!?
Mm!!
Mmm!!
KON !?
WHAT'RE YOU DOING BACK THERE?
I DIDN'T KNOW YOU WERE INTO THAT KIND OF STUFF.
YOU SEEM AGITATED.
YOU'RE LUCKY YOU CAN FIND TIME TO ENJOY YOUR-SELF.
Mm --
Mmm-mm! Mm!
WUP WUP
Mmmm-mmm!!!
WHAM

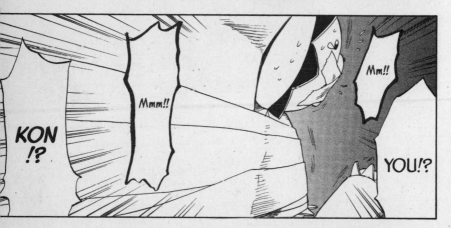

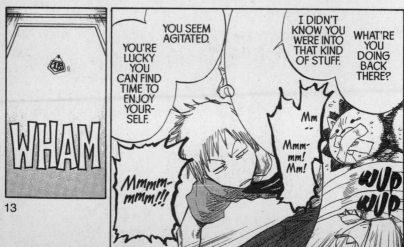

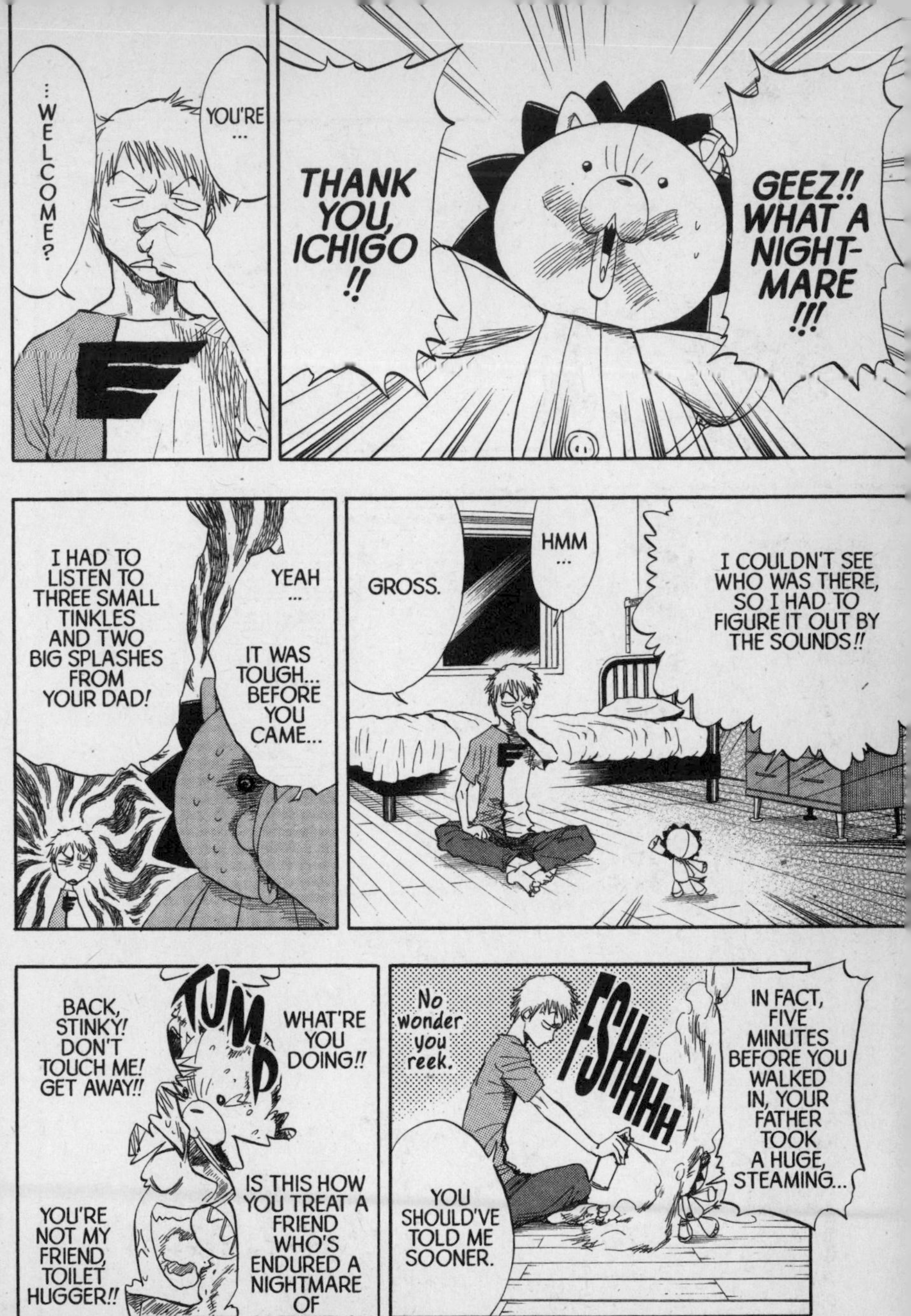
GEEZ!! WHAT A NIGHTMARE!!!
THANK YOU, ICHIGO!!
YOU'RE...
...WELCOME?
I COULDN'T SEE WHO WAS THERE, SO I HAD TO FIGURE IT OUT BY THE SOUNDS!!
HMM...
GROSS.
YEAH...
IT WAS TOUGH... BEFORE YOU CAME...
I HAD TO LISTEN TO THREE SMALL TINKLES AND TWO BIG SPLASHES FROM YOUR DAD!
IN FACT, FIVE MINUTES BEFORE YOU WALKED IN, YOUR FATHER TOOK A HUGE, STEAMING...
FSHHHH
No wonder you reek.
YOU SHOULD'VE TOLD ME SOONER.
WHAT'RE YOU DOING!!
TUMP
BACK, STINKY! DON'T TOUCH ME! GET AWAY!!
IS THIS HOW YOU TREAT A FRIEND WHO'S ENDURED A NIGHTMARE OF CAPTIVITY!?
YOU'RE NOT MY FRIEND, TOILET HUGGER!!

READ THIS WAY

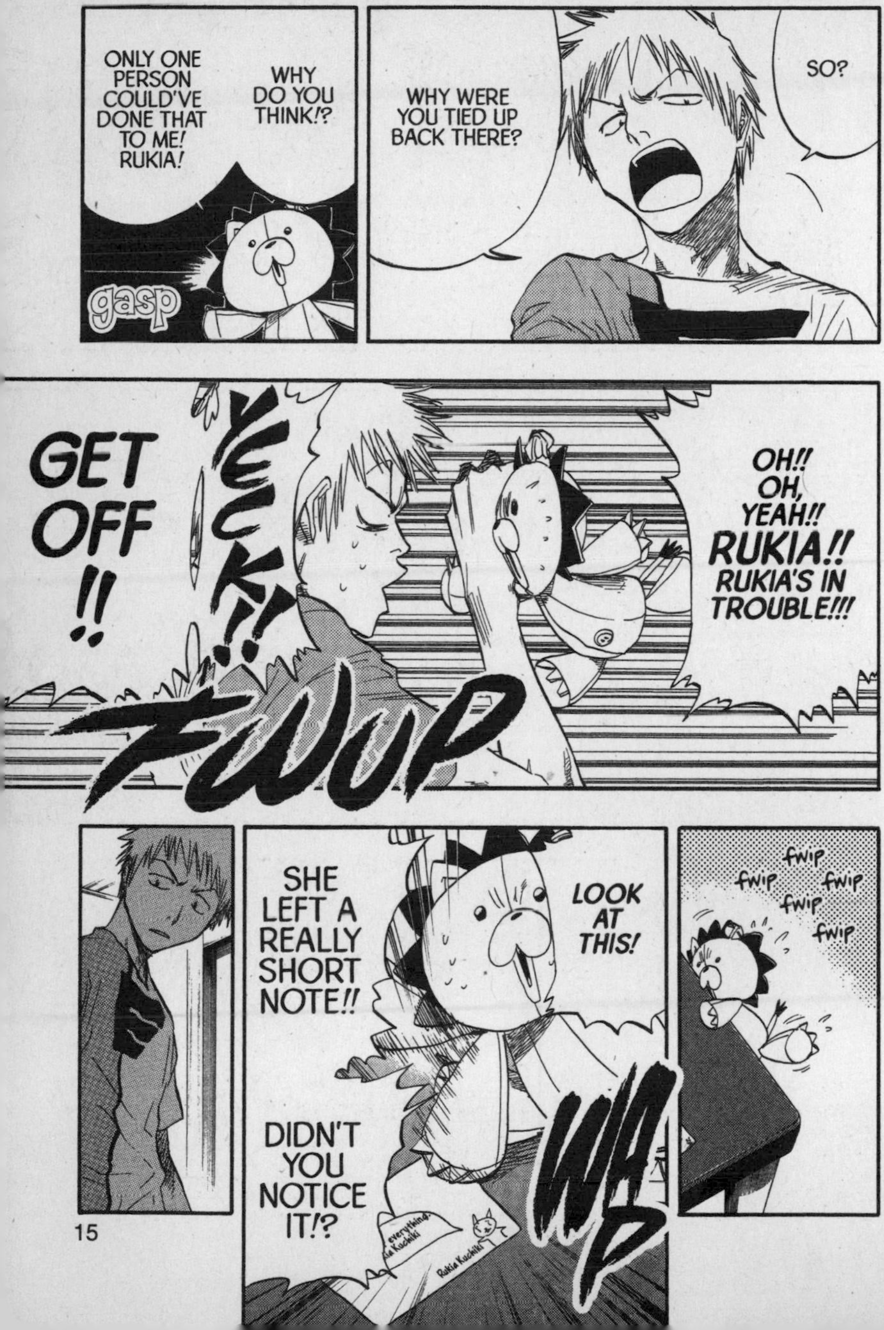

SO?
WHY WERE YOU TIED UP BACK THERE?
WHY DO YOU THINK!?
ONLY ONE PERSON COULD'VE DONE THAT TO ME! RUKIA!
gasp
OH!! OH, YEAH!! RUKIA!! RUKIA'S IN TROUBLE!!!
YECK!!
GET OFF!!
FWUP
fwip
fwip
fwip
fwip
fwip
LOOK AT THIS!
SHE LEFT A REALLY SHORT NOTE!!
DIDN'T YOU NOTICE IT!?
Rukia Kuchiki

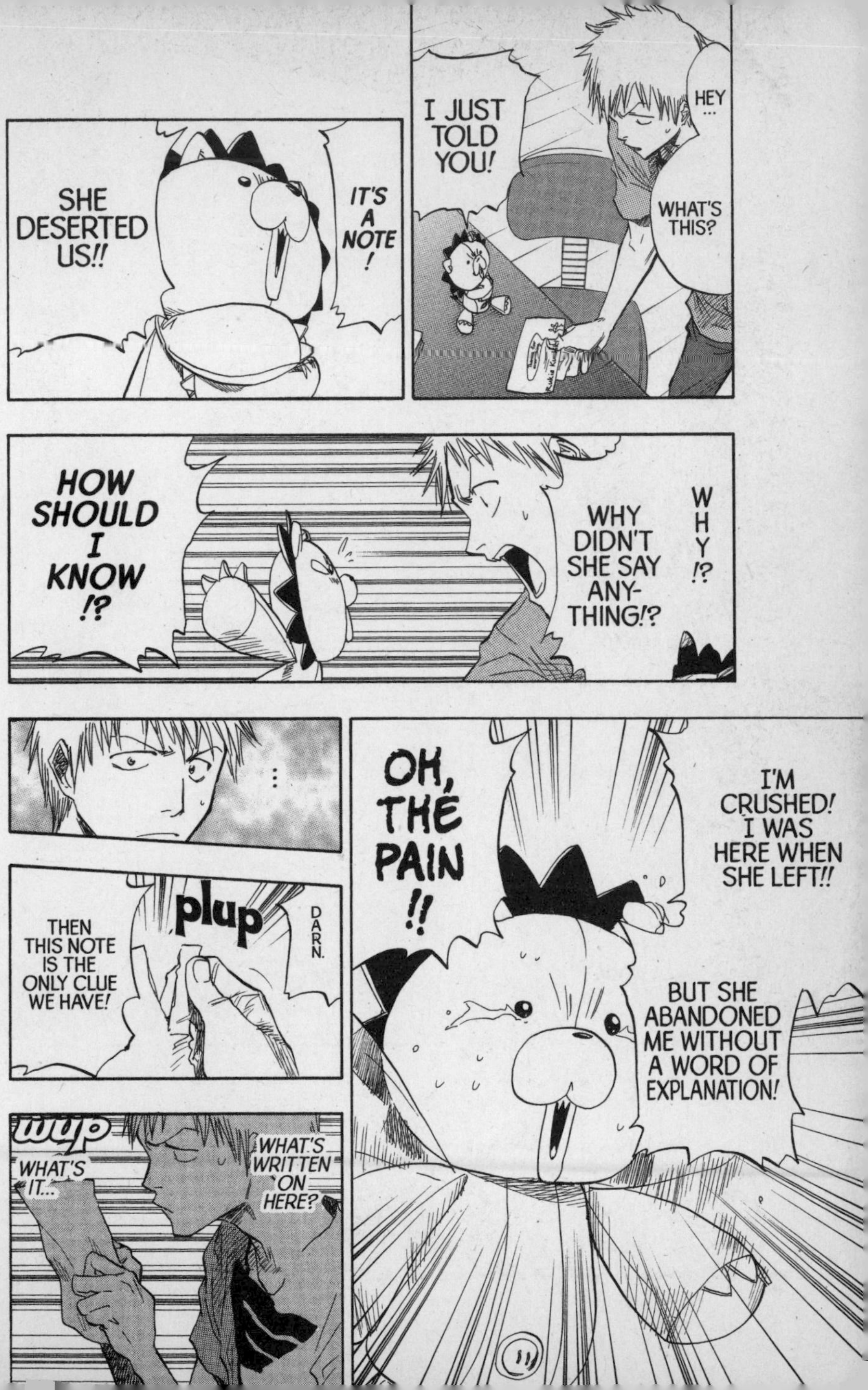
HEY...
WHAT'S THIS?
I JUST TOLD YOU!
IT'S A NOTE!
SHE DESERTED US!!
WHY!?
WHY DIDN'T SHE SAY ANYTHING!?
HOW SHOULD I KNOW!?
I'M CRUSHED! I WAS HERE WHEN SHE LEFT!!
BUT SHE ABANDONED ME WITHOUT A WORD OF EXPLANATION!
OH, THE PAIN!!
...
DARN.
plup
THEN THIS NOTE IS THE ONLY CLUE WE HAVE!
wup
WHAT'S WRITTEN ON HERE?
WHAT'S IT...

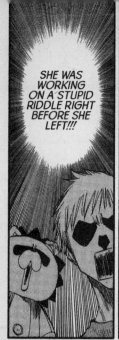

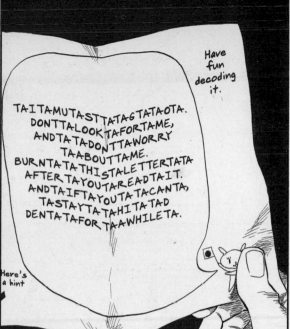

Have fun decoding it.
TAITAMUTASTTATAGTATAOTA.
DONTTALOOKTAFORTAME,
ANDTATADONTTAWORRY
TAABOUTTAME.
BURNTATATHISTALETTERTATA
AFTERTAYOUTAREADTAIT.
ANDTAIFTAYOUTATACANTA,
TASTAYTATAHITATAD
DENTATAFORTAAWHILETA.
Here's a hint
SHE WAS WORKING ON A STUPID RIDDLE RIGHT BEFORE SHE LEFT!!!
Here's a hint
WHAT'S THIS!?
WHY A TANUKI?!! OH, I GET IT, "TA-NUKI"! "NUKI" MEANS "WITHOUT"!
SO I'LL READ IT WITHOUT THE TA'S!!
UM...
"I... MUST... GO."

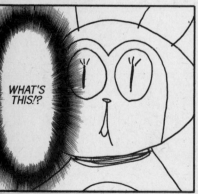

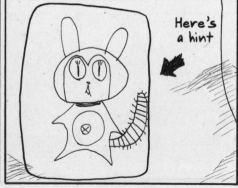

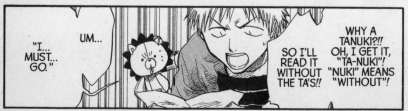

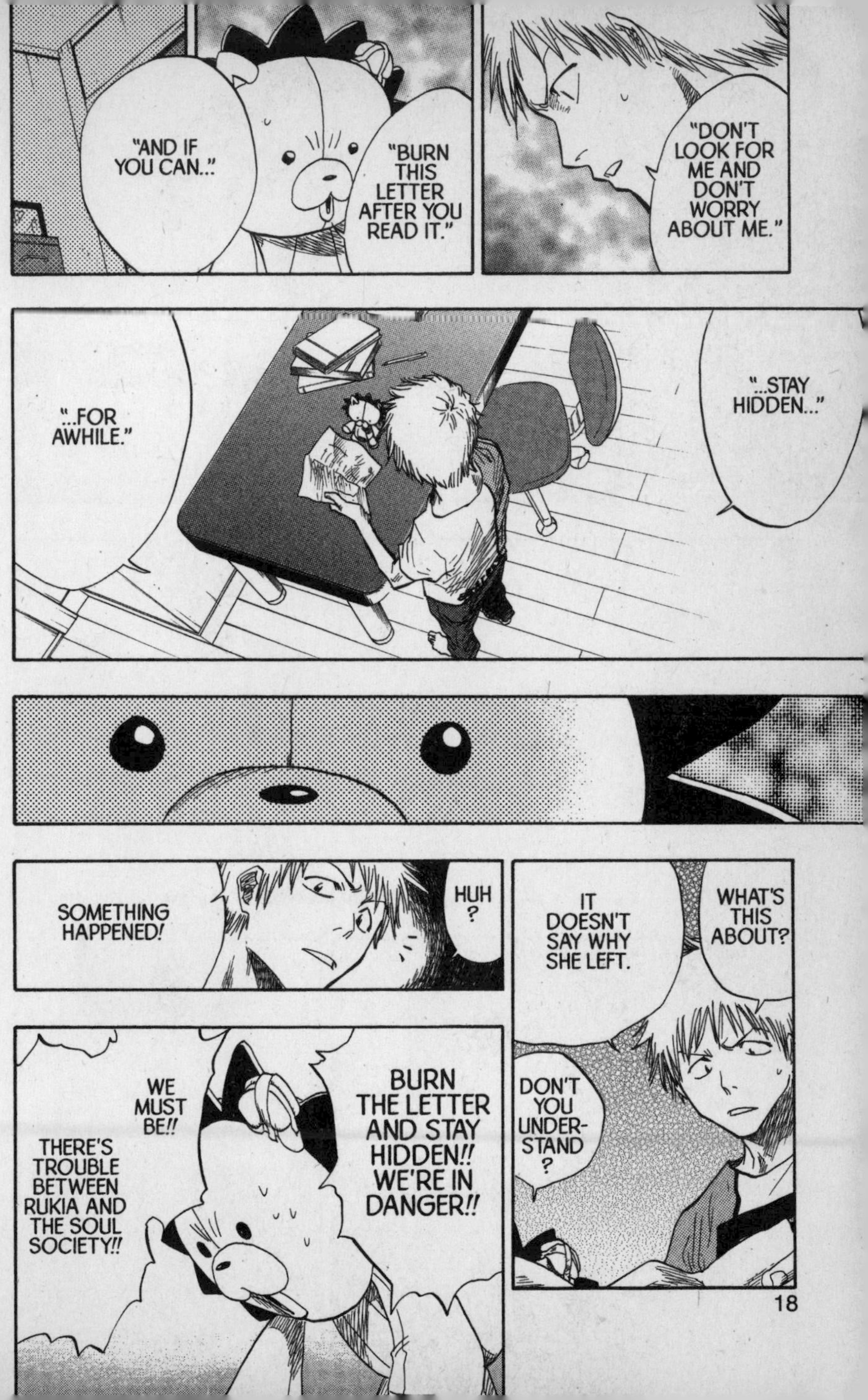
"DON'T LOOK FOR ME AND DON'T WORRY ABOUT ME."
"BURN THIS LETTER AFTER YOU READ IT."
"AND IF YOU CAN.."
"...STAY HIDDEN..."
"...FOR AWHILE."
WHAT'S THIS ABOUT?
IT DOESN'T SAY WHY SHE LEFT.
DON'T YOU UNDER-STAND?
HUH?
SOMETHING HAPPENED!
BURN THE LETTER AND STAY HIDDEN!! WE'RE IN DANGER!!
WE MUST BE!!
THERE'S TROUBLE BETWEEN RUKIA AND THE SOUL SOCIETY!!

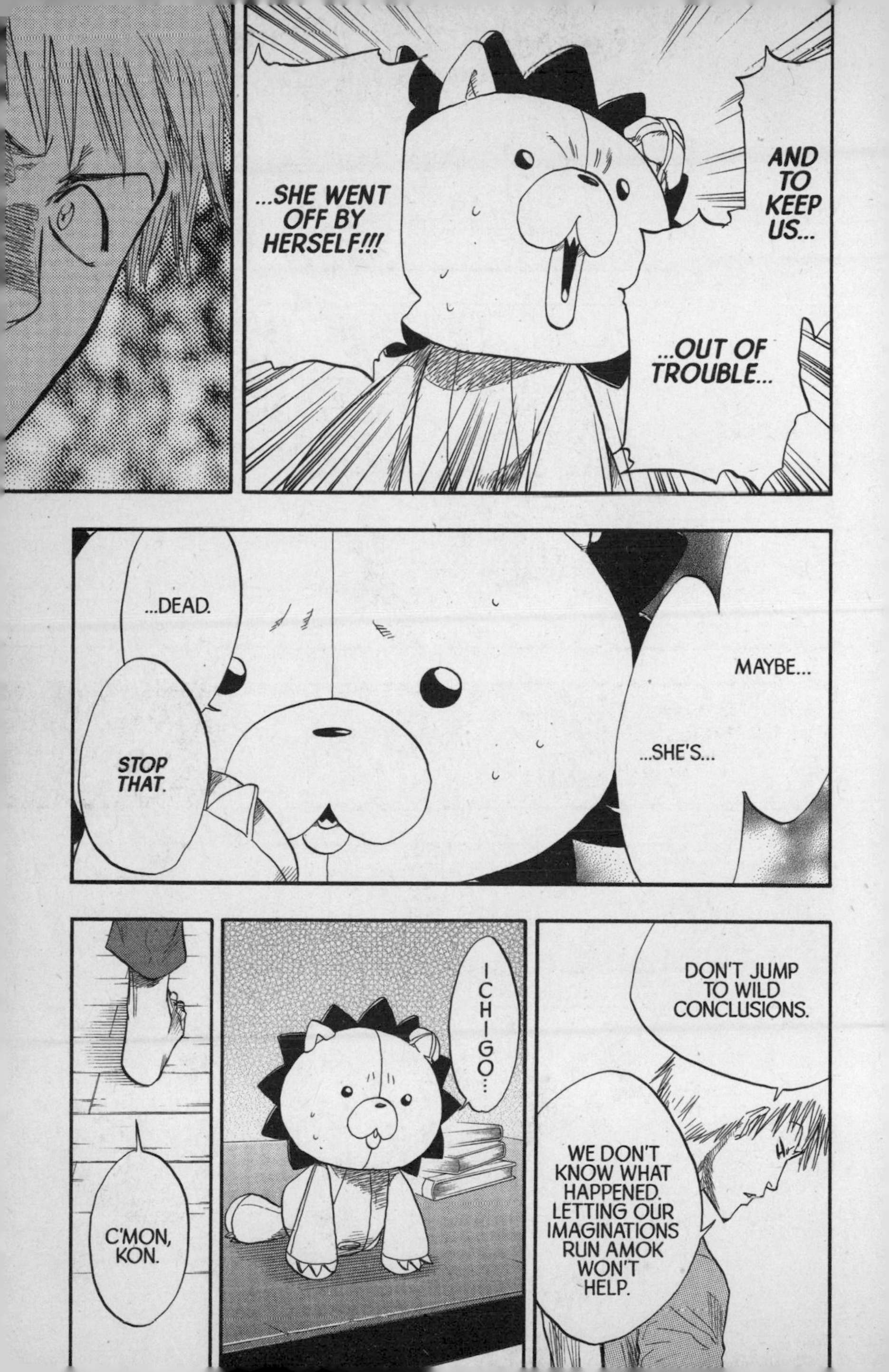
AND TO KEEP US...
...OUT OF TROUBLE...
...SHE WENT OFF BY HERSELF!!!
MAYBE...
...SHE'S...
...DEAD.
STOP THAT.
DON'T JUMP TO WILD CONCLUSIONS.
WE DON'T KNOW WHAT HAPPENED. LETTING OUR IMAGINATIONS RUN AMOK WON'T HELP.
ICHIGO...
C'MON, KON.

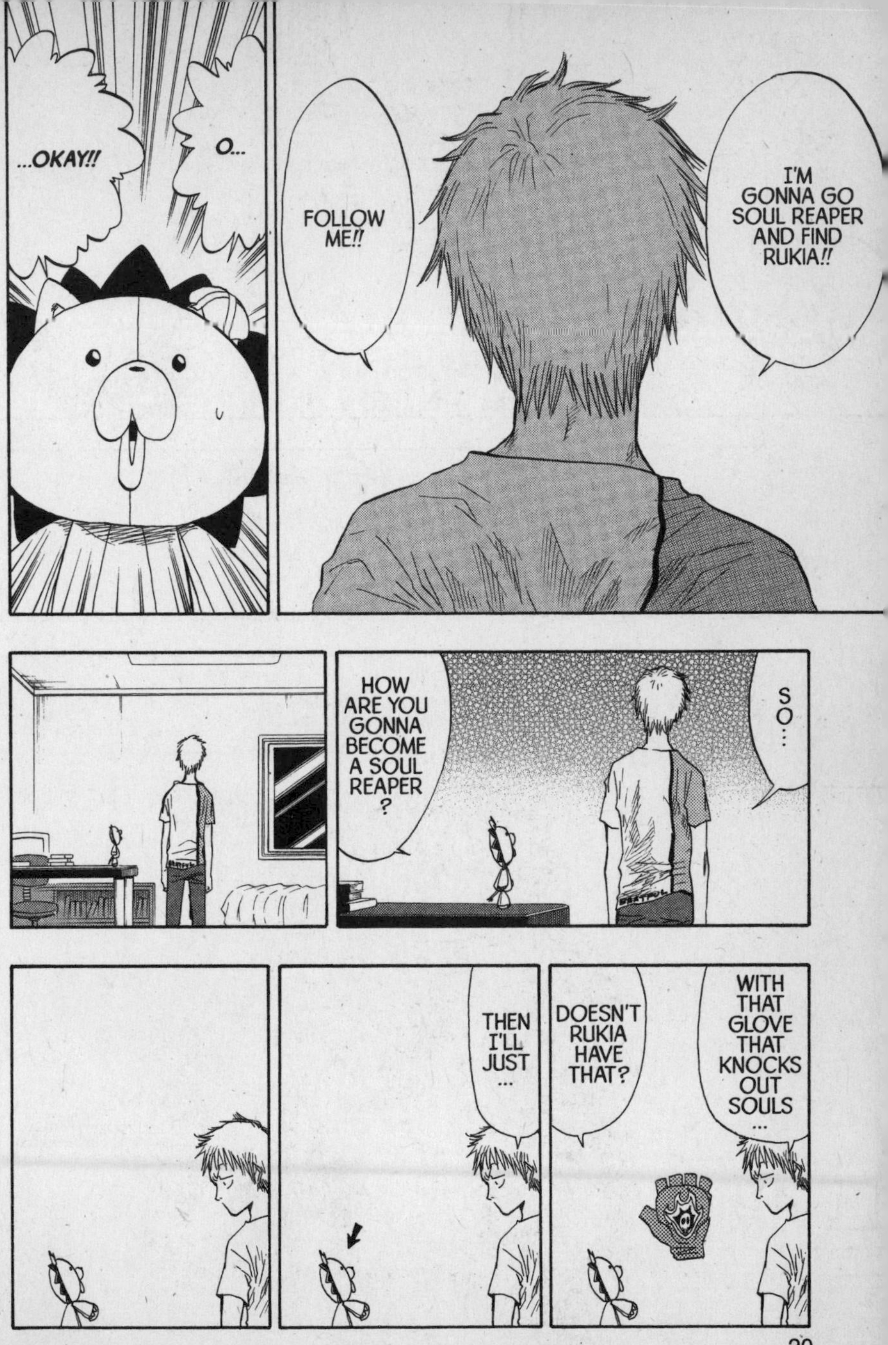
I'M GONNA GO SOUL REAPER AND FIND RUKIA!!
FOLLOW ME!!
O...
...OKAY!!
SO...
HOW ARE YOU GONNA BECOME A SOUL REAPER?
WITH THAT GLOVE THAT KNOCKS OUT SOULS...
DOESN'T RUKIA HAVE THAT?
THEN I'LL JUST...

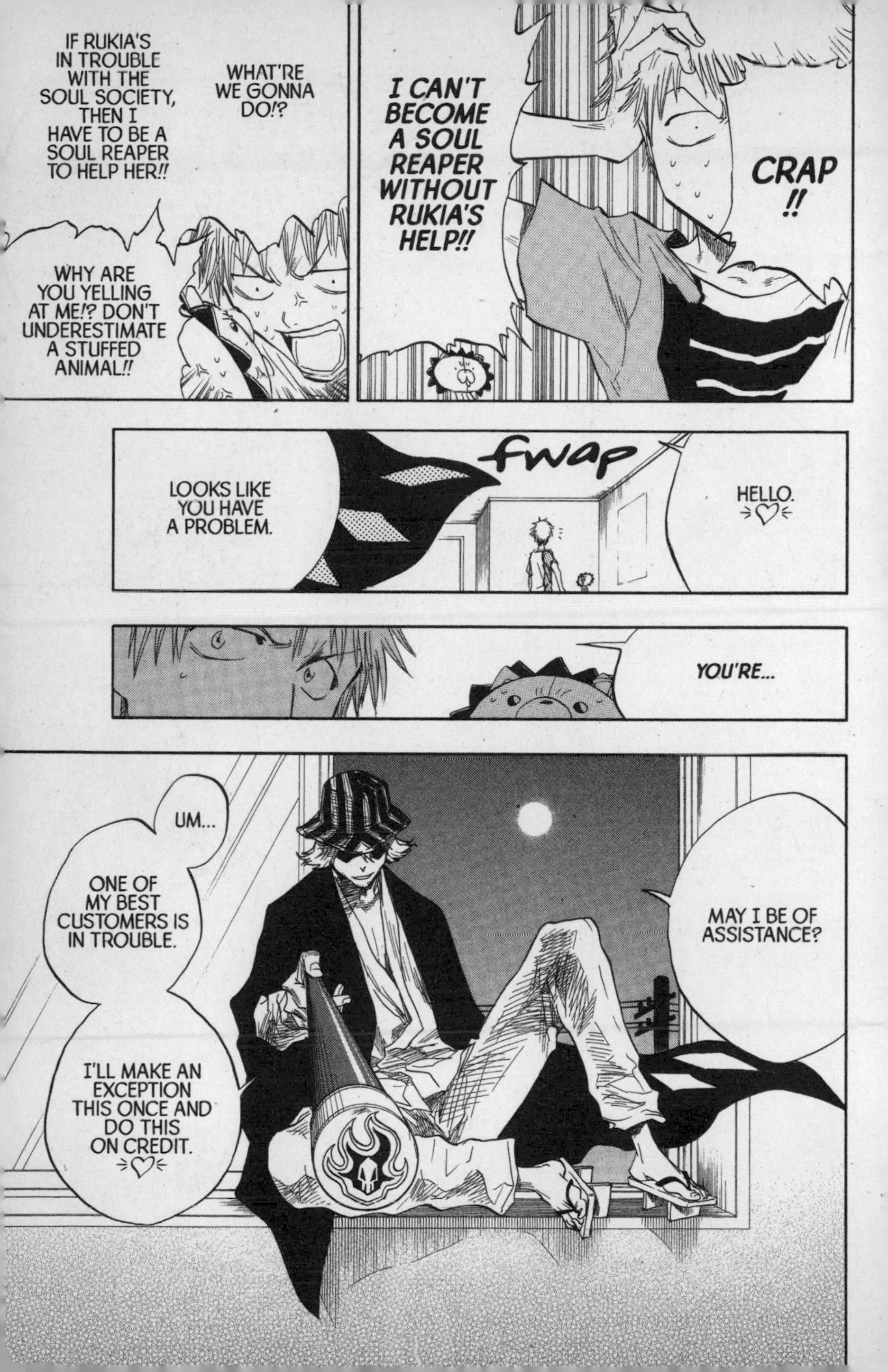
CRAP!!
I CAN'T BECOME A SOUL REAPER WITHOUT RUKIA'S HELP!!
WHAT'RE WE GONNA DO!?
IF RUKIA'S IN TROUBLE WITH THE SOUL SOCIETY, THEN I HAVE TO BE A SOUL REAPER TO HELP HER!!
WHY ARE YOU YELLING AT ME!? DON'T UNDERESTIMATE A STUFFED ANIMAL!!
HELLO. ♡
fwap
LOOKS LIKE YOU HAVE A PROBLEM.
YOU'RE...
MAY I BE OF ASSISTANCE?
UM...
ONE OF MY BEST CUSTOMERS IS IN TROUBLE.
I'LL MAKE AN EXCEPTION THIS ONCE AND DO THIS ON CREDIT. ♡

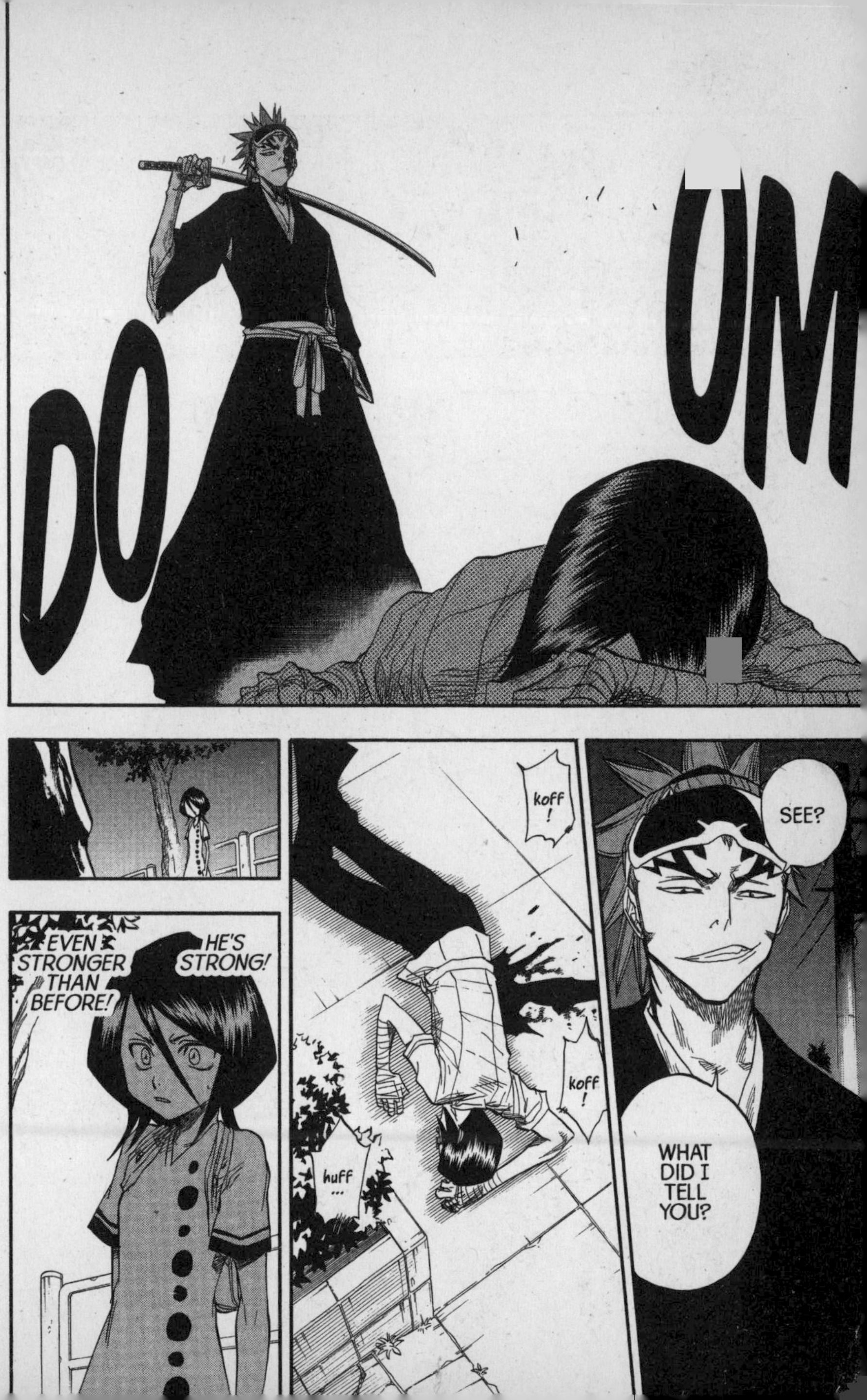
DOOM
SEE?
WHAT DID I TELL YOU?
koff!
koff!
huff...
HE'S STRONG!
EVEN STRONGER THAN BEFORE!

READ THIS WAY

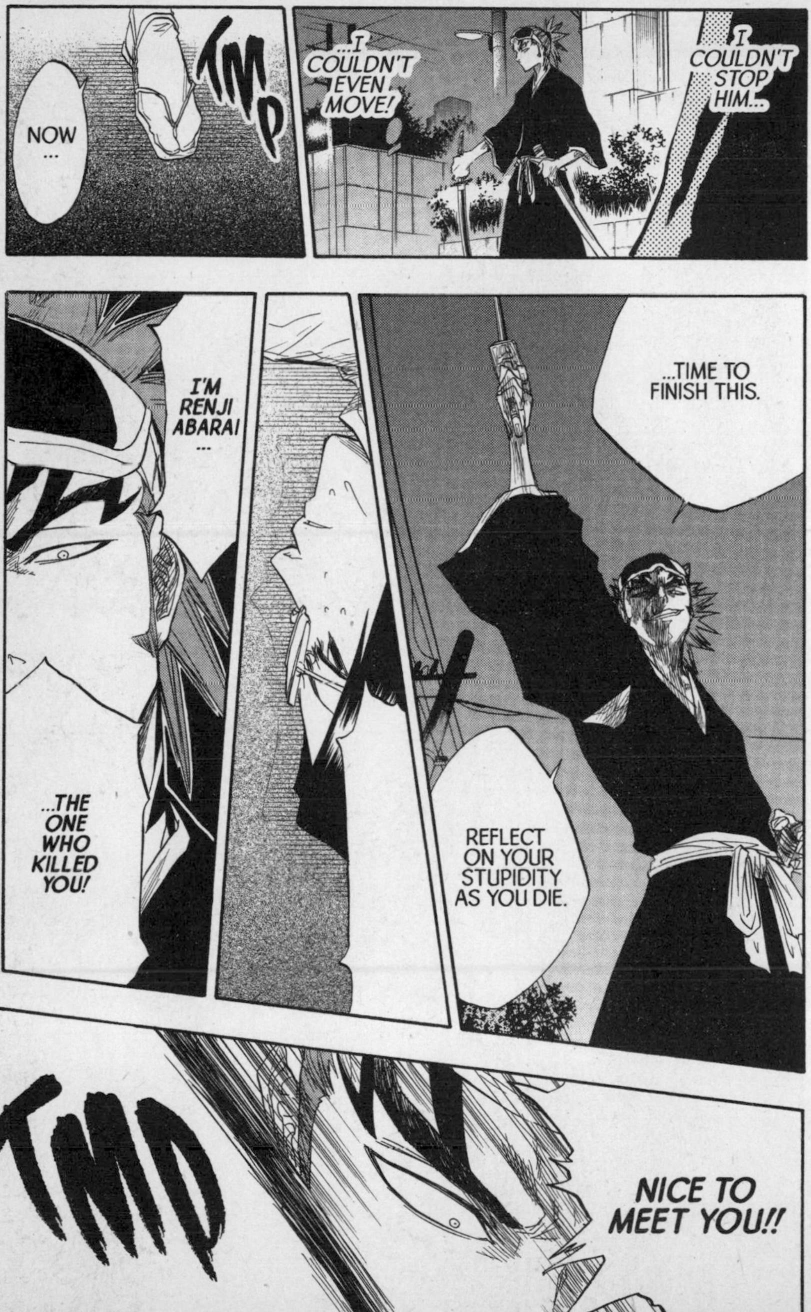
I COULDN'T STOP HIM...
...I COULDN'T EVEN MOVE!
TMP
NOW...
...TIME TO FINISH THIS.
REFLECT ON YOUR STUPIDITY AS YOU DIE.
I'M RENJI ABARAI...
...THE ONE WHO KILLED YOU!
NICE TO MEET YOU!!
TMP

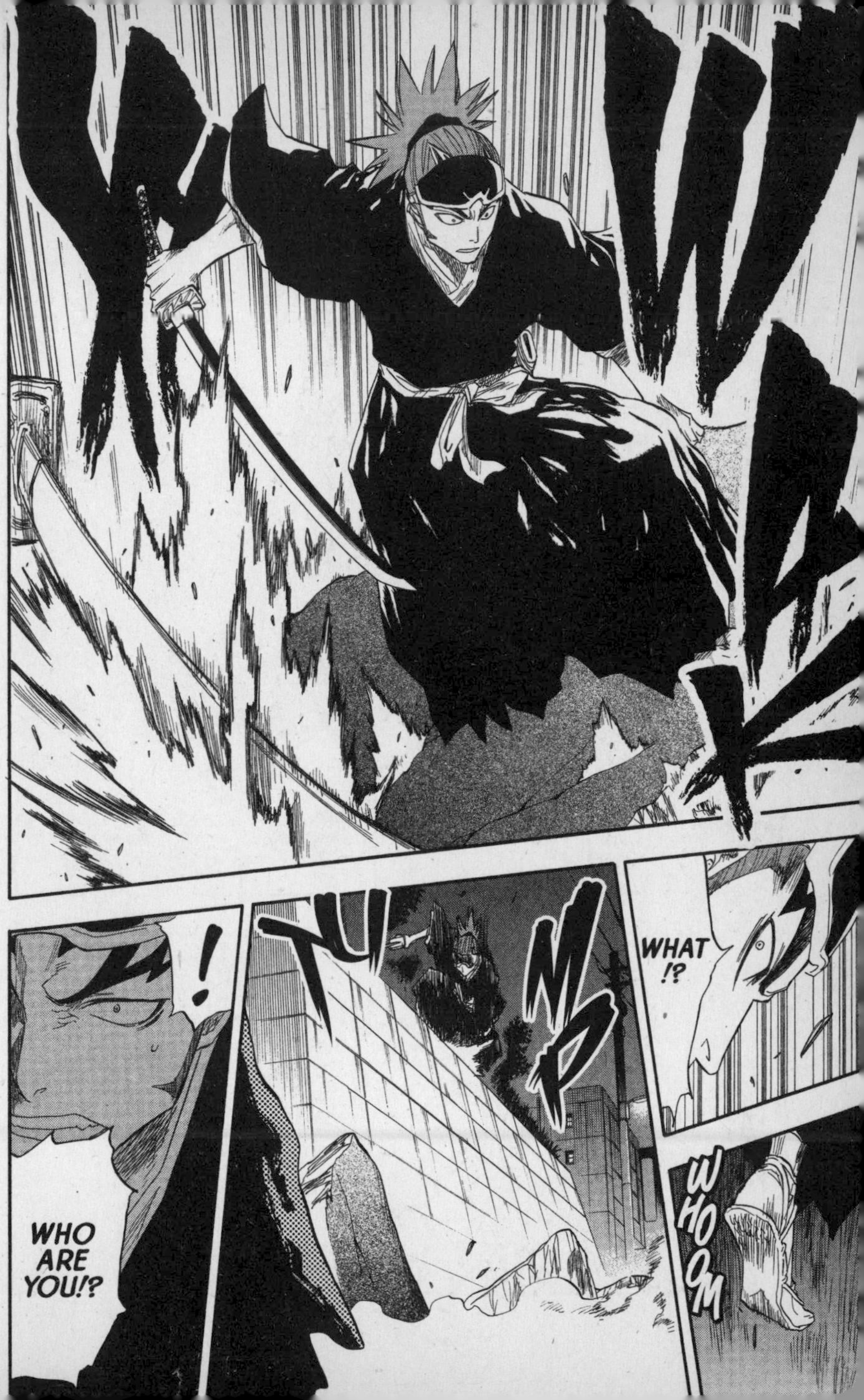
WHAT
!?
WHOOM
!
WHO
ARE
YOU!?

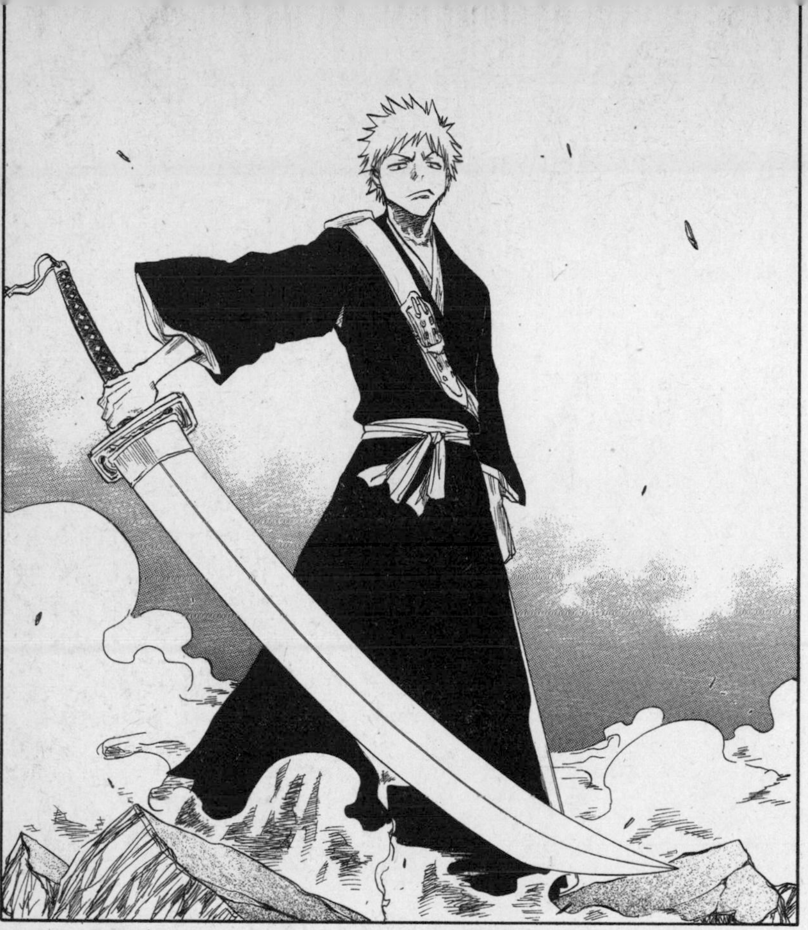

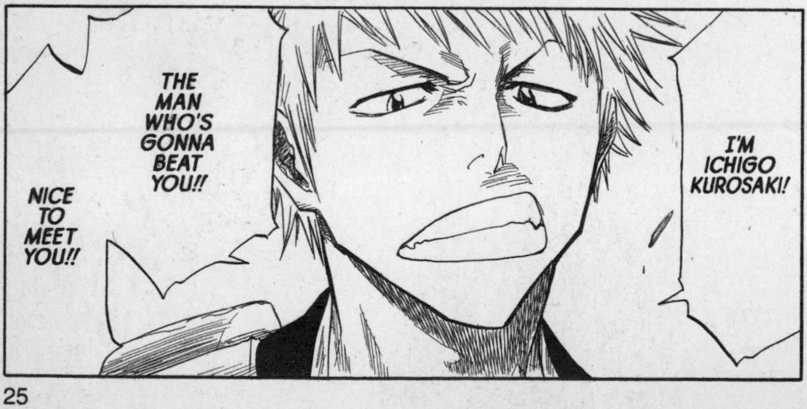
I'M ICHIGO KUROSAKI!
THE MAN WHO'S GONNA BEAT YOU!!
NICE TO MEET YOU!!

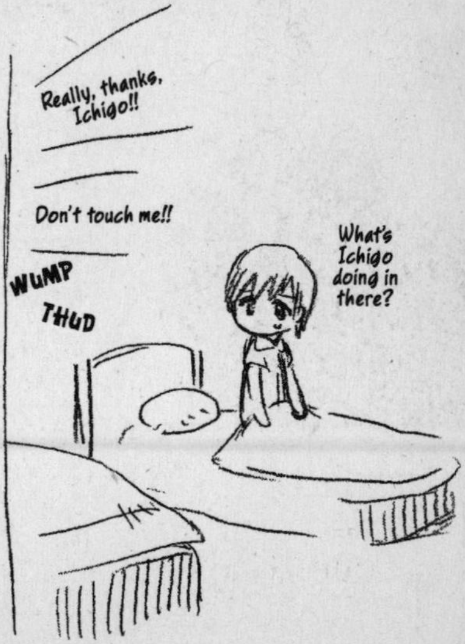

What's Ichigo doing in there?
Really, thanks, Ichigo!!
Don't touch me!!
WUMP
THUD

54. The Nameless Boy

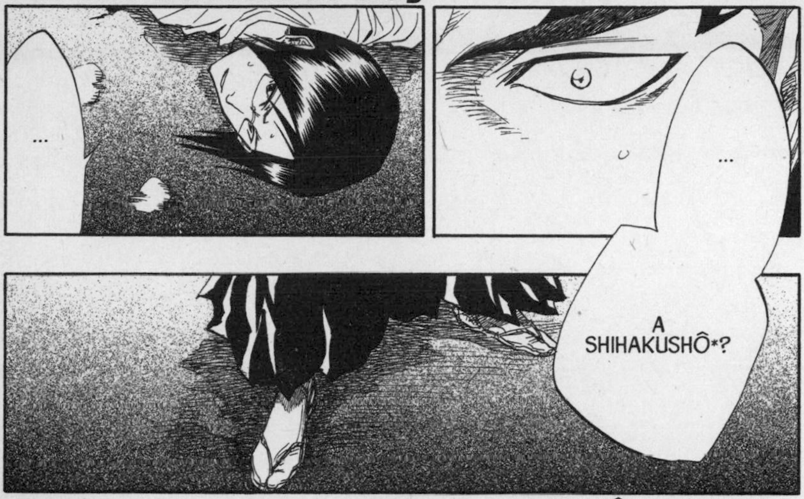
...
...
A SHIHAKUSHÔ*?

*SHIHAKUSHÔ: SOUL REAPER UNIFORM

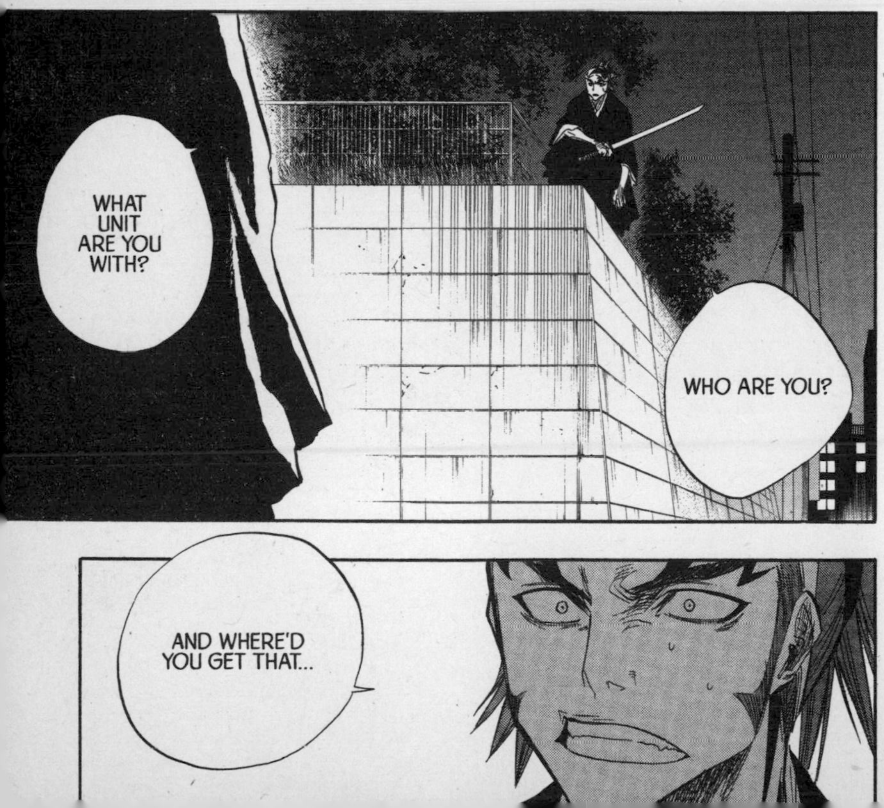
WHO ARE YOU?
WHAT UNIT ARE YOU WITH?
AND WHERE'D YOU GET THAT...

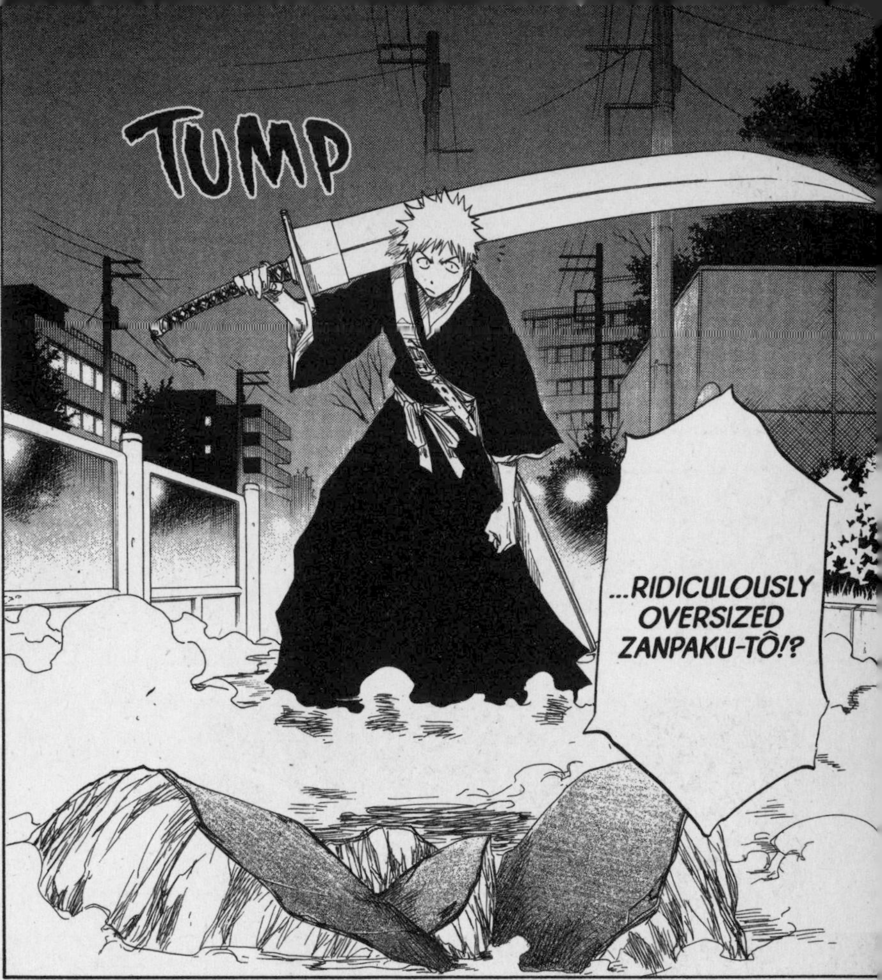
TUMP
...RIDICULOUSLY OVERSIZED ZANPAKU-TÔ!?

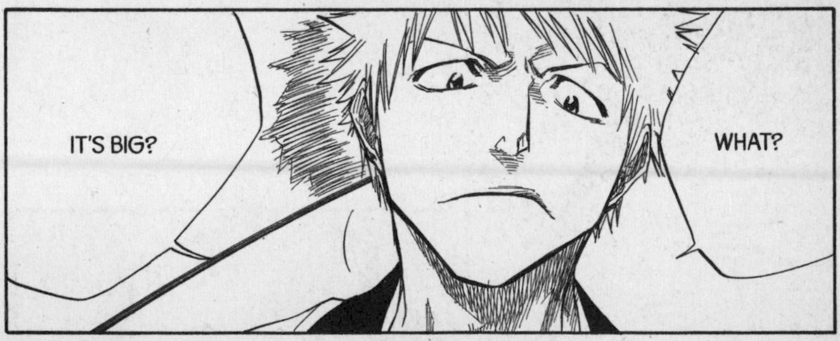
WHAT?
IT'S BIG?

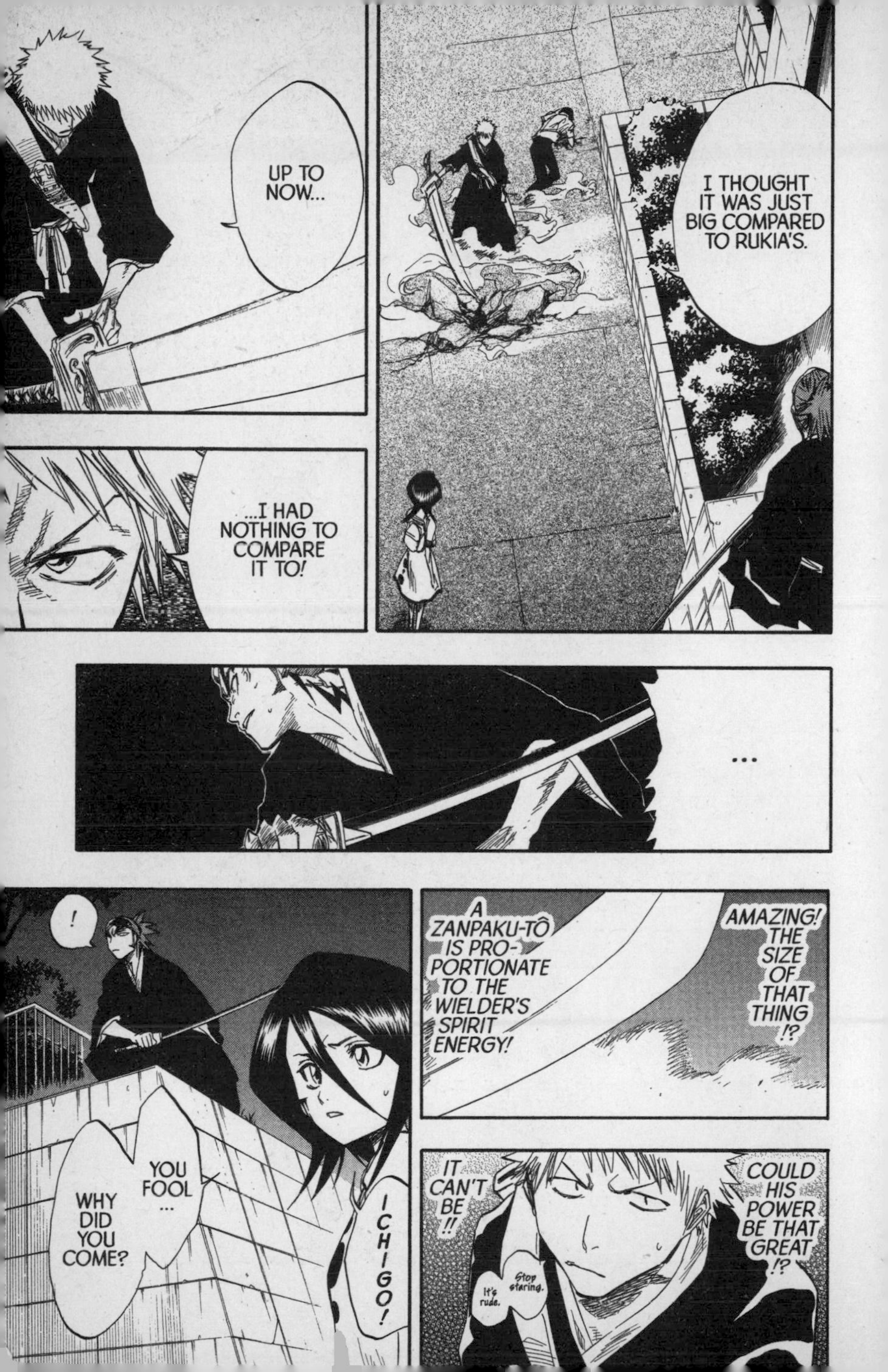
I THOUGHT IT WAS JUST BIG COMPARED TO RUKIA'S.
UP TO NOW...
...I HAD NOTHING TO COMPARE IT TO!
...
AMAZING! THE SIZE OF THAT THING!?
A ZANPAKU-TÔ IS PRO-PORTIONATE TO THE WIELDER'S SPIRIT ENERGY!
COULD HIS POWER BE THAT GREAT!?
IT CAN'T BE!!
Stop staring.
It's rude.
!
ICHIGO!
YOU FOOL...
WHY DID YOU COME?

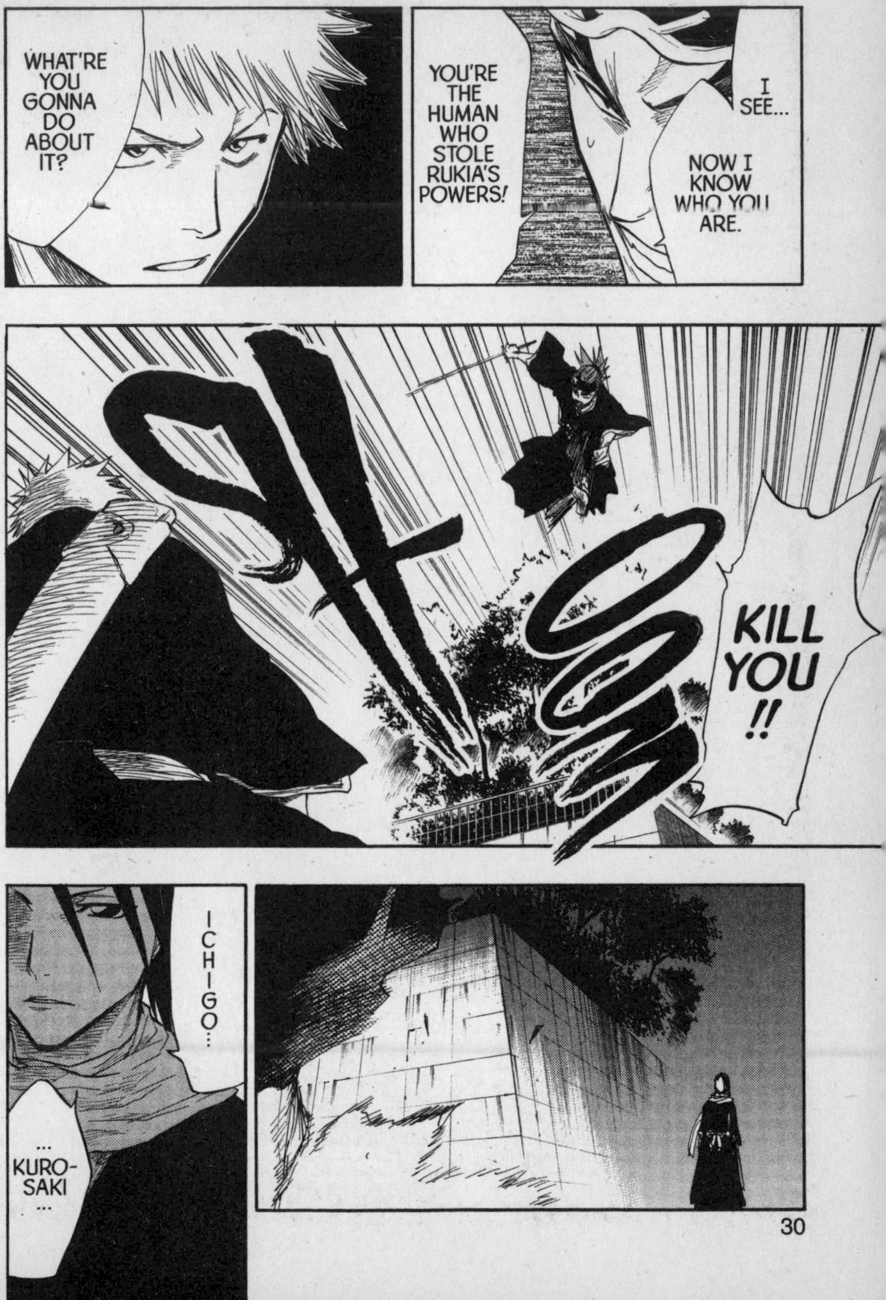
I SEE...
NOW I KNOW WHO YOU ARE.
YOU'RE THE HUMAN WHO STOLE RUKIA'S POWERS!
WHAT'RE YOU GONNA DO ABOUT IT?
KILL YOU!!
ICHIGO...
...KUROSAKI...

54. The Nameless Boy

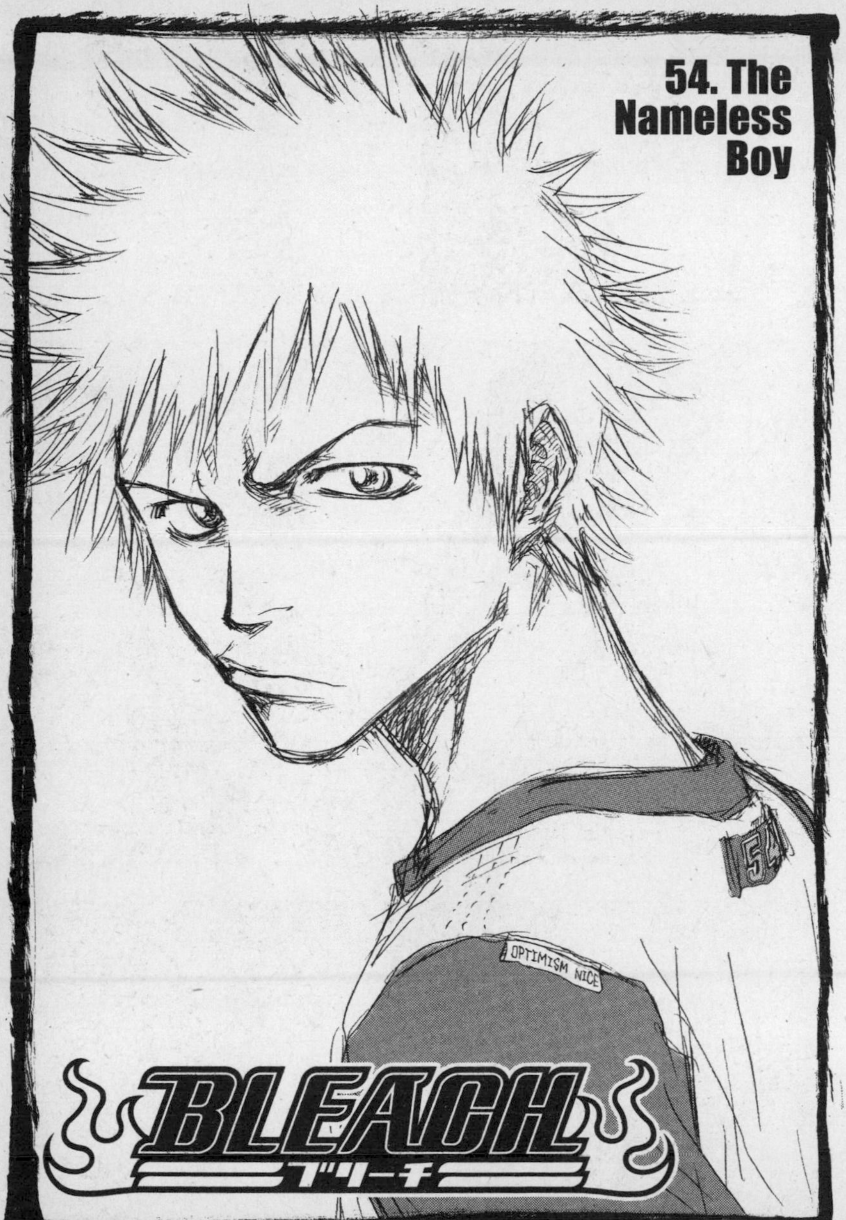
54
OPTIMISM NICE
BLEACH
ブリーチ

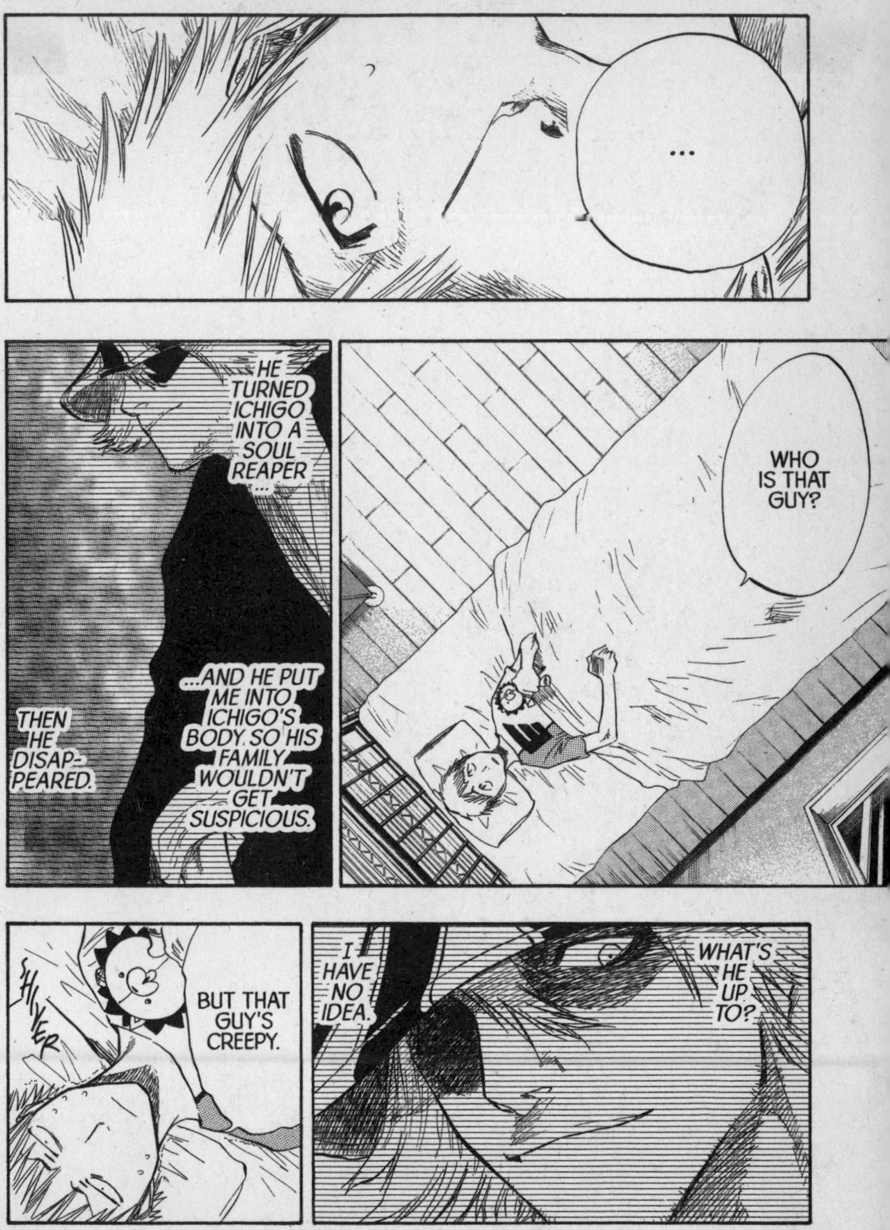
...
WHO IS THAT GUY?
HE TURNED ICHIGO INTO A SOUL REAPER...
...AND HE PUT ME INTO ICHIGO'S BODY SO HIS FAMILY WOULDN'T GET SUSPICIOUS.
THEN HE DISAPPEARED.
WHAT'S HE UP TO?
I HAVE NO IDEA.
BUT THAT GUY'S CREEPY.
SHIVER

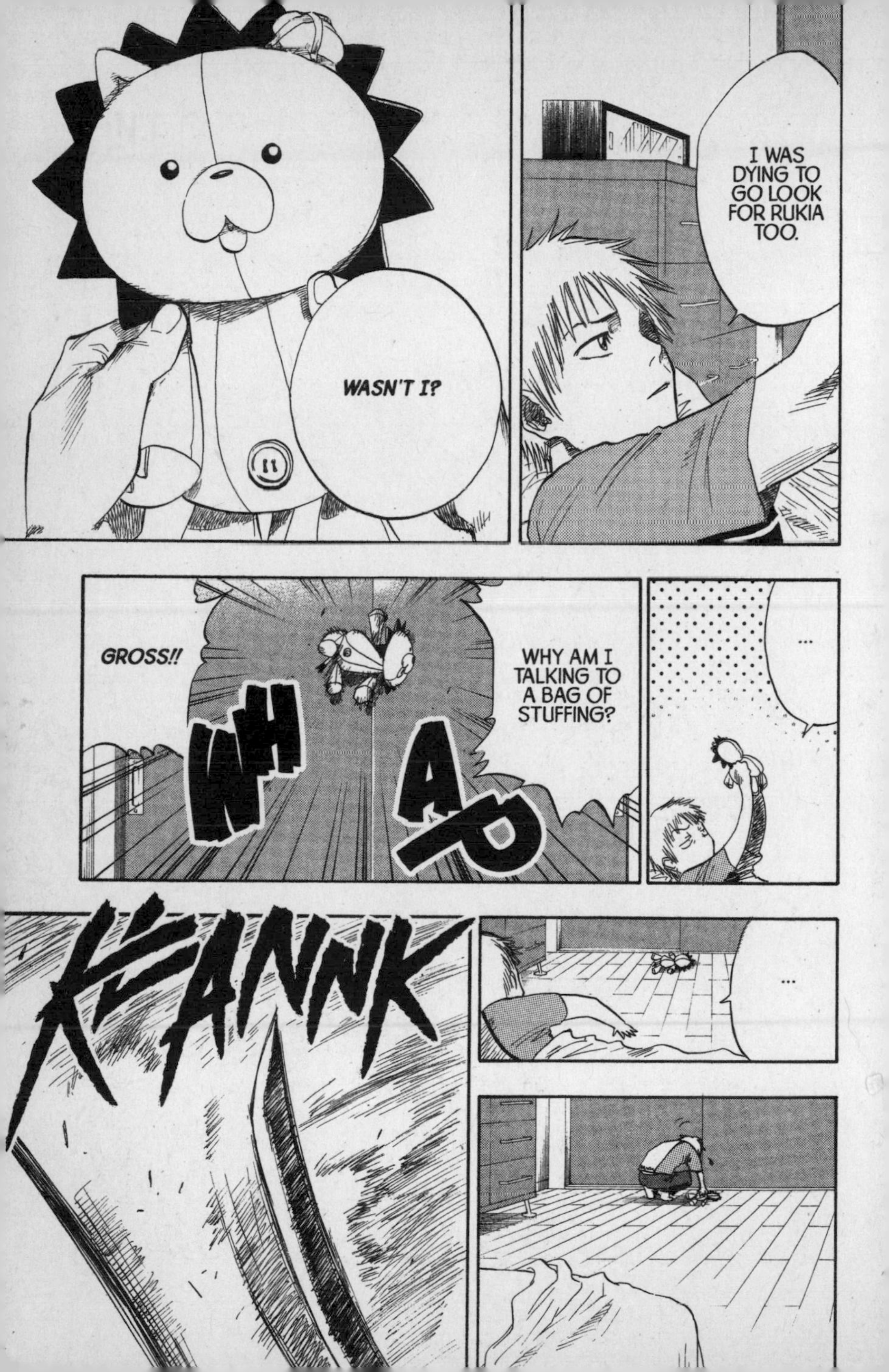
I WAS DYING TO GO LOOK FOR RUKIA TOO.
WASN'T I?
...
WHY AM I TALKING TO A BAG OF STUFFING?
GROSS!!
WHAP
...
KLANNK

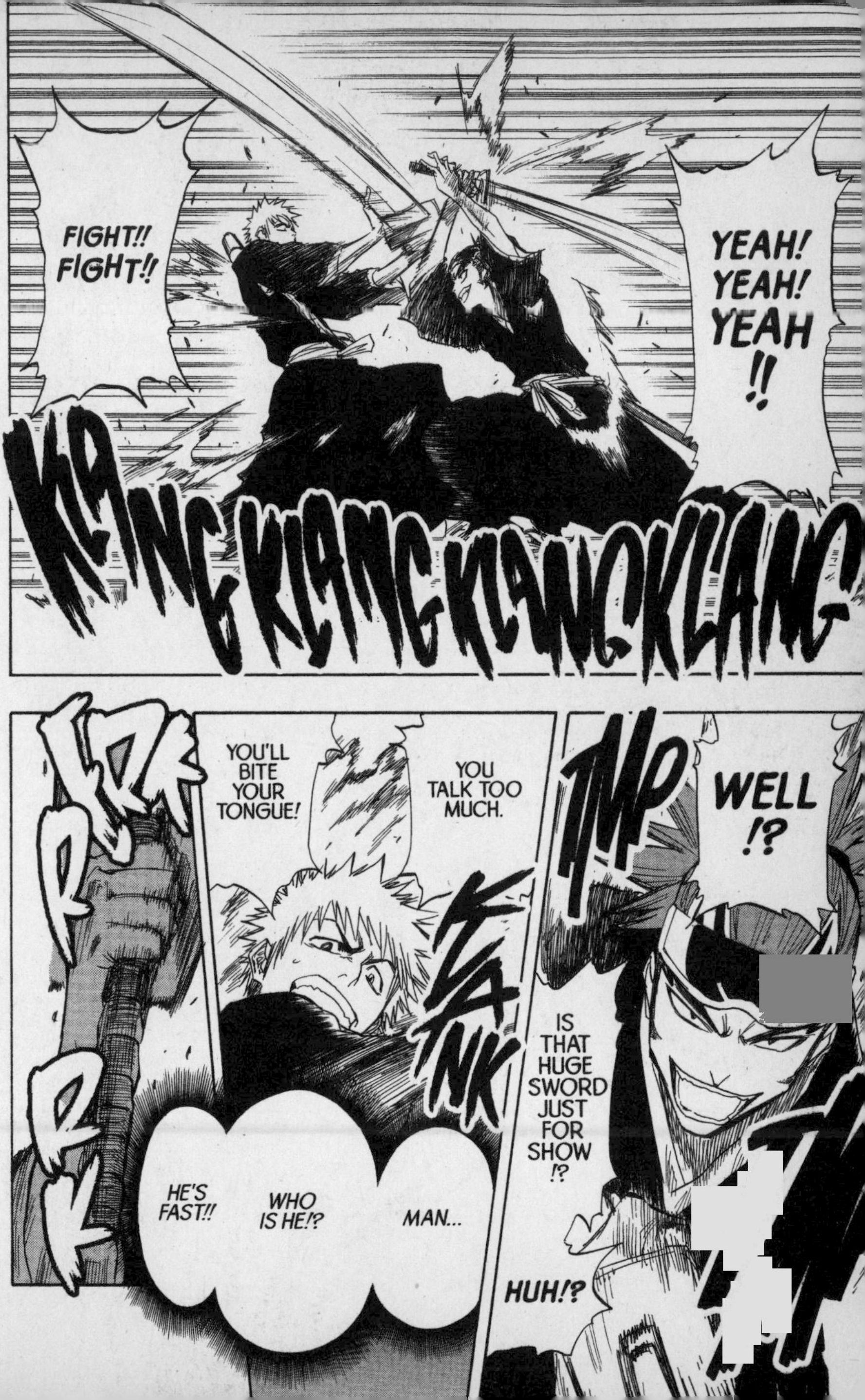
YEAH! YEAH! YEAH!!
FIGHT!! FIGHT!!
KLANG KLANG KLANG KLANG
WELL!?
IS THAT HUGE SWORD JUST FOR SHOW!?
HUH!?
YOU TALK TOO MUCH.
YOU'LL BITE YOUR TONGUE!
MAN...
WHO IS HE!?
HE'S FAST!!

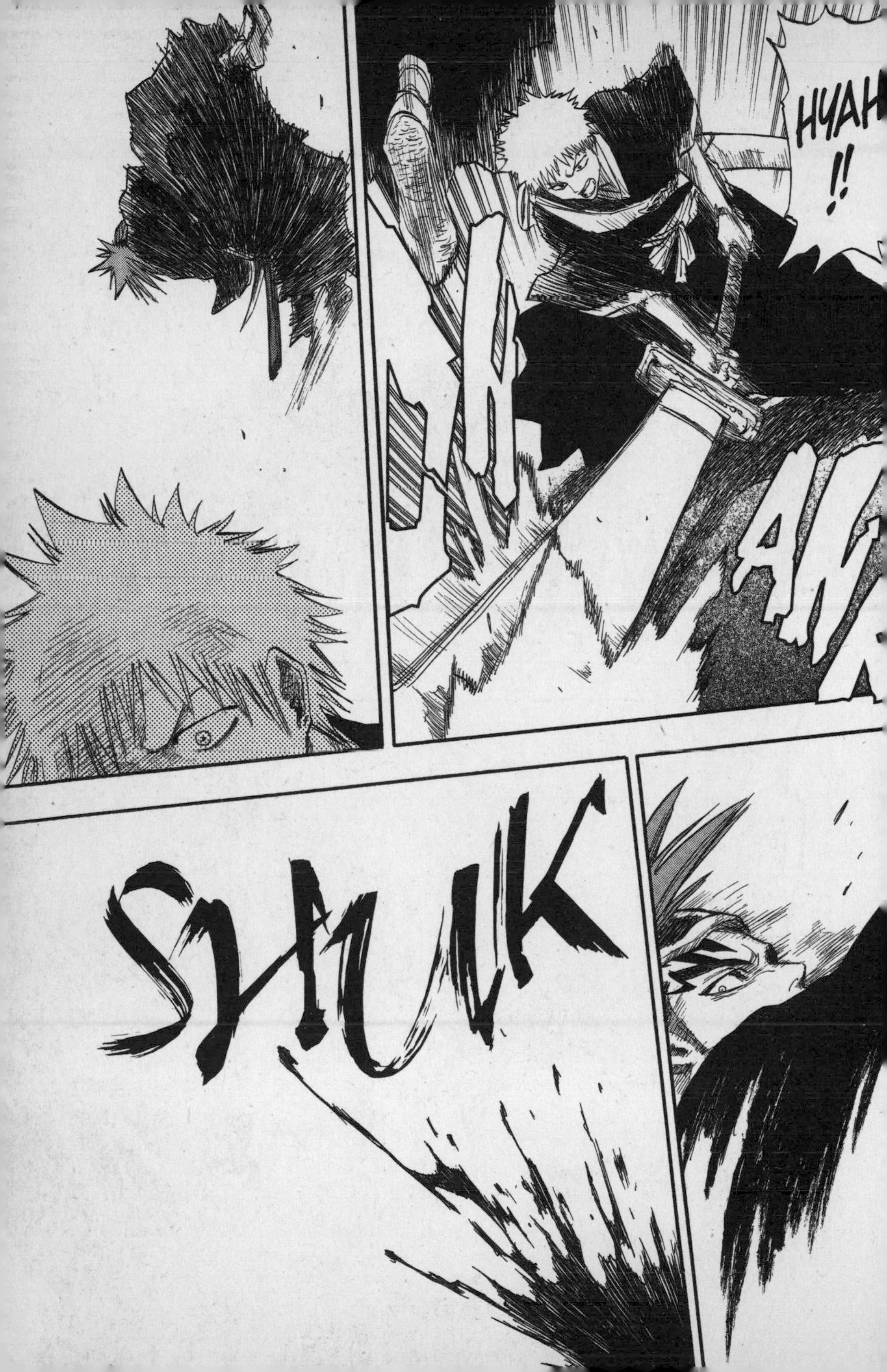

HYAH !!
SHUK

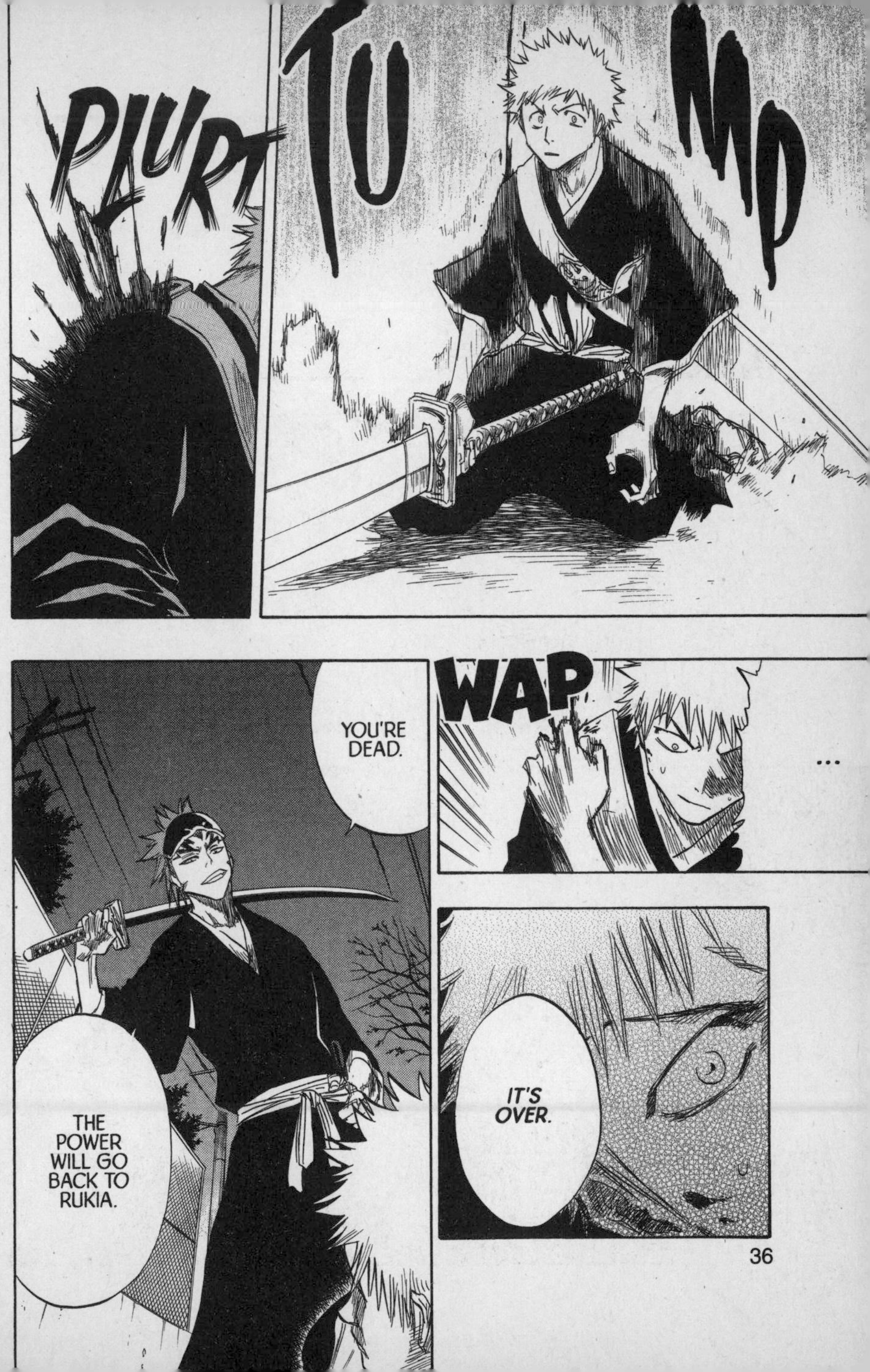
TUMP
PAURT
WAP
...
IT'S OVER.
YOU'RE DEAD.
THE POWER WILL GO BACK TO RUKIA.

READ THIS WAY

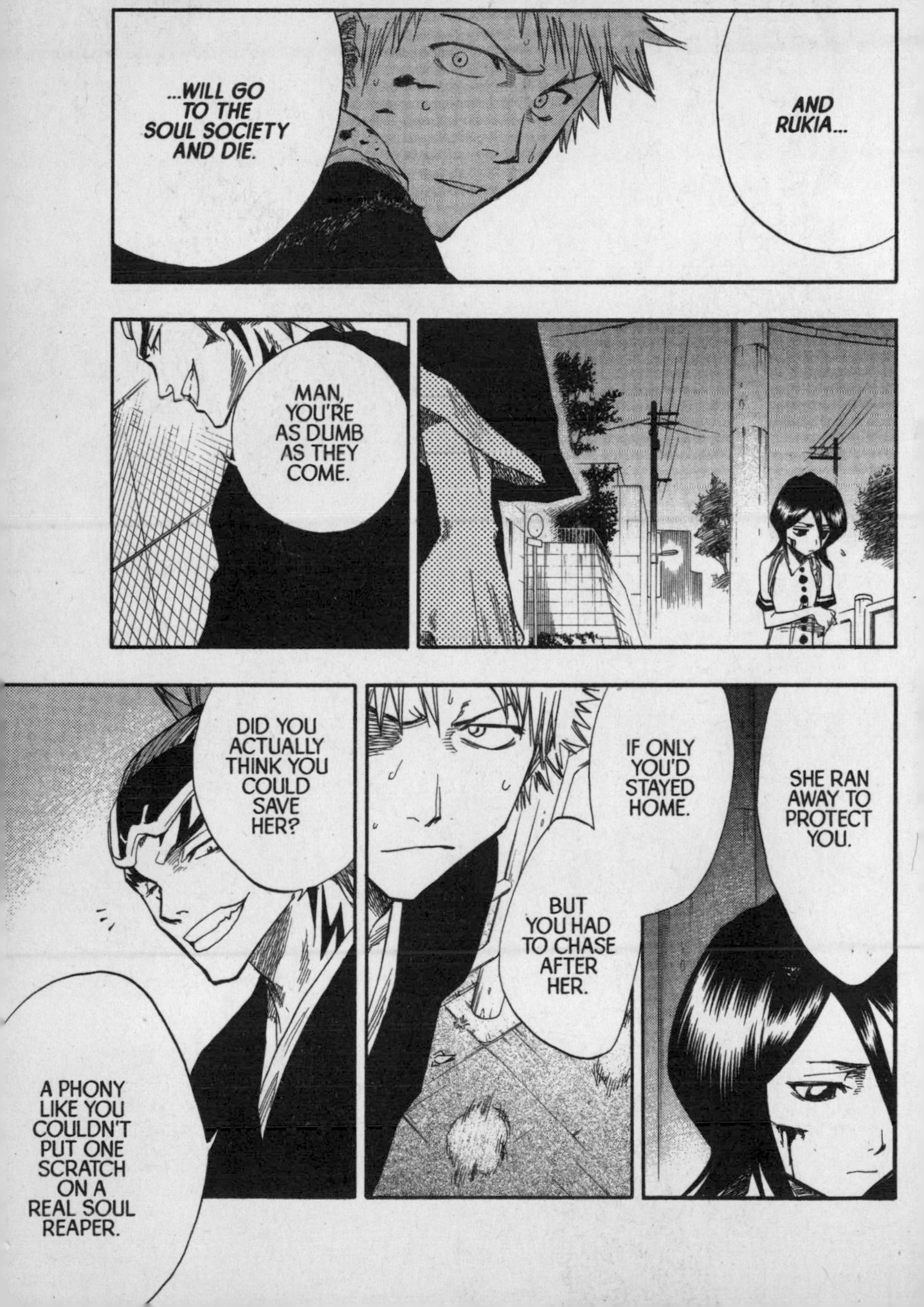
AND RUKIA...
...WILL GO TO THE SOUL SOCIETY AND DIE.
MAN, YOU'RE AS DUMB AS THEY COME.
SHE RAN AWAY TO PROTECT YOU.
IF ONLY YOU'D STAYED HOME.
BUT YOU HAD TO CHASE AFTER HER.
DID YOU ACTUALLY THINK YOU COULD SAVE HER?
A PHONY LIKE YOU COULDN'T PUT ONE SCRATCH ON A REAL SOUL REAPER.

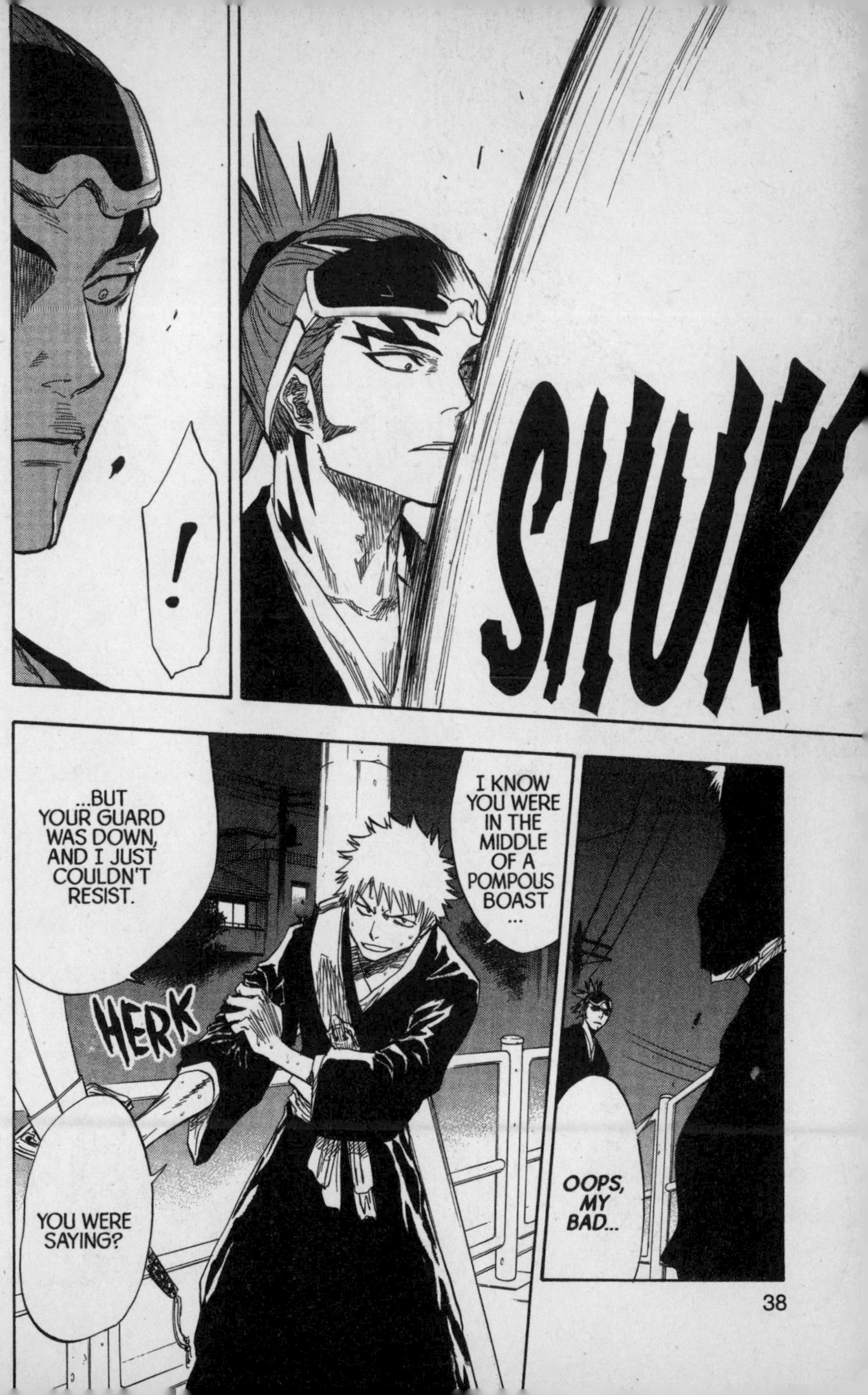
SHUK
!
OOPS, MY BAD...
I KNOW YOU WERE IN THE MIDDLE OF A POMPOUS BOAST...
...BUT YOUR GUARD WAS DOWN, AND I JUST COULDN'T RESIST.
HERK
YOU WERE SAYING?

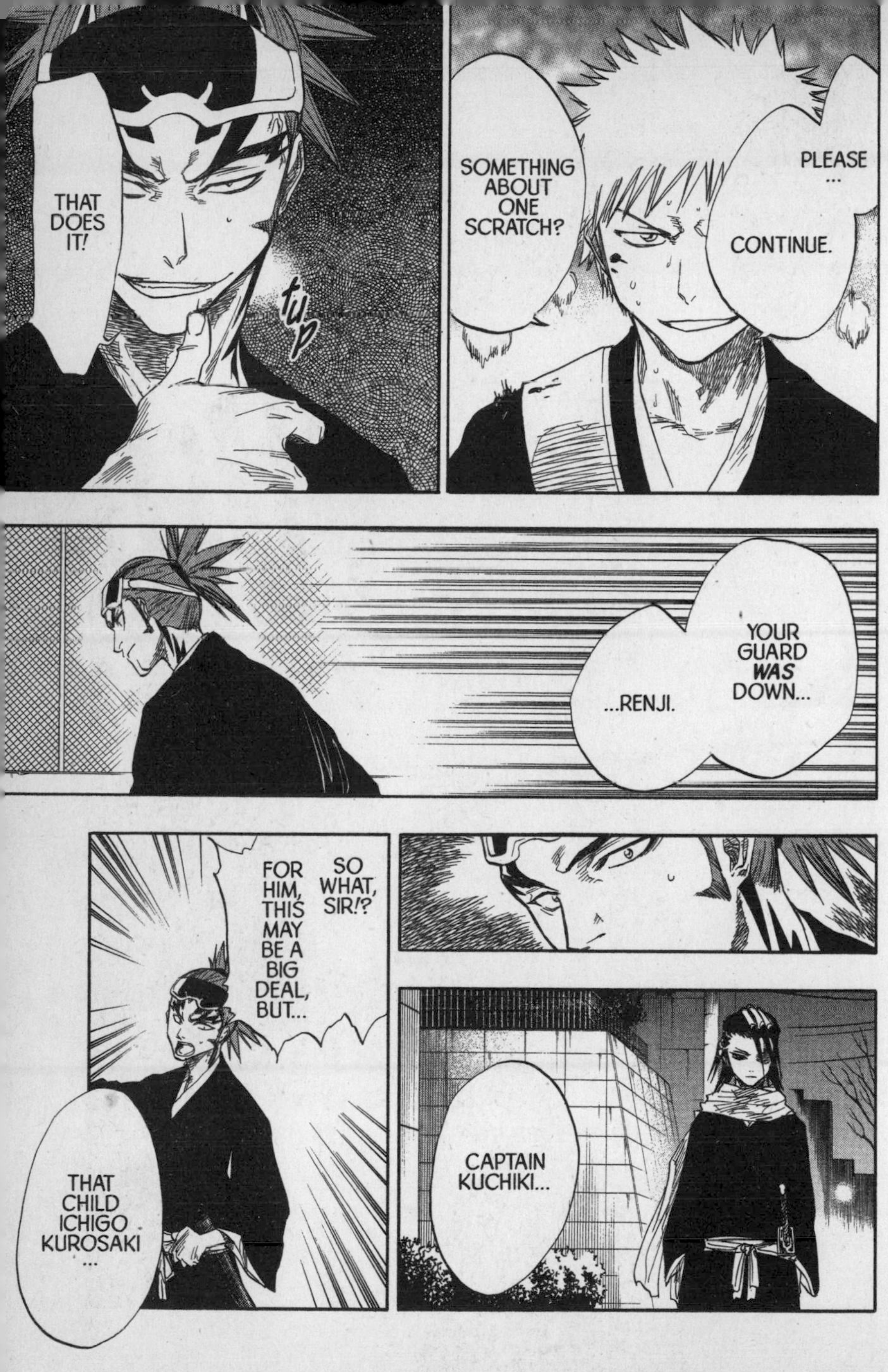
PLEASE ... CONTINUE.
SOMETHING ABOUT ONE SCRATCH?
THAT DOES IT!
tup
YOUR GUARD WAS DOWN...
...RENJI.
CAPTAIN KUCHIKI...
SO WHAT, SIR!?
FOR HIM, THIS MAY BE A BIG DEAL, BUT...
THAT CHILD ICHIGO KUROSAKI ...

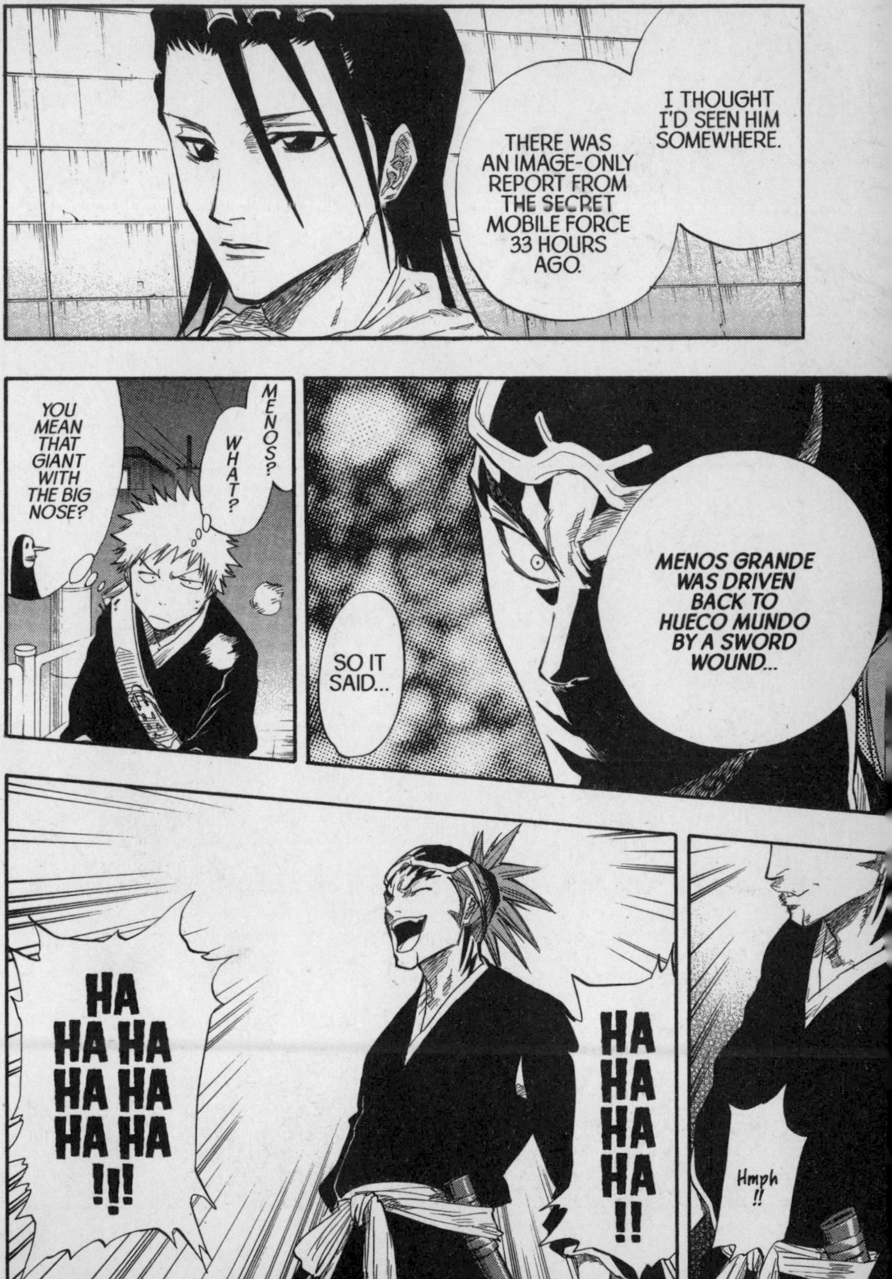
I THOUGHT I'D SEEN HIM SOMEWHERE.
THERE WAS AN IMAGE-ONLY REPORT FROM THE SECRET MOBILE FORCE 33 HOURS AGO.
MENOS GRANDE WAS DRIVEN BACK TO HUECO MUNDO BY A SWORD WOUND...
SO IT SAID...
MENOS? WHAT?
YOU MEAN THAT GIANT WITH THE BIG NOSE?
Hmph !!
HA HA HA HA HA!!
HA HA HA HA HA HA HA HA !!!

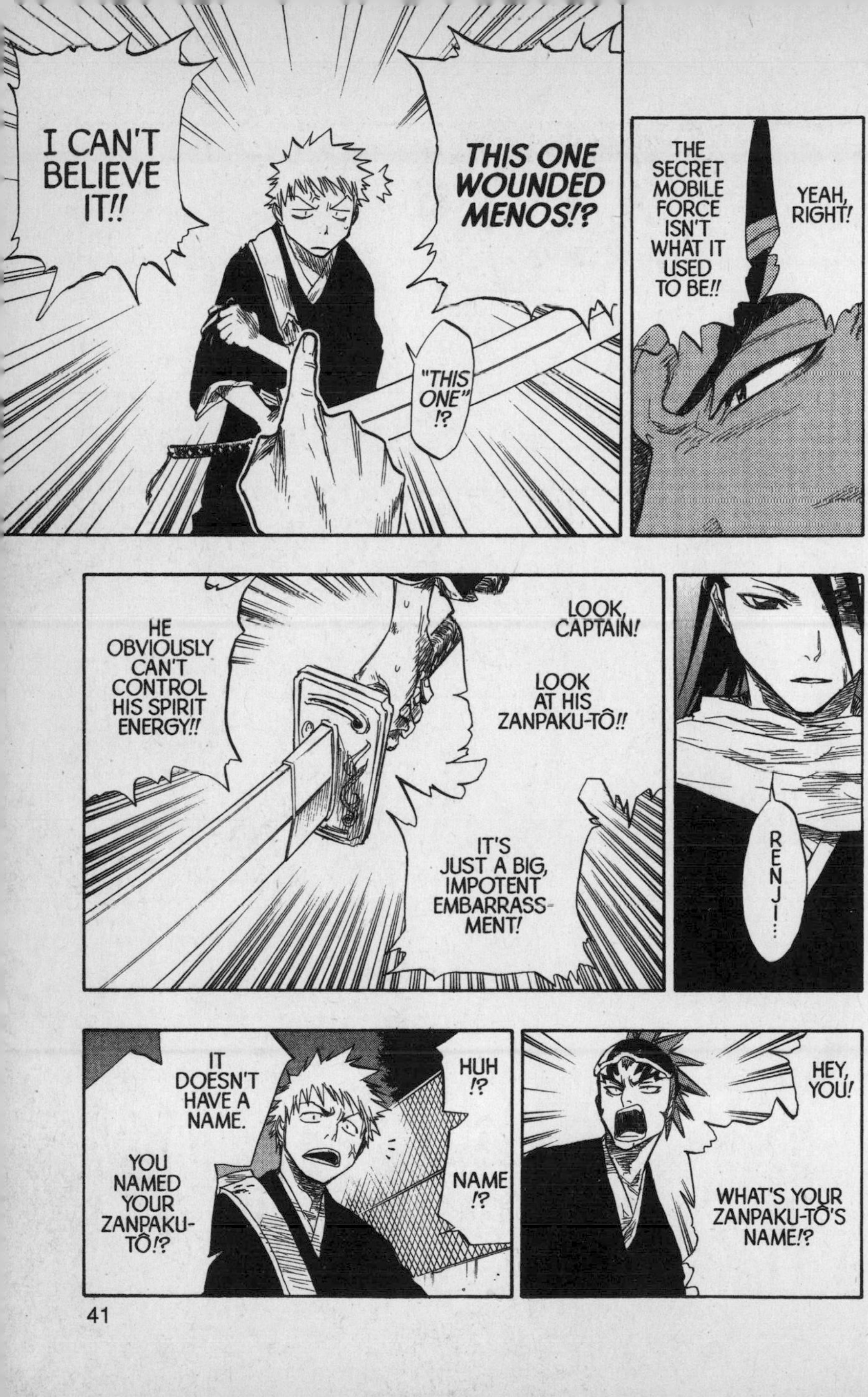
YEAH, RIGHT!
THE SECRET MOBILE FORCE ISN'T WHAT IT USED TO BE!!
THIS ONE WOUNDED MENOS!?
I CAN'T BELIEVE IT!!
"THIS ONE"!?
RENJI…
LOOK, CAPTAIN!
LOOK AT HIS ZANPAKU-TÔ!!
HE OBVIOUSLY CAN'T CONTROL HIS SPIRIT ENERGY!!
IT'S JUST A BIG, IMPOTENT EMBARRASS-MENT!
HEY, YOU!
WHAT'S YOUR ZANPAKU-TÔ'S NAME!?
HUH!?
IT DOESN'T HAVE A NAME.
NAME!?
YOU NAMED YOUR ZANPAKU-TÔ!?

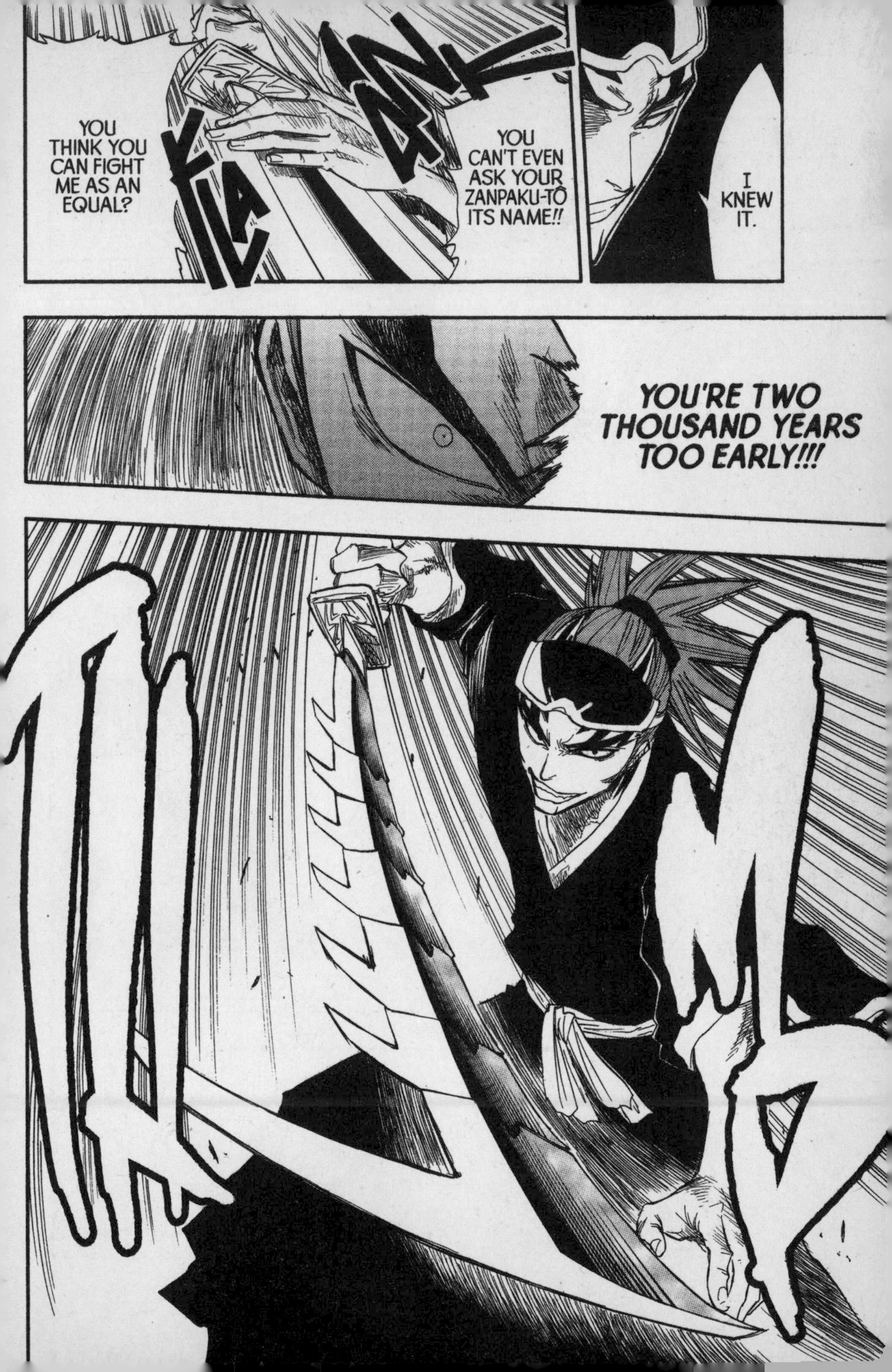
I KNEW IT.
YOU CAN'T EVEN ASK YOUR ZANPAKU-TÔ ITS NAME!!
YOU THINK YOU CAN FIGHT ME AS AN EQUAL?
YOU'RE TWO THOUSAND YEARS TOO EARLY!!!

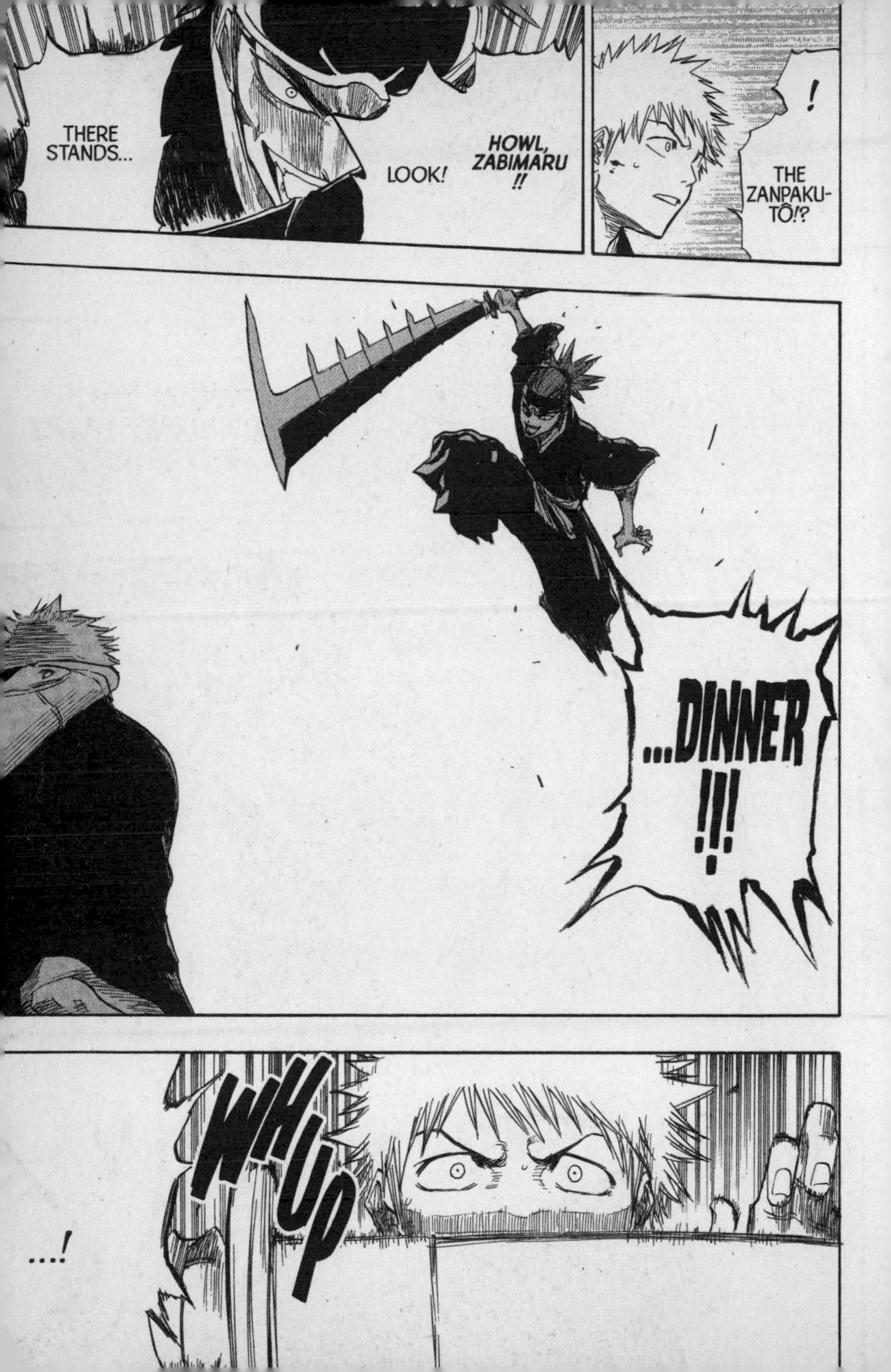
!
THE ZANPAKUTÔ!?
HOWL, ZABIMARU!!
LOOK!
THERE STANDS...
...DINNER!!!
WHUP
...!

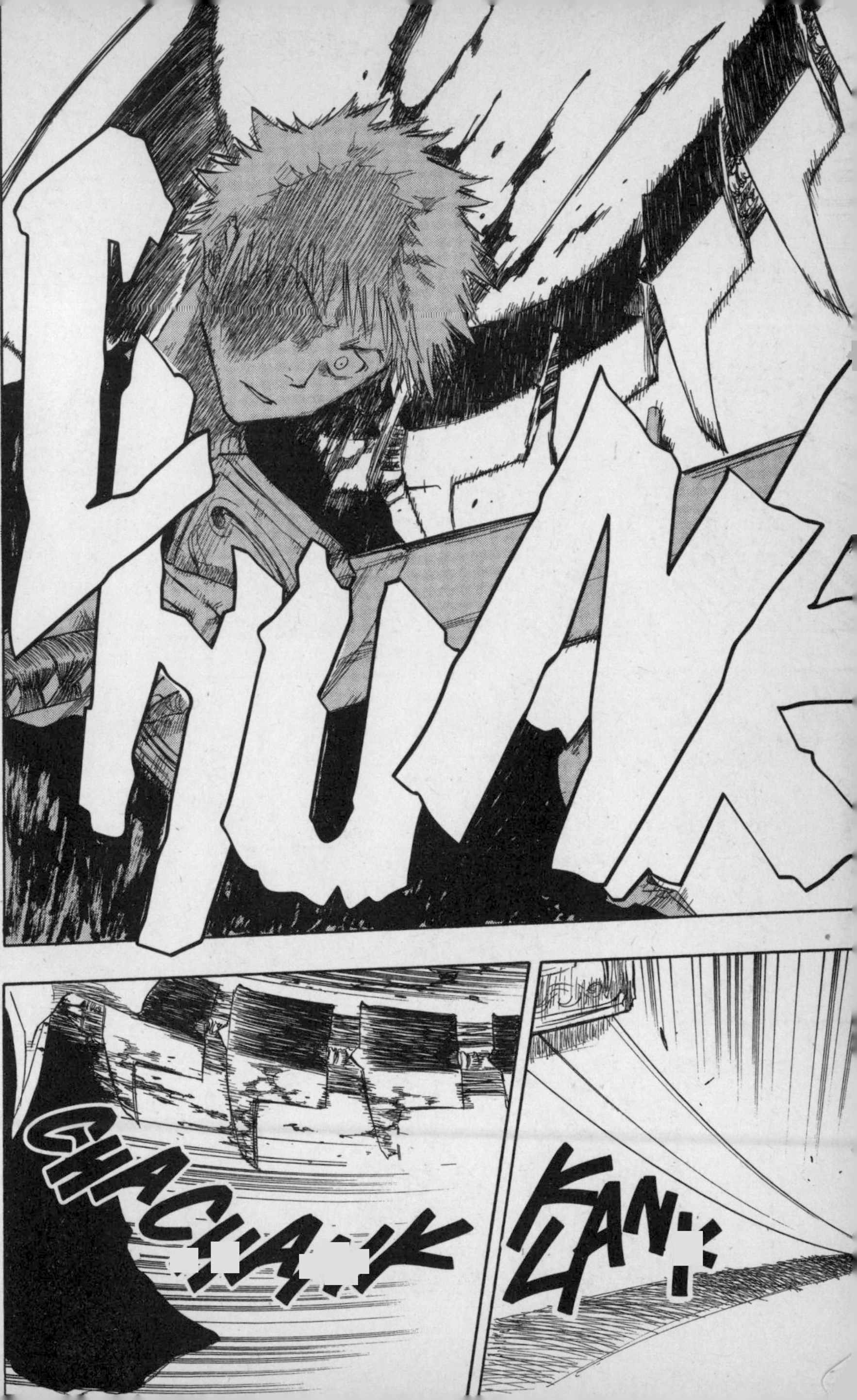
CHUNK
KAN
CHACHAK

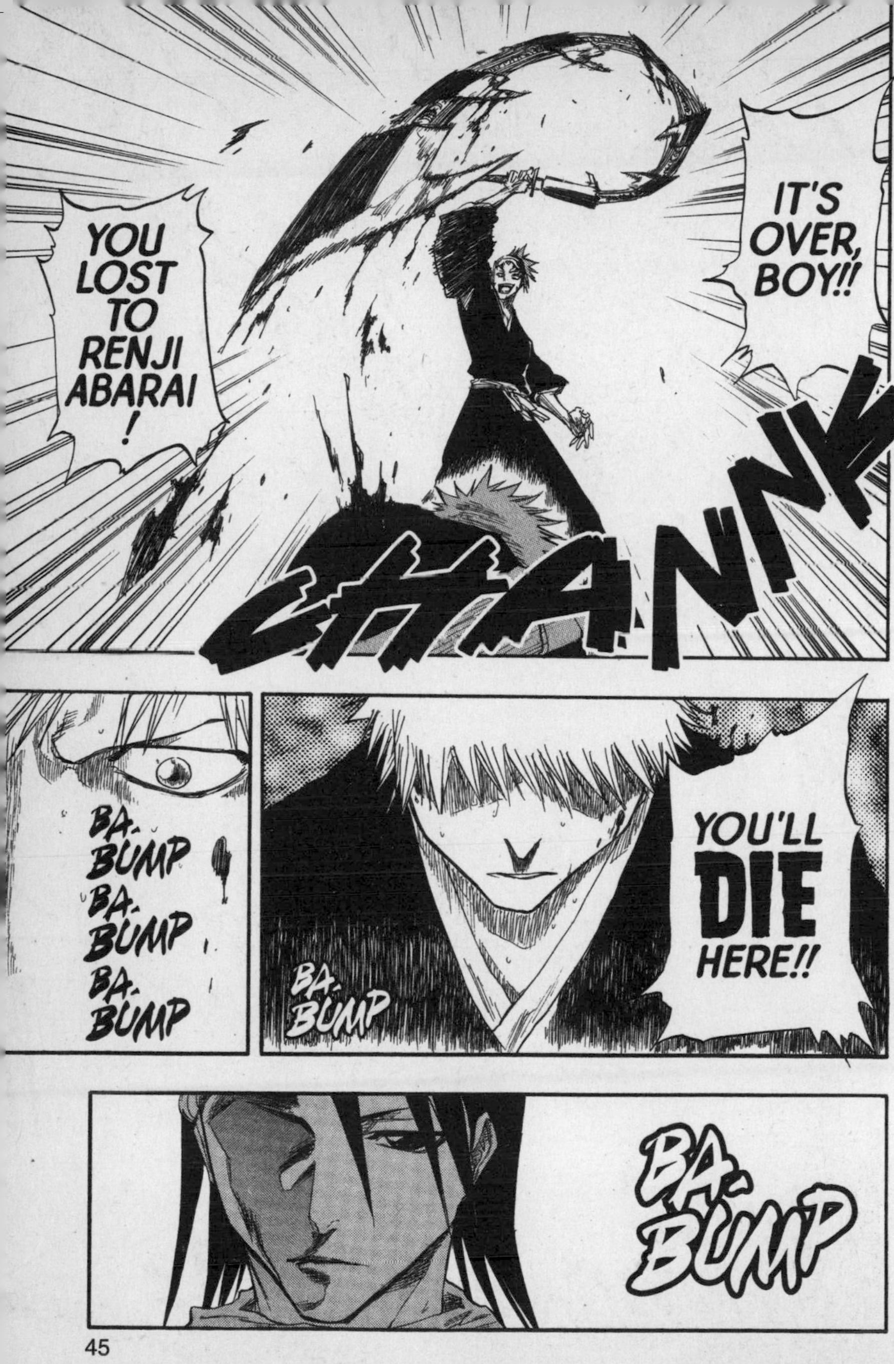
IT'S OVER, BOY!!
YOU LOST TO RENJI ABARAI!
CHANNK
YOU'LL DIE HERE!!
BA-BUMP
BA-BUMP BA-BUMP BA-BUMP
BA-BUMP

55. SHUT

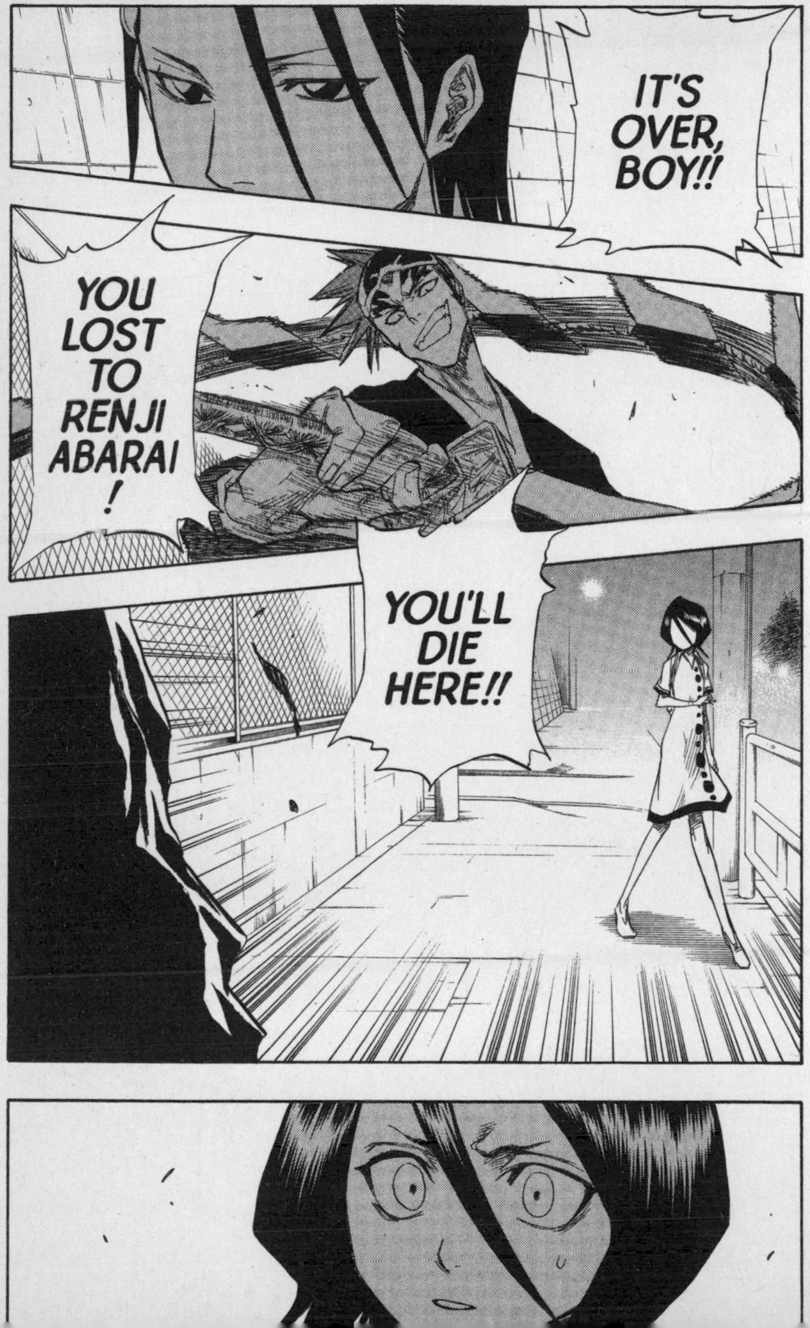
IT'S OVER, BOY!!
YOU LOST TO RENJI ABARAI!
YOU'LL DIE HERE!!

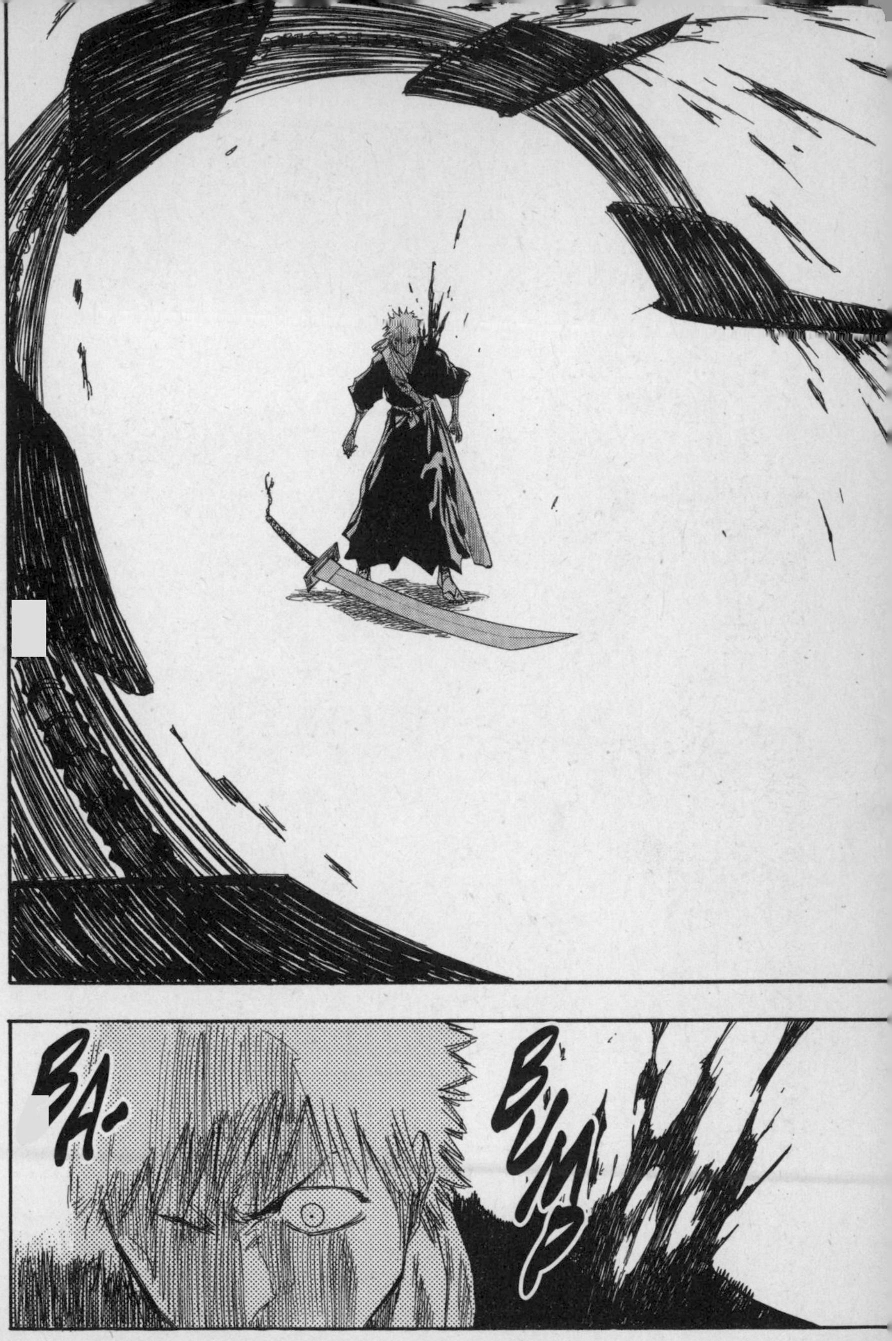
BA-
BUMP

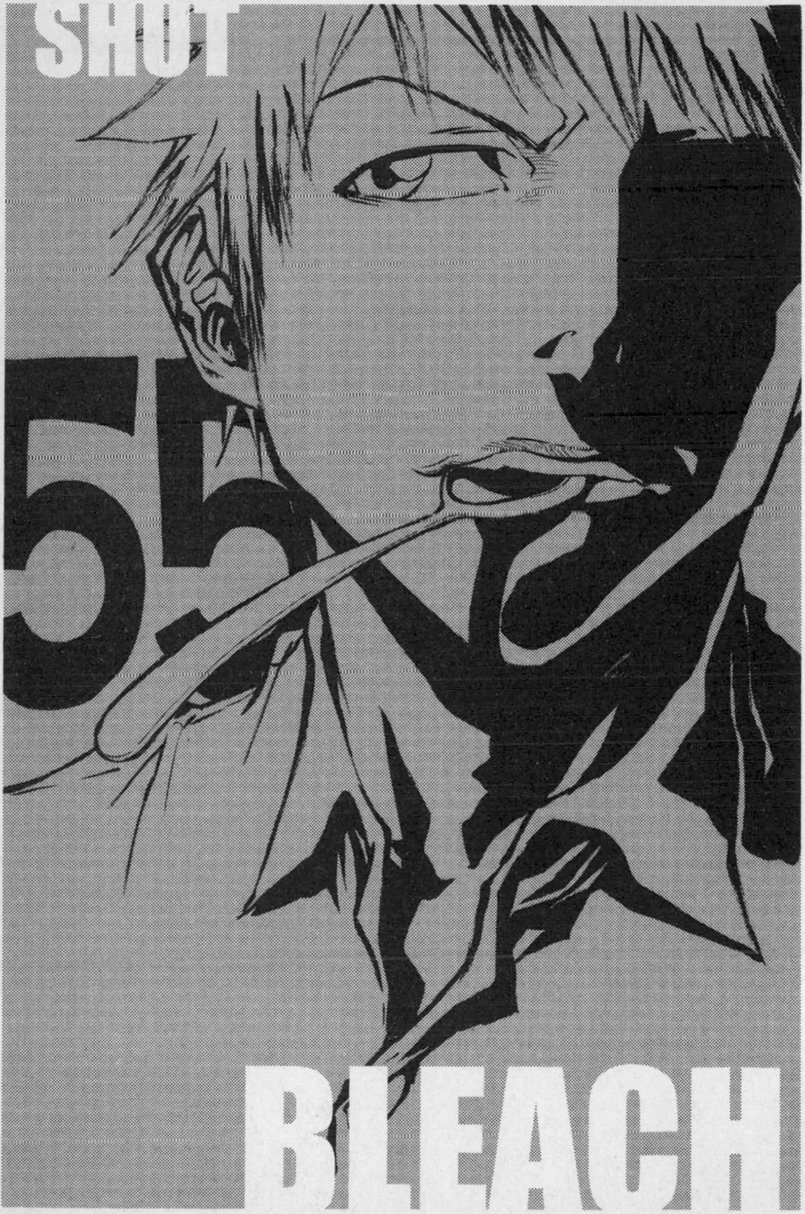
SHOT
55
BLEACH

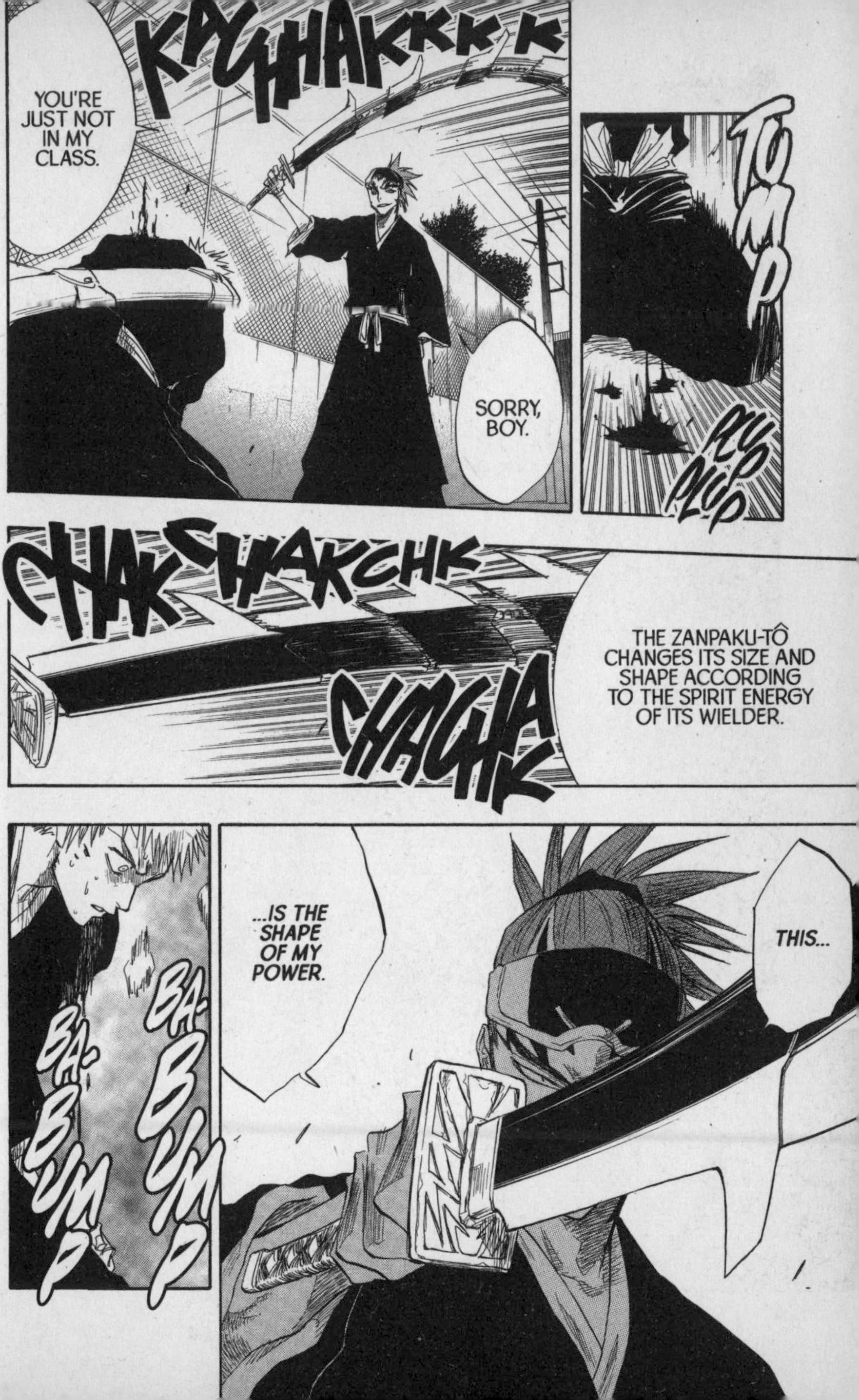
TOMP
PLIP PLOP
KPCHHAKKKK
YOU'RE JUST NOT IN MY CLASS.
SORRY, BOY.
THE ZANPAKU-TÔ CHANGES ITS SIZE AND SHAPE ACCORDING TO THE SPIRIT ENERGY OF ITS WIELDER.
SHAKCHK
CHAK
CHACHAK
THIS...
...IS THE SHAPE OF MY POWER.
BA-BUMP
BA-BUMP

READ THIS WAY

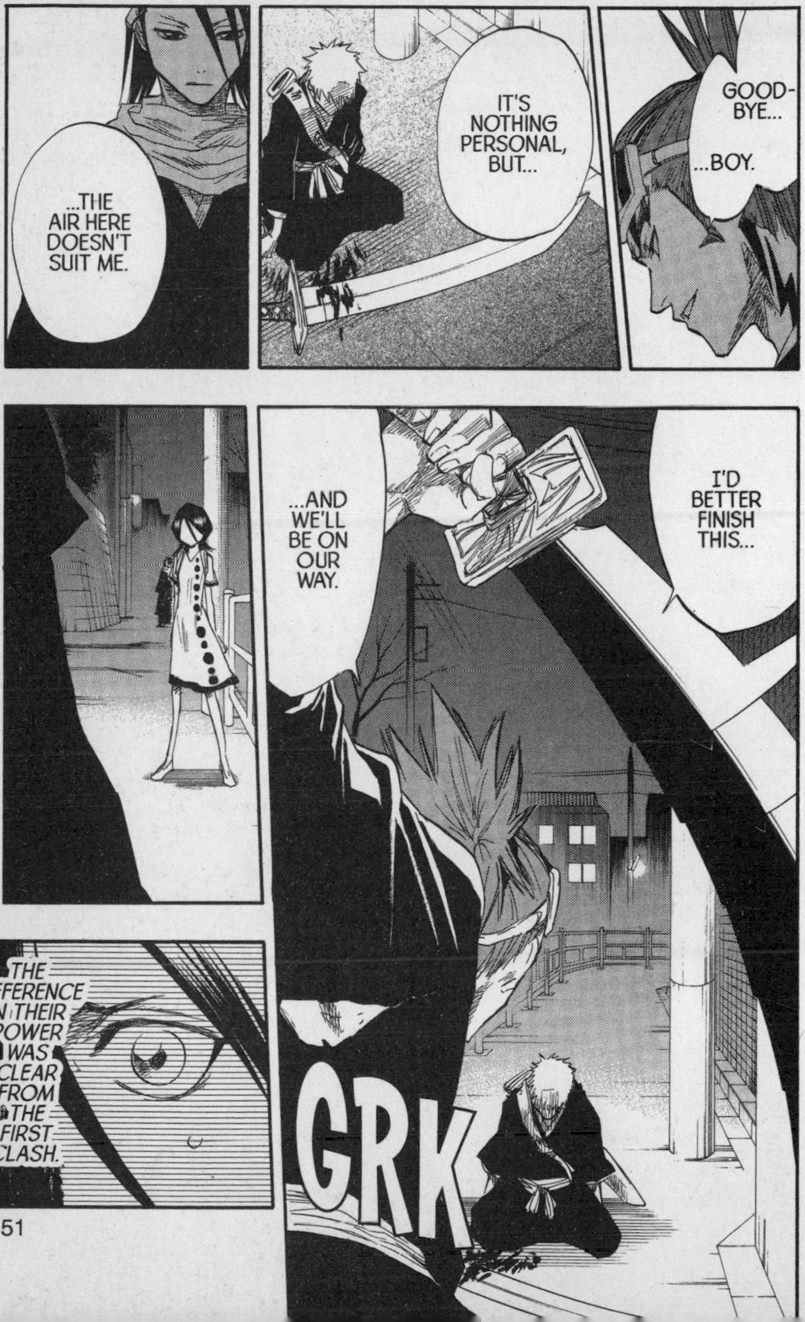

GOOD-BYE...
...BOY.
IT'S NOTHING PERSONAL, BUT...
...THE AIR HERE DOESN'T SUIT ME.
I'D BETTER FINISH THIS...
...AND WE'LL BE ON OUR WAY.
GRK
THE DIFFERENCE IN THEIR POWER WAS CLEAR FROM THE FIRST CLASH.

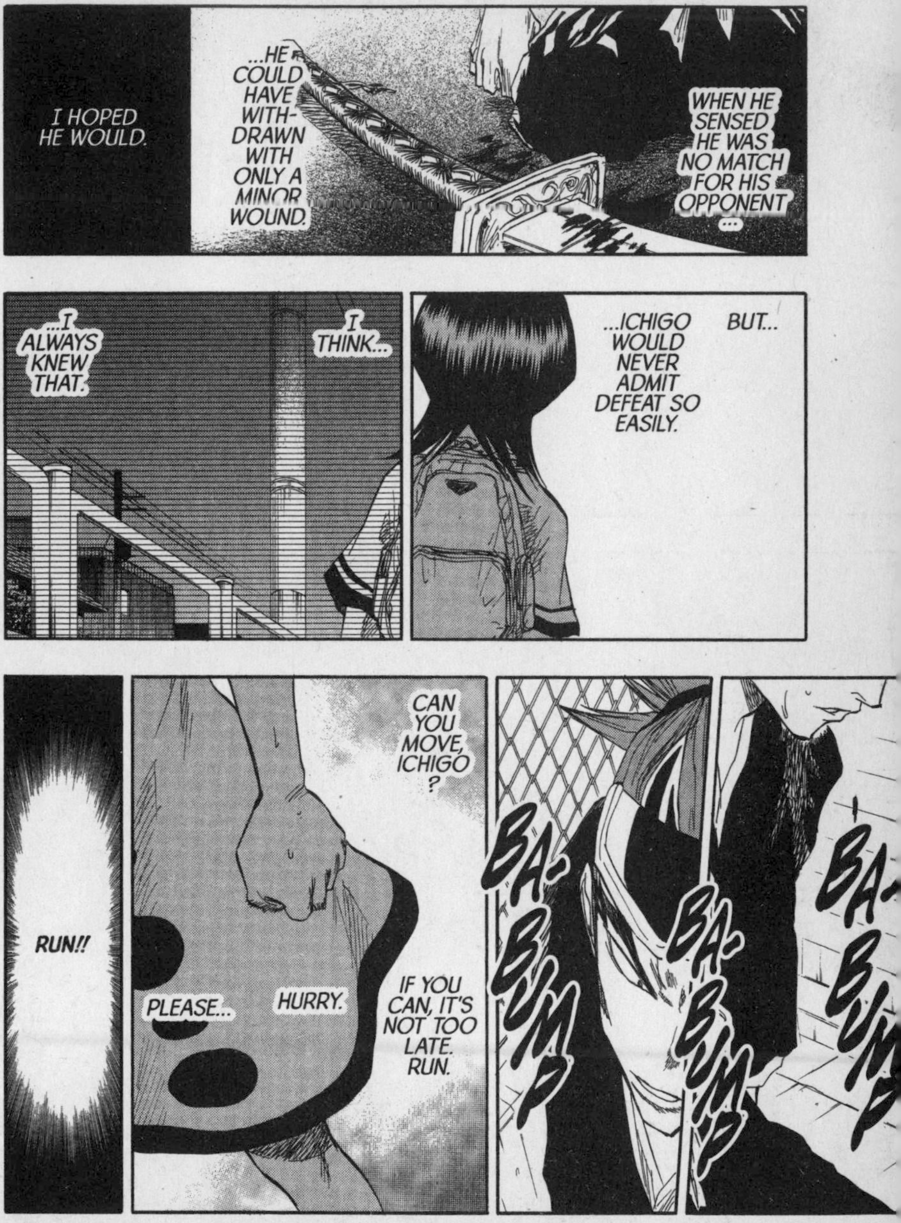
WHEN HE SENSED HE WAS NO MATCH FOR HIS OPPONENT...
...HE COULD HAVE WITH-DRAWN WITH ONLY A MINOR WOUND.
I HOPED HE WOULD.
BUT...
...ICHIGO WOULD NEVER ADMIT DEFEAT SO EASILY.
I THINK...
...I ALWAYS KNEW THAT.
BA-BUMP
BA-BUMP
BA-BUMP
CAN YOU MOVE, ICHIGO?
IF YOU CAN, IT'S NOT TOO LATE. RUN.
HURRY.
PLEASE...
RUN!!

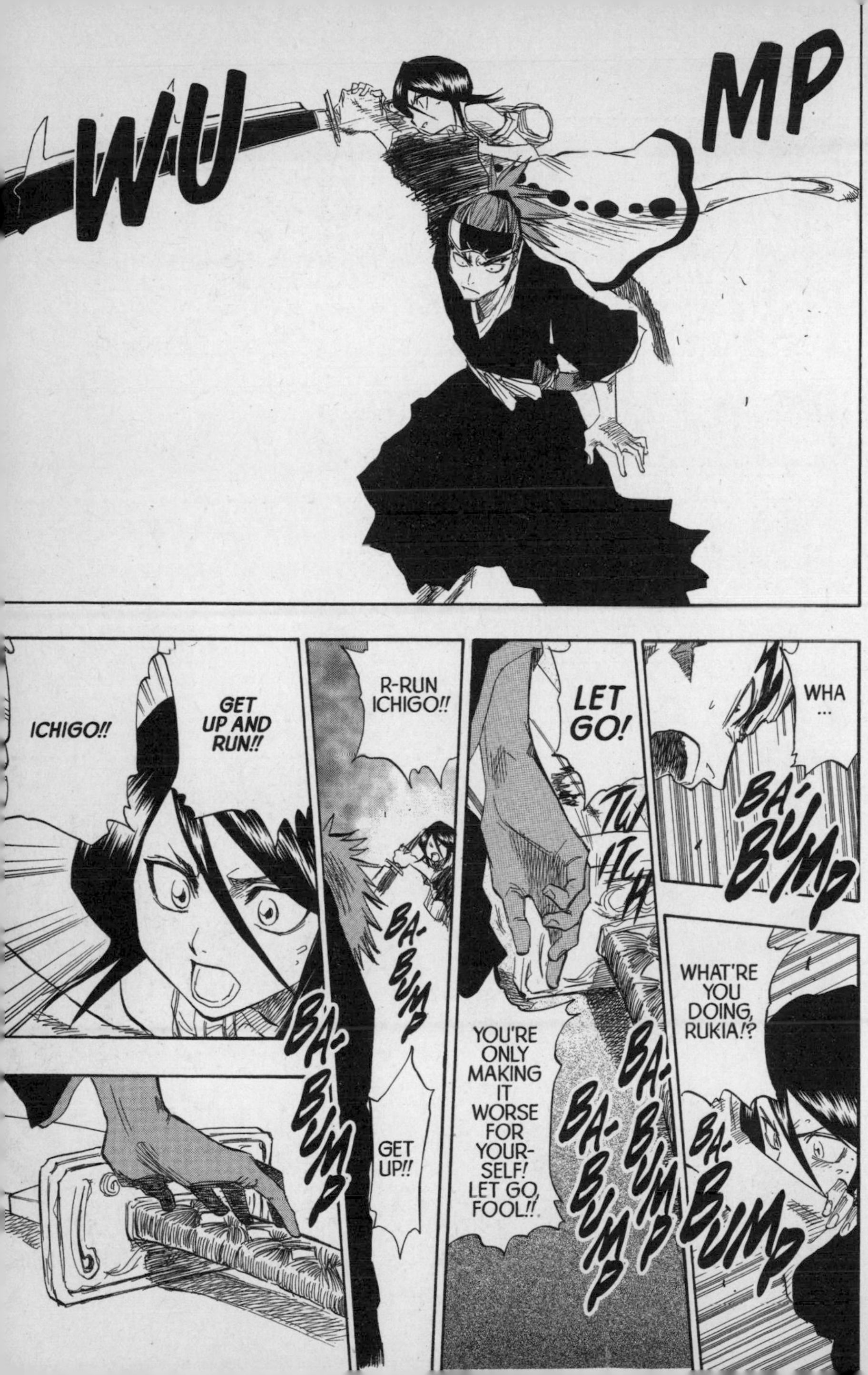
WUMP
WHA ...
BA-BUMP
WHAT'RE YOU DOING, RUKIA!?
BA-BUMP
LET GO!
TWITCH
YOU'RE ONLY MAKING IT WORSE FOR YOURSELF! LET GO, FOOL!!
BA-BUMP
BA-BUMP
R-RUN ICHIGO!!
BA-BUMP
GET UP!!
GET UP AND RUN!!
ICHIGO!!
BA-BUMP

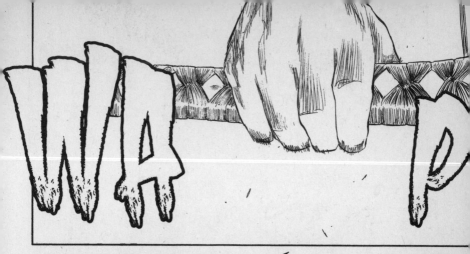

WAP

!!

WUMP

WHAT?

YOU CAN STILL MOVE?

EXCELLENT.

IT'S NO FUN BUTCHERING A CRIPPLED PIG, ANYWAY.

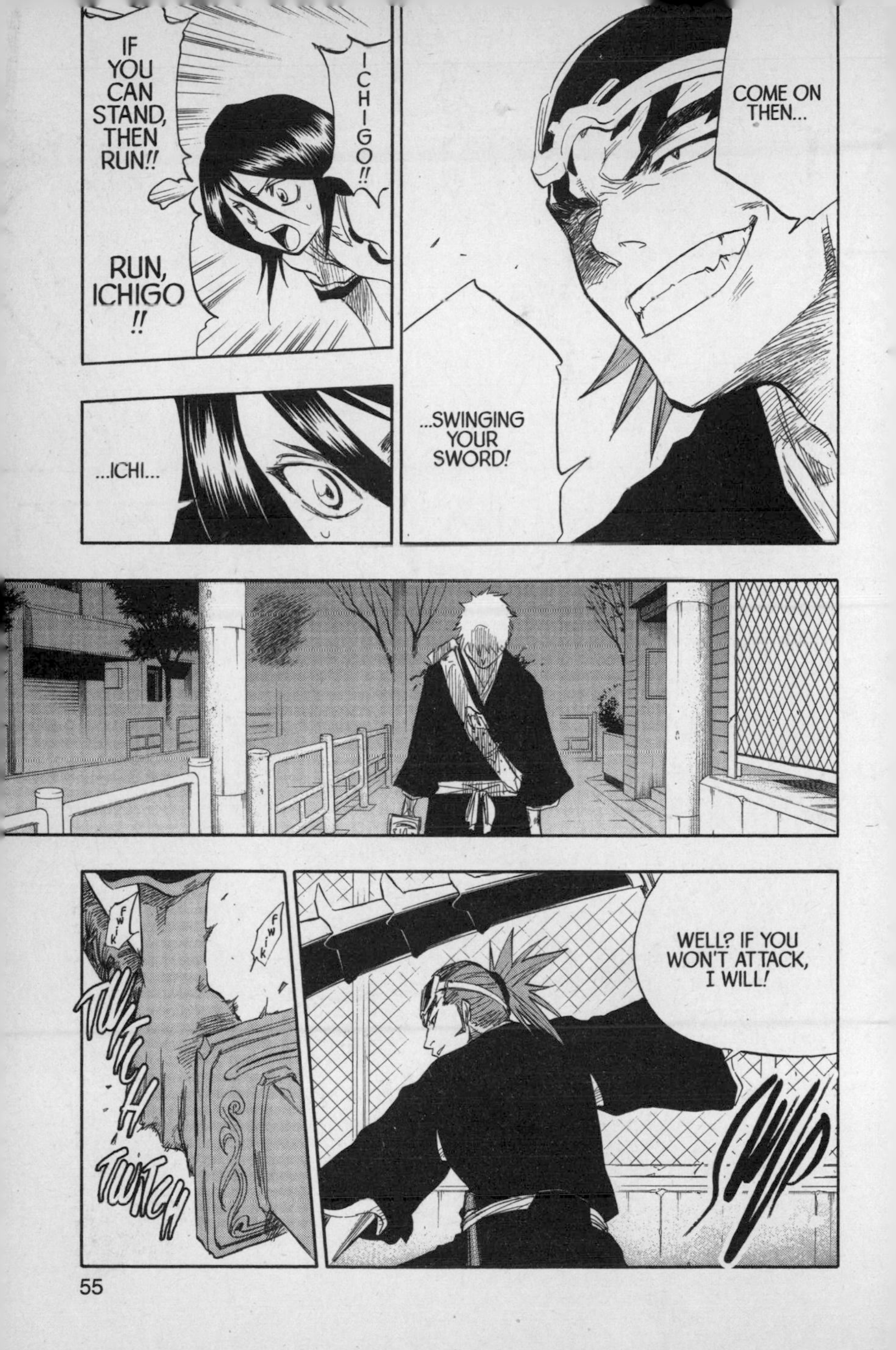
COME ON THEN...
...SWINGING YOUR SWORD!
ICHIGO!!
IF YOU CAN STAND, THEN RUN!!
RUN, ICHIGO!!
...ICHI...
WELL? IF YOU WON'T ATTACK, I WILL!
FWIK
FWIK
TWITCH
TWITCH

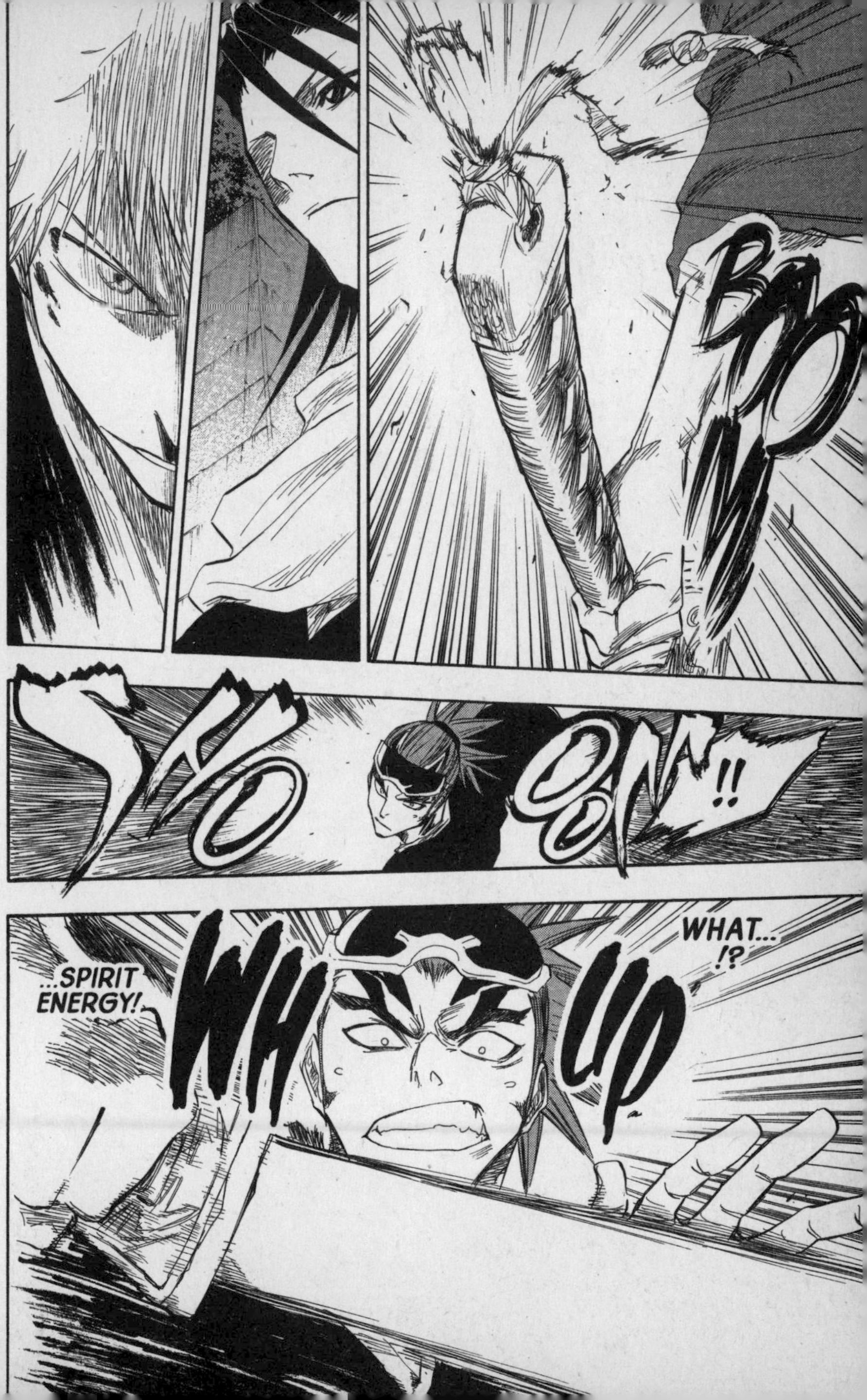
BOOM
SHOOOM!!
WHAT... !?
WHUP
...SPIRIT ENERGY!

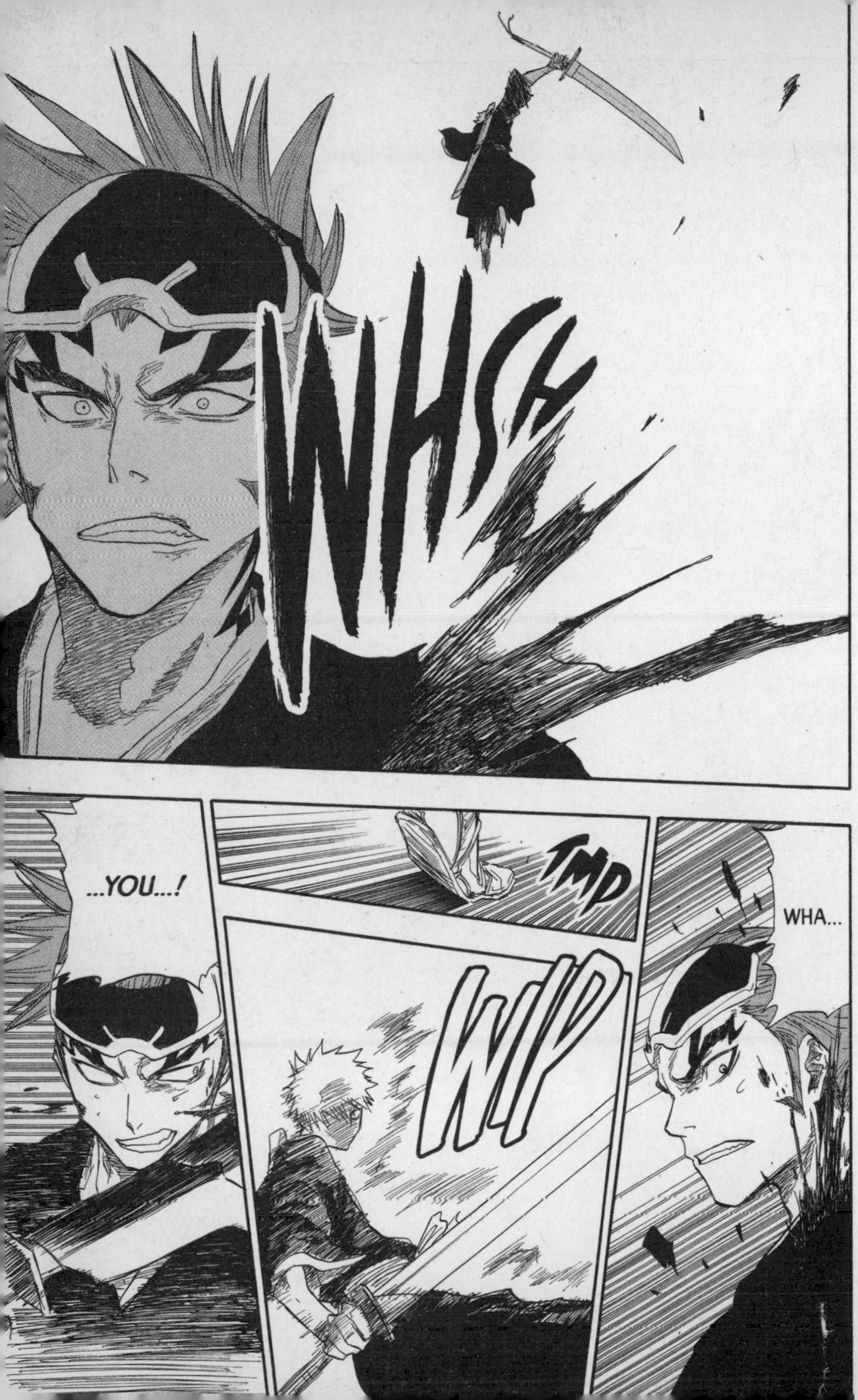
WHSH
WHA...
TMP
WIP
...YOU...!

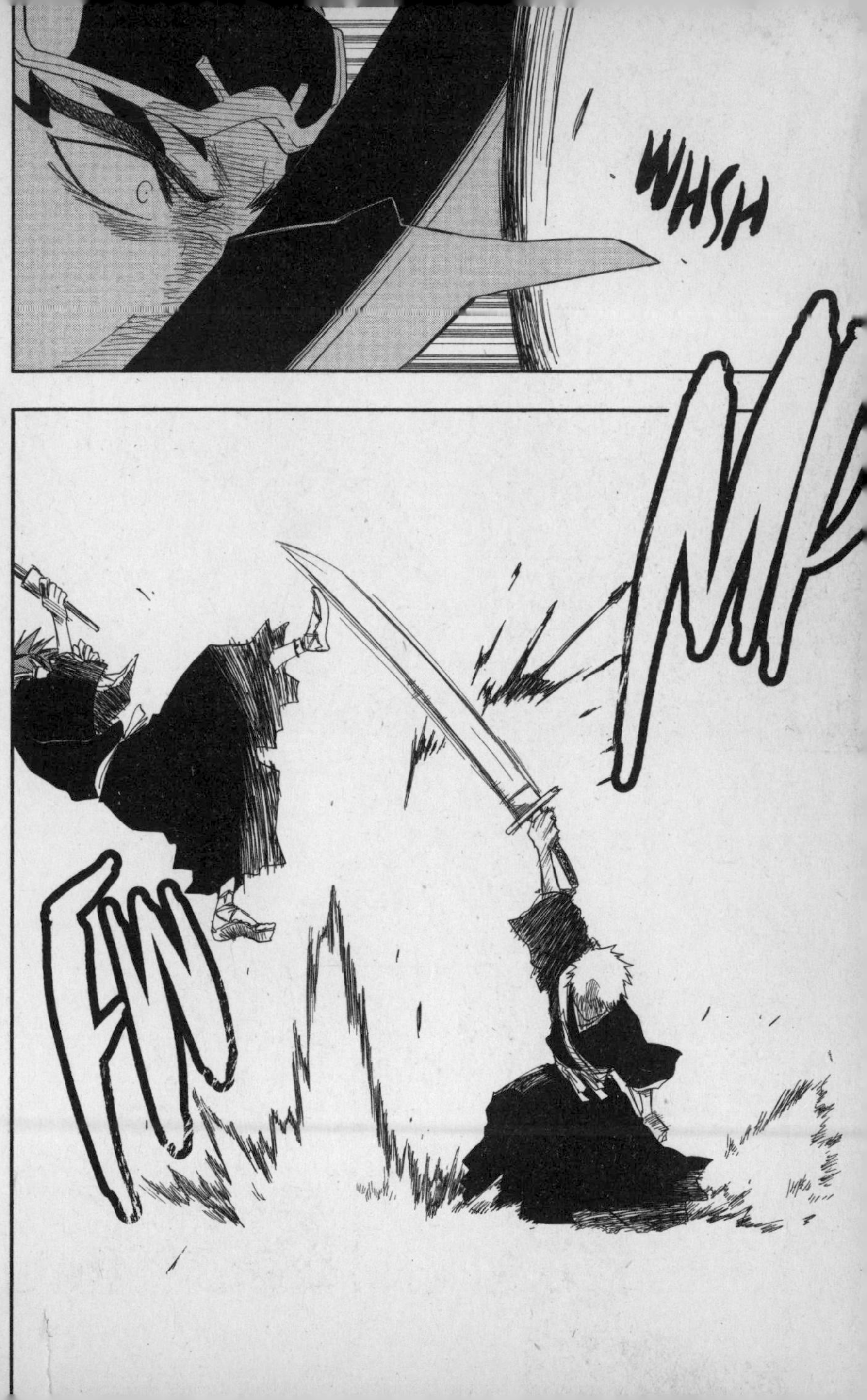
WHSH

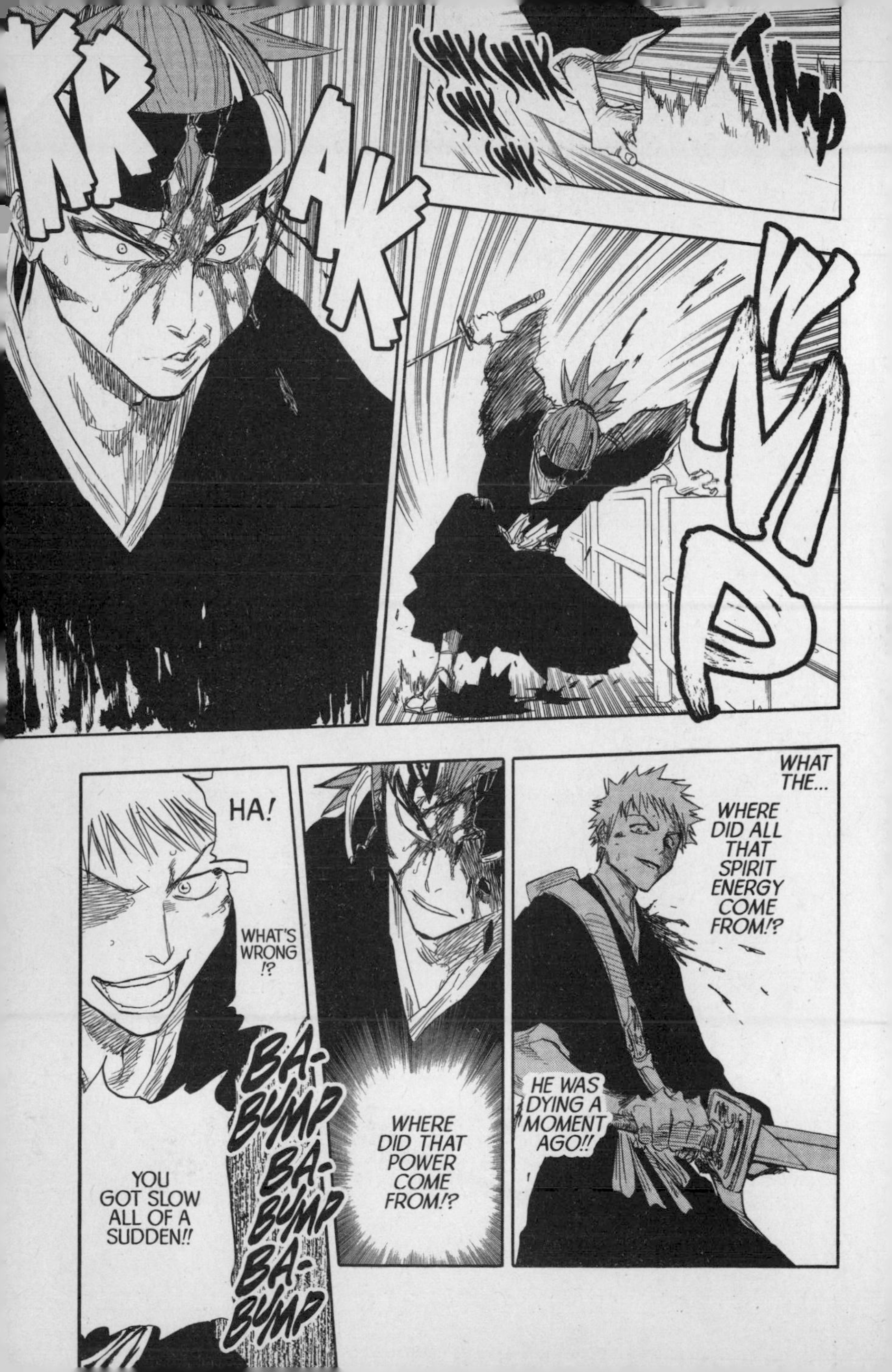
SWIK SWIK SWIK SWIK
TMP
KRAK
WHAT THE...
WHERE DID ALL THAT SPIRIT ENERGY COME FROM!?
HE WAS DYING A MOMENT AGO!!
WHERE DID THAT POWER COME FROM!?
BA-BUMP BA-BUMP BA-BUMP
HA!
WHAT'S WRONG!?
YOU GOT SLOW ALL OF A SUDDEN!!

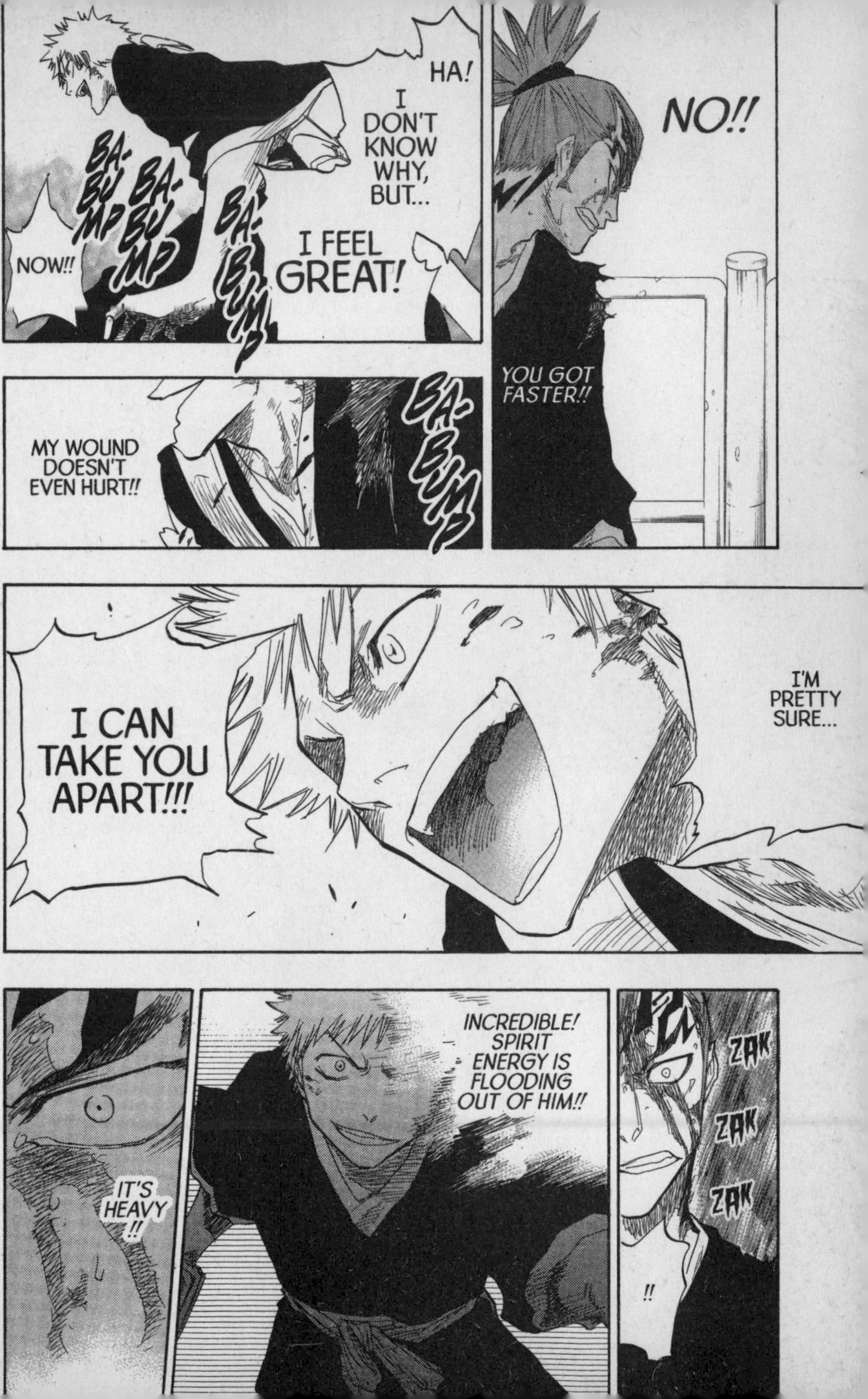
NO!!
YOU GOT FASTER!!
HA!
I DON'T KNOW WHY, BUT...
I FEEL GREAT!
BA-BUMP
BA-BUMP
BA-BUMP
NOW!!
BA-BUMP
MY WOUND DOESN'T EVEN HURT!!
I'M PRETTY SURE...
I CAN TAKE YOU APART!!!
ZAK
ZAK
ZAK
!!
INCREDIBLE! SPIRIT ENERGY IS FLOODING OUT OF HIM!!
IT'S HEAVY!!

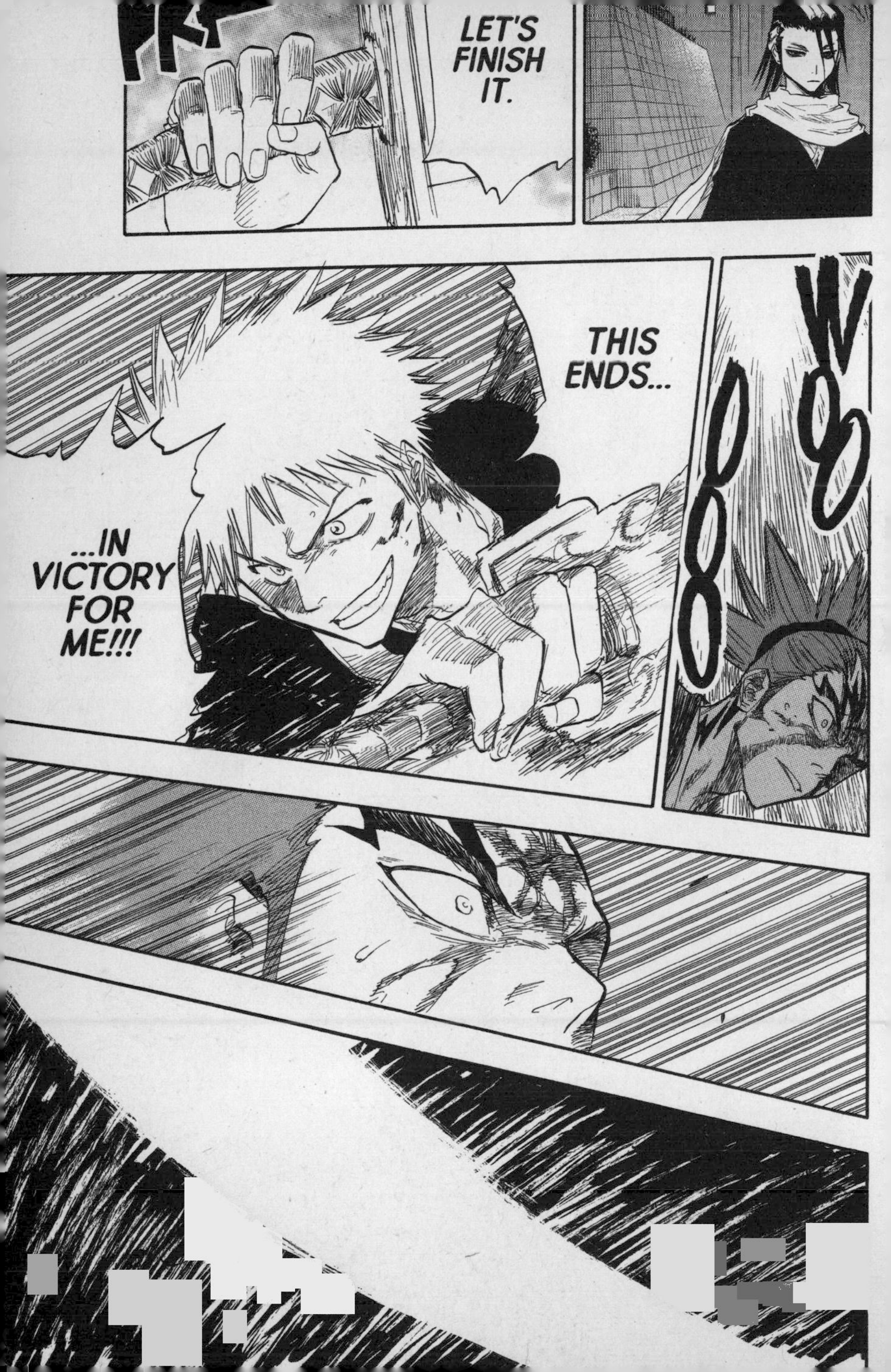
LET'S FINISH IT.
WOOOO
THIS ENDS...
...IN VICTORY FOR ME!!!

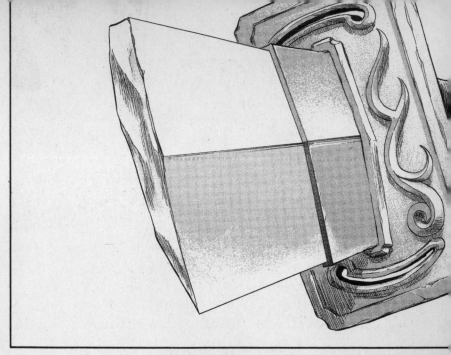

THE BLADE... DIS- APPEARED !?

WHAT !?

HE DIDN'T DO ANY- THING.

BUT...

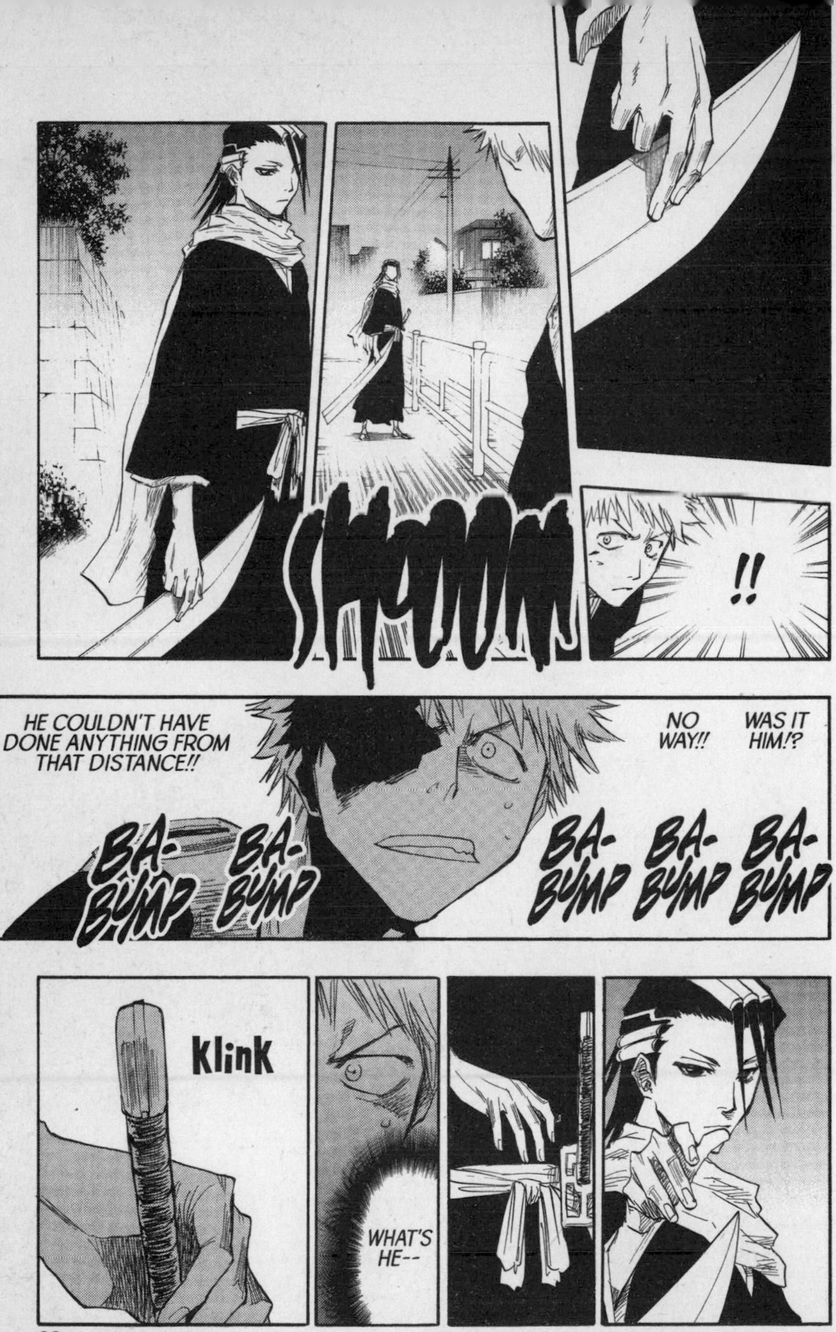
SHYOOM
!!
WAS IT HIM!?
NO WAY!!
HE COULDN'T HAVE DONE ANYTHING FROM THAT DISTANCE!!
BA-BUMP BA-BUMP BA-BUMP
BA-BUMP BA-BUMP
Klink
WHAT'S HE--

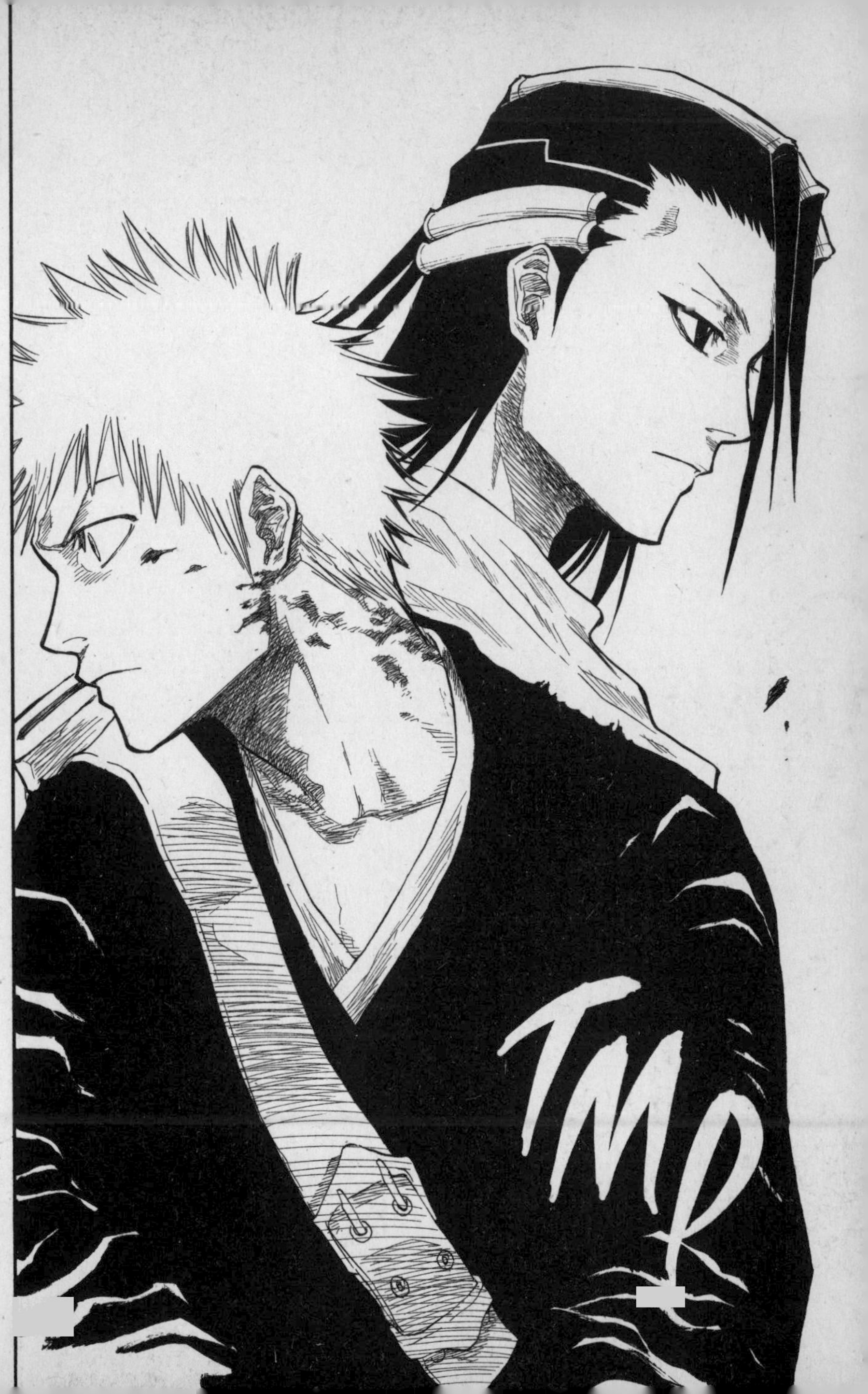
TMP

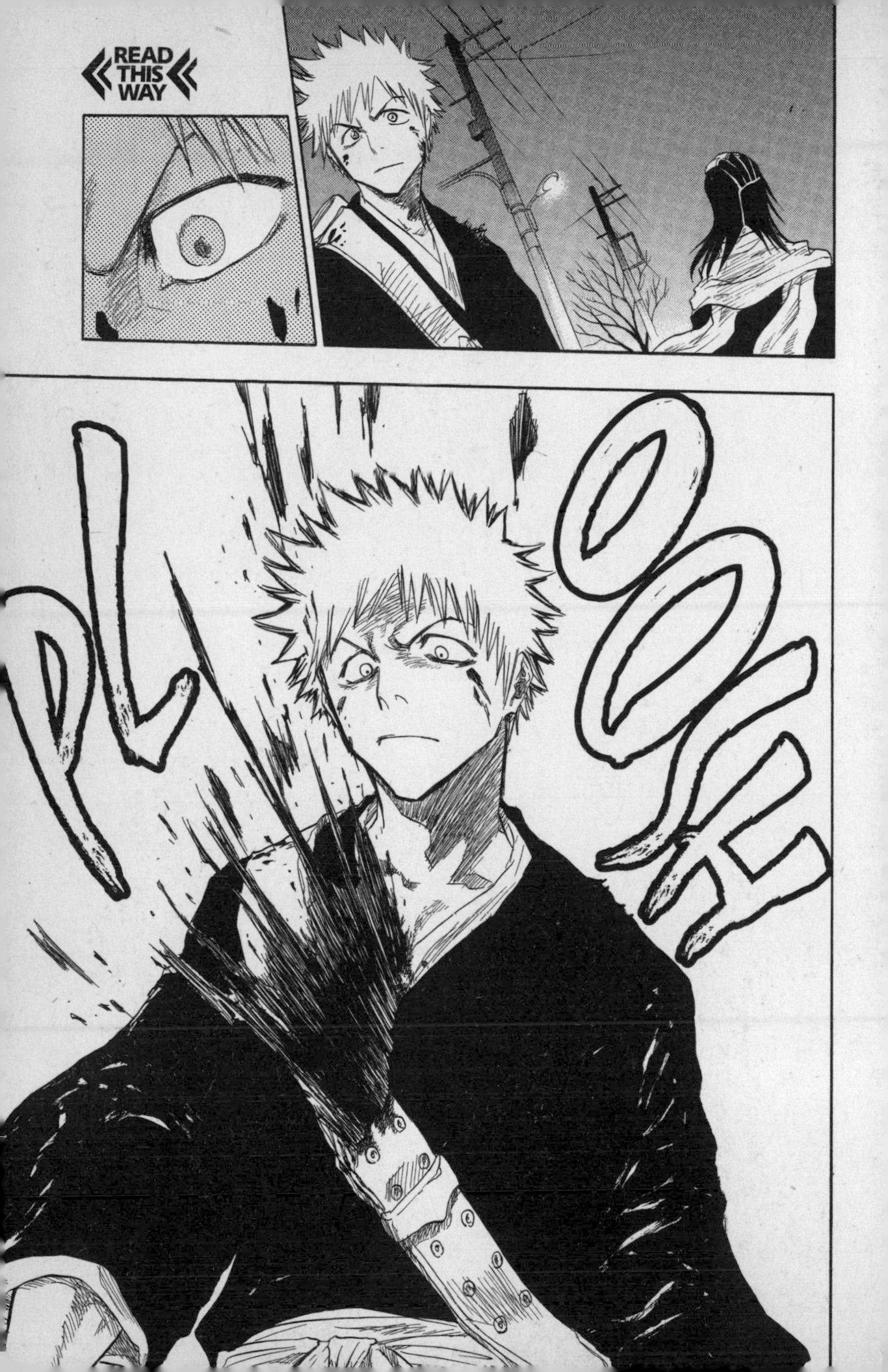
READ THIS WAY
PLOOSH

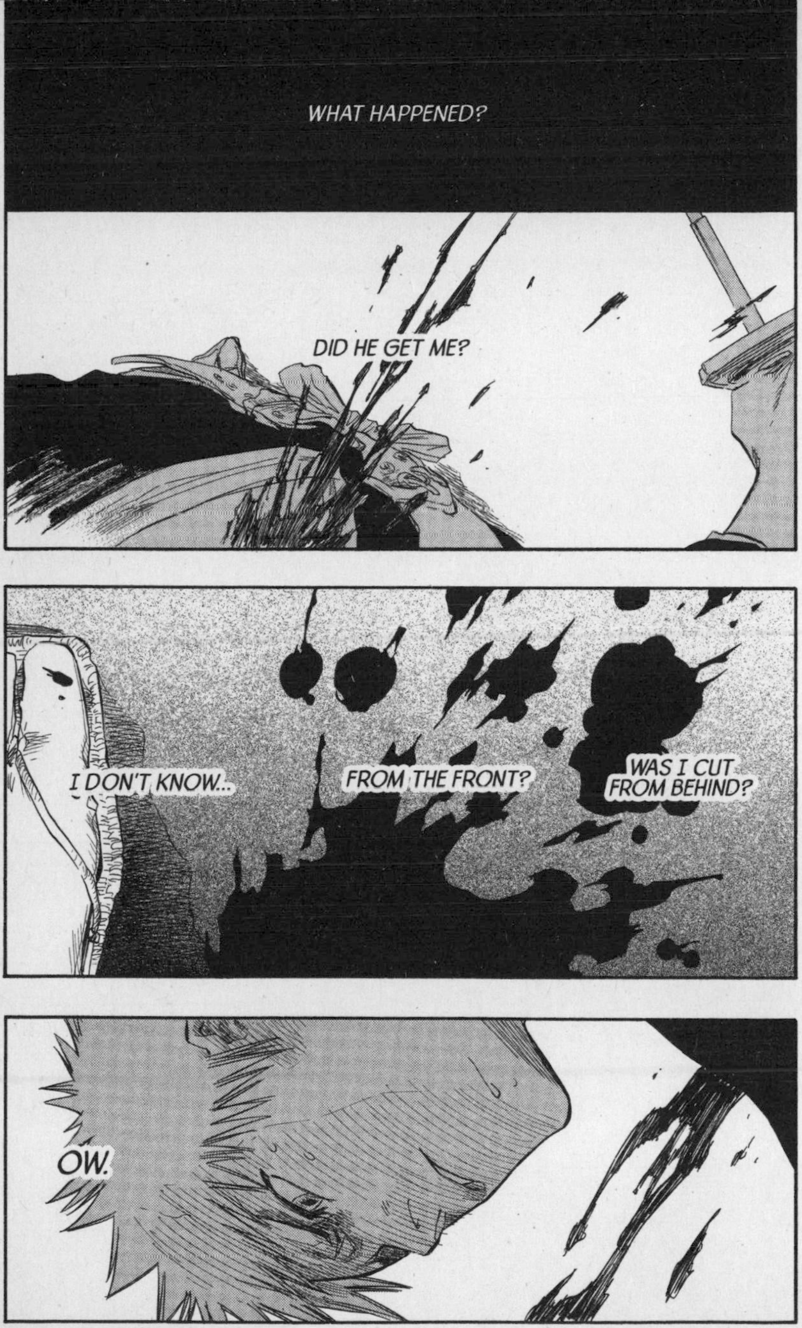
WHAT HAPPENED?
DID HE GET ME?
WAS I CUT FROM BEHIND?
FROM THE FRONT?
I DON'T KNOW...
OW.

56. broken coda

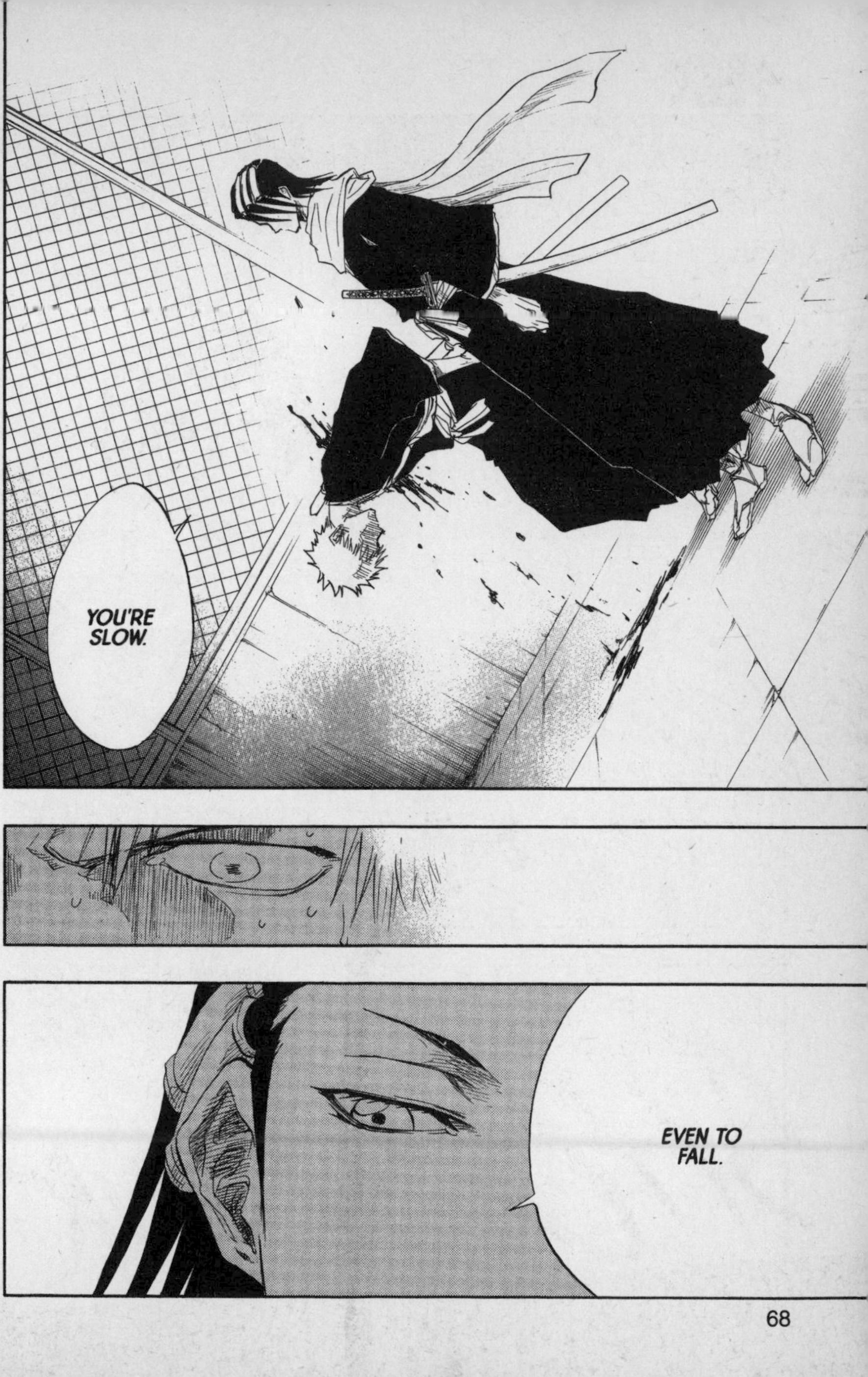
YOU'RE SLOW.
EVEN TO FALL.

READ THIS WAY

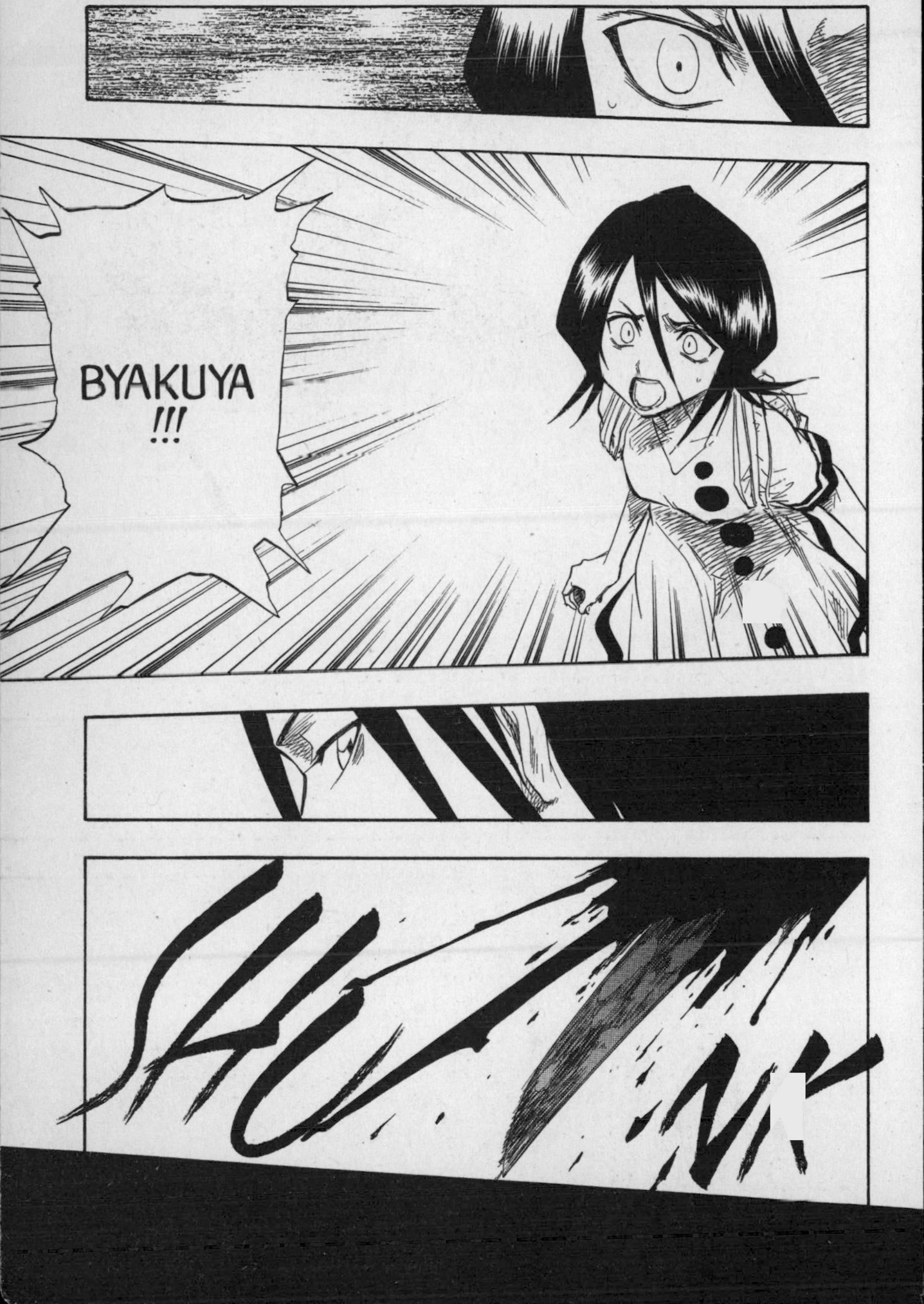
BYAKUYA !!!
SHUNK

56. broken coda

BLEACH

READ THIS WAY

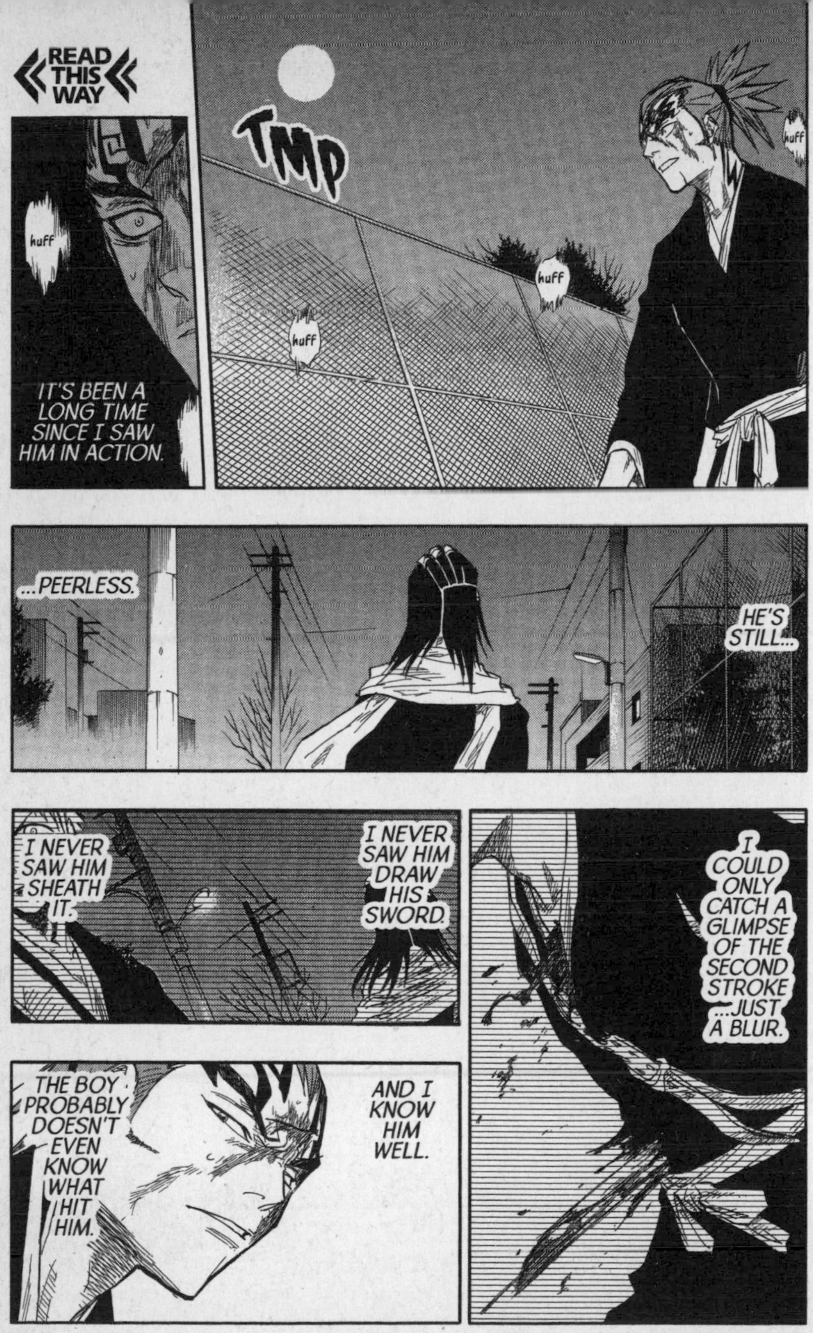

huff
TMP
huff
huff
huff
IT'S BEEN A LONG TIME SINCE I SAW HIM IN ACTION.
HE'S STILL...
...PEERLESS.
I COULD ONLY CATCH A GLIMPSE OF THE SECOND STROKE ...JUST A BLUR.
I NEVER SAW HIM DRAW HIS SWORD.
I NEVER SAW HIM SHEATH IT.
AND I KNOW HIM WELL.
THE BOY PROBABLY DOESN'T EVEN KNOW WHAT HIT HIM.

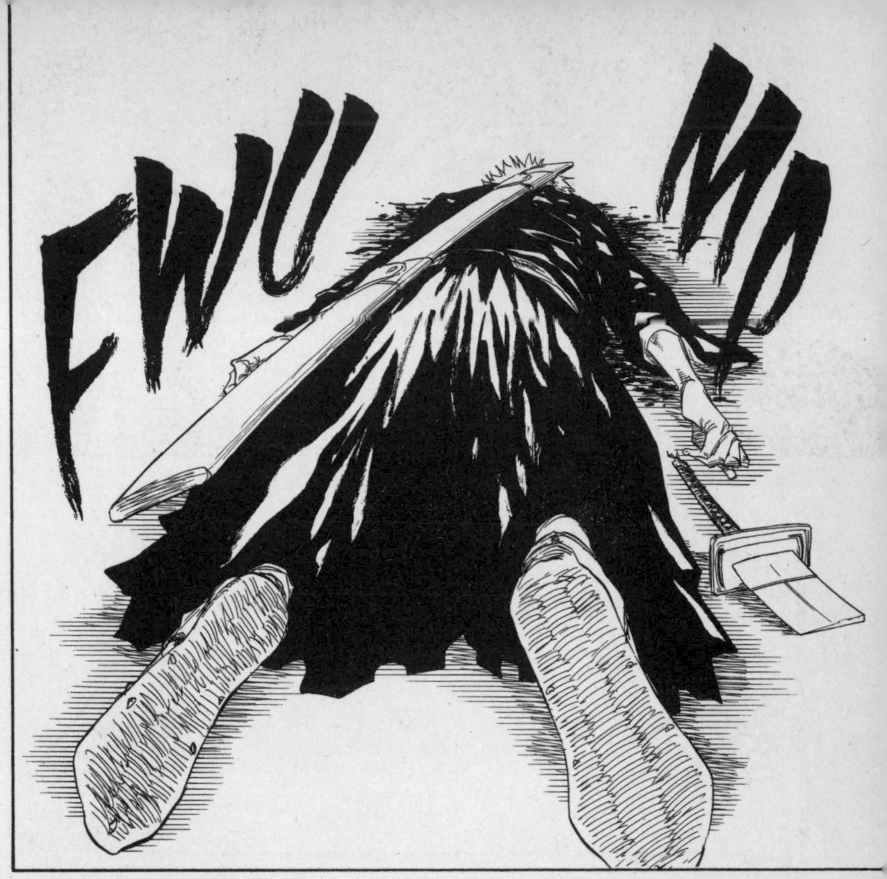
FWUMP
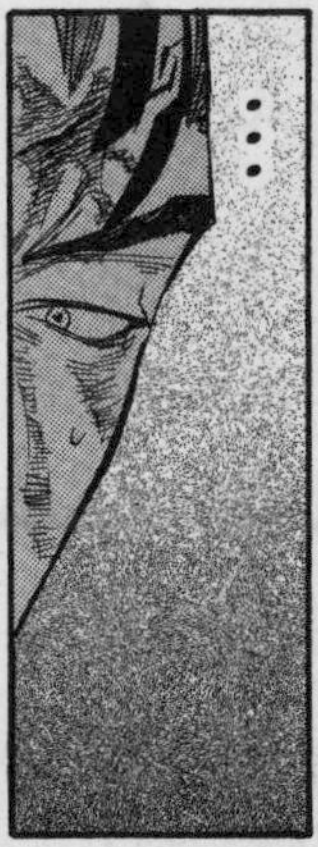
...
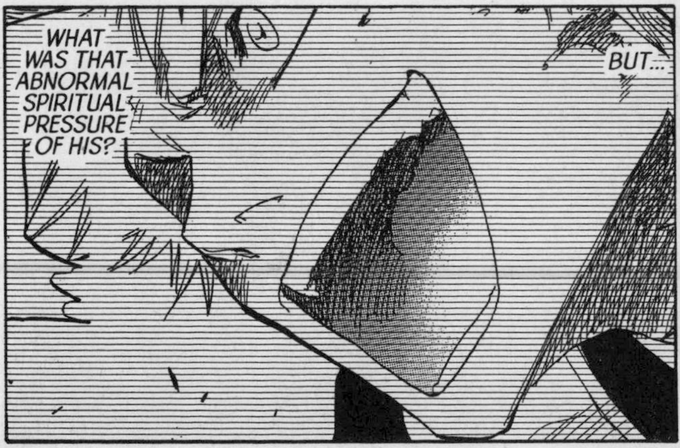
BUT...
WHAT WAS THAT ABNORMAL SPIRITUAL PRESSURE OF HIS?

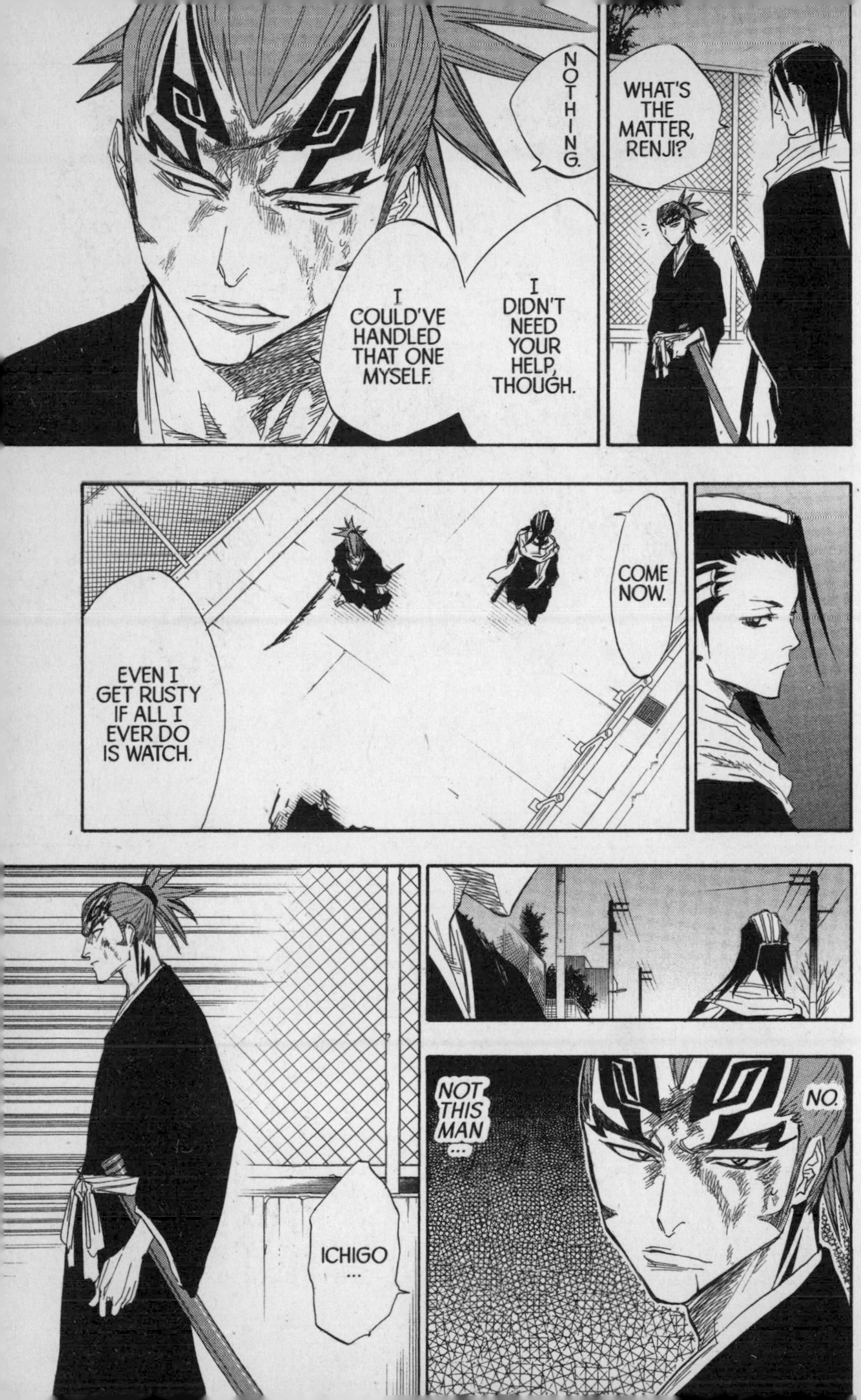
WHAT'S THE MATTER, RENJI?
NOTHING.
I DIDN'T NEED YOUR HELP, THOUGH.
I COULD'VE HANDLED THAT ONE MYSELF.
COME NOW.
EVEN I GET RUSTY IF ALL I EVER DO IS WATCH.
NO.
NOT THIS MAN...
ICHIGO...

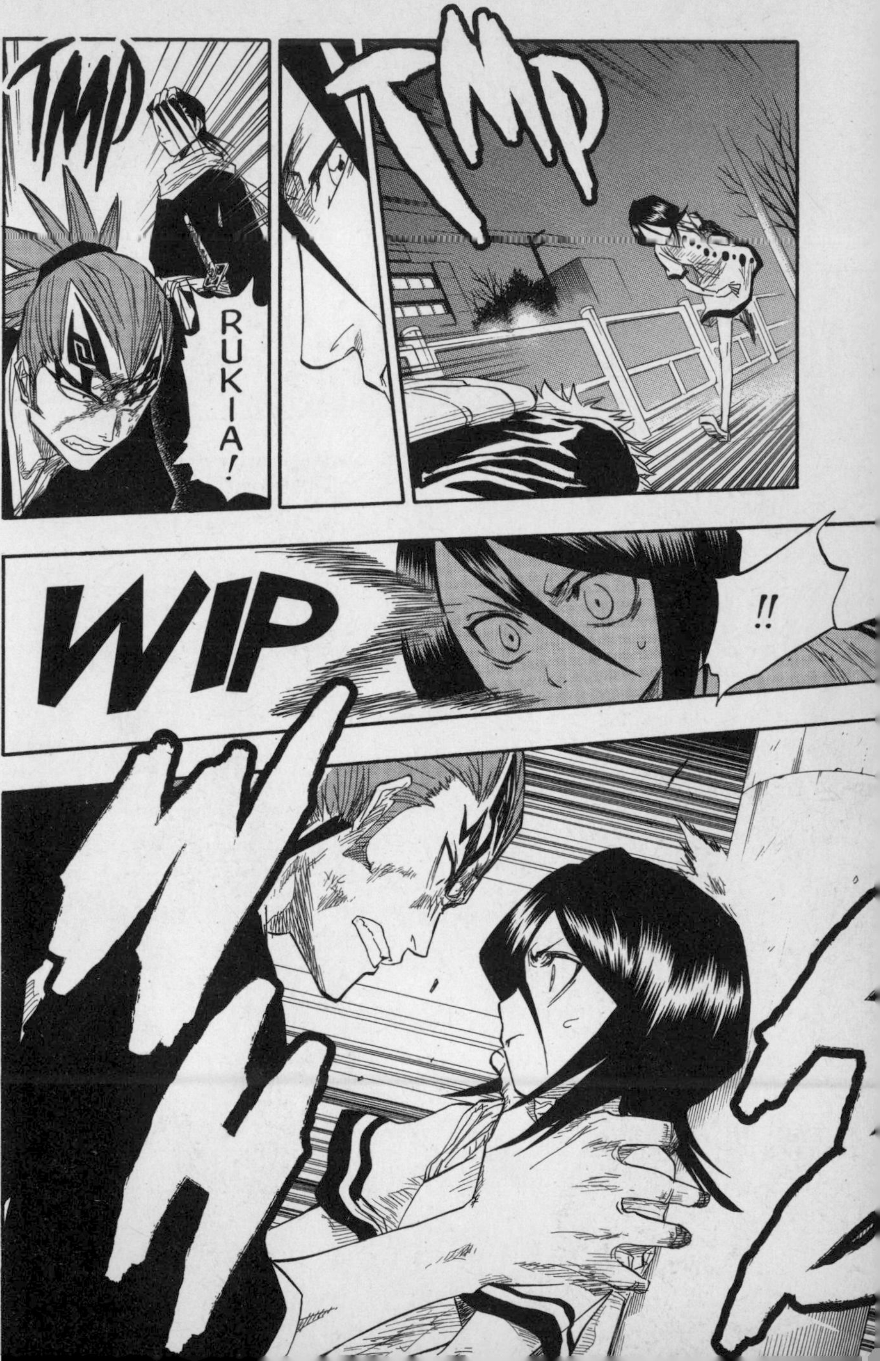
TMP
TMP
RUKIA!
!!
WIP

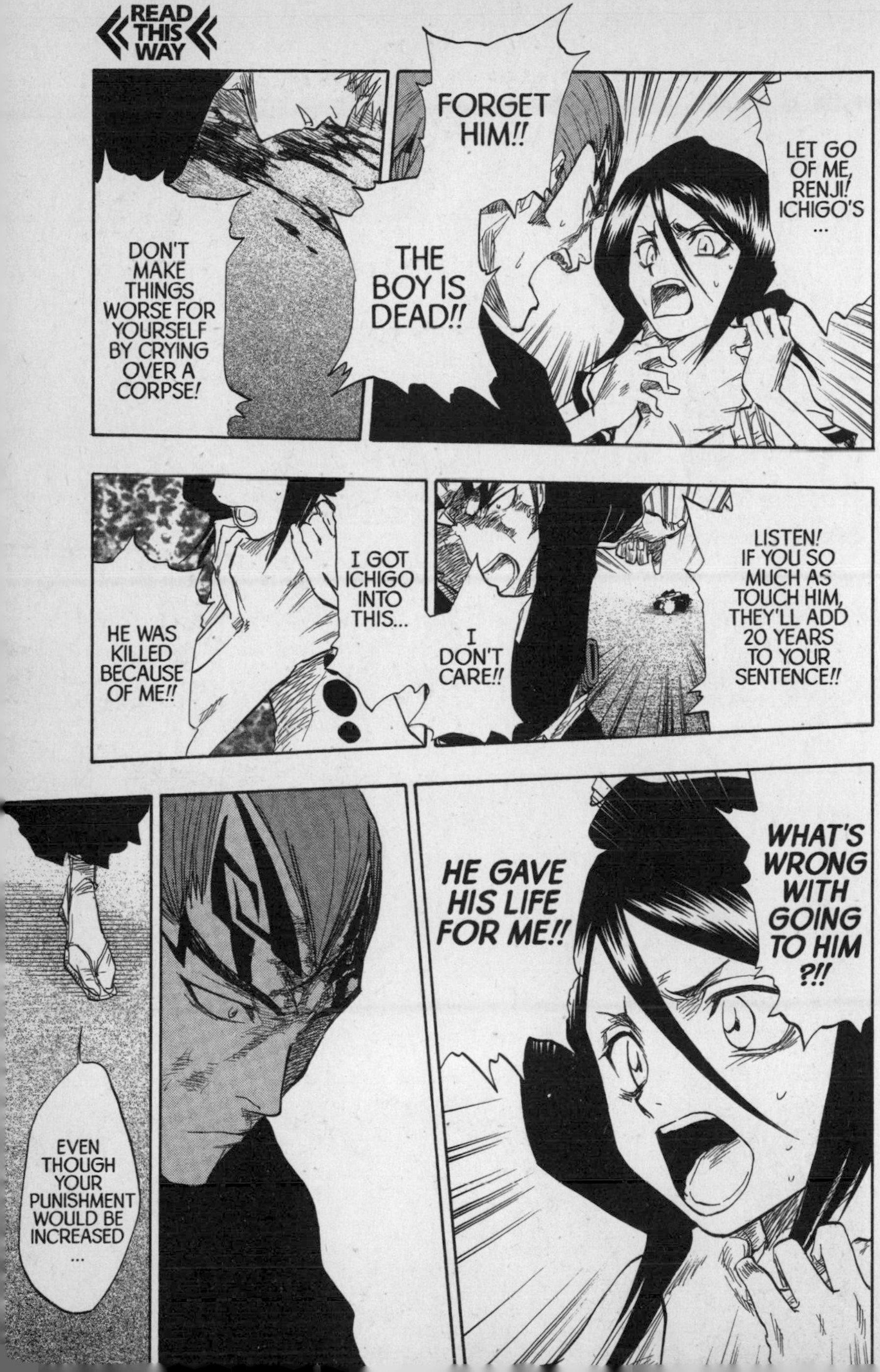
READ THIS WAY
LET GO OF ME, RENJI! ICHIGO'S ...
FORGET HIM!!
THE BOY IS DEAD!!
DON'T MAKE THINGS WORSE FOR YOURSELF BY CRYING OVER A CORPSE!
LISTEN! IF YOU SO MUCH AS TOUCH HIM, THEY'LL ADD 20 YEARS TO YOUR SENTENCE!!
I DON'T CARE!!
I GOT ICHIGO INTO THIS...
HE WAS KILLED BECAUSE OF ME!!
WHAT'S WRONG WITH GOING TO HIM ?!!
HE GAVE HIS LIFE FOR ME!!
EVEN THOUGH YOUR PUNISHMENT WOULD BE INCREASED ...

BRO-THER...

...GO TO THIS BOY?

YOU FEEL YOU MUST...

TMP

I UNDERSTAND, RUKIA...

THIS CHILD...

...LOOKS VERY MUCH LIKE HIM.

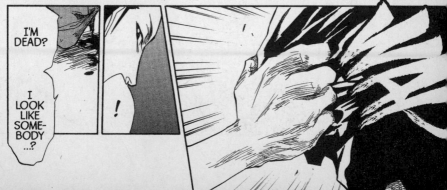

I'M DEAD?

I LOOK LIKE SOMEBODY...?

!

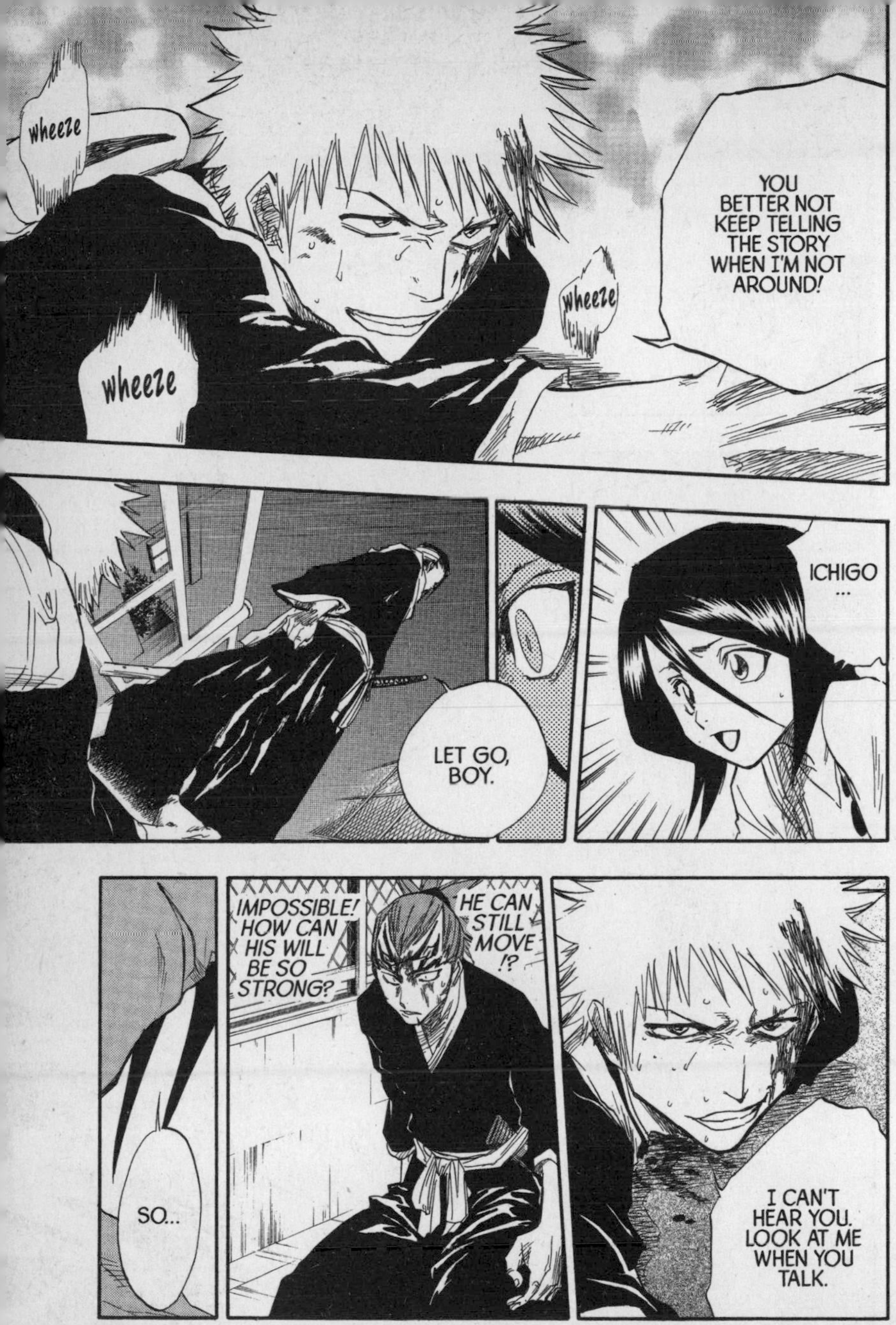
YOU BETTER NOT KEEP TELLING THE STORY WHEN I'M NOT AROUND!
wheeze
wheeze
wheeze
ICHIGO ...
LET GO, BOY.
I CAN'T HEAR YOU. LOOK AT ME WHEN YOU TALK.
HE CAN STILL MOVE !?
IMPOSSIBLE! HOW CAN HIS WILL BE SO STRONG?
SO...

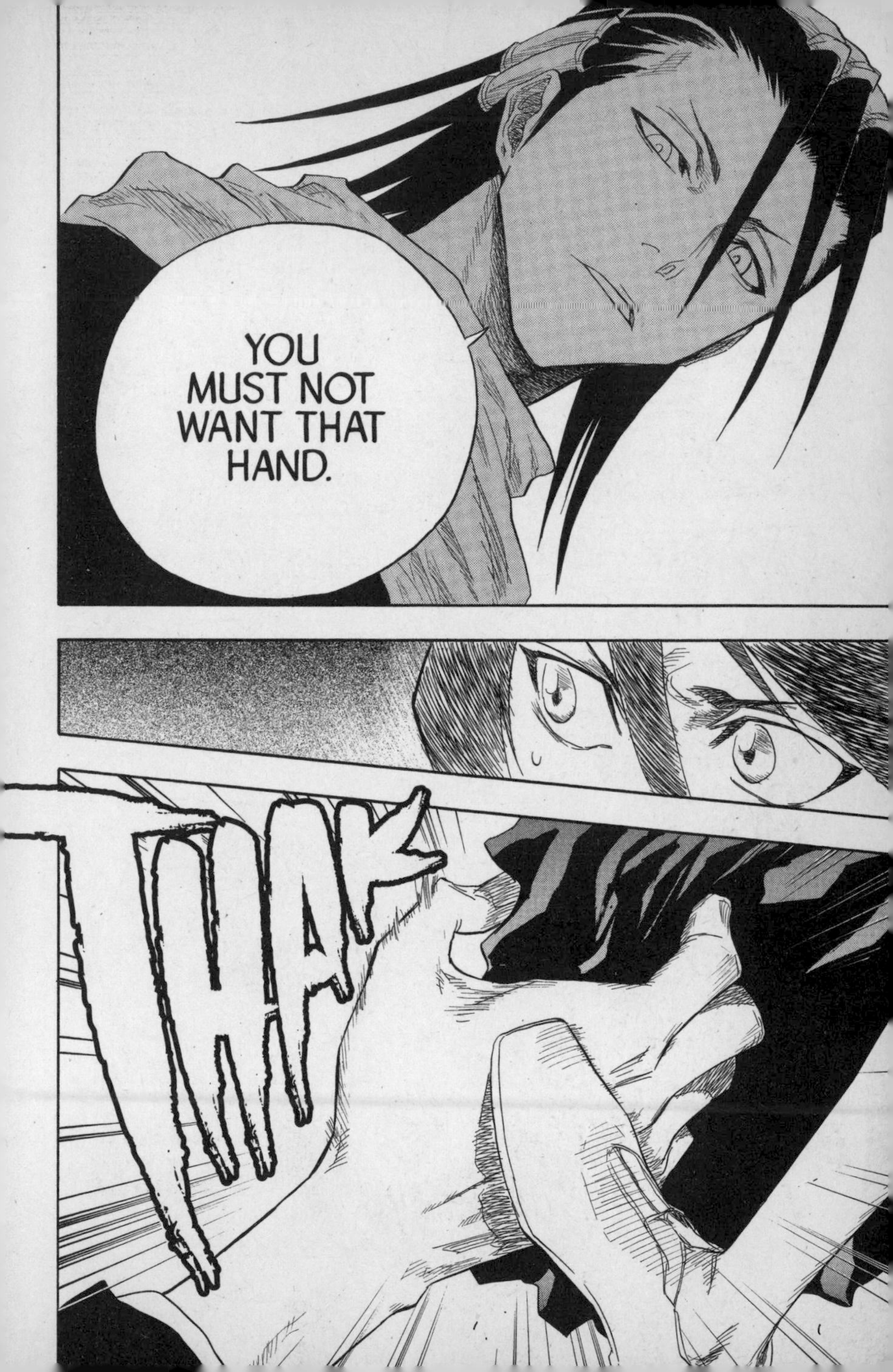
YOU MUST NOT WANT THAT HAND.
THAK

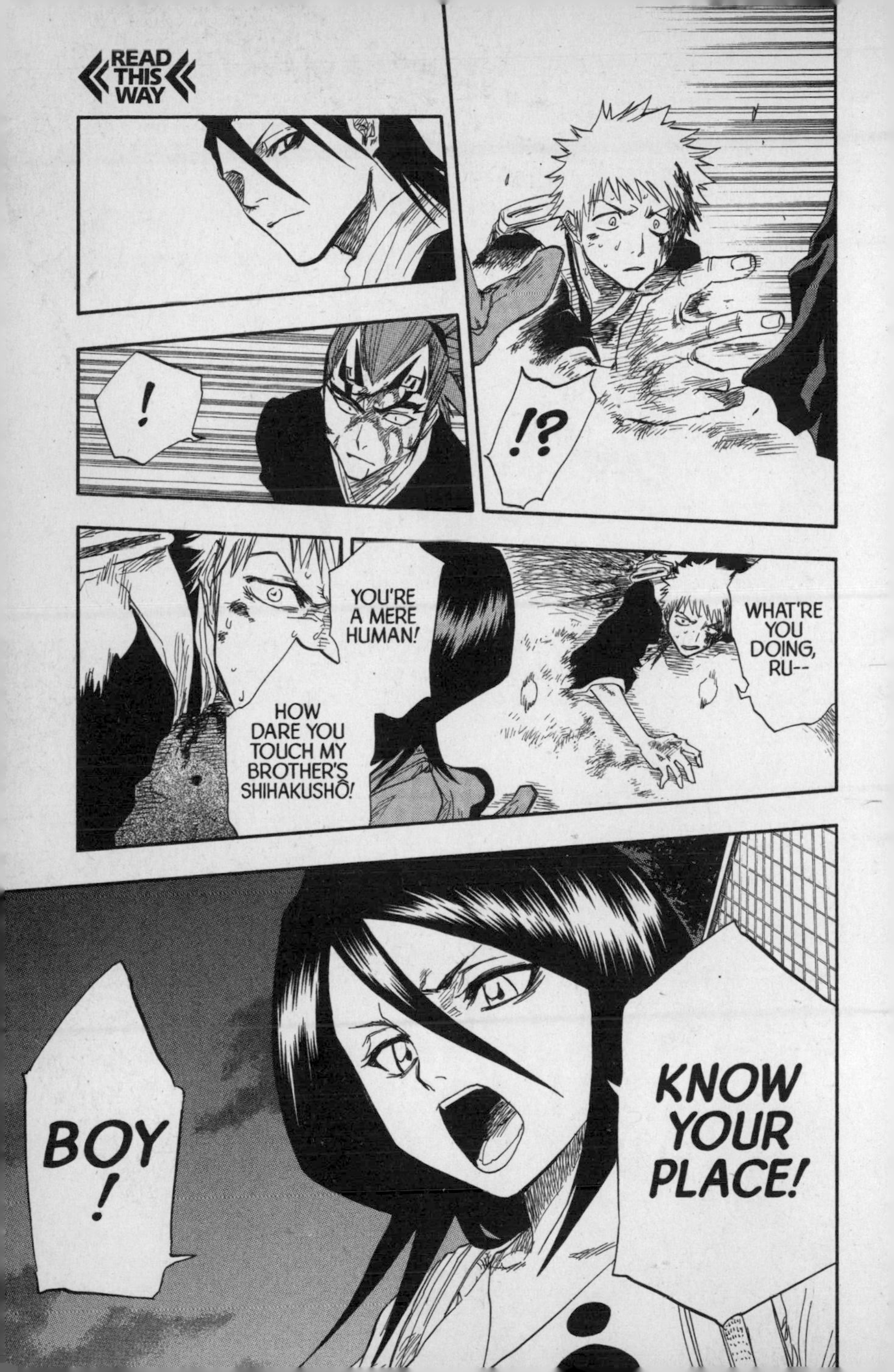
READ THIS WAY
!?
!
WHAT'RE YOU DOING, RU--
YOU'RE A MERE HUMAN!
HOW DARE YOU TOUCH MY BROTHER'S SHIHAKUSHŌ!
KNOW YOUR PLACE!
BOY!

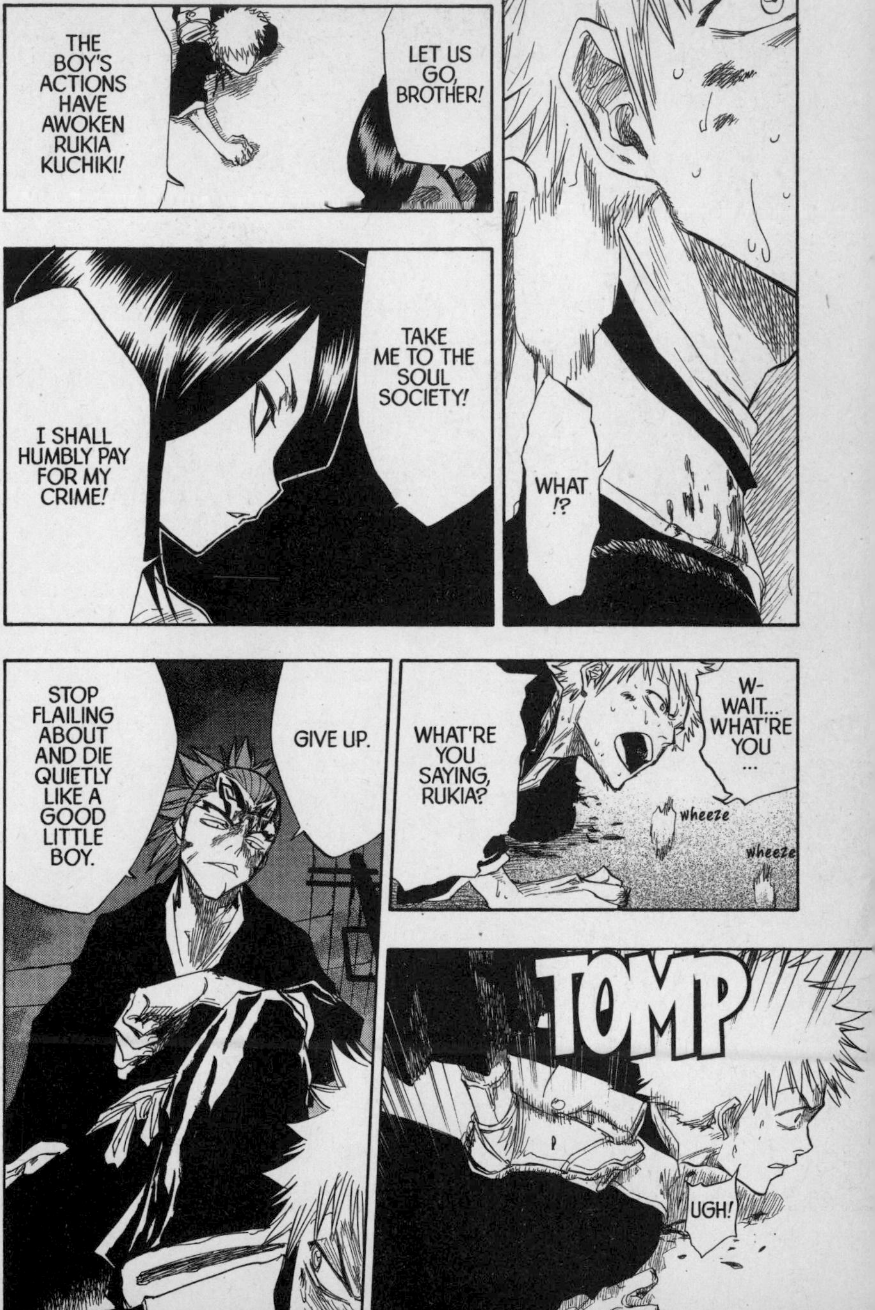
WHAT !?
LET US GO, BROTHER!
THE BOY'S ACTIONS HAVE AWOKEN RUKIA KUCHIKI!
TAKE ME TO THE SOUL SOCIETY!
I SHALL HUMBLY PAY FOR MY CRIME!
W-WAIT... WHAT'RE YOU ...
wheeze
wheeze
WHAT'RE YOU SAYING, RUKIA?
TOMP
UGH!
GIVE UP.
STOP FLAILING ABOUT AND DIE QUIETLY LIKE A GOOD LITTLE BOY.

READ THIS WAY

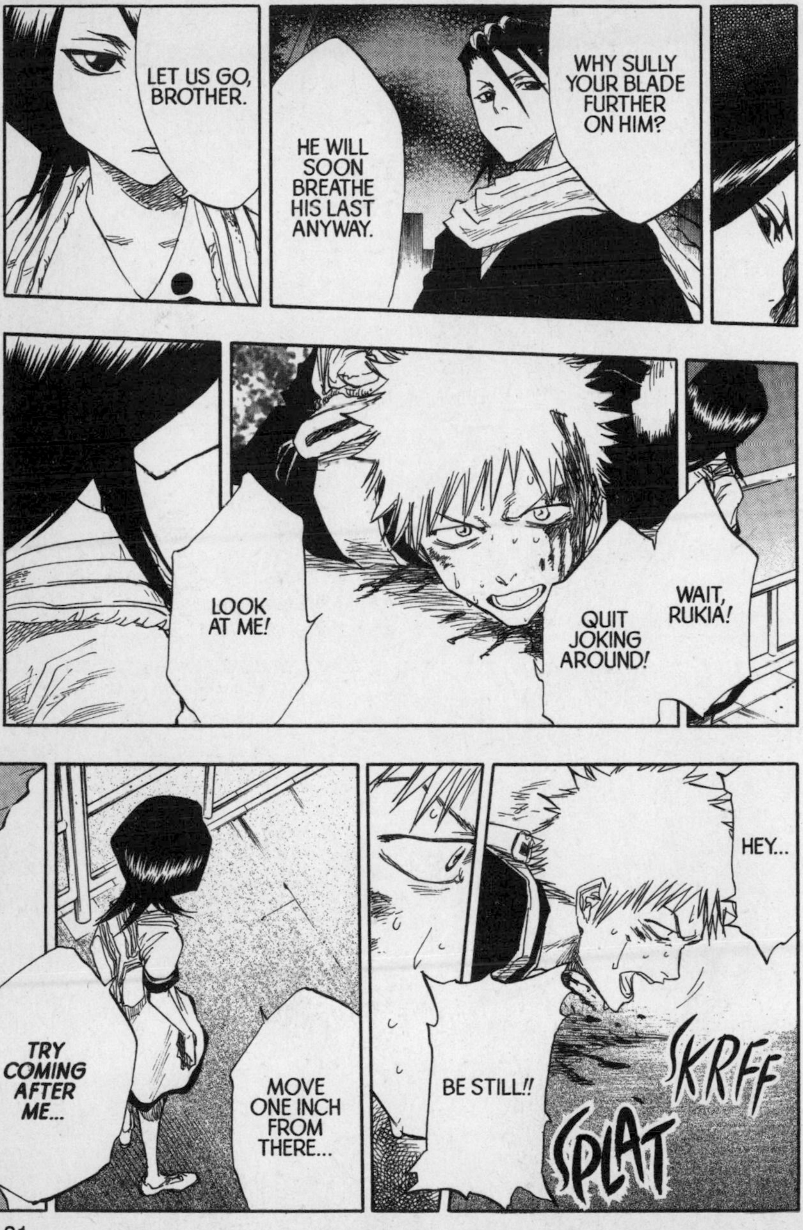

WHY SULLY YOUR BLADE FURTHER ON HIM?
HE WILL SOON BREATHE HIS LAST ANYWAY.
LET US GO, BROTHER.
WAIT, RUKIA!
QUIT JOKING AROUND!
LOOK AT ME!
HEY...
SKRFF
SPLAT
BE STILL!!
MOVE ONE INCH FROM THERE...
TRY COMING AFTER ME...

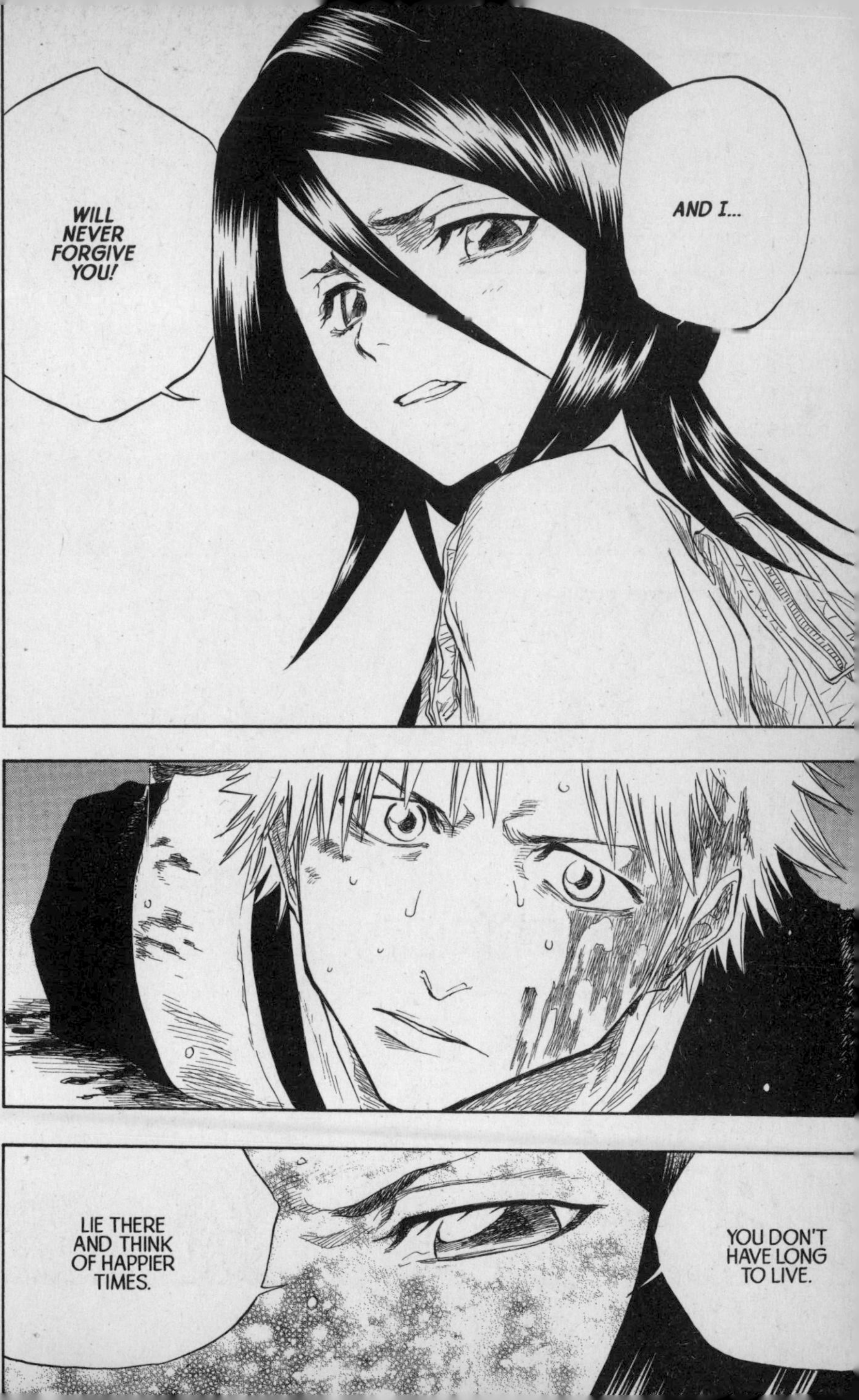
AND I...
WILL NEVER FORGIVE YOU!
YOU DON'T HAVE LONG TO LIVE.
LIE THERE AND THINK OF HAPPIER TIMES.

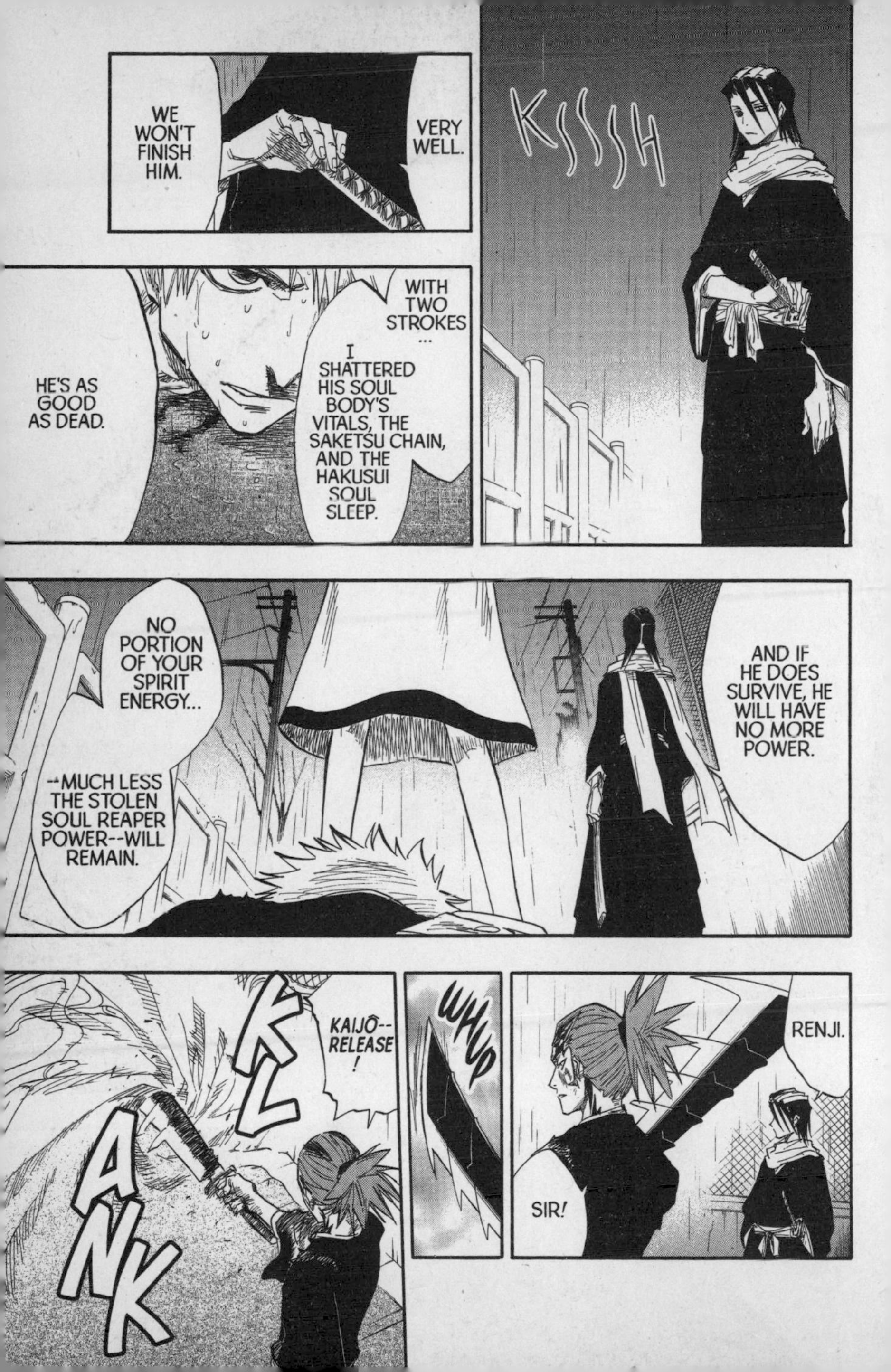
KSSSH
VERY WELL.
WE WON'T FINISH HIM.
WITH TWO STROKES...
I SHATTERED HIS SOUL BODY'S VITALS, THE SAKETSU CHAIN, AND THE HAKUSUI SOUL SLEEP.
HE'S AS GOOD AS DEAD.
AND IF HE DOES SURVIVE, HE WILL HAVE NO MORE POWER.
NO PORTION OF YOUR SPIRIT ENERGY...
--MUCH LESS THE STOLEN SOUL REAPER POWER--WILL REMAIN.
RENJI.
SIR!
WHUP
KAIJÔ--RELEASE!
KLANK

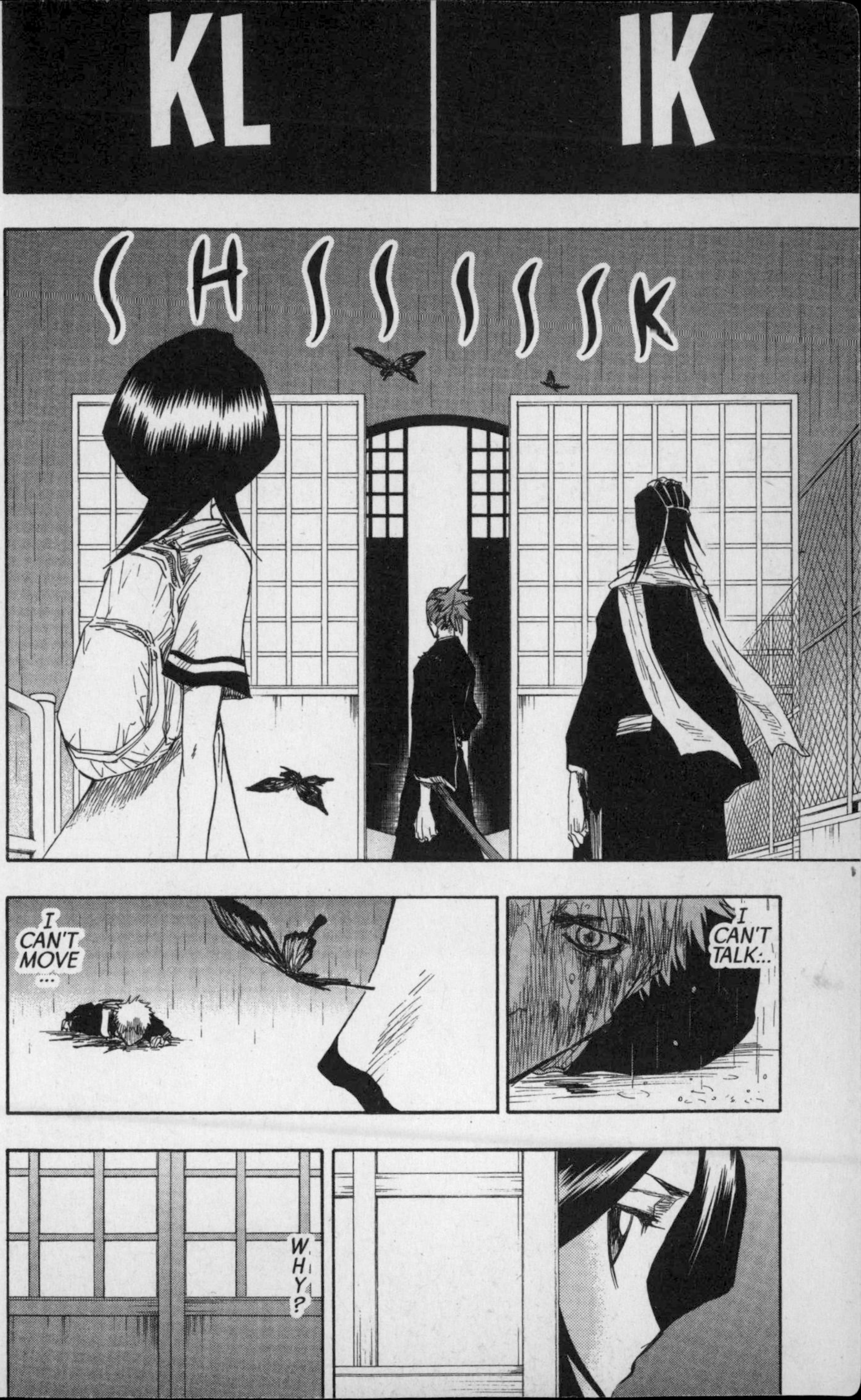
KLIK
CHIIIIIK
I CAN'T TALK...
I CAN'T MOVE...
WHY?

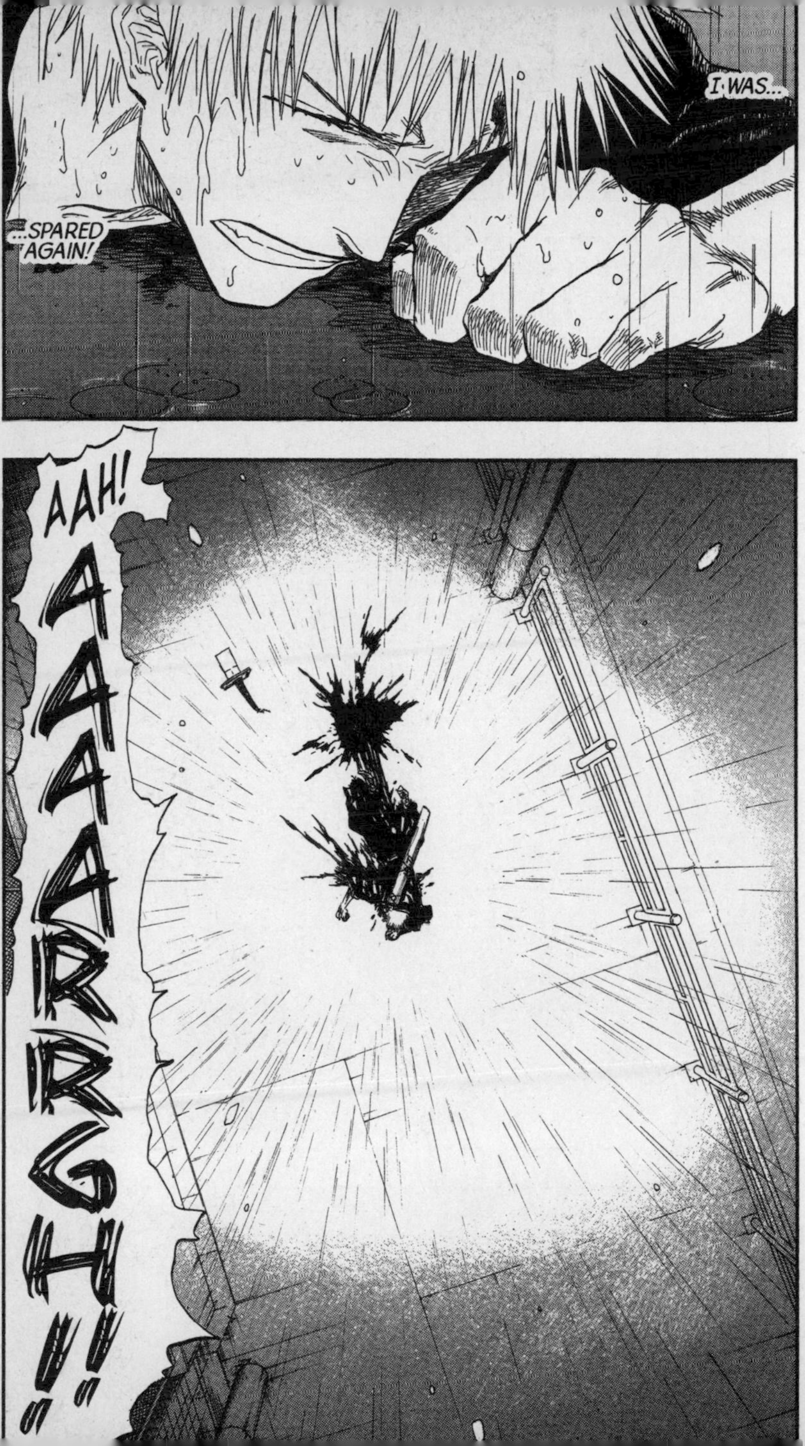
I WAS...
...SPARED AGAIN!
AAH!
AAARRGH!!

57. July Rain, Interrupted

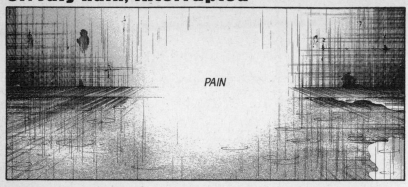

PAIN

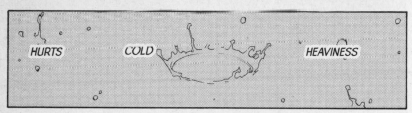

HURTS   COLD   HEAVINESS

WON'T
STOP   BLEEDING

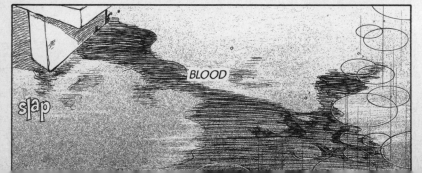

BLOOD

slap

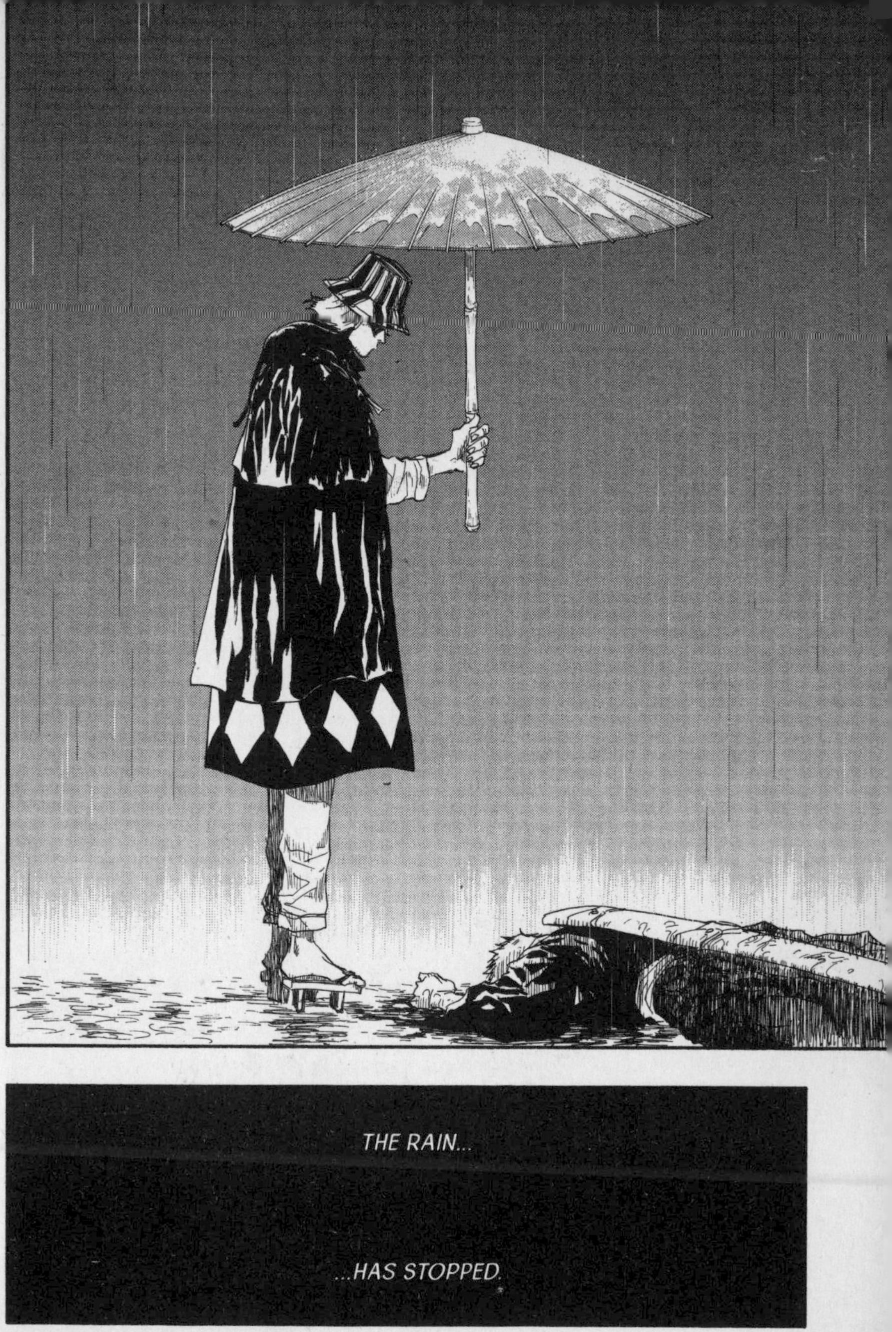
THE RAIN...
...HAS STOPPED.

57. July Rain,
Interrupted

BLEACH

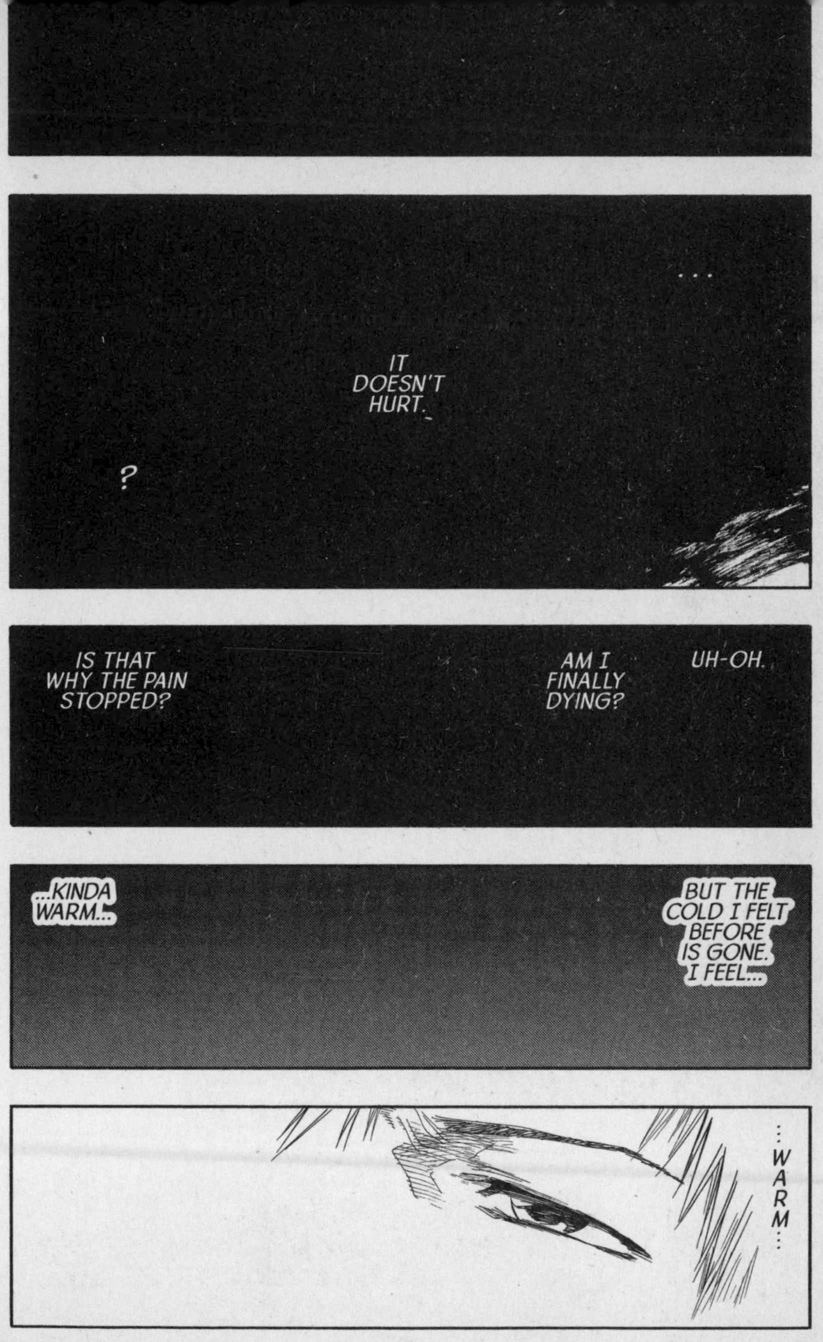
...
IT DOESN'T HURT.
?
UH-OH.
AM I FINALLY DYING?
IS THAT WHY THE PAIN STOPPED?
BUT THE COLD I FELT BEFORE IS GONE. I FEEL...
...KINDA WARM...
...WARM...

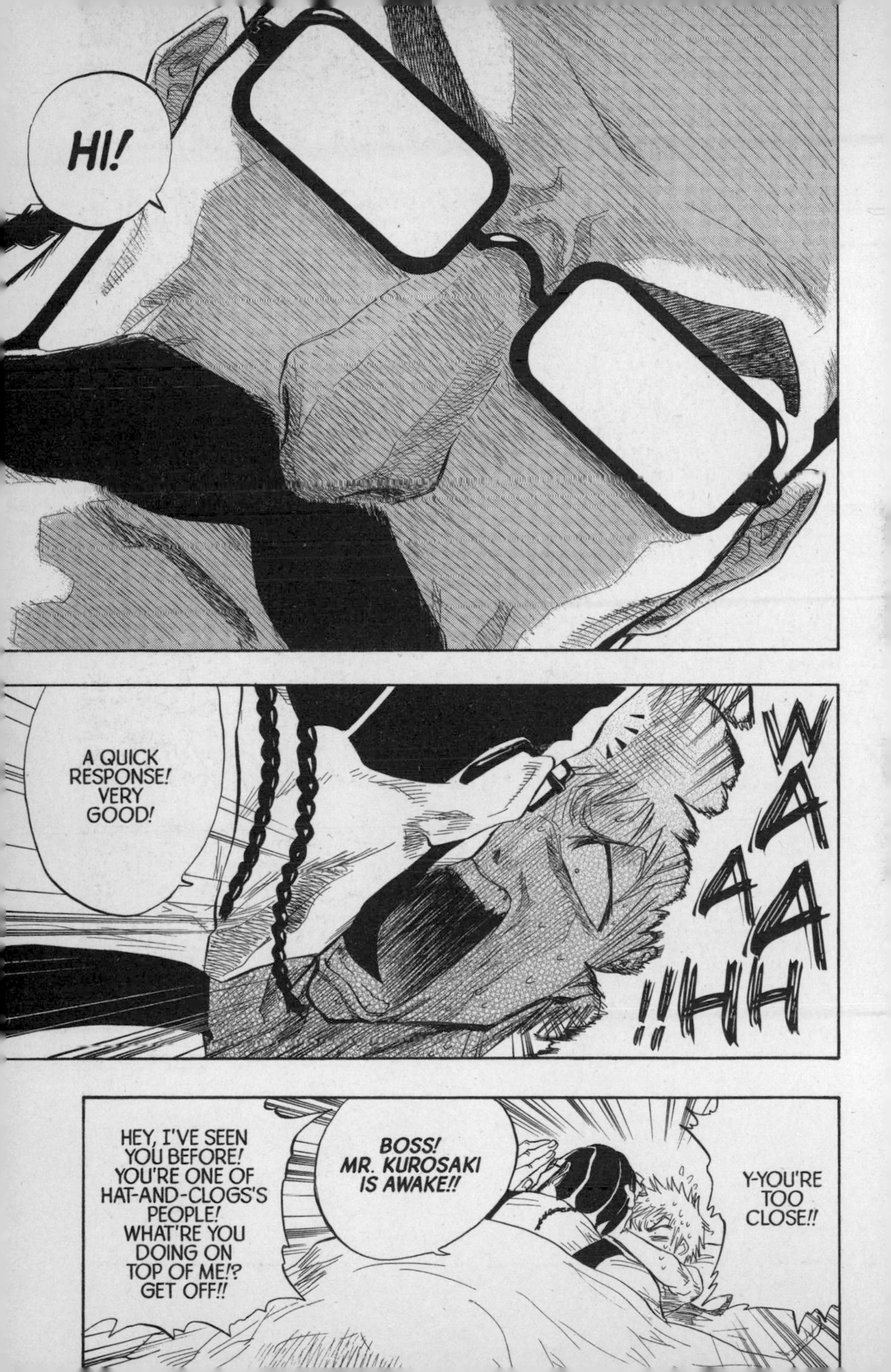
HI!
WAAAHH!!
A QUICK RESPONSE! VERY GOOD!
Y-YOU'RE TOO CLOSE!!
BOSS! MR. KUROSAKI IS AWAKE!!
HEY, I'VE SEEN YOU BEFORE! YOU'RE ONE OF HAT-AND-CLOGS'S PEOPLE! WHAT'RE YOU DOING ON TOP OF ME!? GET OFF!!

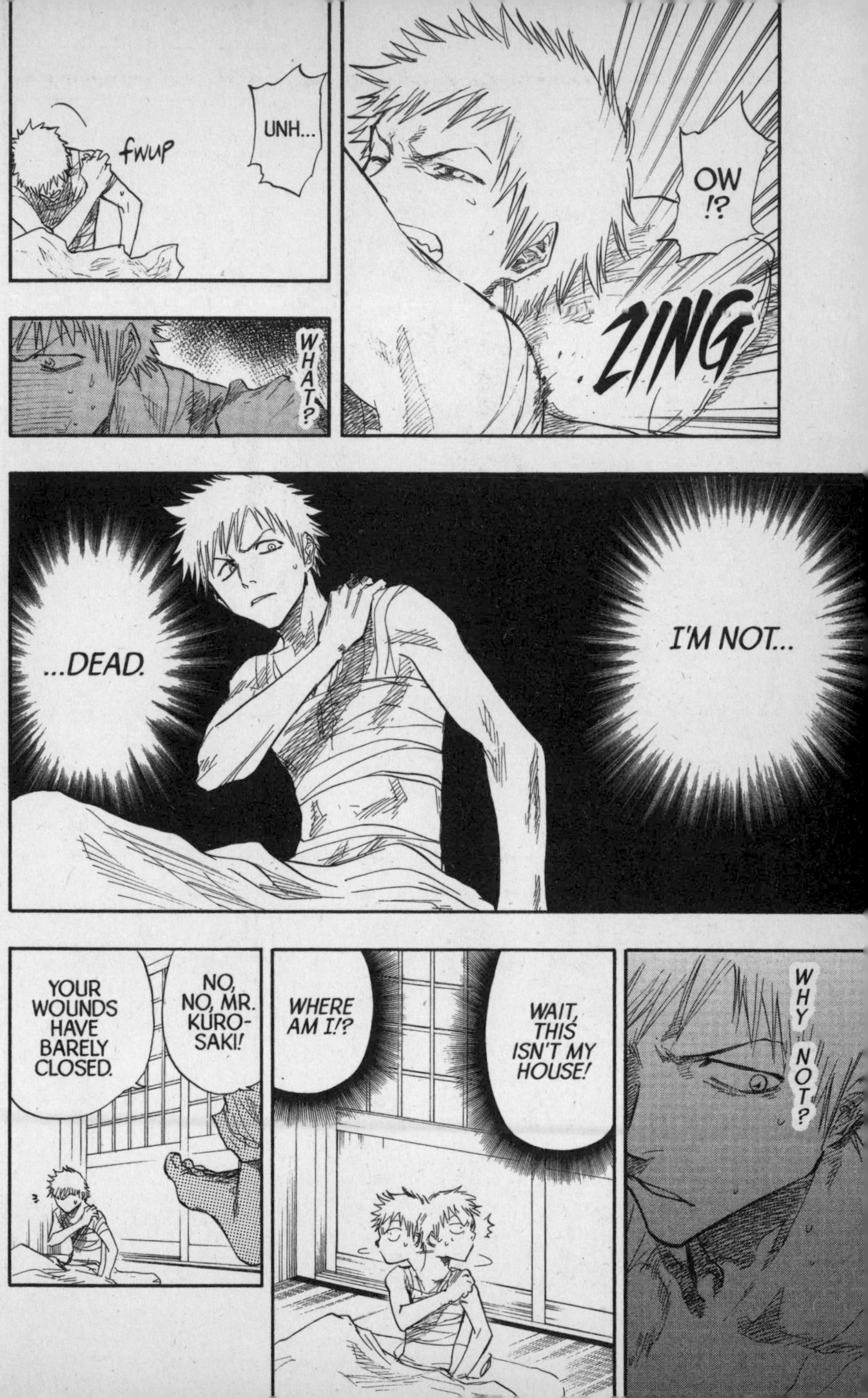
OW!?
ZING
UNH...
fwup
WHAT?
I'M NOT...
...DEAD.
WHY NOT?
WAIT, THIS ISN'T MY HOUSE!
WHERE AM I!?
NO, NO, MR. KUROSAKI!
YOUR WOUNDS HAVE BARELY CLOSED.

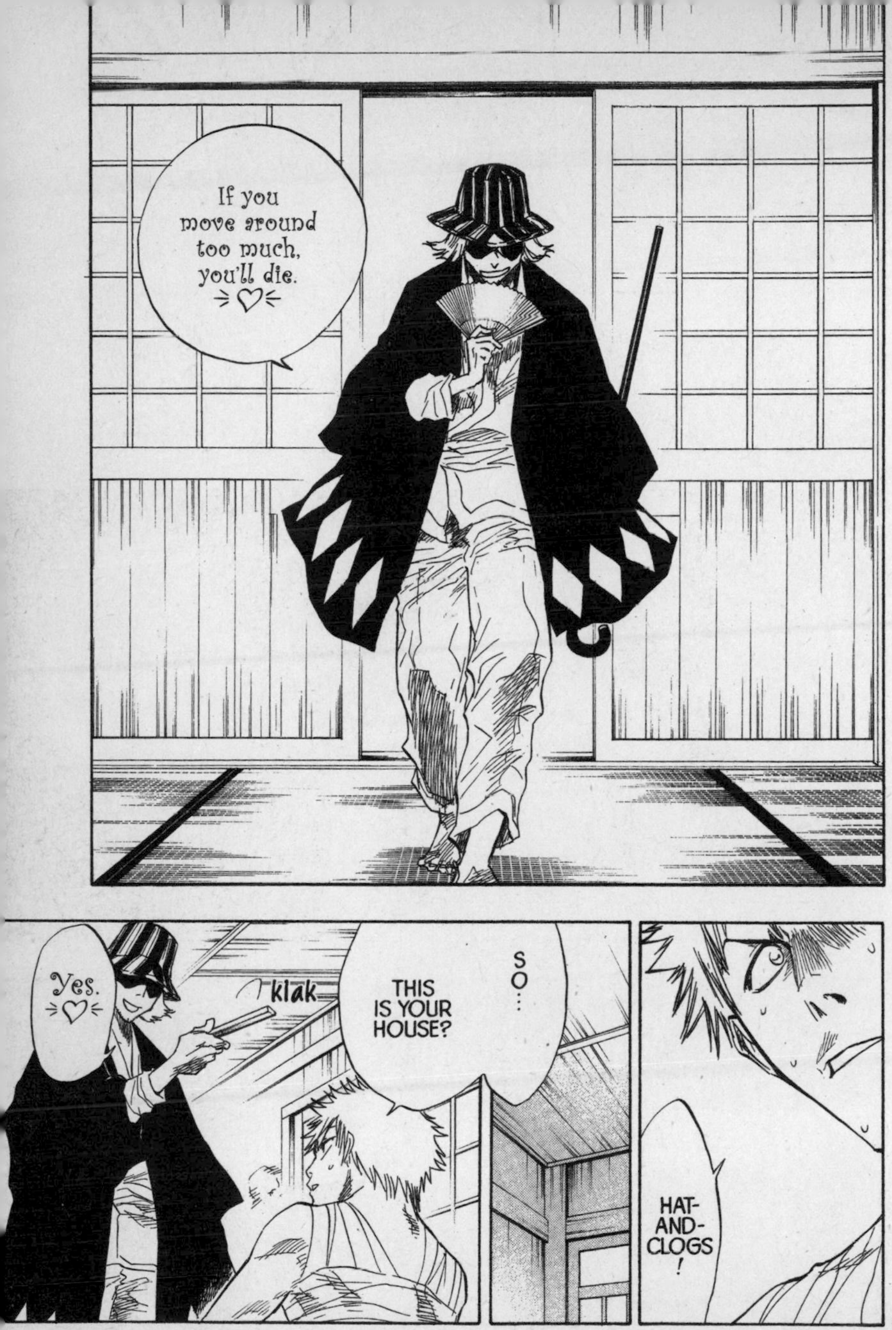
If you move around too much, you'll die. ♡
HAT-AND-CLOGS!
SO…
THIS IS YOUR HOUSE?
klak
Yes. ♡

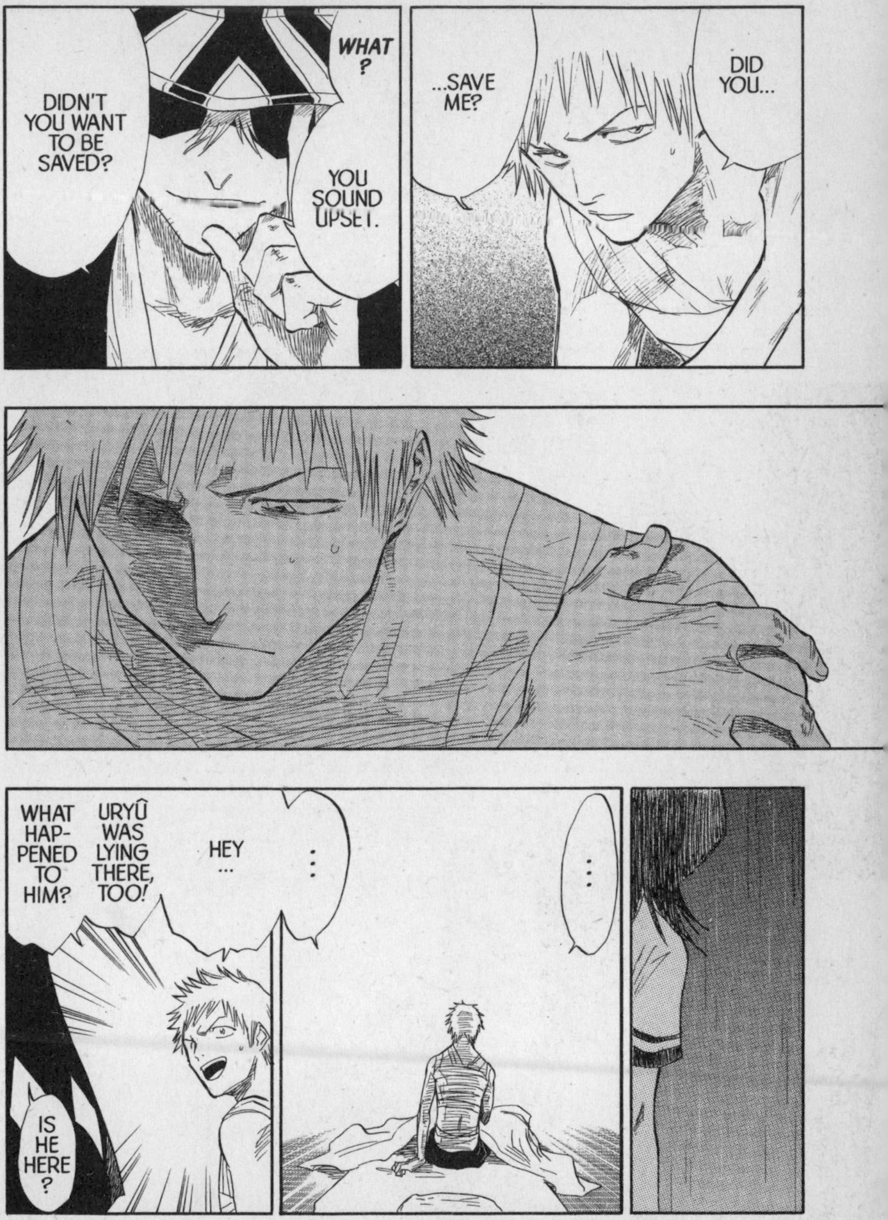
DID YOU...
...SAVE ME?
WHAT?
YOU SOUND UPSET.
DIDN'T YOU WANT TO BE SAVED?
...
...
HEY...
URYÛ WAS LYING THERE, TOO!
WHAT HAPPENED TO HIM?
IS HE HERE?

READ THIS WAY

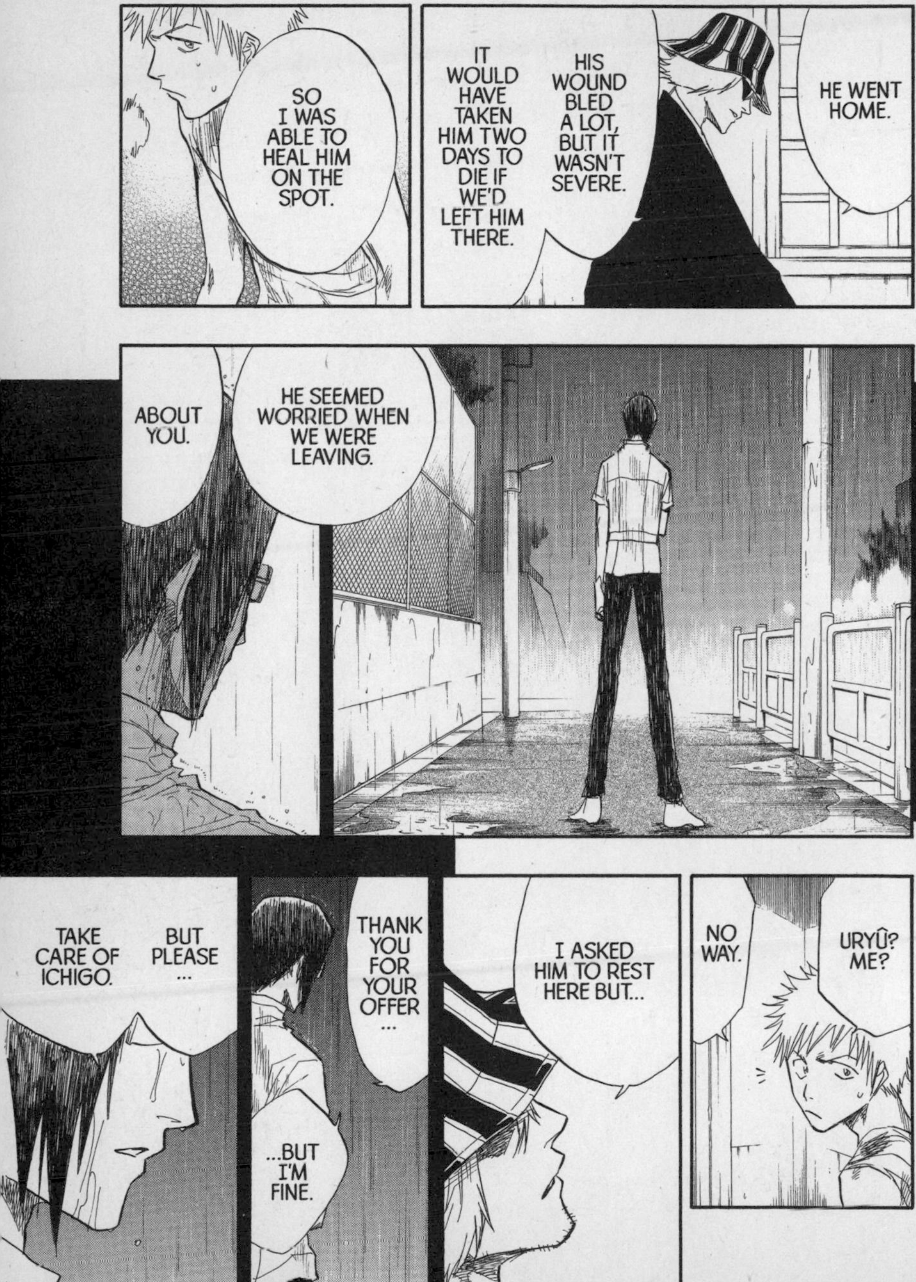
HE WENT HOME.
HIS WOUND BLED A LOT, BUT IT WASN'T SEVERE.
IT WOULD HAVE TAKEN HIM TWO DAYS TO DIE IF WE'D LEFT HIM THERE.
SO I WAS ABLE TO HEAL HIM ON THE SPOT.
HE SEEMED WORRIED WHEN WE WERE LEAVING.
ABOUT YOU.
URYÛ? ME?
NO WAY.
I ASKED HIM TO REST HERE BUT...
THANK YOU FOR YOUR OFFER...
...BUT I'M FINE.
BUT PLEASE...
TAKE CARE OF ICHIGO.

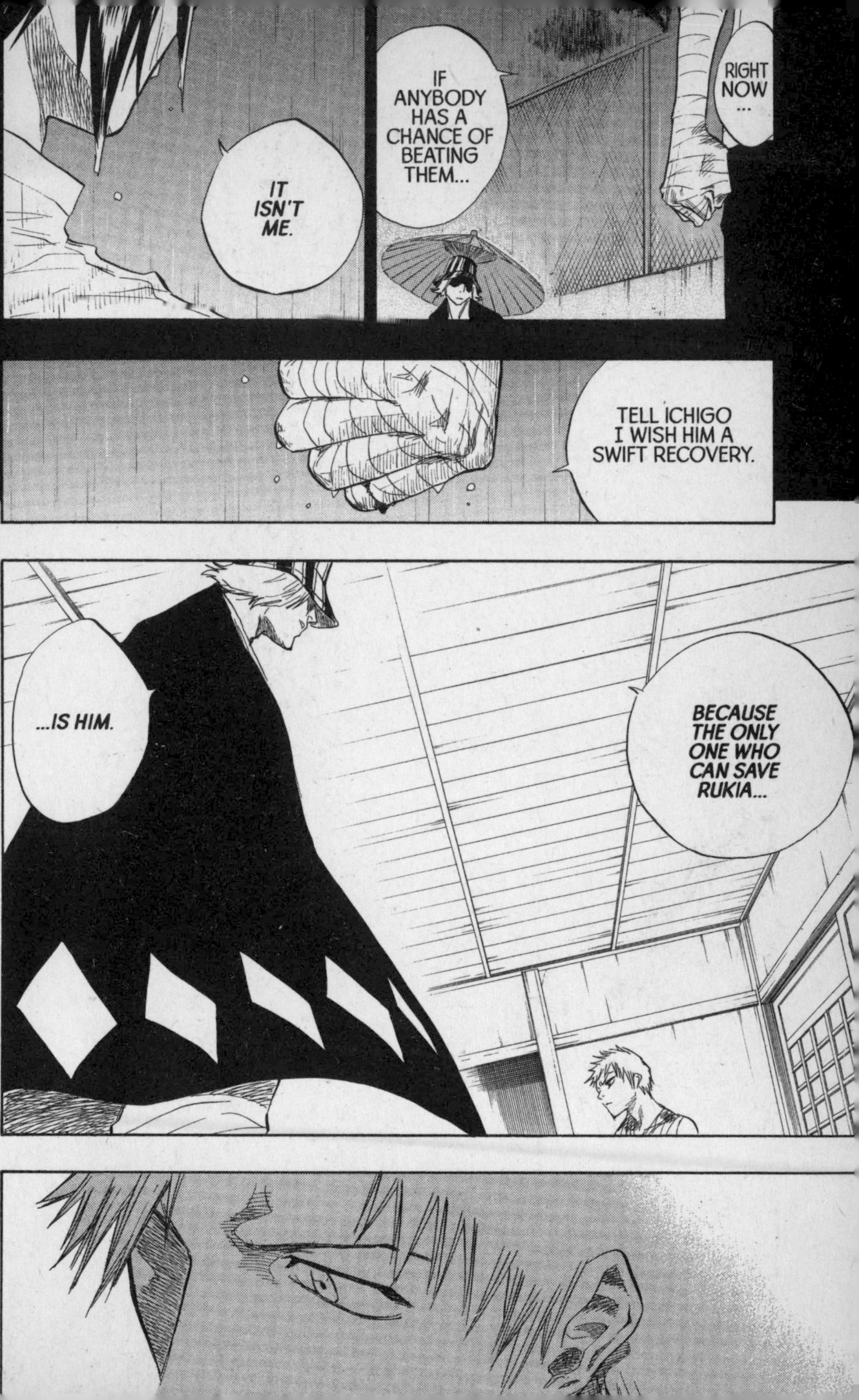
RIGHT NOW ...
IF ANYBODY HAS A CHANCE OF BEATING THEM...
IT ISN'T ME.
TELL ICHIGO I WISH HIM A SWIFT RECOVERY.
BECAUSE THE ONLY ONE WHO CAN SAVE RUKIA...
...IS HIM.

READ THIS WAY

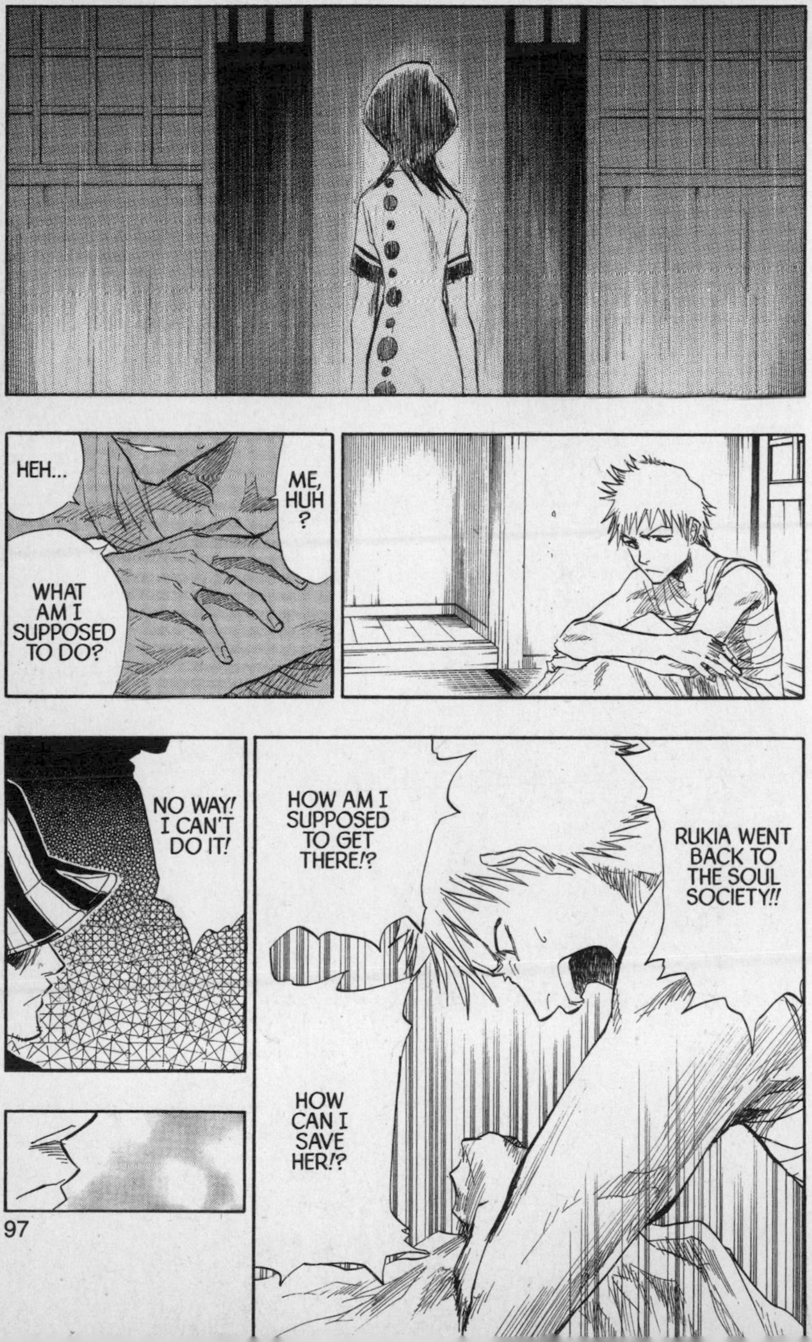
HEH...
ME, HUH?
WHAT AM I SUPPOSED TO DO?
RUKIA WENT BACK TO THE SOUL SOCIETY!!
HOW AM I SUPPOSED TO GET THERE!?
HOW CAN I SAVE HER!?
NO WAY! I CAN'T DO IT!

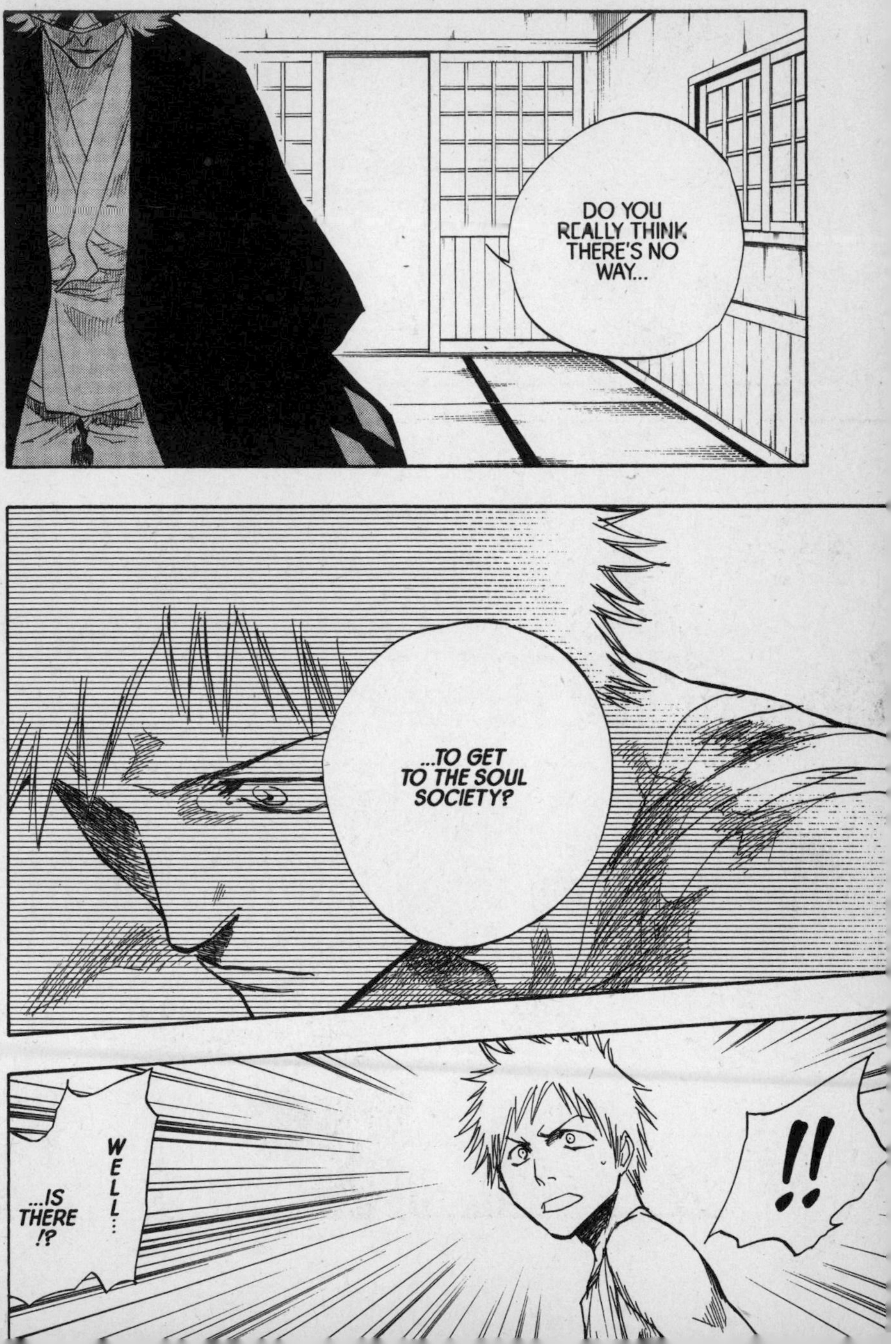
DO YOU REALLY THINK THERE'S NO WAY...
...TO GET TO THE SOUL SOCIETY?
!!
WELL...
...IS THERE!?

READ THIS WAY

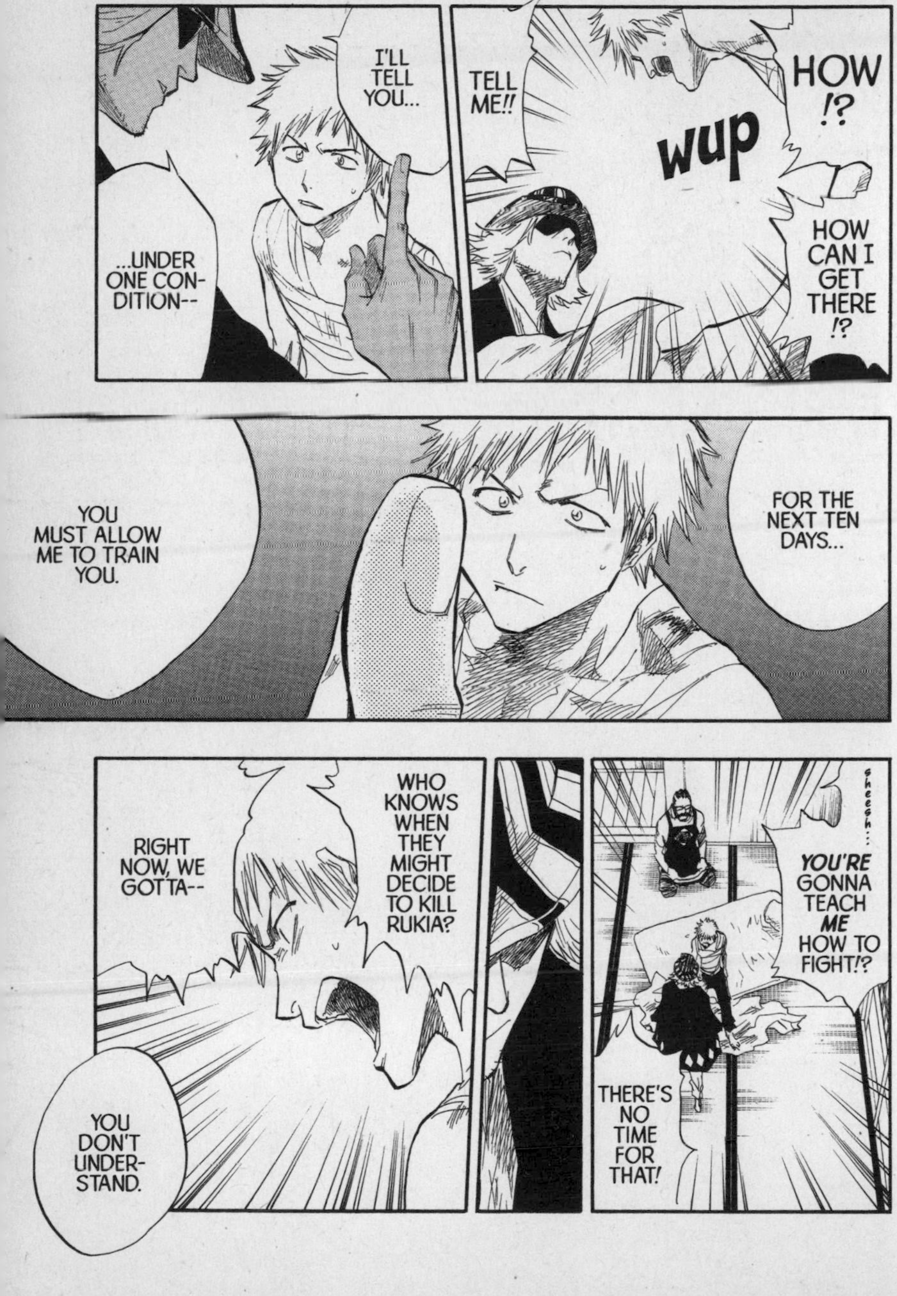
HOW !?
wup
HOW CAN I GET THERE !?
TELL ME!!
I'LL TELL YOU...
...UNDER ONE CONDITION--
FOR THE NEXT TEN DAYS...
YOU MUST ALLOW ME TO TRAIN YOU.
sheesh...
YOU'RE GONNA TEACH ME HOW TO FIGHT!?
THERE'S NO TIME FOR THAT!
WHO KNOWS WHEN THEY MIGHT DECIDE TO KILL RUKIA?
RIGHT NOW, WE GOTTA--
YOU DON'T UNDERSTAND.

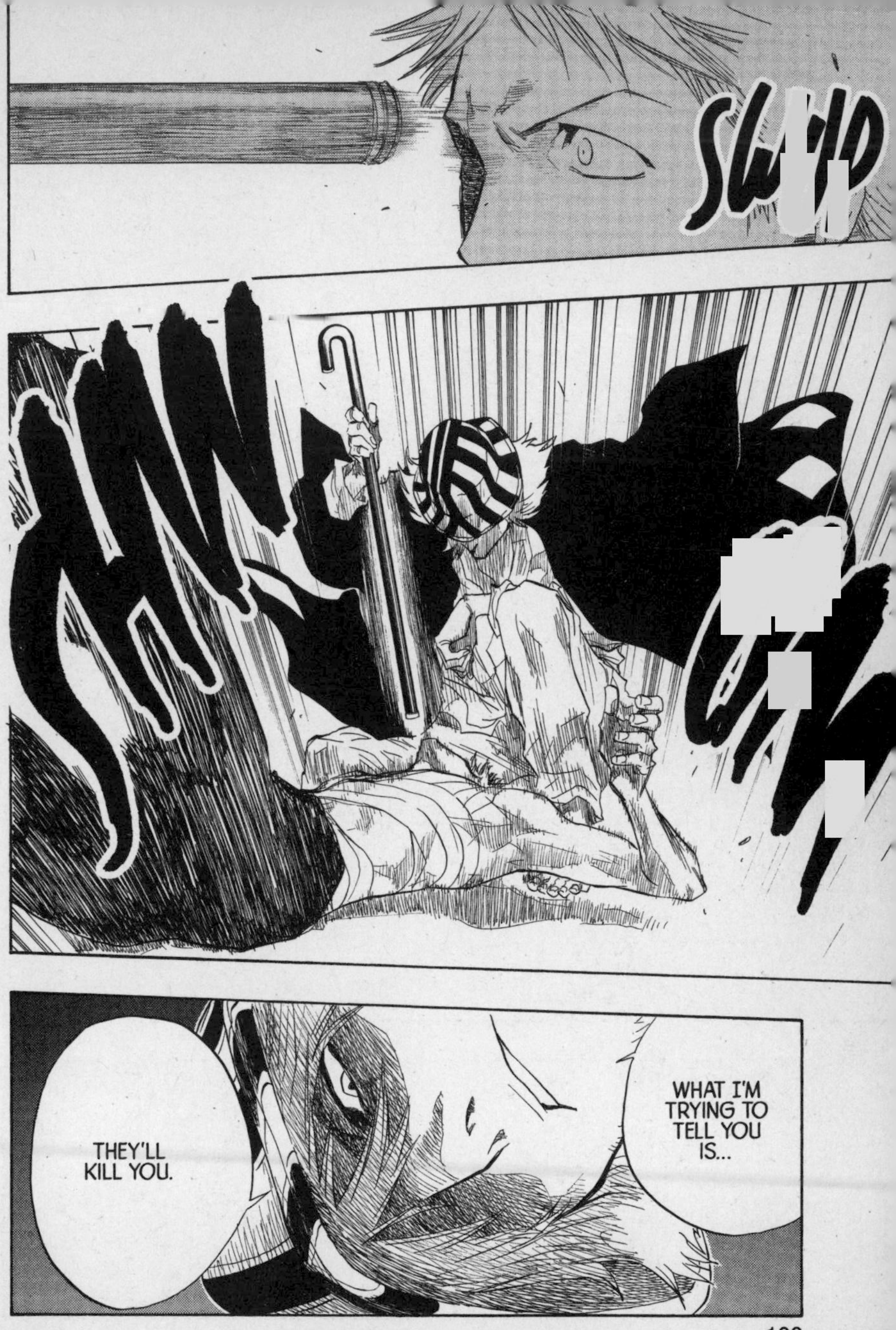
WHAT I'M TRYING TO TELL YOU IS...
THEY'LL KILL YOU.

READ THIS WAY

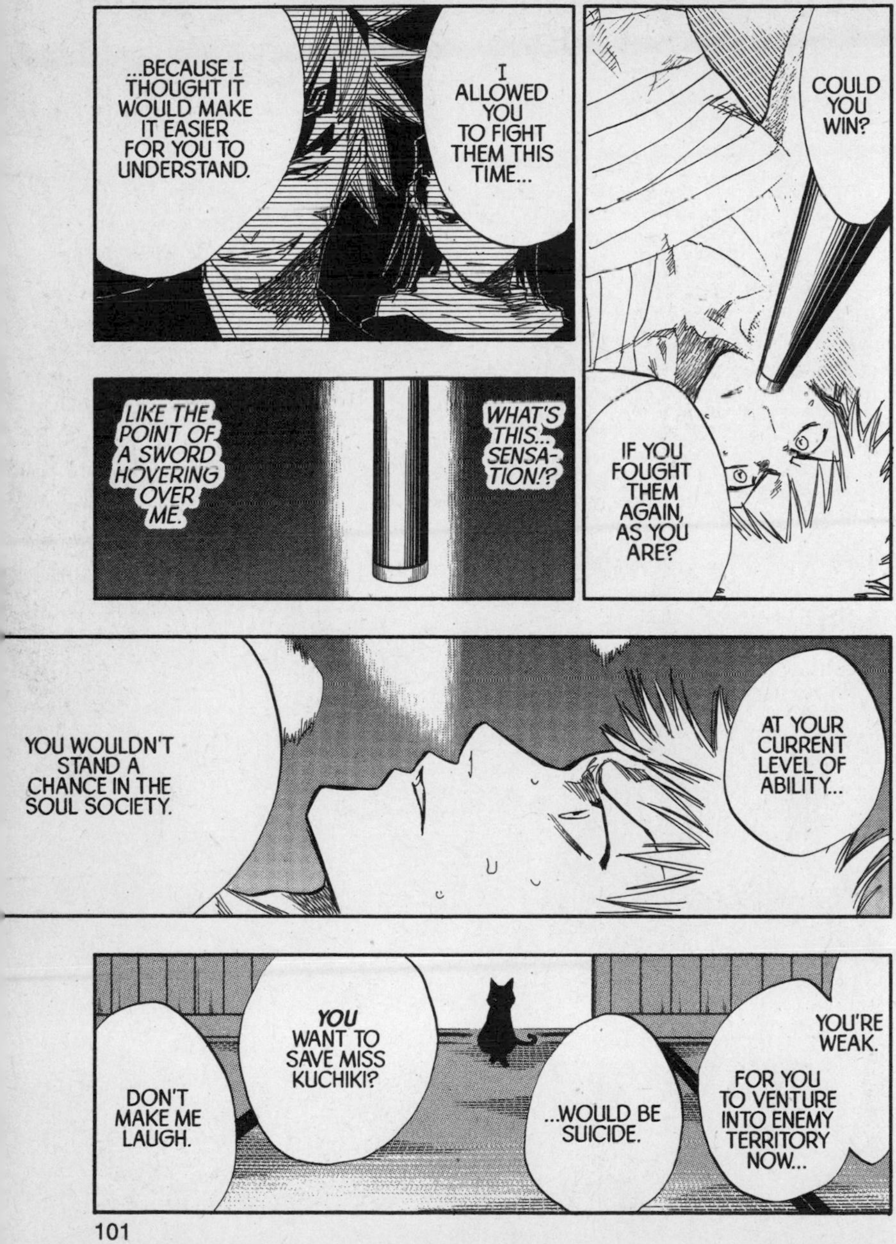
COULD YOU WIN?
IF YOU FOUGHT THEM AGAIN, AS YOU ARE?
I ALLOWED YOU TO FIGHT THEM THIS TIME...
...BECAUSE I THOUGHT IT WOULD MAKE IT EASIER FOR YOU TO UNDERSTAND.
WHAT'S THIS... SENSATION!?
LIKE THE POINT OF A SWORD HOVERING OVER ME.
AT YOUR CURRENT LEVEL OF ABILITY...
YOU WOULDN'T STAND A CHANCE IN THE SOUL SOCIETY.
YOU'RE WEAK.
FOR YOU TO VENTURE INTO ENEMY TERRITORY NOW...
...WOULD BE SUICIDE.
YOU WANT TO SAVE MISS KUCHIKI?
DON'T MAKE ME LAUGH.

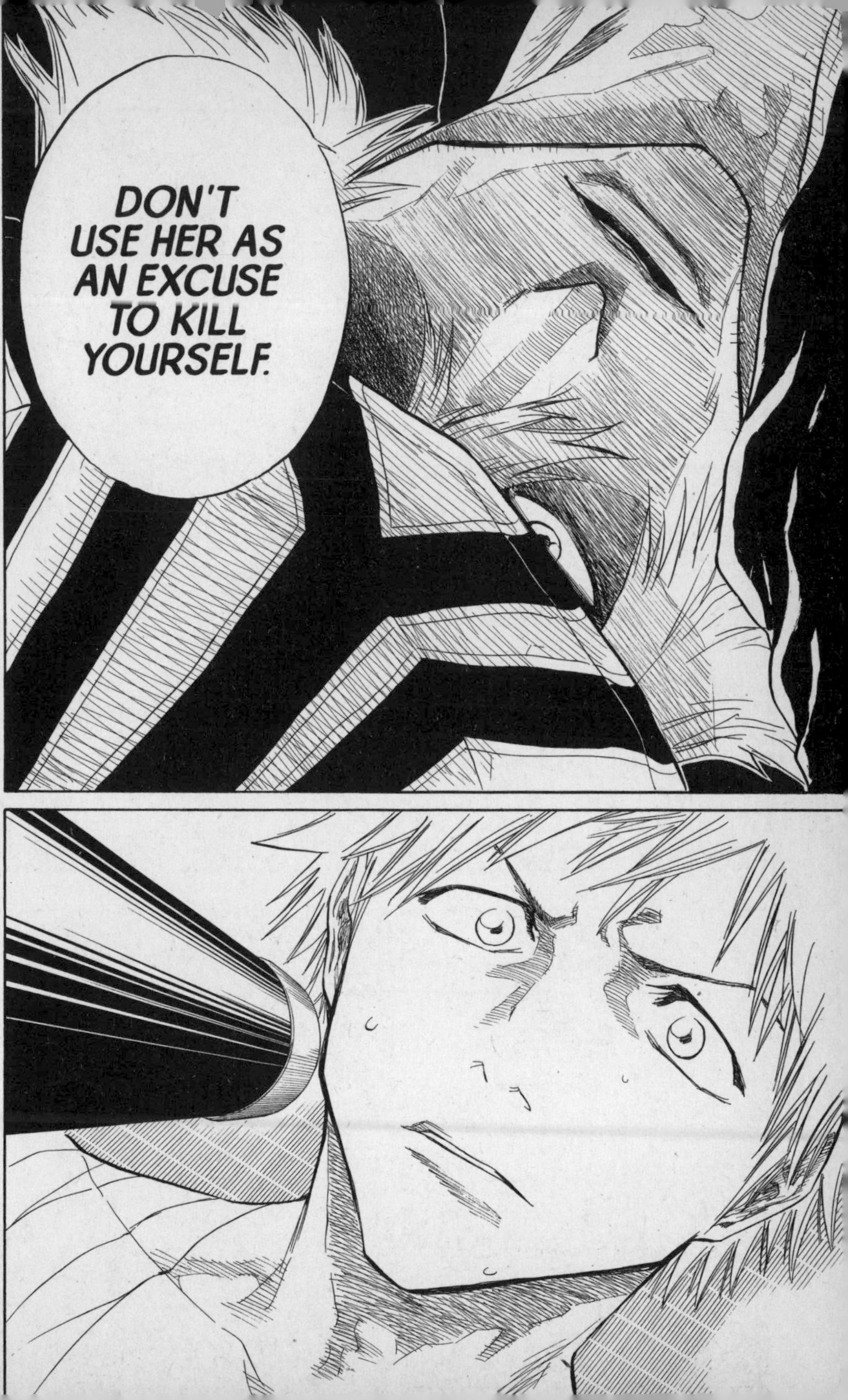
DON'T USE HER AS AN EXCUSE TO KILL YOURSELF.

READ THIS WAY

*KYOKUSHÛ: A CAPITAL OFFENDER.

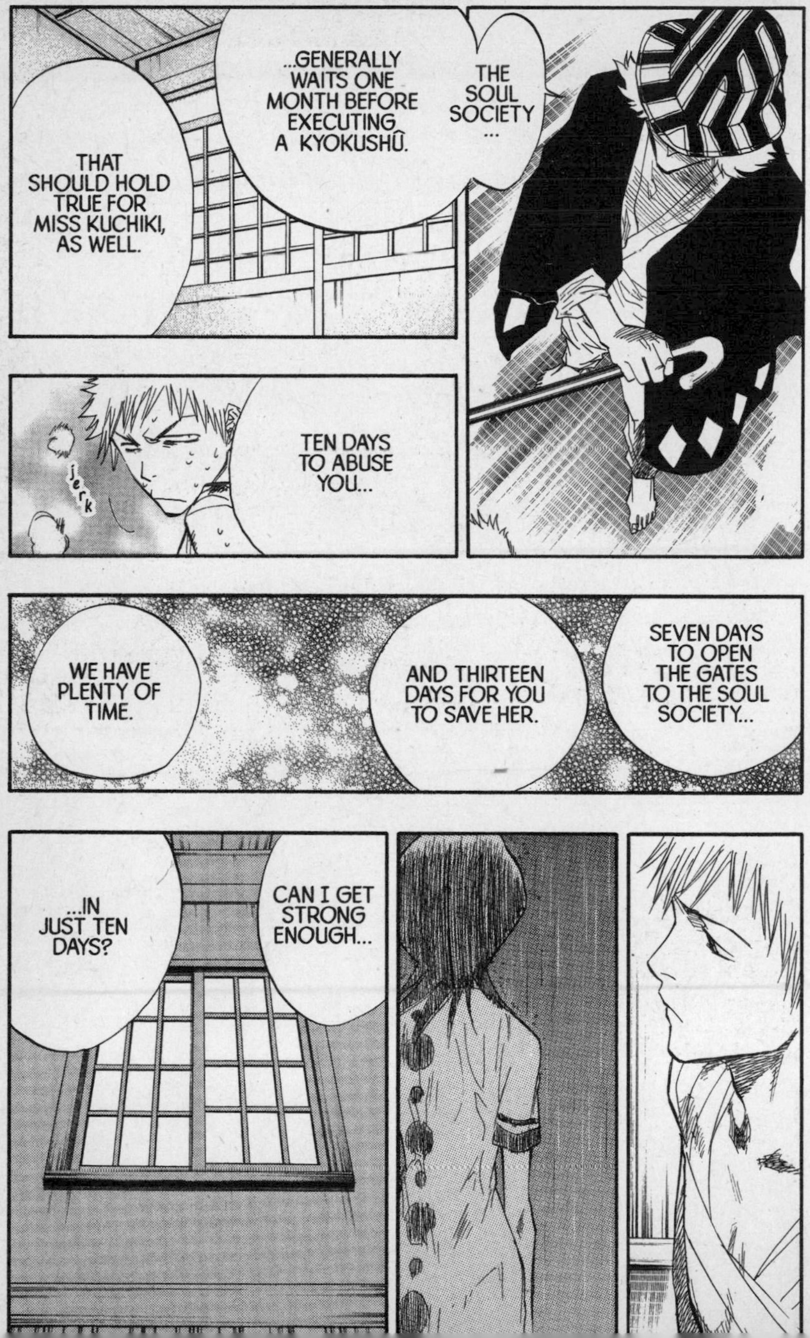
THE SOUL SOCIETY ...
...GENERALLY WAITS ONE MONTH BEFORE EXECUTING A KYOKUSHÛ.
THAT SHOULD HOLD TRUE FOR MISS KUCHIKI, AS WELL.
TEN DAYS TO ABUSE YOU...
jerk
SEVEN DAYS TO OPEN THE GATES TO THE SOUL SOCIETY...
AND THIRTEEN DAYS FOR YOU TO SAVE HER.
WE HAVE PLENTY OF TIME.
CAN I GET STRONG ENOUGH...
...IN JUST TEN DAYS?

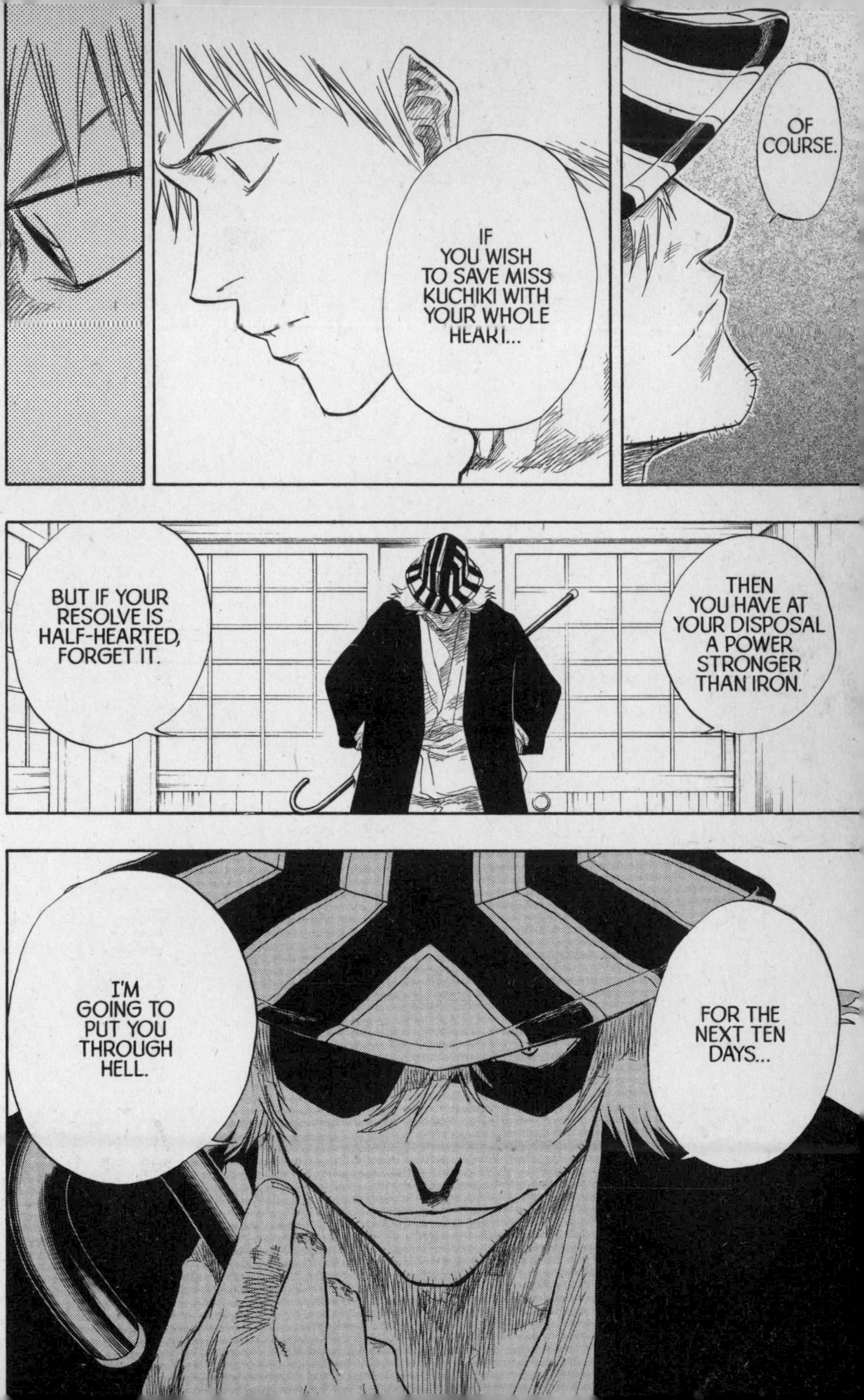
OF COURSE.
IF YOU WISH TO SAVE MISS KUCHIKI WITH YOUR WHOLE HEART...
THEN YOU HAVE AT YOUR DISPOSAL A POWER STRONGER THAN IRON.
BUT IF YOUR RESOLVE IS HALF-HEARTED, FORGET IT.
FOR THE NEXT TEN DAYS...
I'M GOING TO PUT YOU THROUGH HELL.

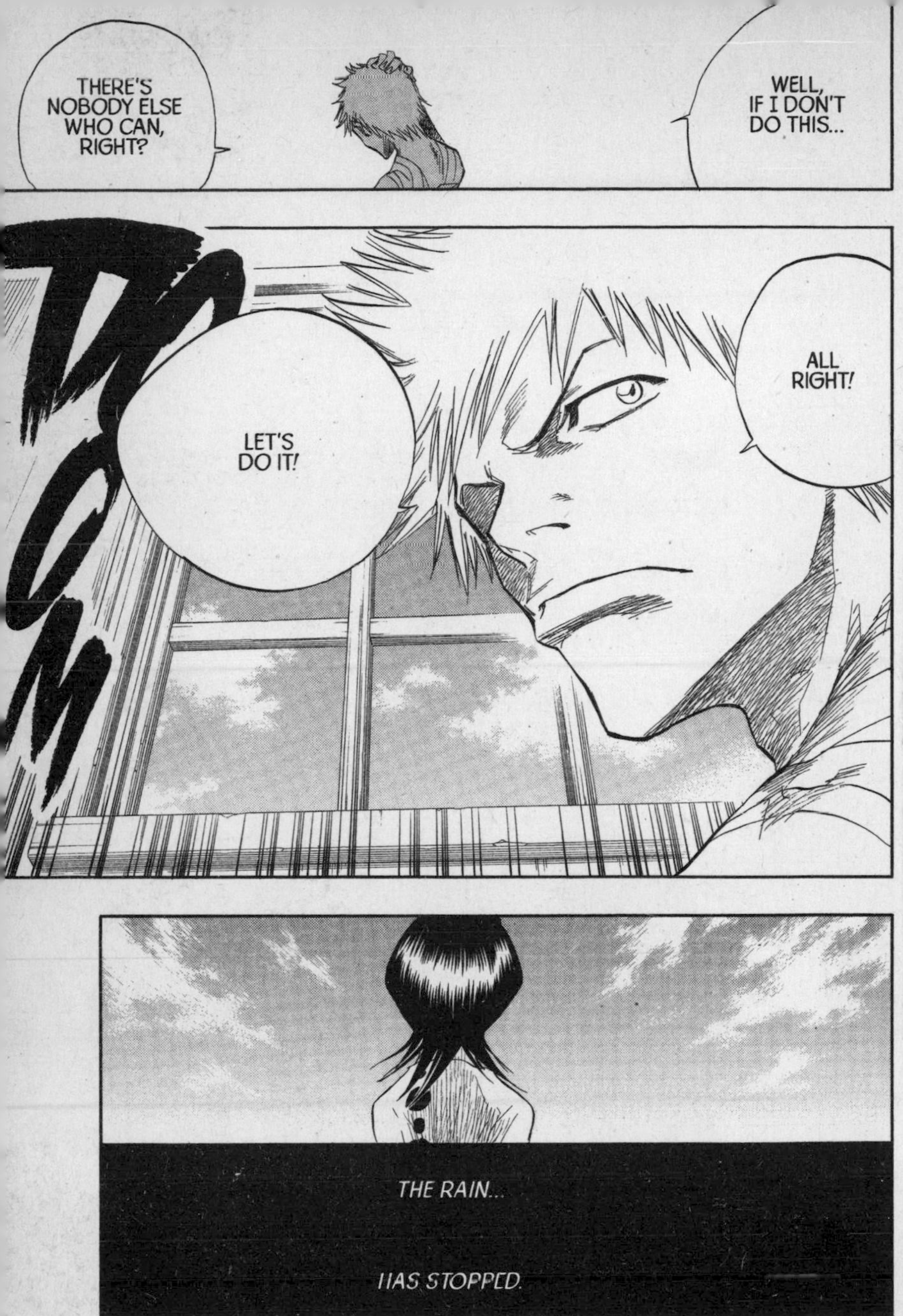
WELL, IF I DON'T DO THIS...
THERE'S NOBODY ELSE WHO CAN, RIGHT?
ALL RIGHT!
LET'S DO IT!
THE RAIN...
HAS STOPPED.

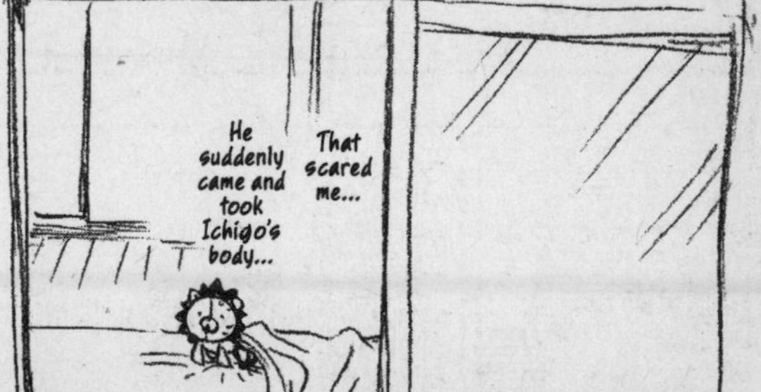
That scared me...
He suddenly came and took Ichigo's body...

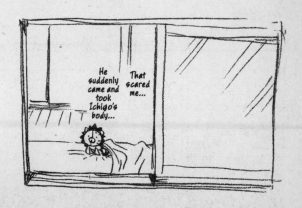

58. blank

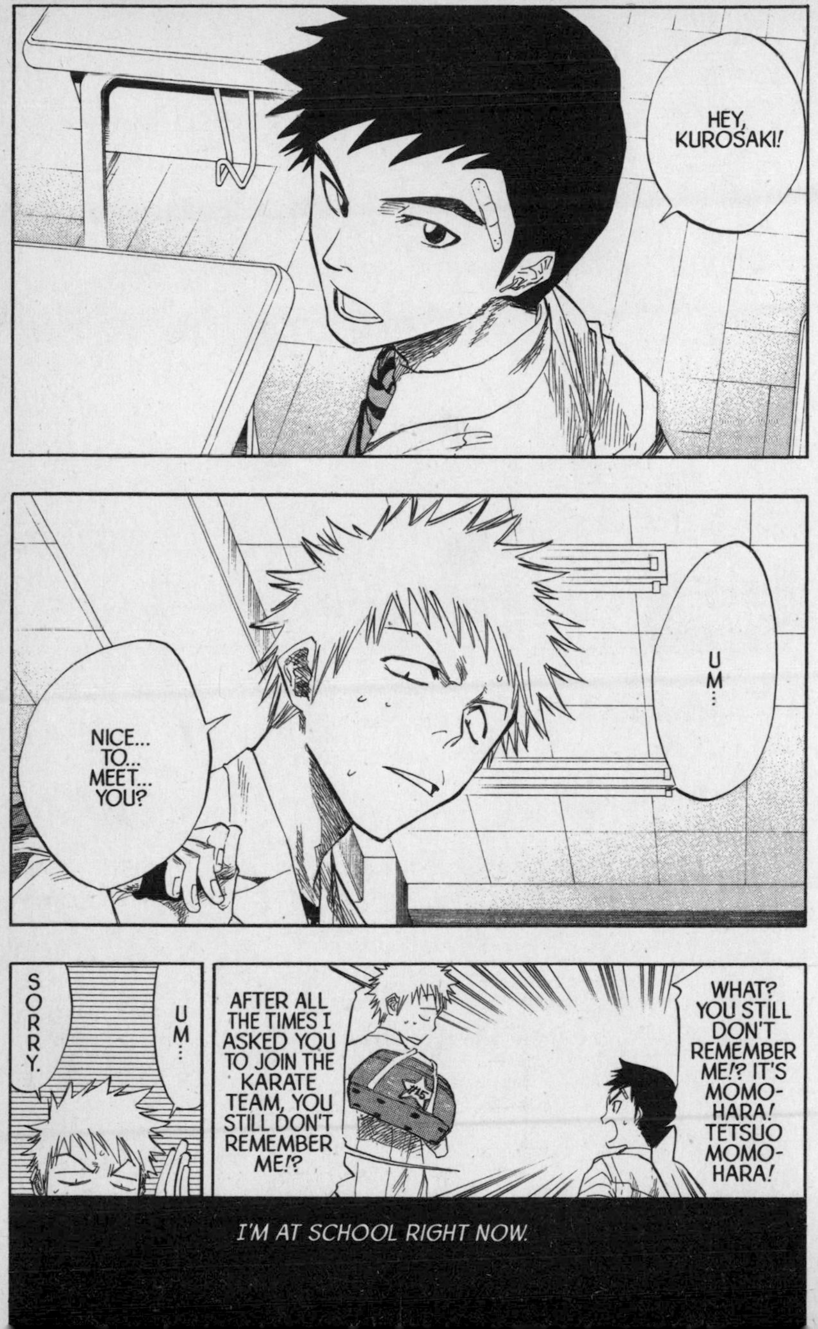
HEY, KUROSAKI!
UM...
NICE... TO... MEET... YOU?
WHAT? YOU STILL DON'T REMEMBER ME!? IT'S MOMO-HARA! TETSUO MOMO-HARA!
AFTER ALL THE TIMES I ASKED YOU TO JOIN THE KARATE TEAM, YOU STILL DON'T REMEMBER ME!?
UM...
SORRY.
I'M AT SCHOOL RIGHT NOW.

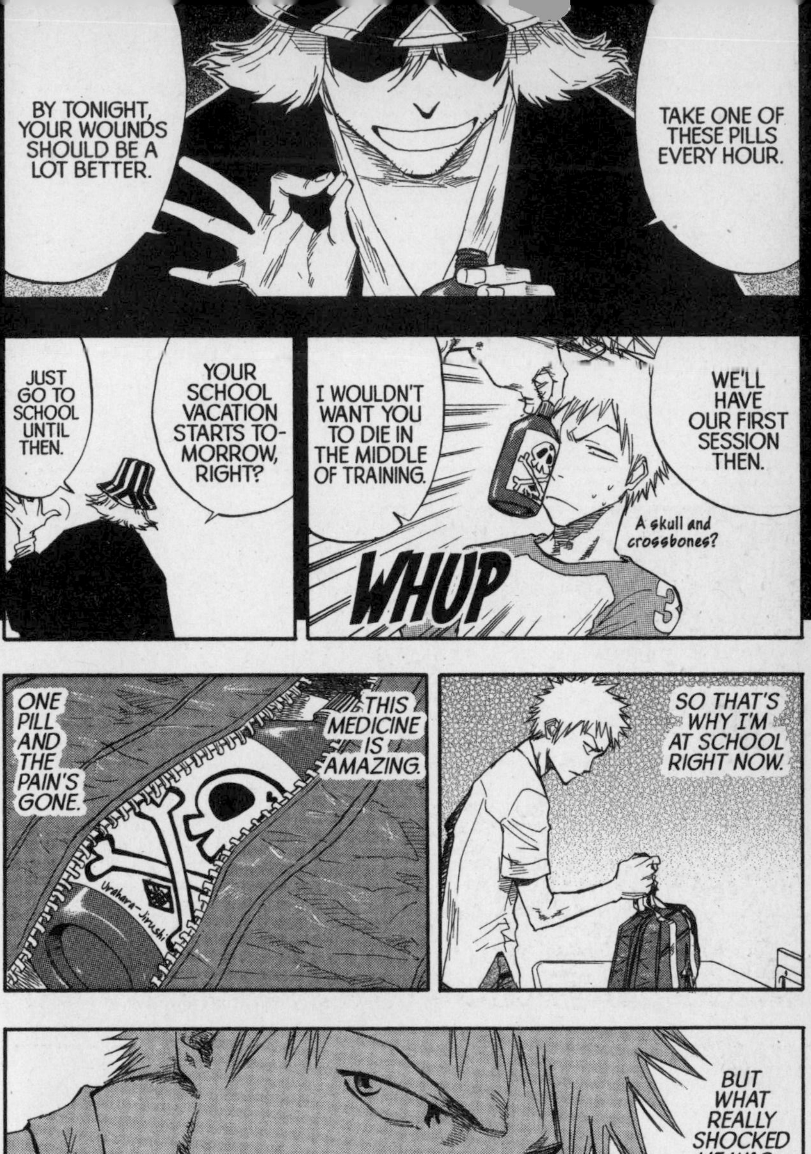
TAKE ONE OF THESE PILLS EVERY HOUR.
BY TONIGHT, YOUR WOUNDS SHOULD BE A LOT BETTER.
WE'LL HAVE OUR FIRST SESSION THEN.
I WOULDN'T WANT YOU TO DIE IN THE MIDDLE OF TRAINING.
WHUP
A skull and crossbones?
YOUR SCHOOL VACATION STARTS TO-MORROW, RIGHT?
JUST GO TO SCHOOL UNTIL THEN.
SO THAT'S WHY I'M AT SCHOOL RIGHT NOW.
THIS MEDICINE IS AMAZING.
ONE PILL AND THE PAIN'S GONE.
Urahara-Jirushi
BUT WHAT REALLY SHOCKED ME WAS...

READ THIS WAY

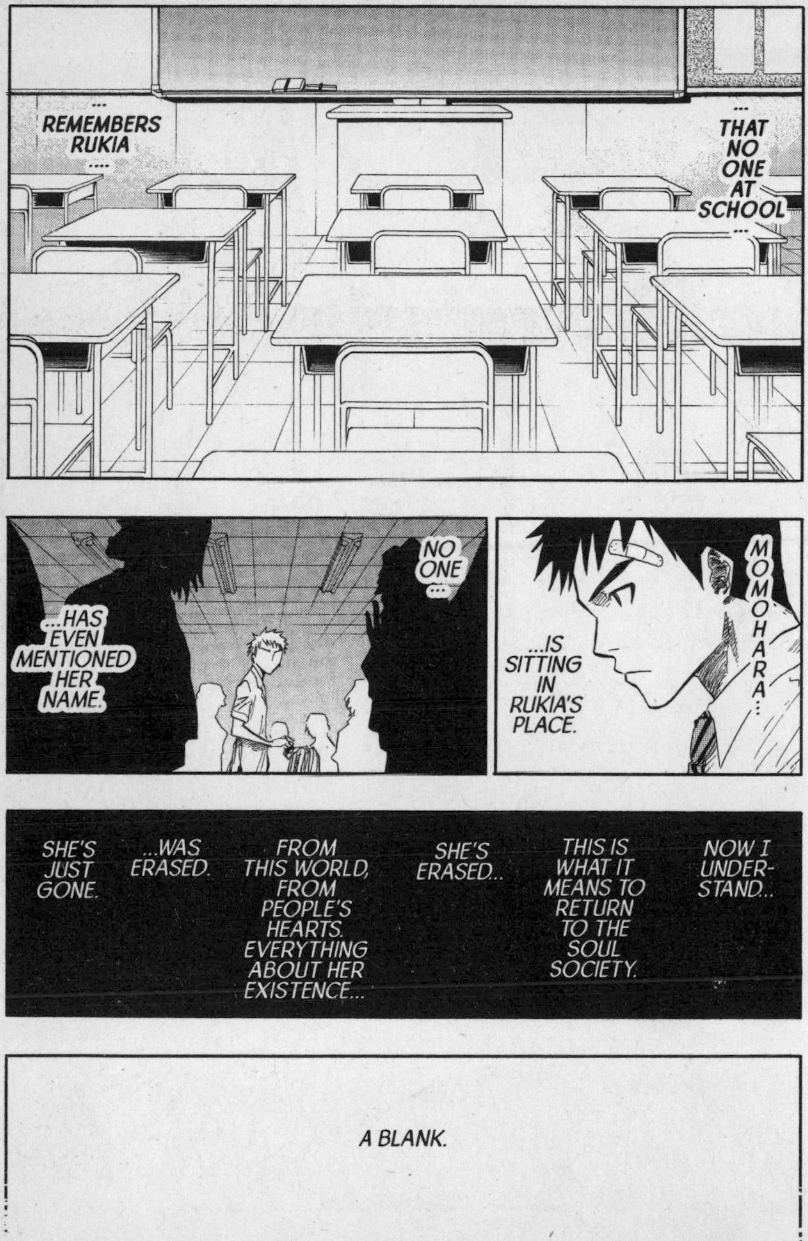
...THAT NO ONE AT SCHOOL...
...REMEMBERS RUKIA....
MOMOHARA...
...IS SITTING IN RUKIA'S PLACE.
NO ONE...
...HAS EVEN MENTIONED HER NAME.
NOW I UNDERSTAND...
THIS IS WHAT IT MEANS TO RETURN TO THE SOUL SOCIETY.
SHE'S ERASED...
FROM THIS WORLD, FROM PEOPLE'S HEARTS. EVERYTHING ABOUT HER EXISTENCE...
...WAS ERASED.
SHE'S JUST GONE.
A BLANK.

BLEACH
ブリーチ

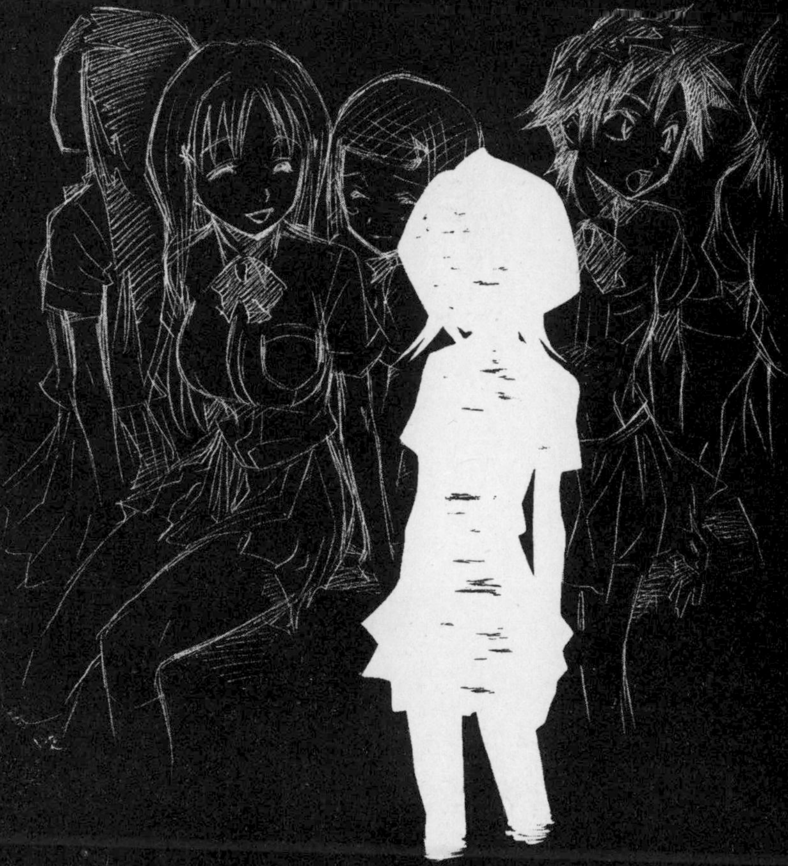

58. blank

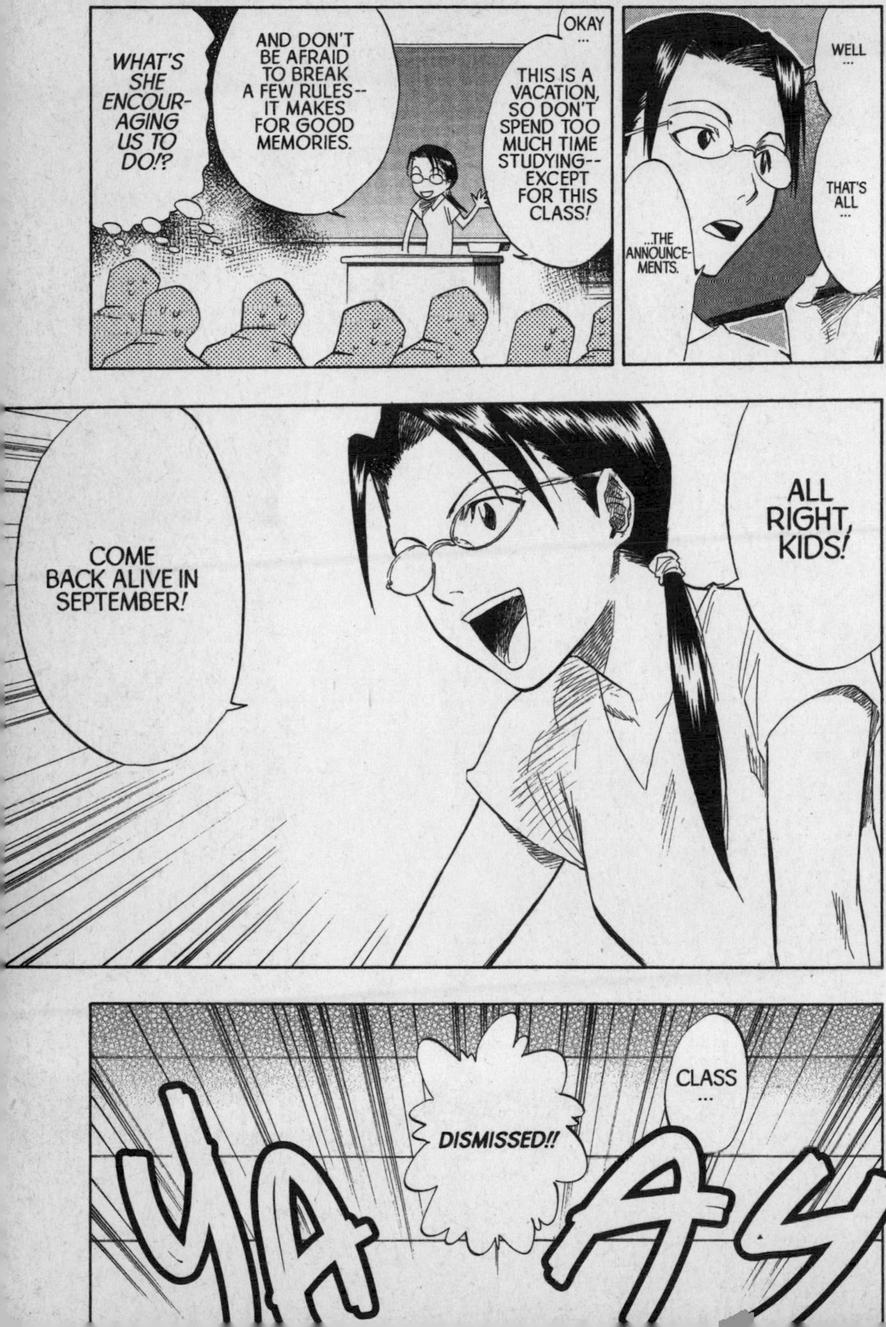
WELL ...
THAT'S ALL ...
...THE ANNOUNCEMENTS.
OKAY ...
THIS IS A VACATION, SO DON'T SPEND TOO MUCH TIME STUDYING-- EXCEPT FOR THIS CLASS!
AND DON'T BE AFRAID TO BREAK A FEW RULES-- IT MAKES FOR GOOD MEMORIES.
WHAT'S SHE ENCOURAGING US TO DO!?
ALL RIGHT, KIDS!
COME BACK ALIVE IN SEPTEMBER!
CLASS ...
DISMISSED!!
YAAY

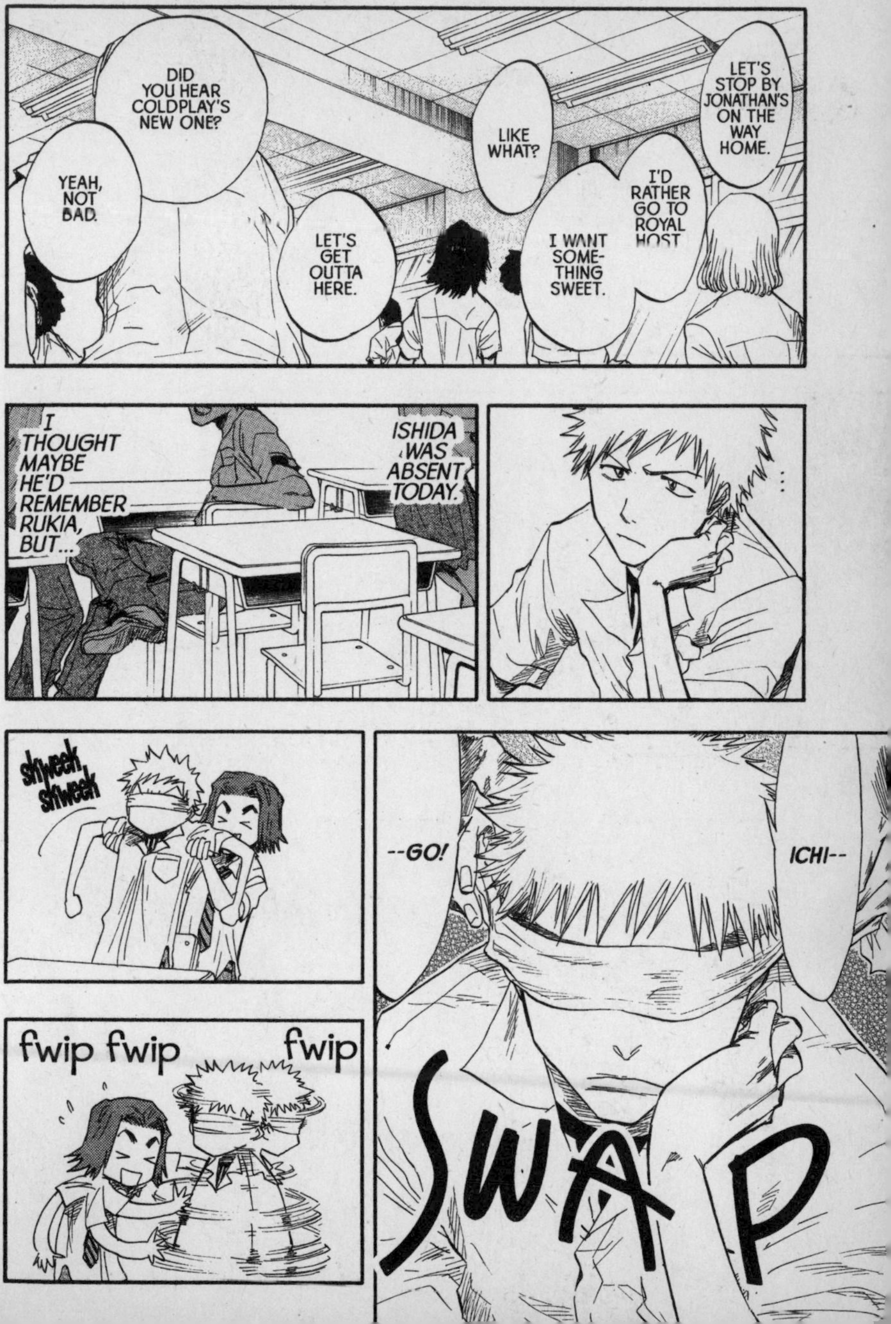
LET'S STOP BY JONATHAN'S ON THE WAY HOME.
I'D RATHER GO TO ROYAL HOST
LIKE WHAT?
I WANT SOME-THING SWEET.
LET'S GET OUTTA HERE.
DID YOU HEAR COLDPLAY'S NEW ONE?
YEAH, NOT BAD.
...
ISHIDA WAS ABSENT TODAY.
I THOUGHT MAYBE HE'D REMEMBER RUKIA, BUT...
ICHI--
--GO!
SWAP
shweek shweek
fwip fwip fwip

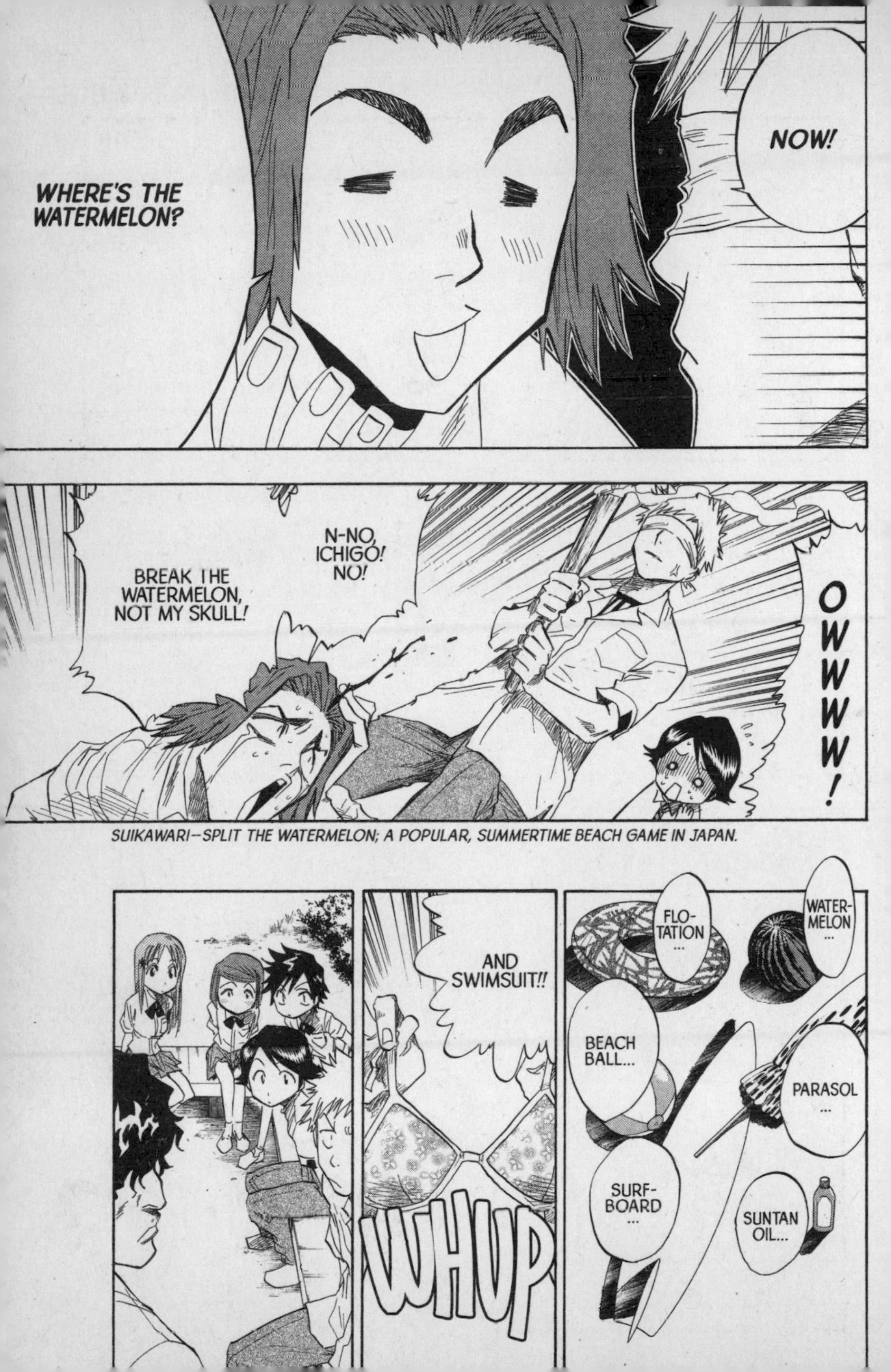
NOW!
WHERE'S THE WATERMELON?
OWWWWW!
N-NO, ICHIGO! NO!
BREAK THE WATERMELON, NOT MY SKULL!
SUIKAWARI--SPLIT THE WATERMELON; A POPULAR, SUMMERTIME BEACH GAME IN JAPAN.
WATER-MELON ...
FLO-TATION ...
PARASOL ...
BEACH BALL...
SUNTAN OIL...
SURF-BOARD ...
AND SWIMSUIT!!
WHUP

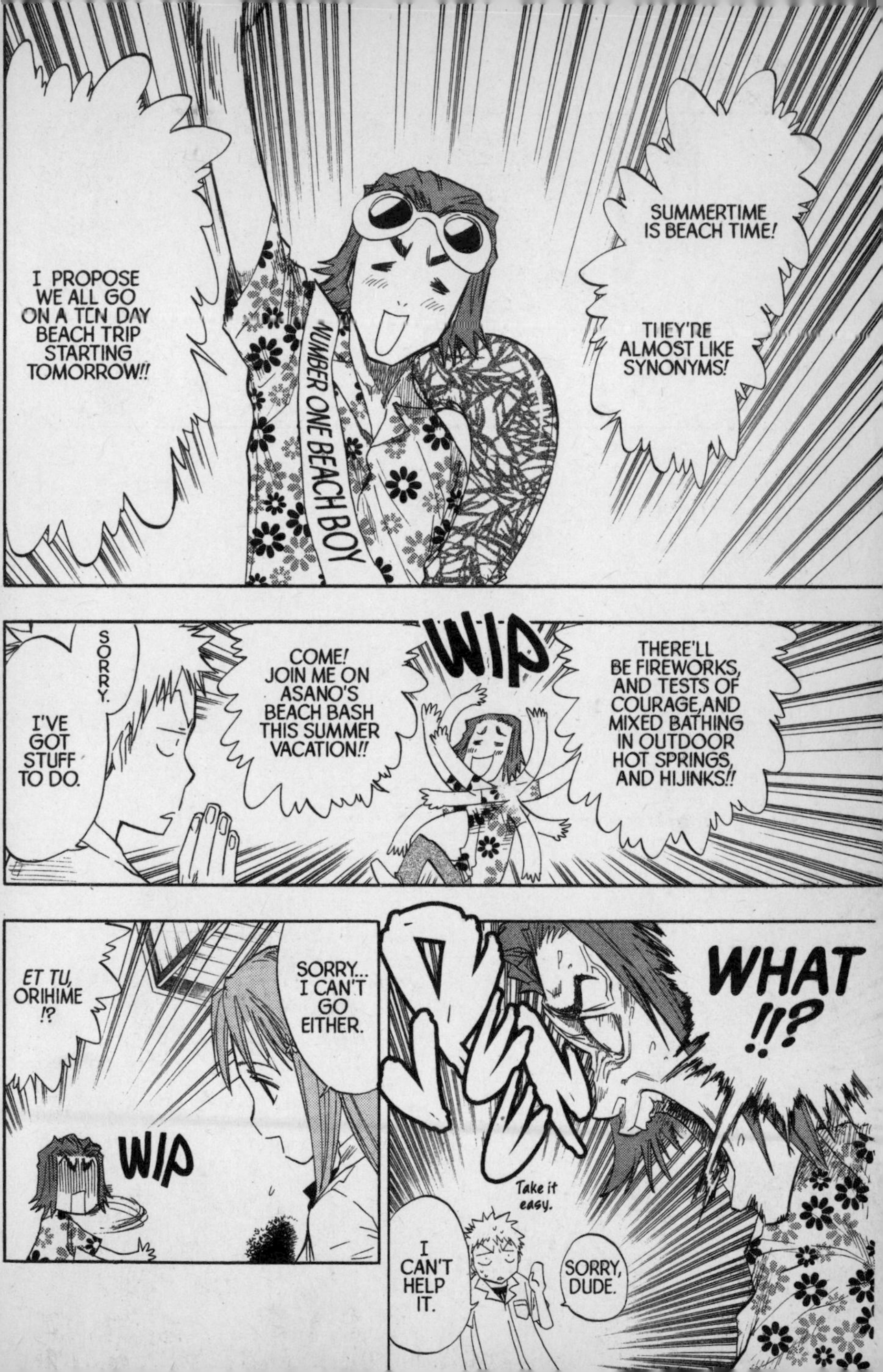
SUMMERTIME IS BEACH TIME!
THEY'RE ALMOST LIKE SYNONYMS!
NUMBER ONE BEACH BOY
I PROPOSE WE ALL GO ON A TEN DAY BEACH TRIP STARTING TOMORROW!!
THERE'LL BE FIREWORKS, AND TESTS OF COURAGE, AND MIXED BATHING IN OUTDOOR HOT SPRINGS, AND HIJINKS!!
WIP
COME! JOIN ME ON ASANO'S BEACH BASH THIS SUMMER VACATION!!
SORRY.
I'VE GOT STUFF TO DO.
WHAT!!?
Take it easy.
SORRY, DUDE.
I CAN'T HELP IT.
SORRY... I CAN'T GO EITHER.
WIP
ET TU, ORIHIME!?

READ THIS WAY

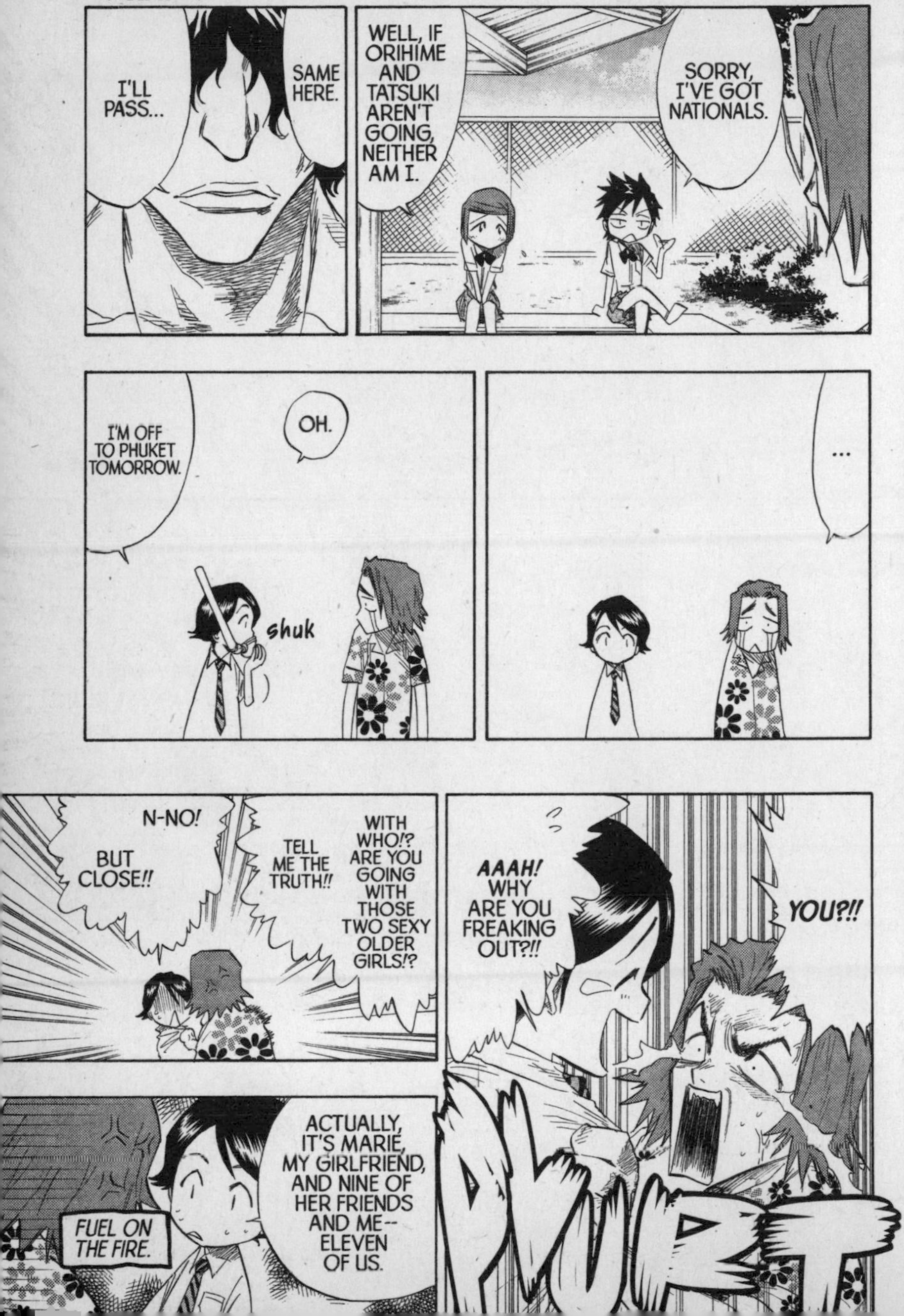
SORRY, I'VE GOT NATIONALS.
WELL, IF ORIHIME AND TATSUKI AREN'T GOING, NEITHER AM I.
SAME HERE.
I'LL PASS...
...
OH.
I'M OFF TO PHUKET TOMORROW.
shuk
YOU?!!
AAAH! WHY ARE YOU FREAKING OUT?!!
PWUPT
WITH WHO!? ARE YOU GOING WITH THOSE TWO SEXY OLDER GIRLS!?
TELL ME THE TRUTH!!
N-NO!
BUT CLOSE!!
ACTUALLY, IT'S MARIE, MY GIRLFRIEND, AND NINE OF HER FRIENDS AND ME-- ELEVEN OF US.
FUEL ON THE FIRE.

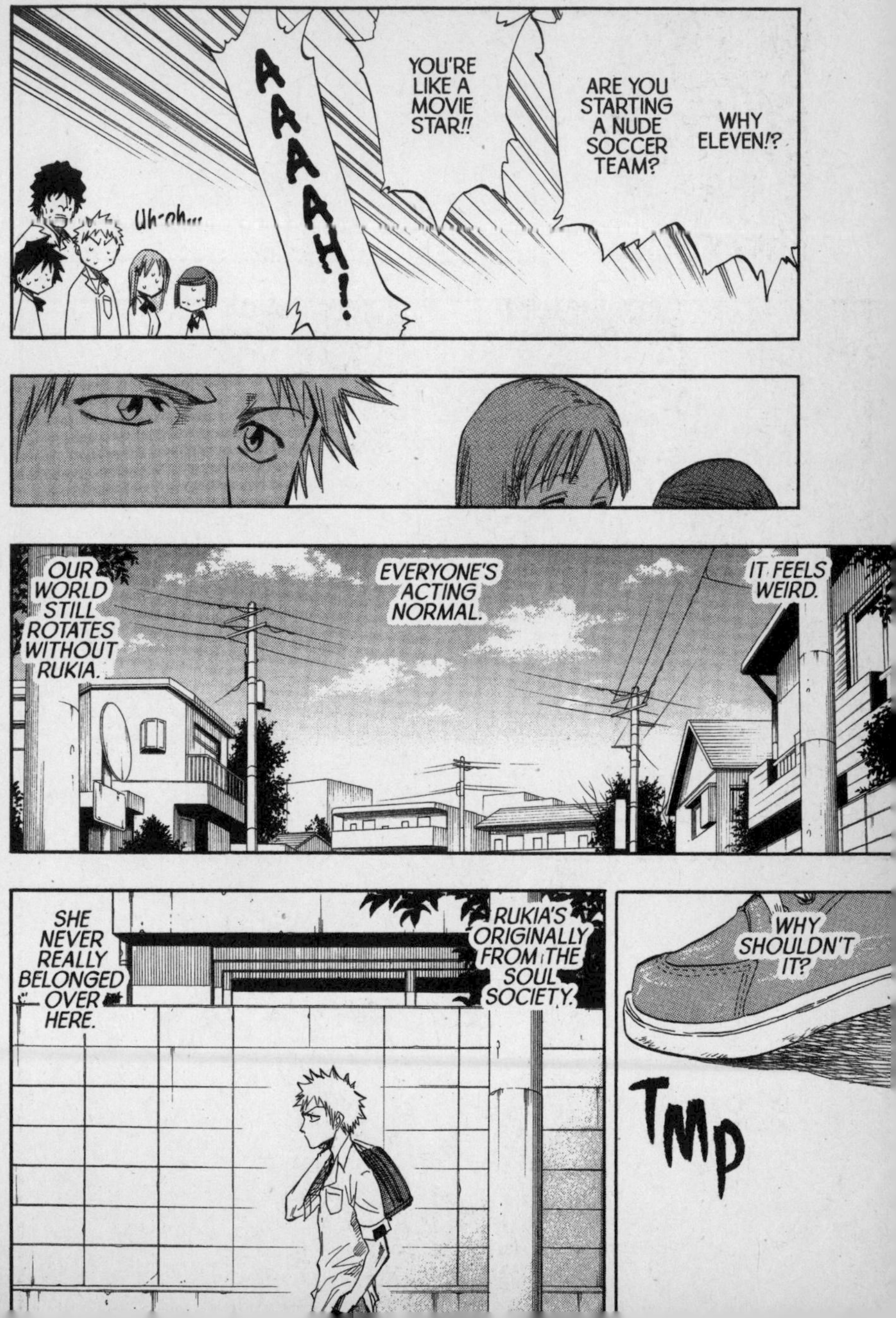
WHY ELEVEN!?
ARE YOU STARTING A NUDE SOCCER TEAM?
YOU'RE LIKE A MOVIE STAR!!
AAAAAH!!
Uh-oh...
IT FEELS WEIRD.
EVERYONE'S ACTING NORMAL.
OUR WORLD STILL ROTATES WITHOUT RUKIA.
WHY SHOULDN'T IT?
TMP
RUKIA'S ORIGINALLY FROM THE SOUL SOCIETY.
SHE NEVER REALLY BELONGED OVER HERE.

READ THIS WAY

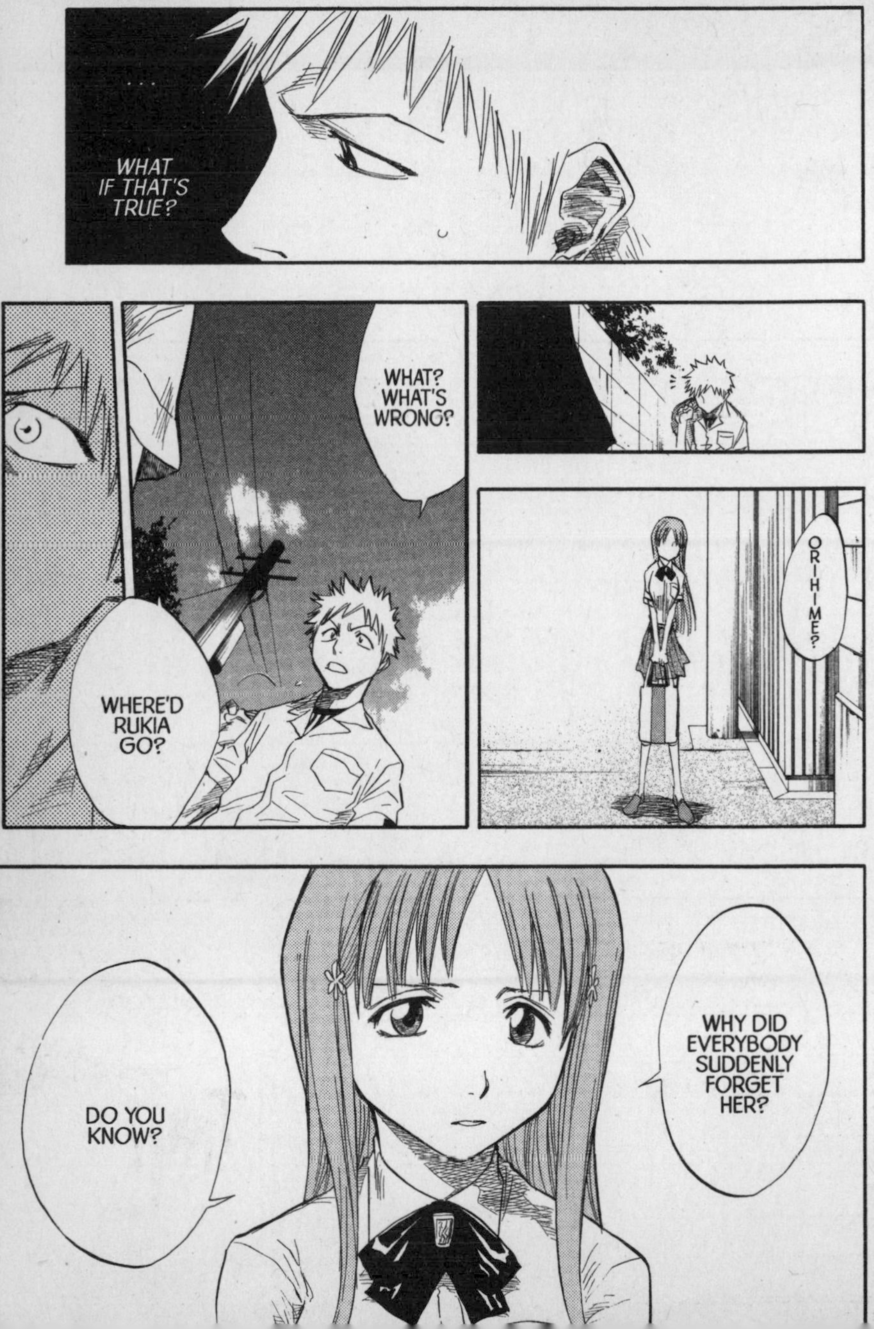
...
WHAT IF THAT'S TRUE?
ORIHIME?
WHAT? WHAT'S WRONG?
WHERE'D RUKIA GO?
WHY DID EVERYBODY SUDDENLY FORGET HER?
DO YOU KNOW?

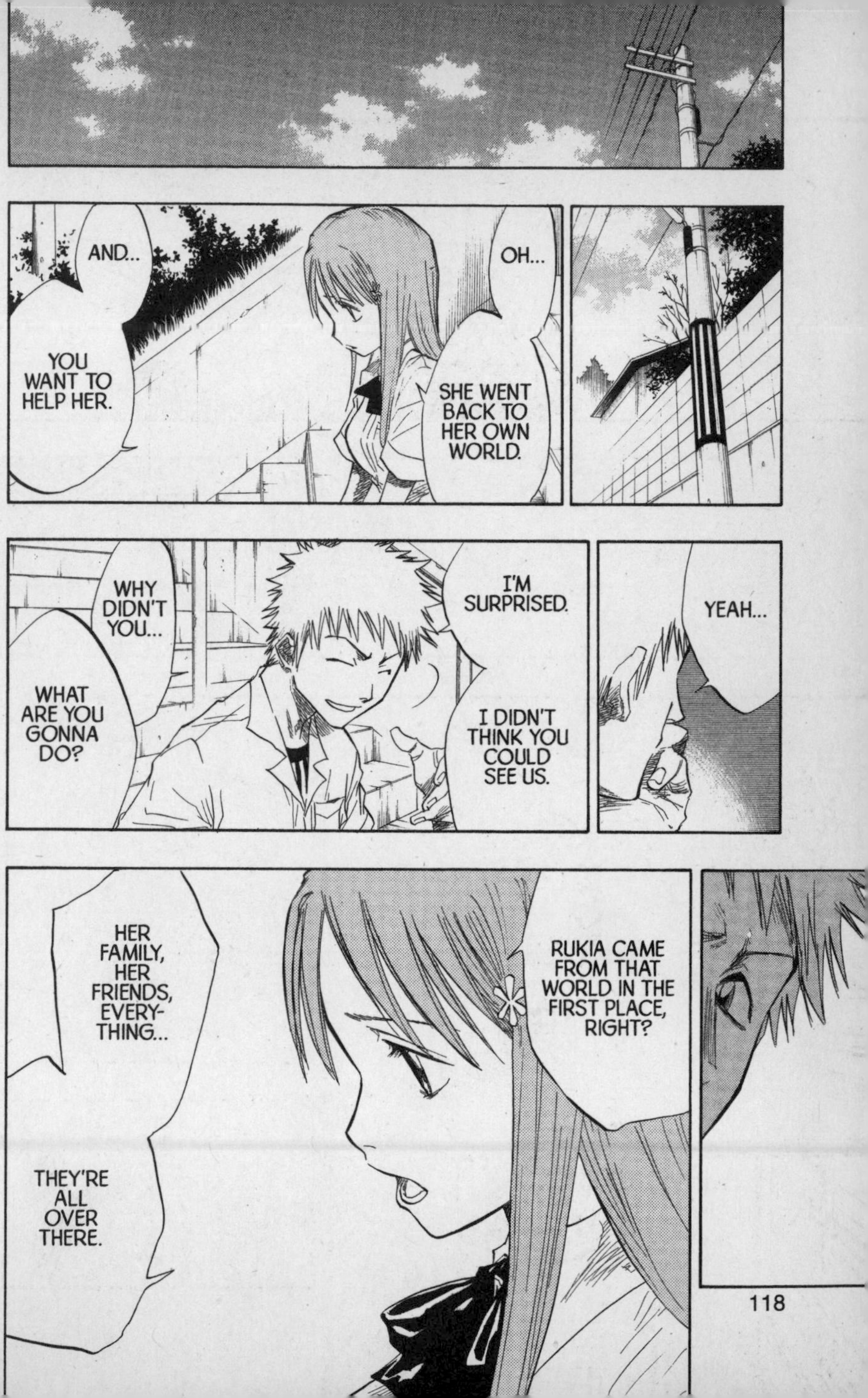
OH...
SHE WENT BACK TO HER OWN WORLD.
AND...
YOU WANT TO HELP HER.
YEAH...
I'M SURPRISED.
I DIDN'T THINK YOU COULD SEE US.
WHY DIDN'T YOU...
WHAT ARE YOU GONNA DO?
RUKIA CAME FROM THAT WORLD IN THE FIRST PLACE, RIGHT?
HER FAMILY, HER FRIENDS, EVERY-THING...
THEY'RE ALL OVER THERE.

READ THIS WAY

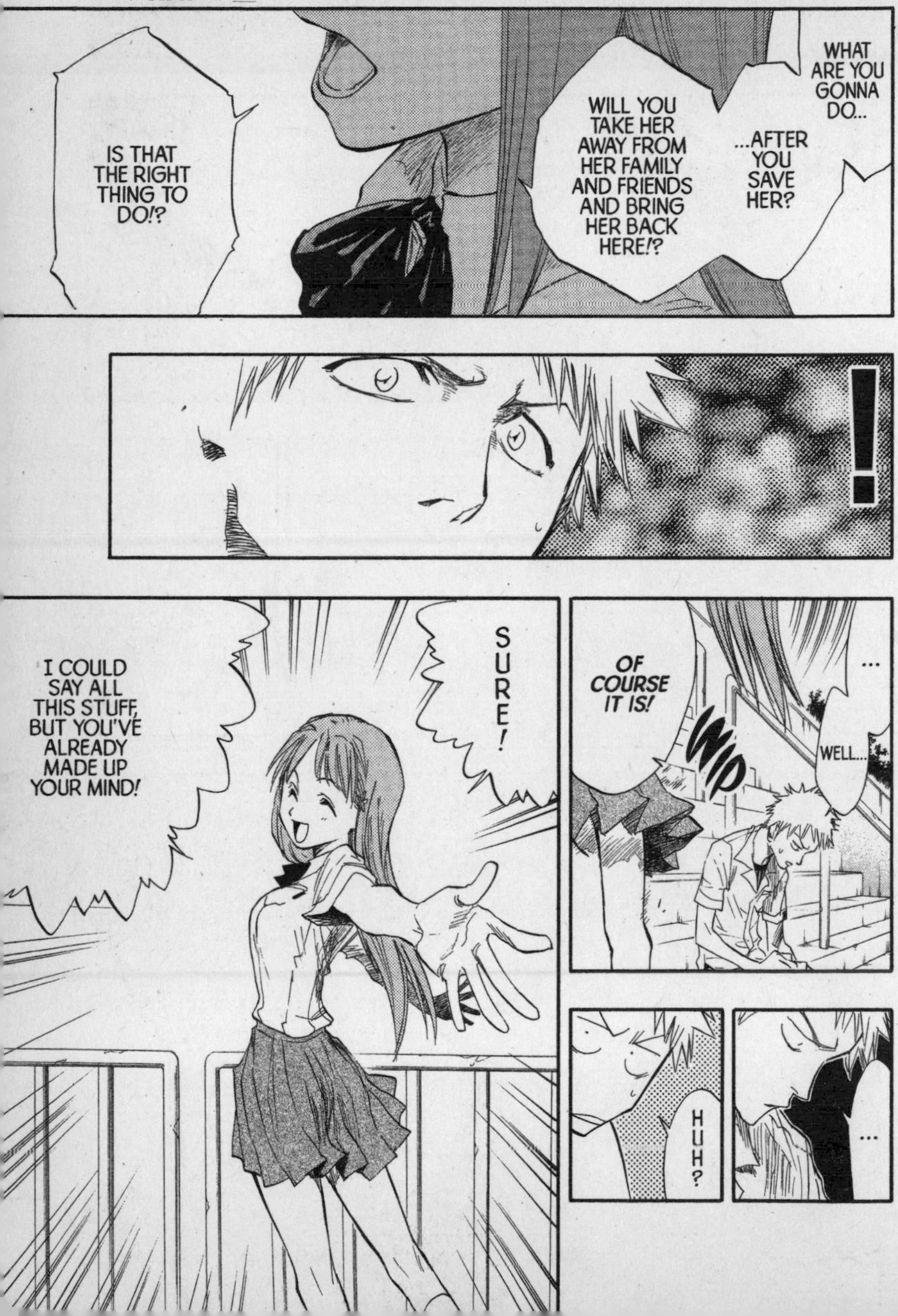
WHAT ARE YOU GONNA DO...
...AFTER YOU SAVE HER?
WILL YOU TAKE HER AWAY FROM HER FAMILY AND FRIENDS AND BRING HER BACK HERE!?
IS THAT THE RIGHT THING TO DO!?
!
...
WELL...
WIP
OF COURSE IT IS!
...
HUH?
SURE!
I COULD SAY ALL THIS STUFF, BUT YOU'VE ALREADY MADE UP YOUR MIND!

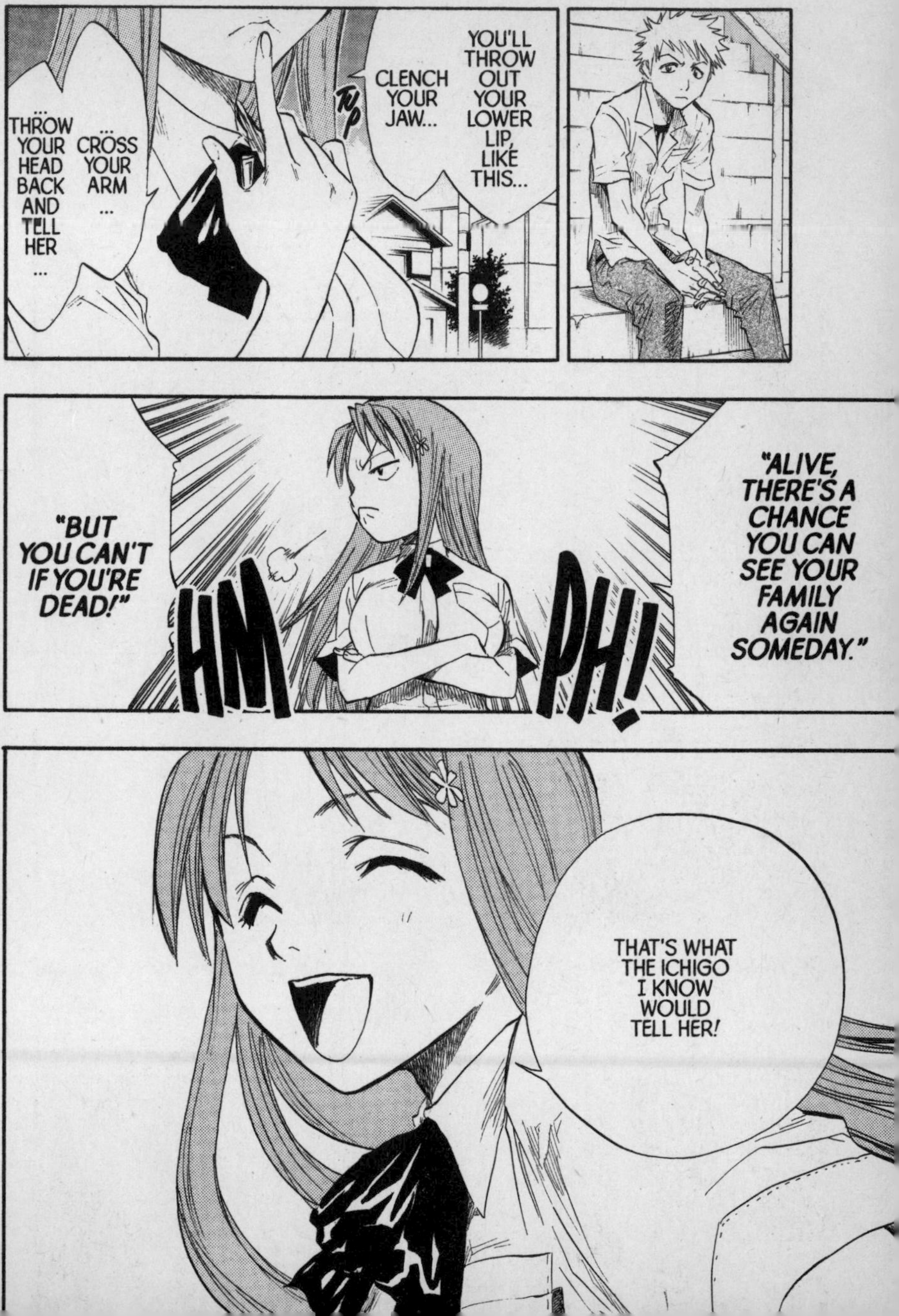
YOU'LL THROW OUT YOUR LOWER LIP, LIKE THIS...
CLENCH YOUR JAW...
TUP
...CROSS YOUR ARM...
...THROW YOUR HEAD BACK AND TELL HER...
"ALIVE, THERE'S A CHANCE YOU CAN SEE YOUR FAMILY AGAIN SOMEDAY."
HMPH!
"BUT YOU CAN'T IF YOU'RE DEAD!"
THAT'S WHAT THE ICHIGO I KNOW WOULD TELL HER!

READ THIS WAY

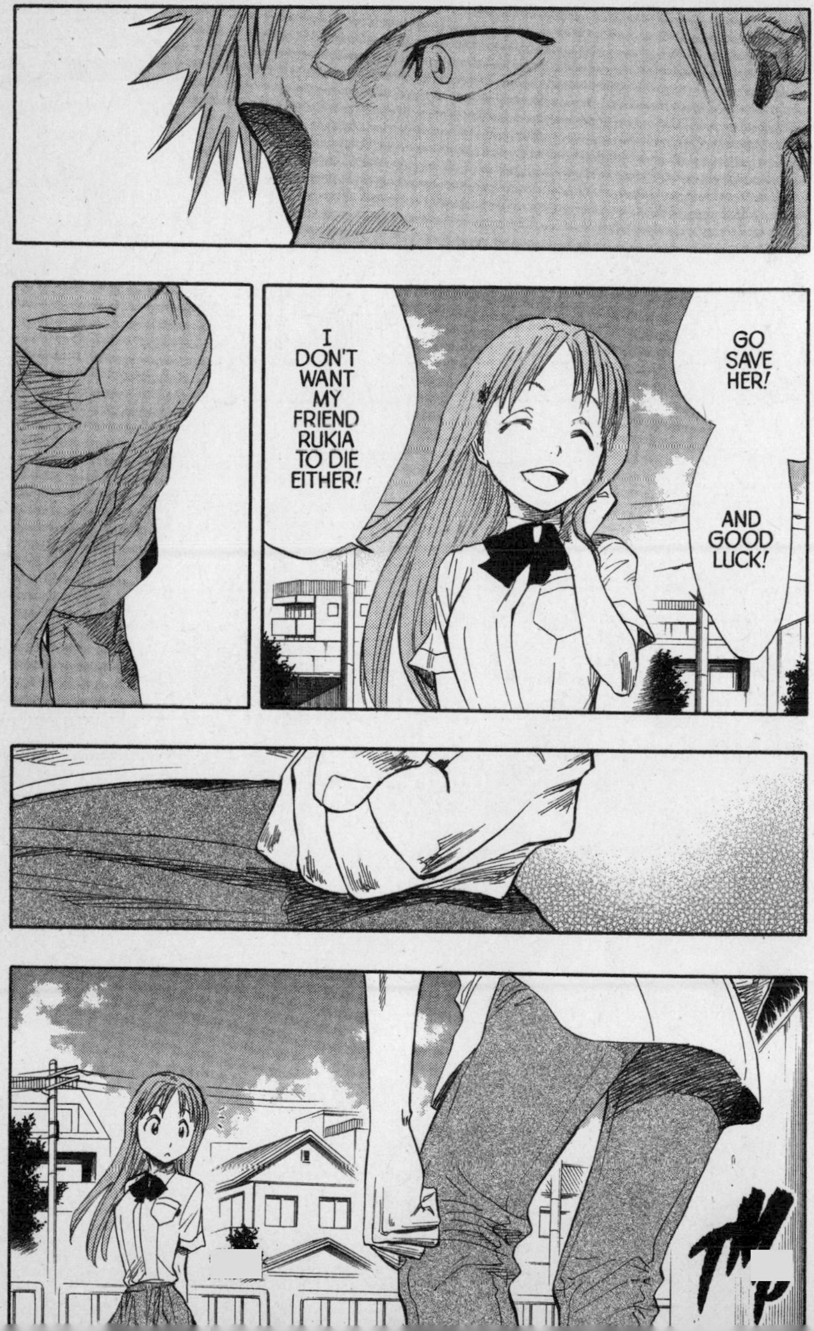
GO SAVE HER!
AND GOOD LUCK!
I DON'T WANT MY FRIEND RUKIA TO DIE EITHER!

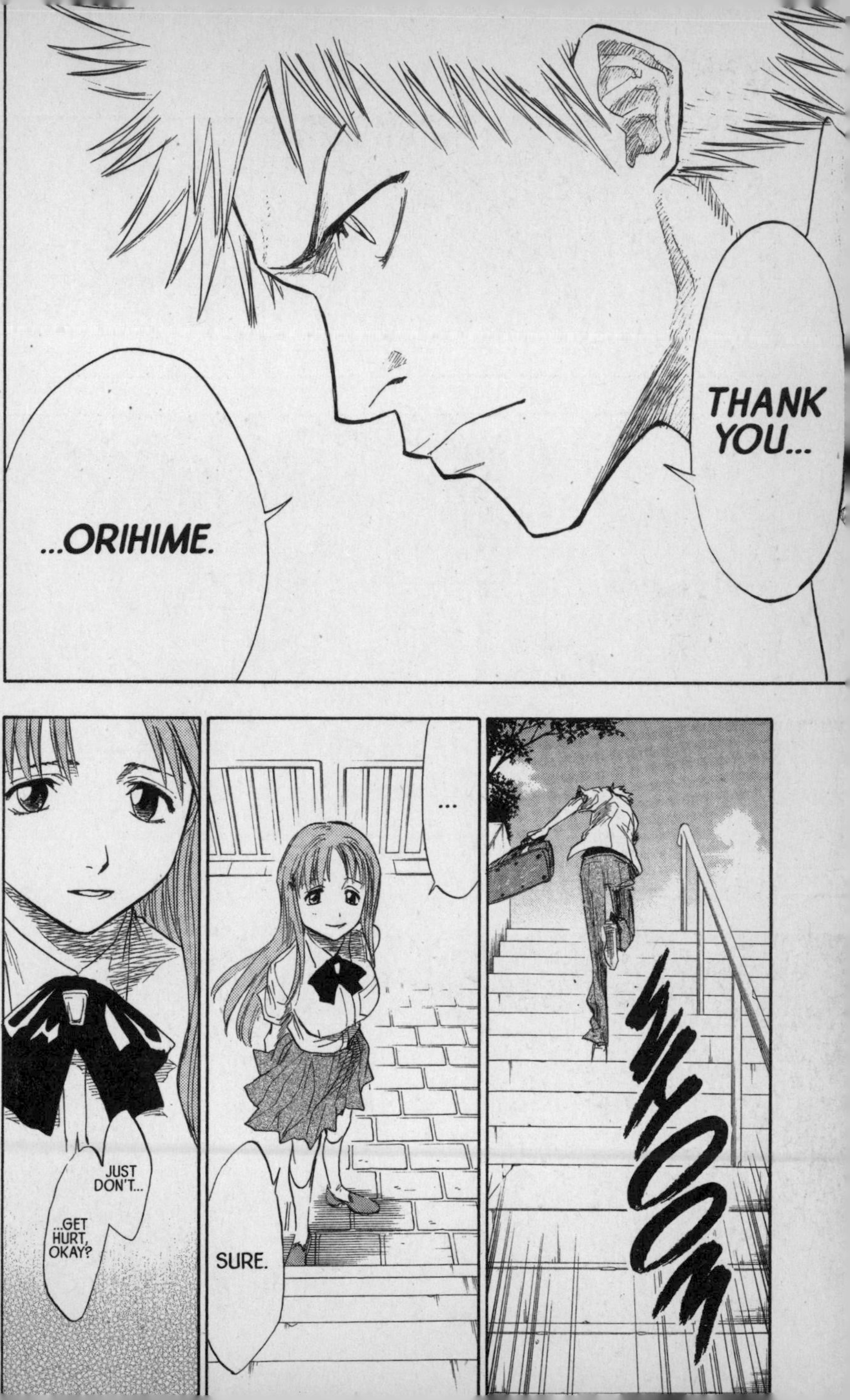
THANK YOU...
...ORIHIME.
WHOOM
...
SURE.
JUST DON'T...
...GET HURT, OKAY?

READ THIS WAY

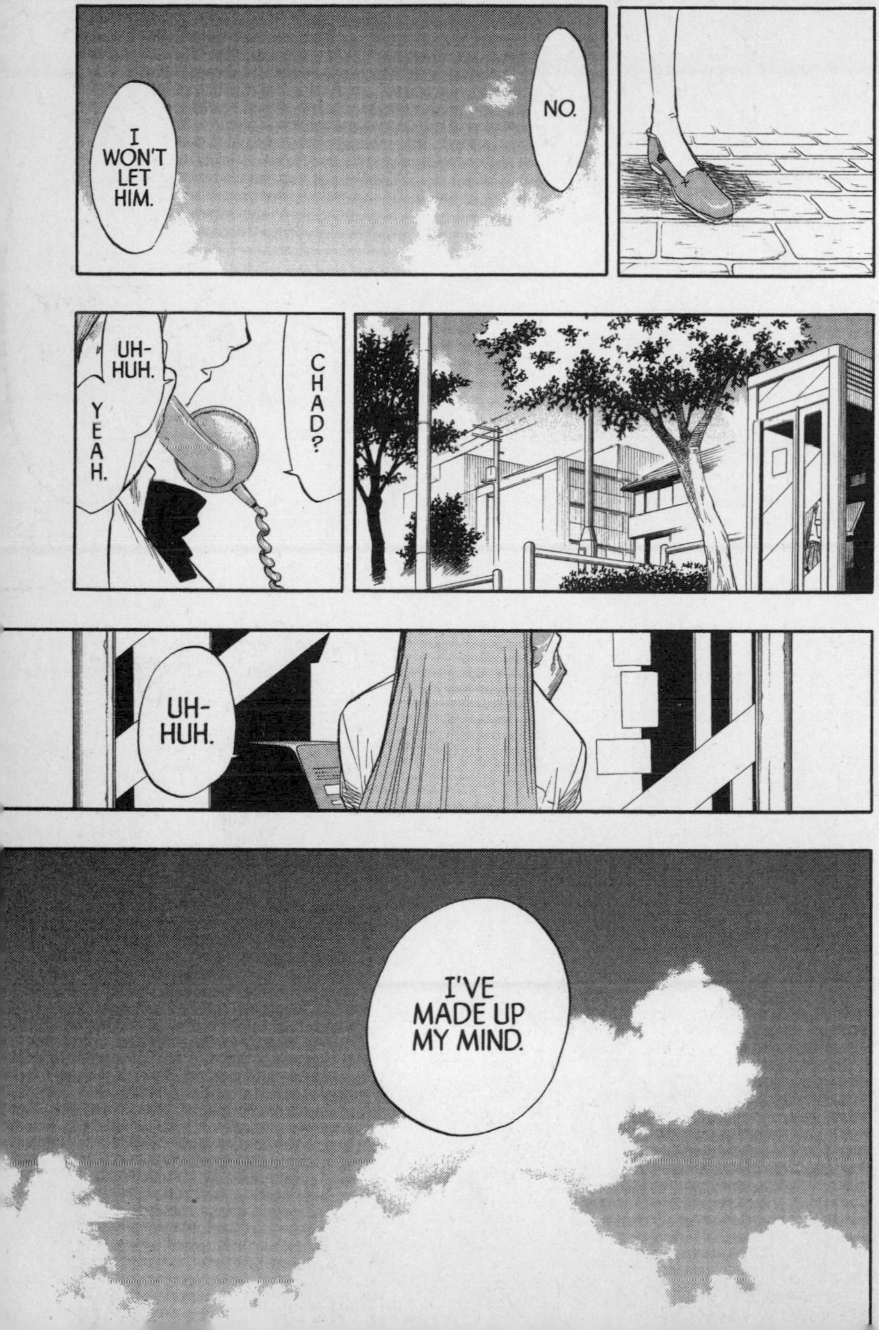
NO.
I WON'T LET HIM.
CHAD?
UH-HUH.
YEAH.
UH-HUH.
I'VE MADE UP MY MIND.

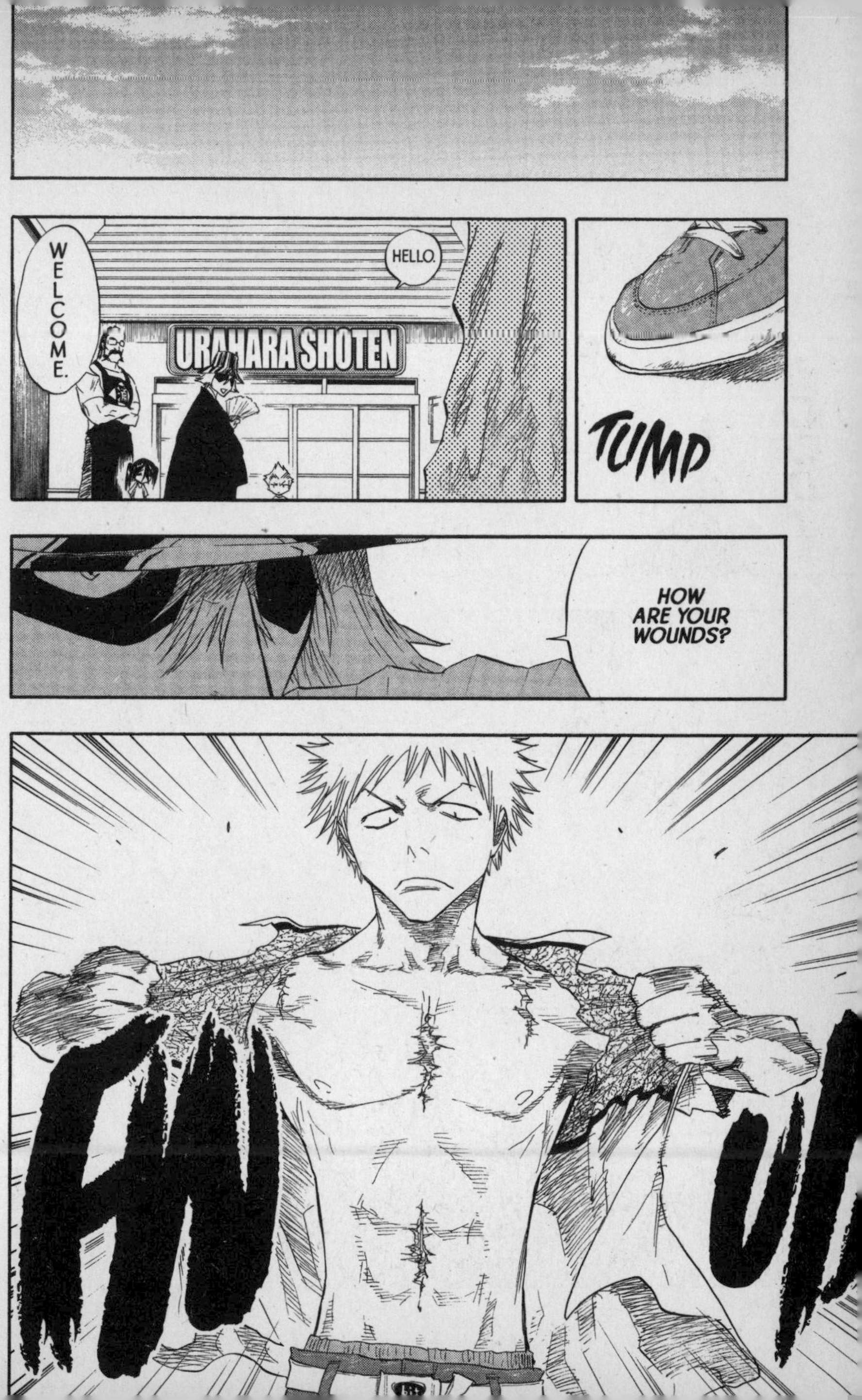
TUMP
HELLO.
WELCOME.
URAHARA SHOTEN
HOW ARE YOUR WOUNDS?

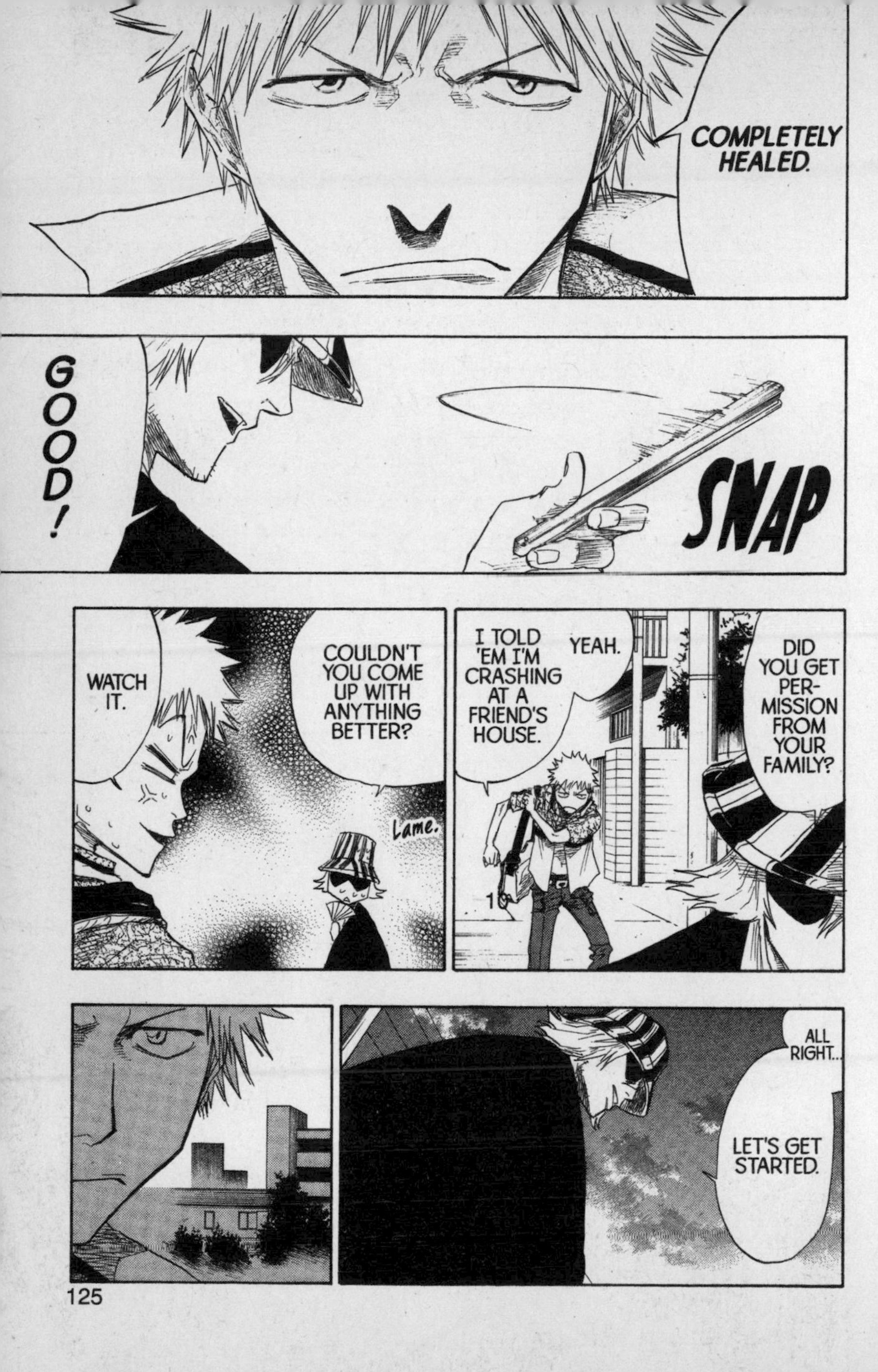
COMPLETELY HEALED.
SNAP
GOOD!
DID YOU GET PER-MISSION FROM YOUR FAMILY?
YEAH.
I TOLD 'EM I'M CRASHING AT A FRIEND'S HOUSE.
COULDN'T YOU COME UP WITH ANYTHING BETTER?
Lame.
WATCH IT.
ALL RIGHT...
LET'S GET STARTED.

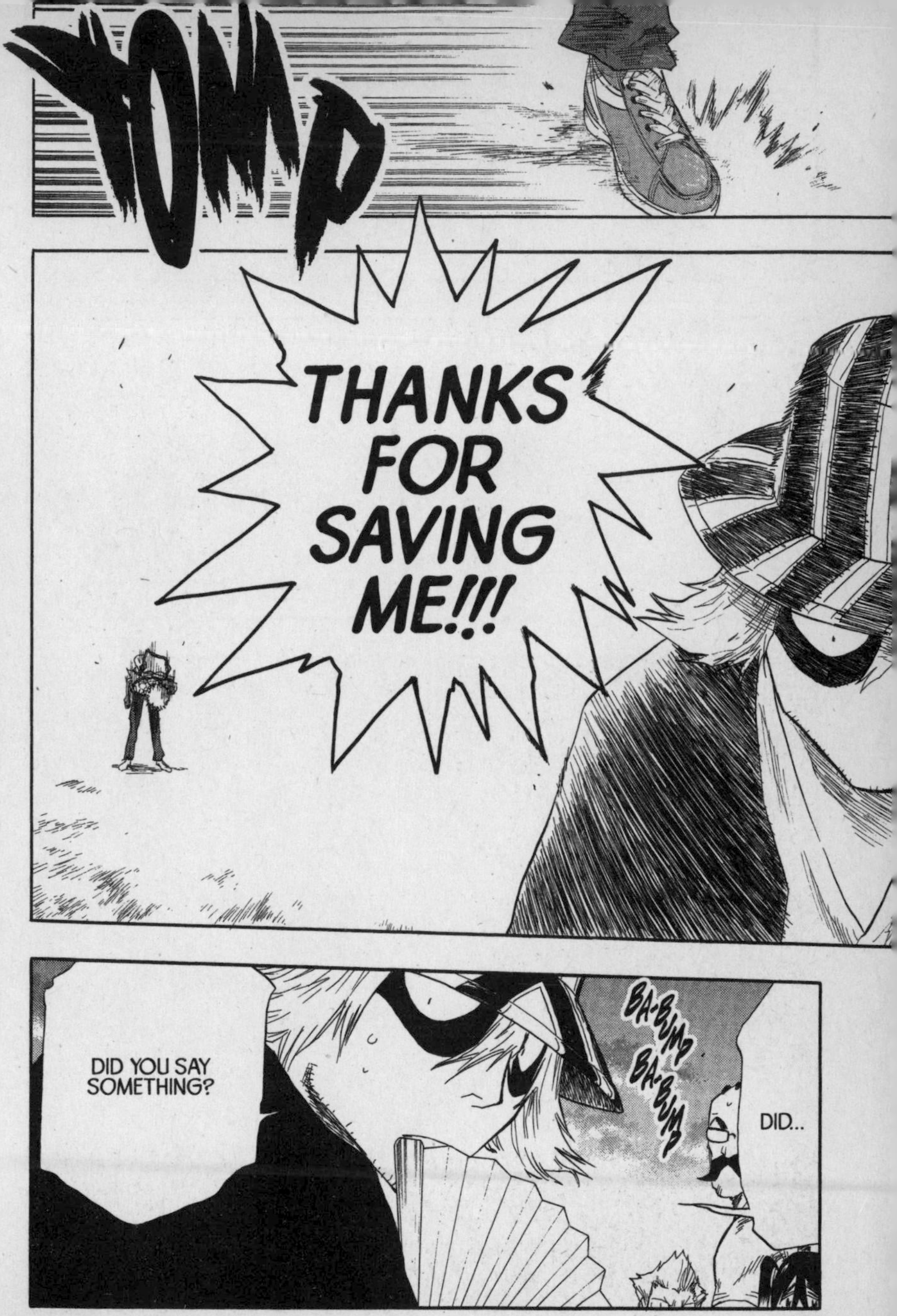
YOMP
THANKS FOR SAVING ME!!!
DID...
BA-BUMP BA-BUMP
DID YOU SAY SOMETHING?

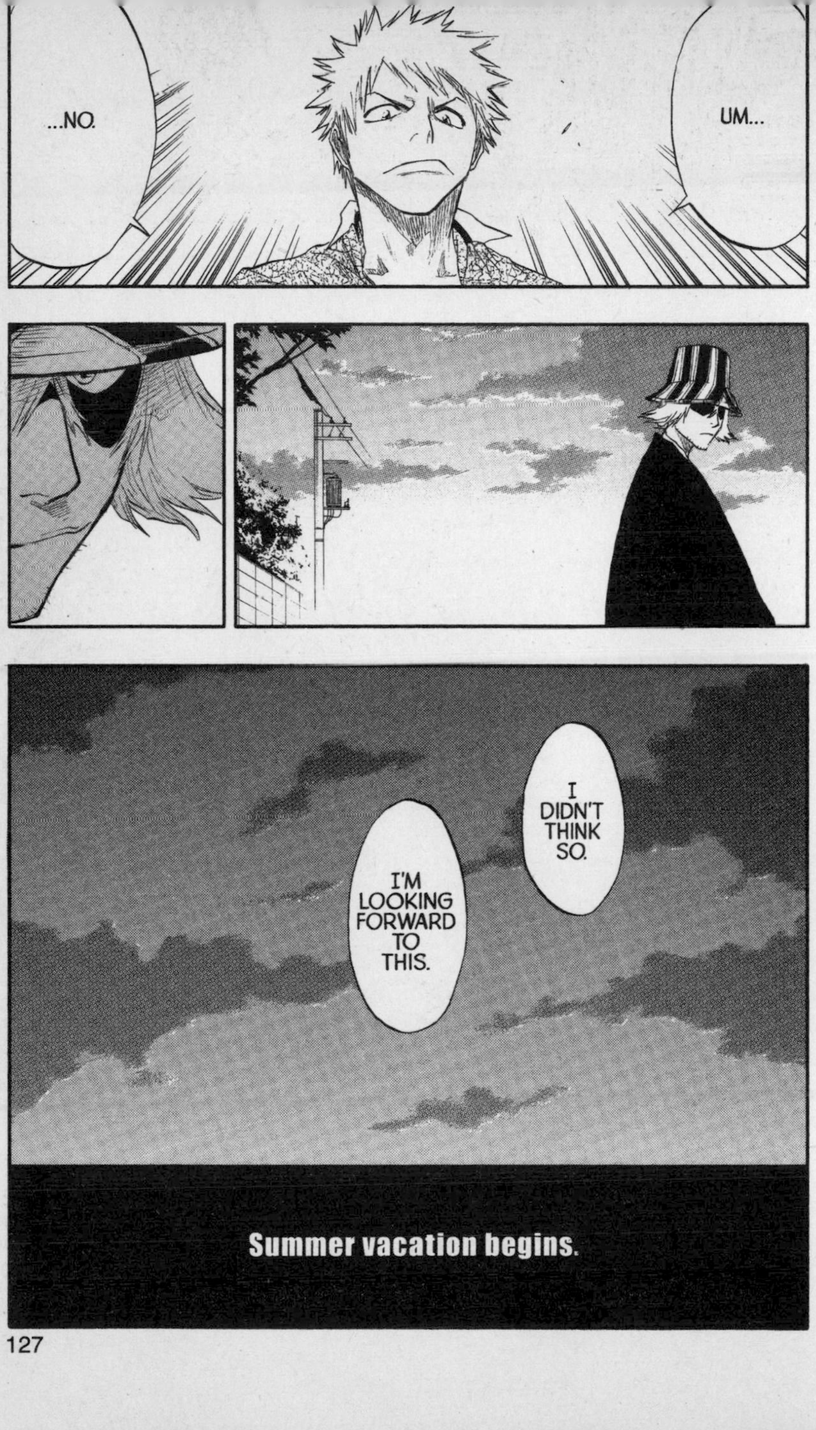
UM...
...NO.
I DIDN'T THINK SO.
I'M LOOKING FORWARD TO THIS.
Summer vacation begins.

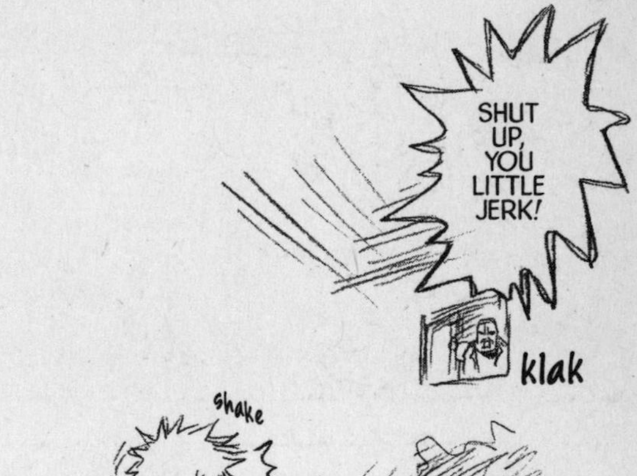
SHUT UP, YOU LITTLE JERK!
klak
shake
S-sorry...

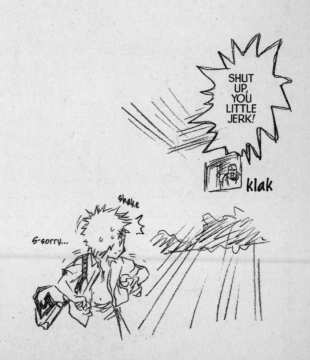

59. Lesson 1: One Strike! + Jailed at Home

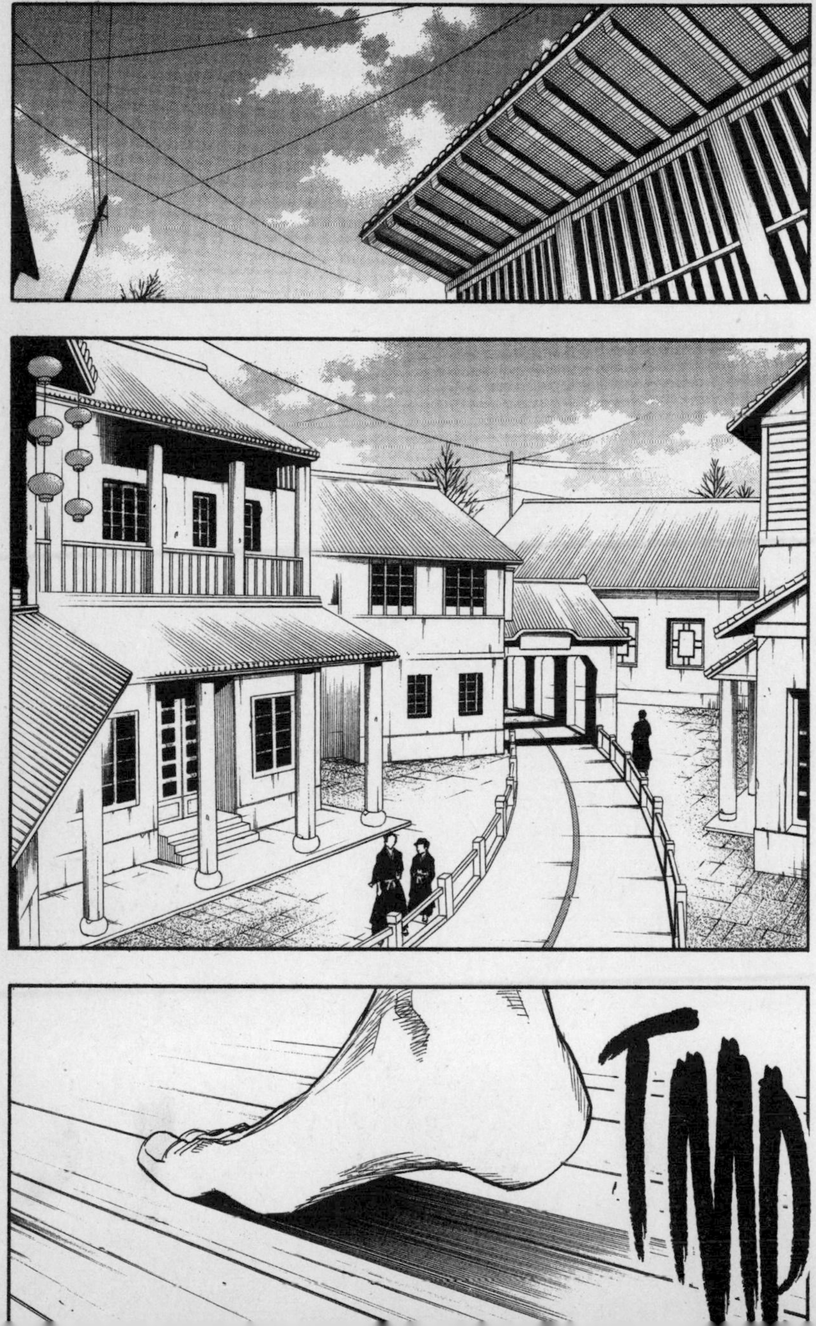
TMP

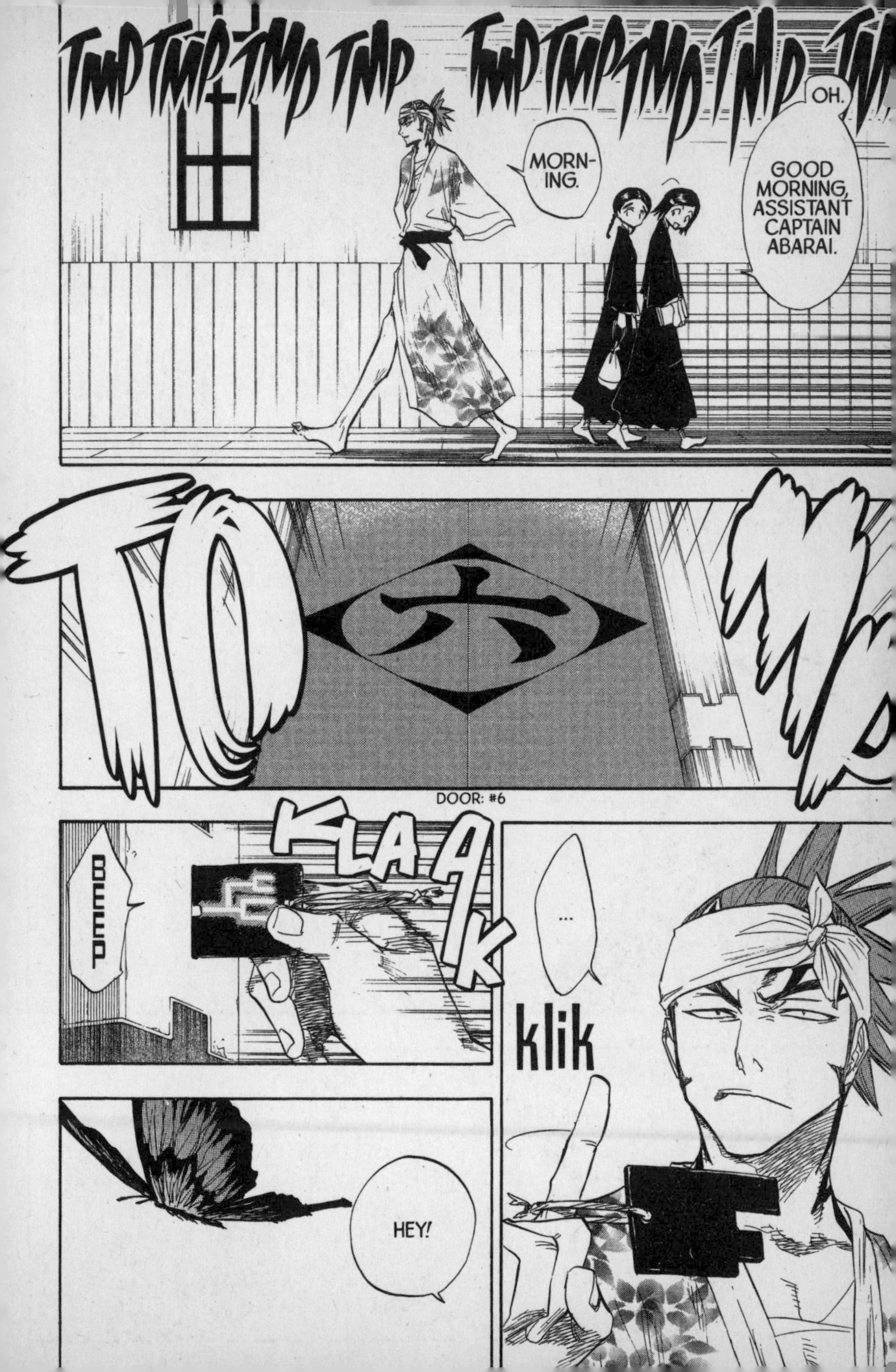
TMP TMP TMP TMP TMP
OH.
GOOD MORNING, ASSISTANT CAPTAIN ABARAI.
MORN-ING.
TMP TMP TMP TMP
DOOR: #6
...
klik
KLAAK
BEEP
HEY!

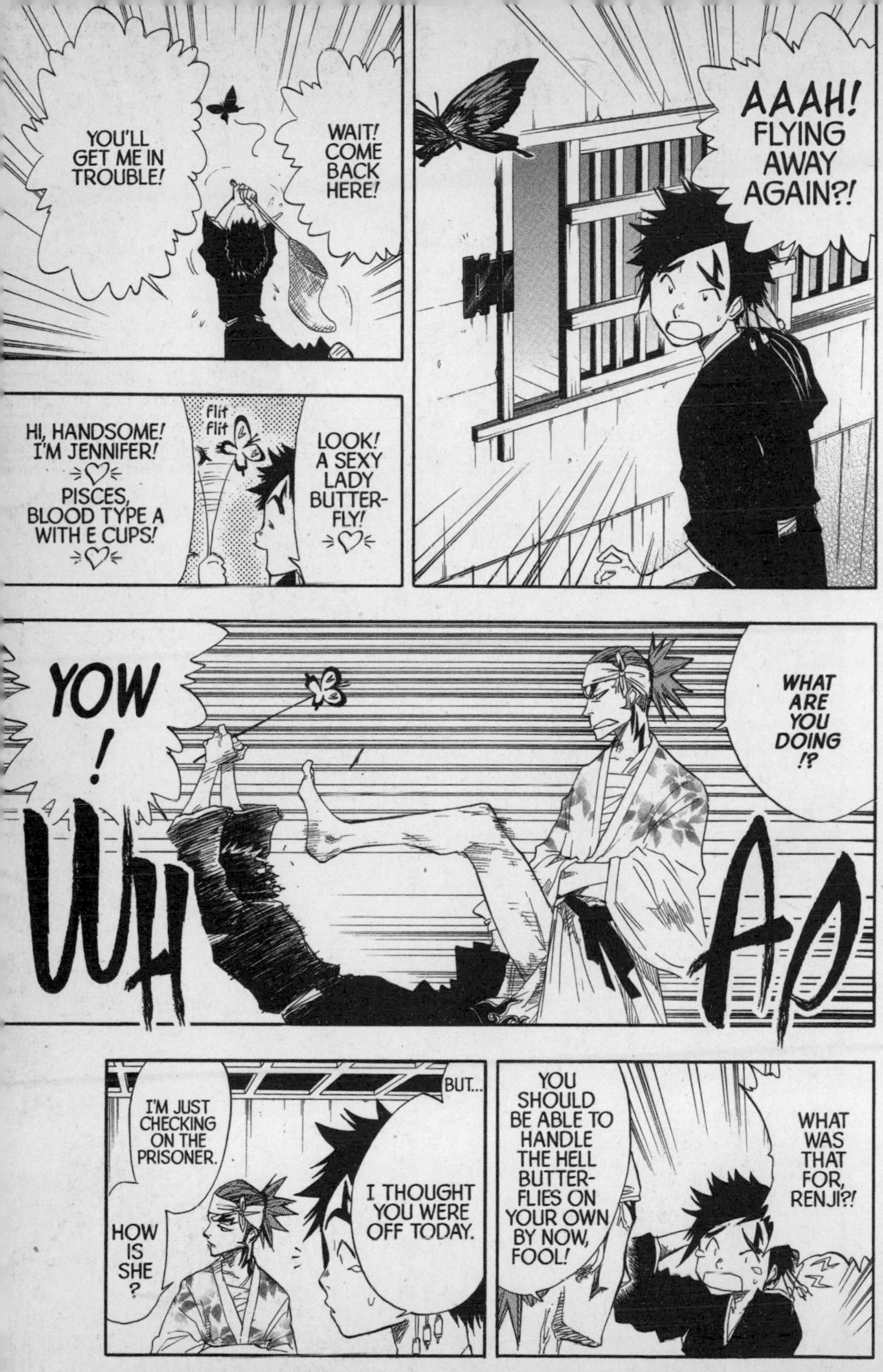
AAAH! FLYING AWAY AGAIN?!
WAIT! COME BACK HERE!
YOU'LL GET ME IN TROUBLE!
LOOK! A SEXY LADY BUTTER-FLY! ♡
Flit Flit
HI, HANDSOME! I'M JENNIFER! ♡ PISCES, BLOOD TYPE A WITH E CUPS! ♡
WHAT ARE YOU DOING !?
WHAP
YOW !
WHAT WAS THAT FOR, RENJI?!
YOU SHOULD BE ABLE TO HANDLE THE HELL BUTTER-FLIES ON YOUR OWN BY NOW, FOOL!
BUT...
I THOUGHT YOU WERE OFF TODAY.
I'M JUST CHECKING ON THE PRISONER.
HOW IS SHE ?

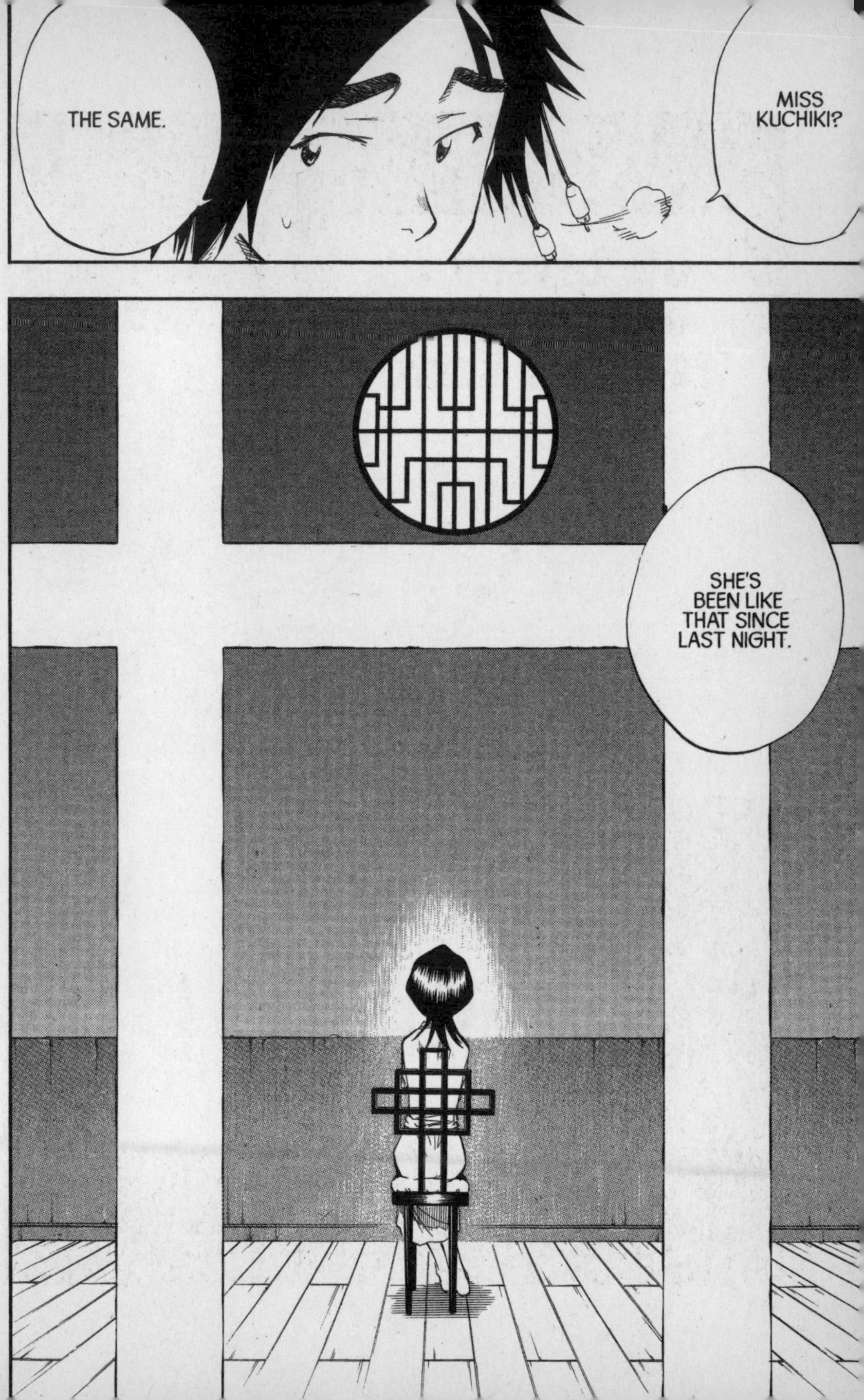
MISS KUCHIKI?
THE SAME.
SHE'S BEEN LIKE THAT SINCE LAST NIGHT.

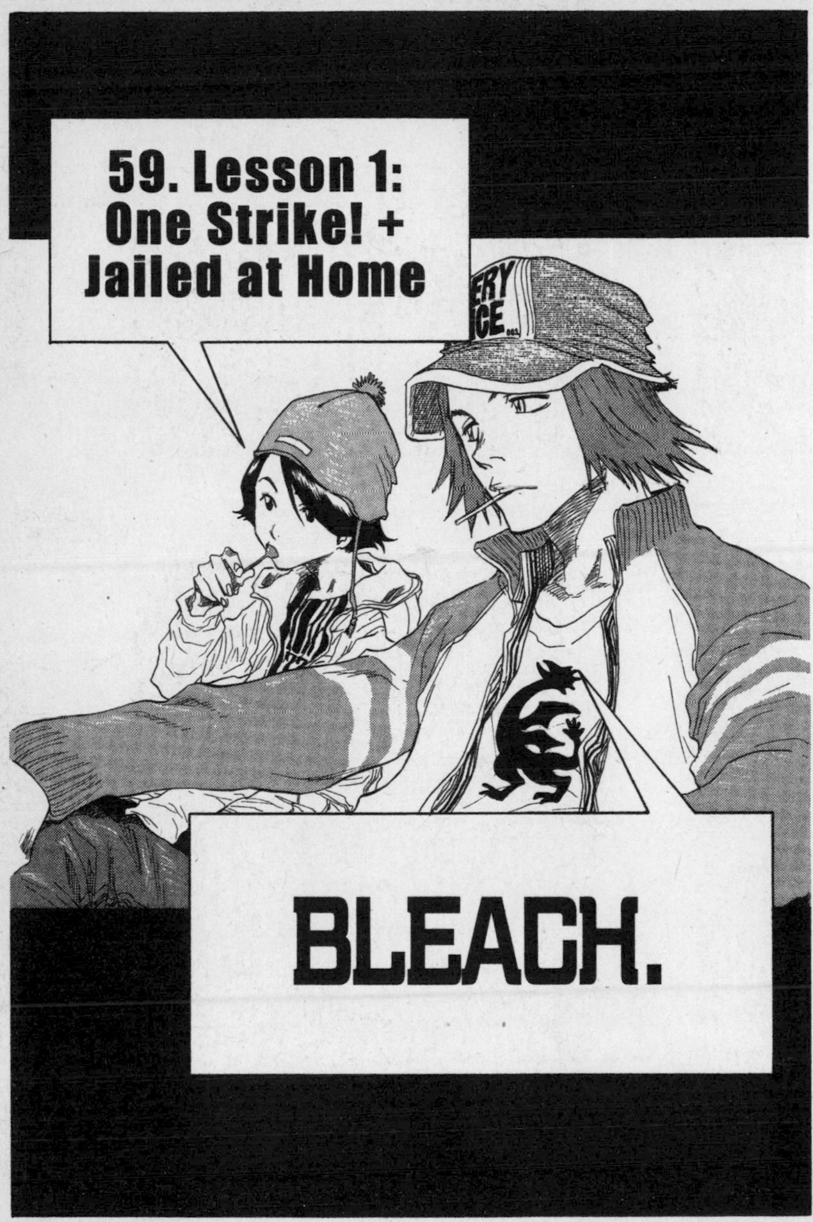
59. Lesson 1: One Strike! + Jailed at Home
BLEACH.

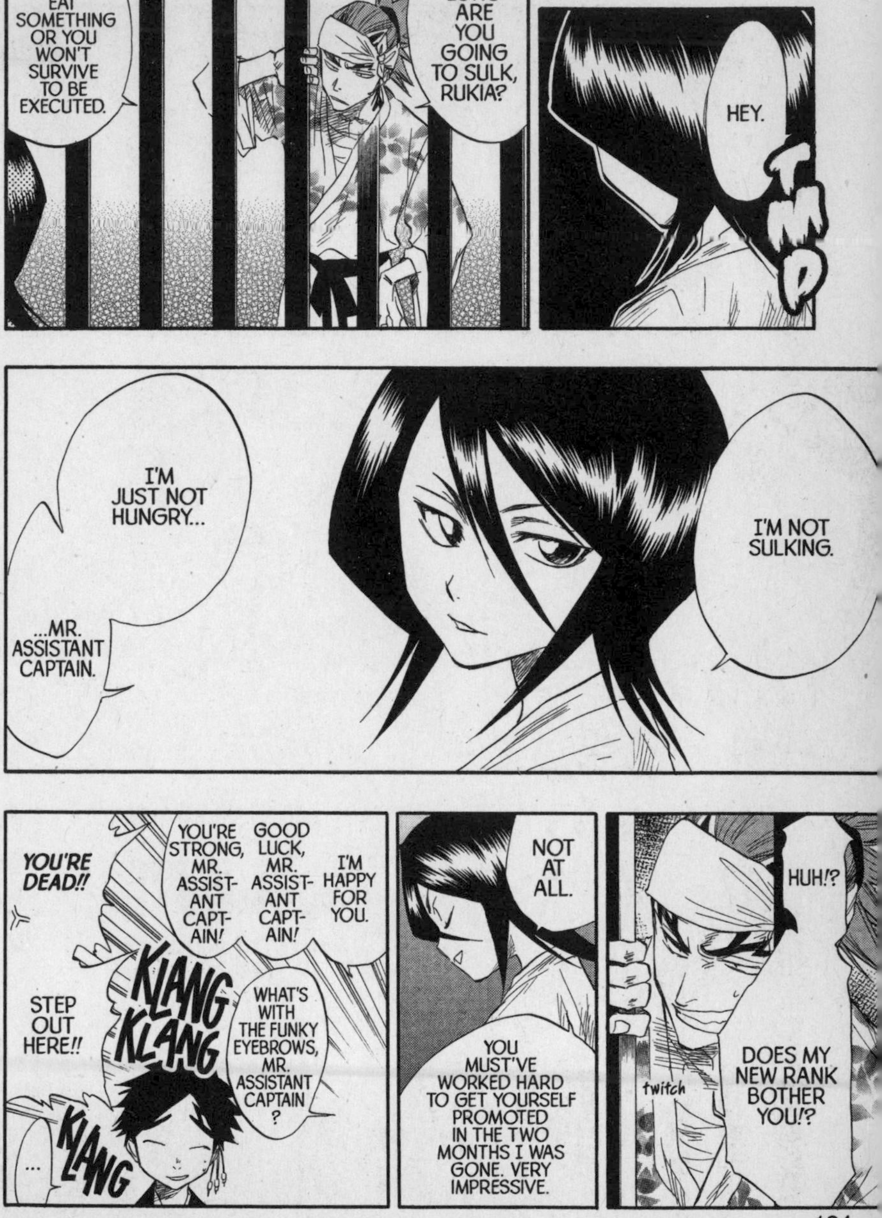
HEY.
TMP
HOW LONG ARE YOU GOING TO SULK, RUKIA?
YOU'D BETTER EAT SOMETHING OR YOU WON'T SURVIVE TO BE EXECUTED.
I'M NOT SULKING.
I'M JUST NOT HUNGRY...
...MR. ASSISTANT CAPTAIN.
HUH!?
DOES MY NEW RANK BOTHER YOU!?
twitch
NOT AT ALL.
YOU MUST'VE WORKED HARD TO GET YOURSELF PROMOTED IN THE TWO MONTHS I WAS GONE. VERY IMPRESSIVE.
I'M HAPPY FOR YOU.
GOOD LUCK, MR. ASSIST-ANT CAPT-AIN!
YOU'RE STRONG, MR. ASSIST-ANT CAPT-AIN!
WHAT'S WITH THE FUNKY EYEBROWS, MR. ASSISTANT CAPTAIN?
YOU'RE DEAD!!
KLANG KLANG
STEP OUT HERE!!
KLANG
...

READ THIS WAY

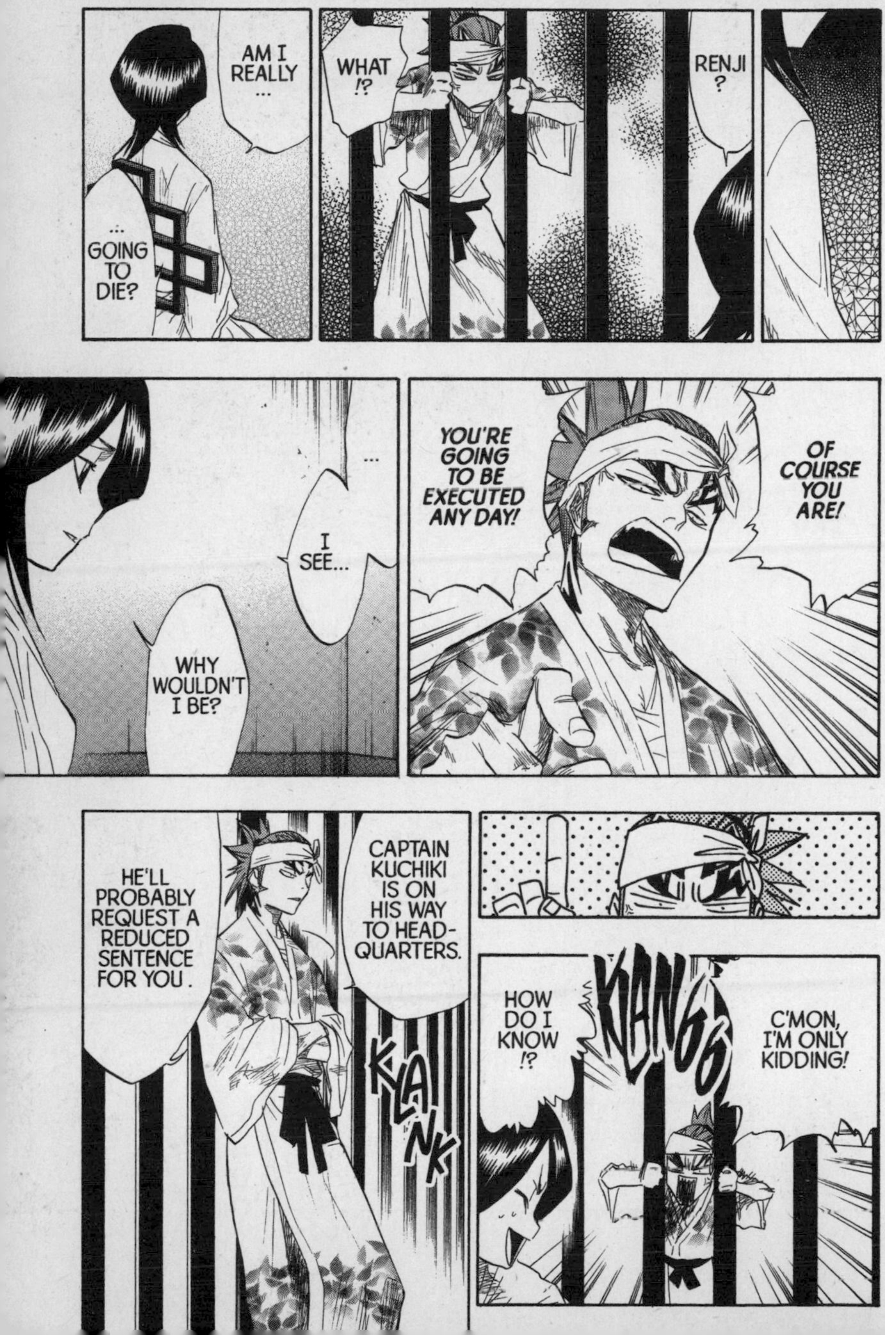
RENJI ?
WHAT !?
AM I REALLY ...
... GOING TO DIE?
OF COURSE YOU ARE!
YOU'RE GOING TO BE EXECUTED ANY DAY!
...
I SEE...
WHY WOULDN'T I BE?
C'MON, I'M ONLY KIDDING!
KLANG
HOW DO I KNOW !?
CAPTAIN KUCHIKI IS ON HIS WAY TO HEAD-QUARTERS.
KLANK
HE'LL PROBABLY REQUEST A REDUCED SENTENCE FOR YOU.

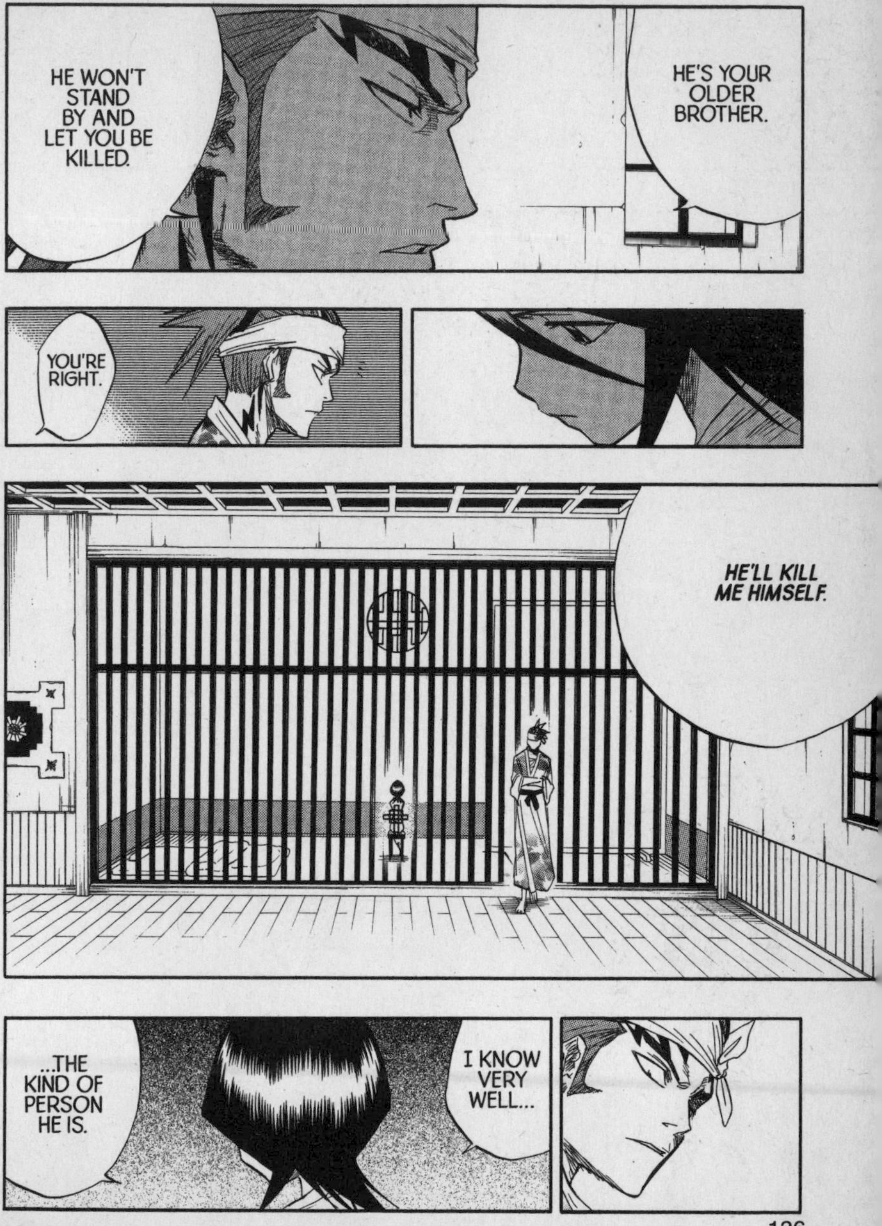
HE'S YOUR OLDER BROTHER.
HE WON'T STAND BY AND LET YOU BE KILLED.
YOU'RE RIGHT.
HE'LL KILL ME HIMSELF.
I KNOW VERY WELL...
...THE KIND OF PERSON HE IS.

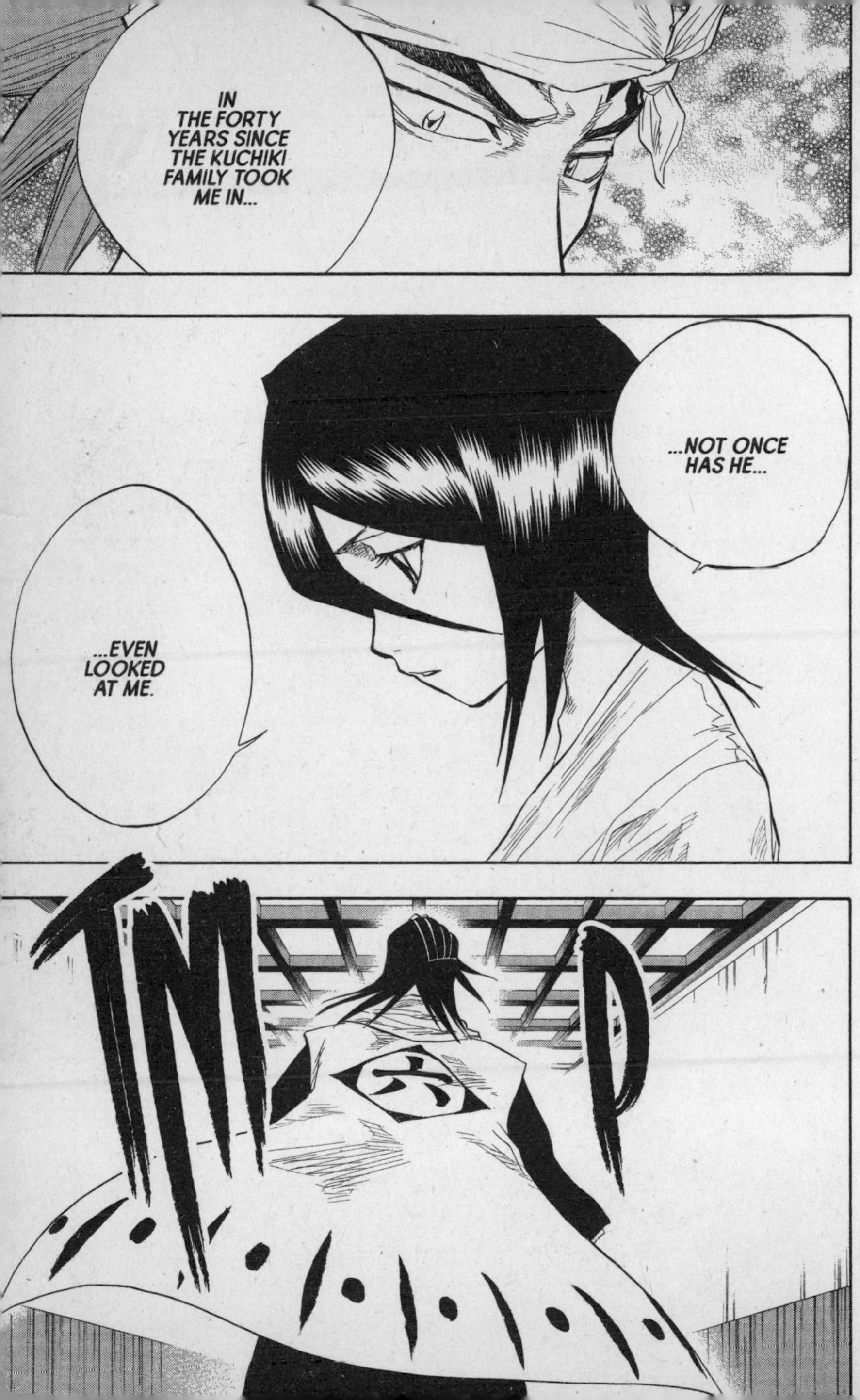
IN THE FORTY YEARS SINCE THE KUCHIKI FAMILY TOOK ME IN...
...NOT ONCE HAS HE...
...EVEN LOOKED AT ME.
TMP

URAHARA SHOTEN
CLOSED
CLOSED

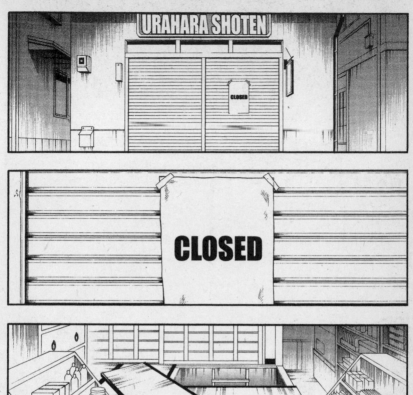

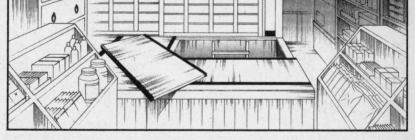

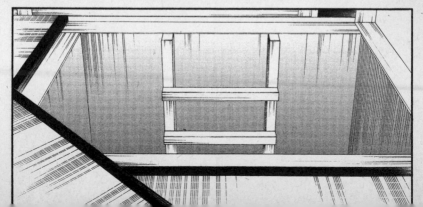

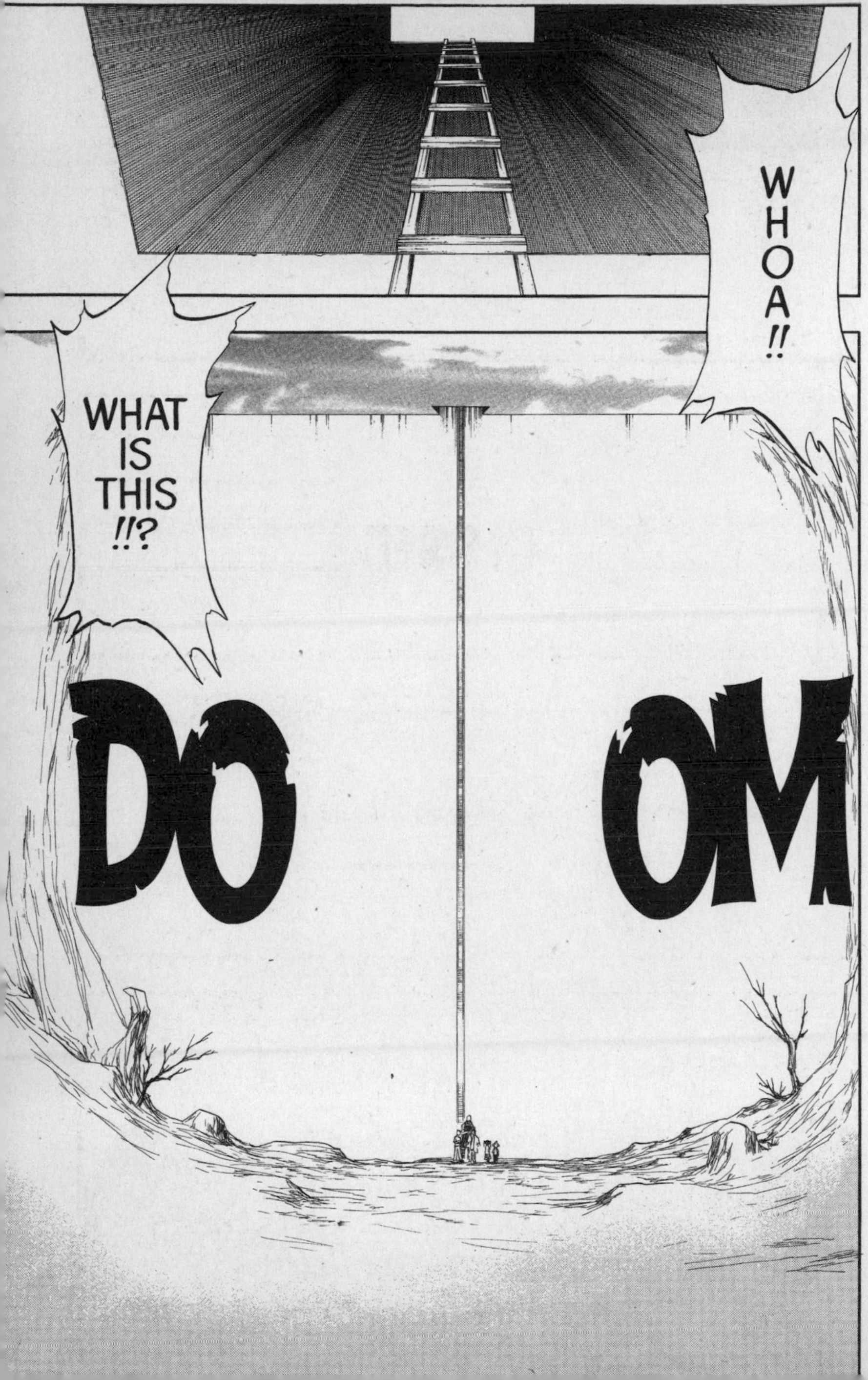
WHOA!!
WHAT IS THIS!!?
DO OM

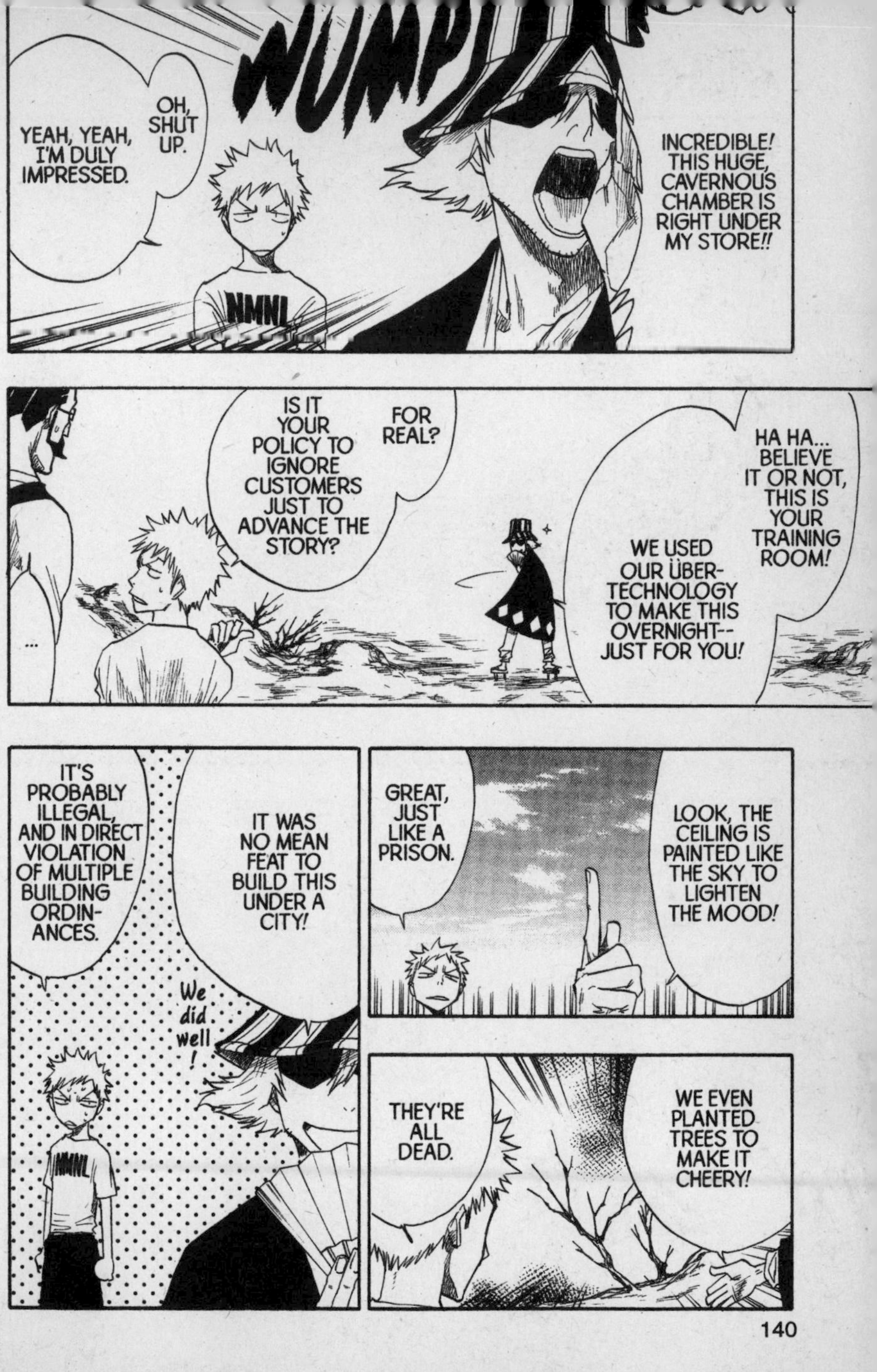

WUMP
INCREDIBLE! THIS HUGE, CAVERNOUS CHAMBER IS RIGHT UNDER MY STORE!!
OH, SHUT UP.
YEAH, YEAH, I'M DULY IMPRESSED.
HA HA... BELIEVE IT OR NOT, THIS IS YOUR TRAINING ROOM!
WE USED OUR ÜBER-TECHNOLOGY TO MAKE THIS OVERNIGHT-- JUST FOR YOU!
FOR REAL?
IS IT YOUR POLICY TO IGNORE CUSTOMERS JUST TO ADVANCE THE STORY?
...
LOOK, THE CEILING IS PAINTED LIKE THE SKY TO LIGHTEN THE MOOD!
GREAT, JUST LIKE A PRISON.
WE EVEN PLANTED TREES TO MAKE IT CHEERY!
THEY'RE ALL DEAD.
IT WAS NO MEAN FEAT TO BUILD THIS UNDER A CITY!
IT'S PROBABLY ILLEGAL, AND IN DIRECT VIOLATION OF MULTIPLE BUILDING ORDIN-ANCES.
We did well!

READ THIS WAY

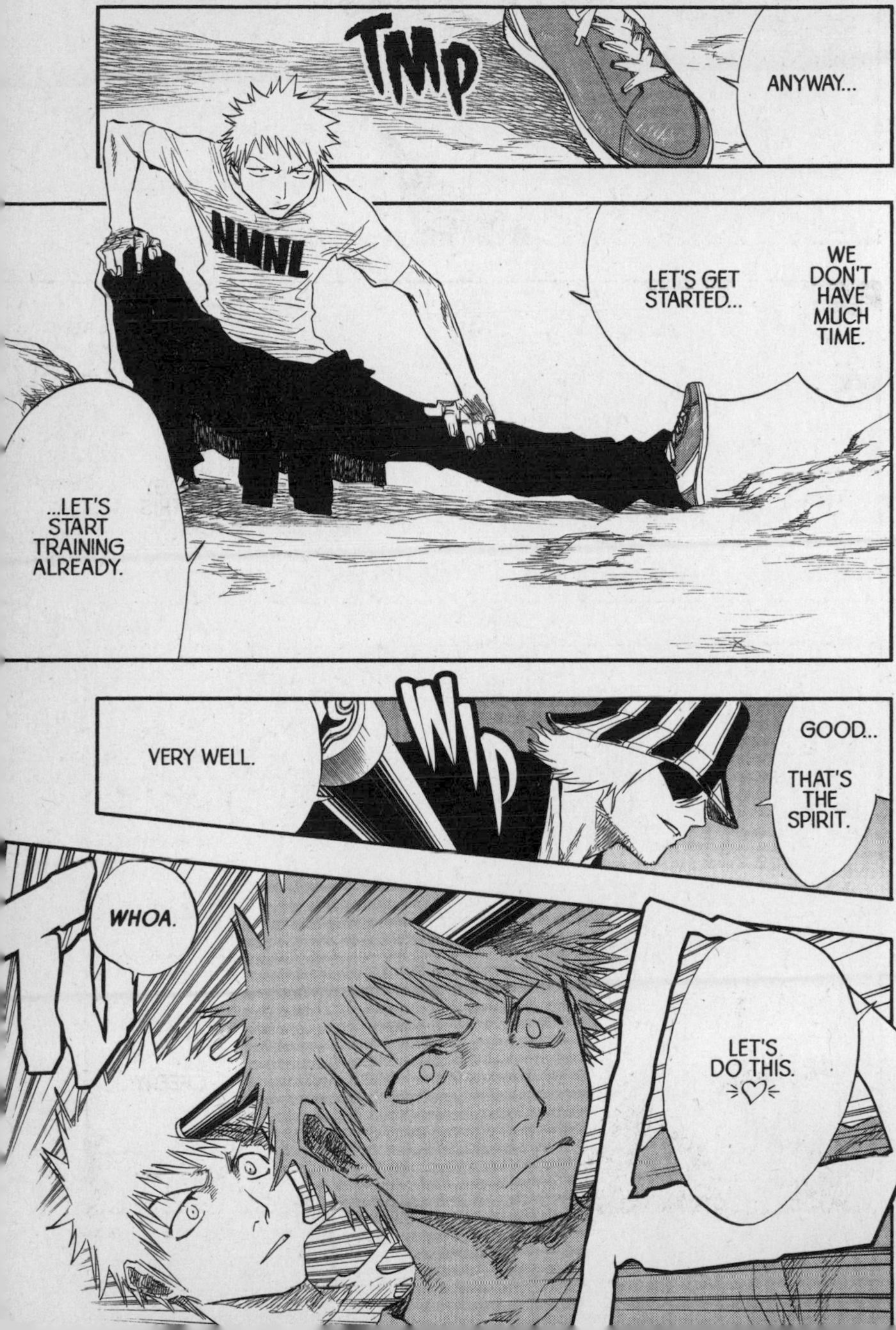
ANYWAY...
TMP
WE DON'T HAVE MUCH TIME.
LET'S GET STARTED...
...LET'S START TRAINING ALREADY.
GOOD...
THAT'S THE SPIRIT.
VERY WELL.
LET'S DO THIS. ♡
WHOA.

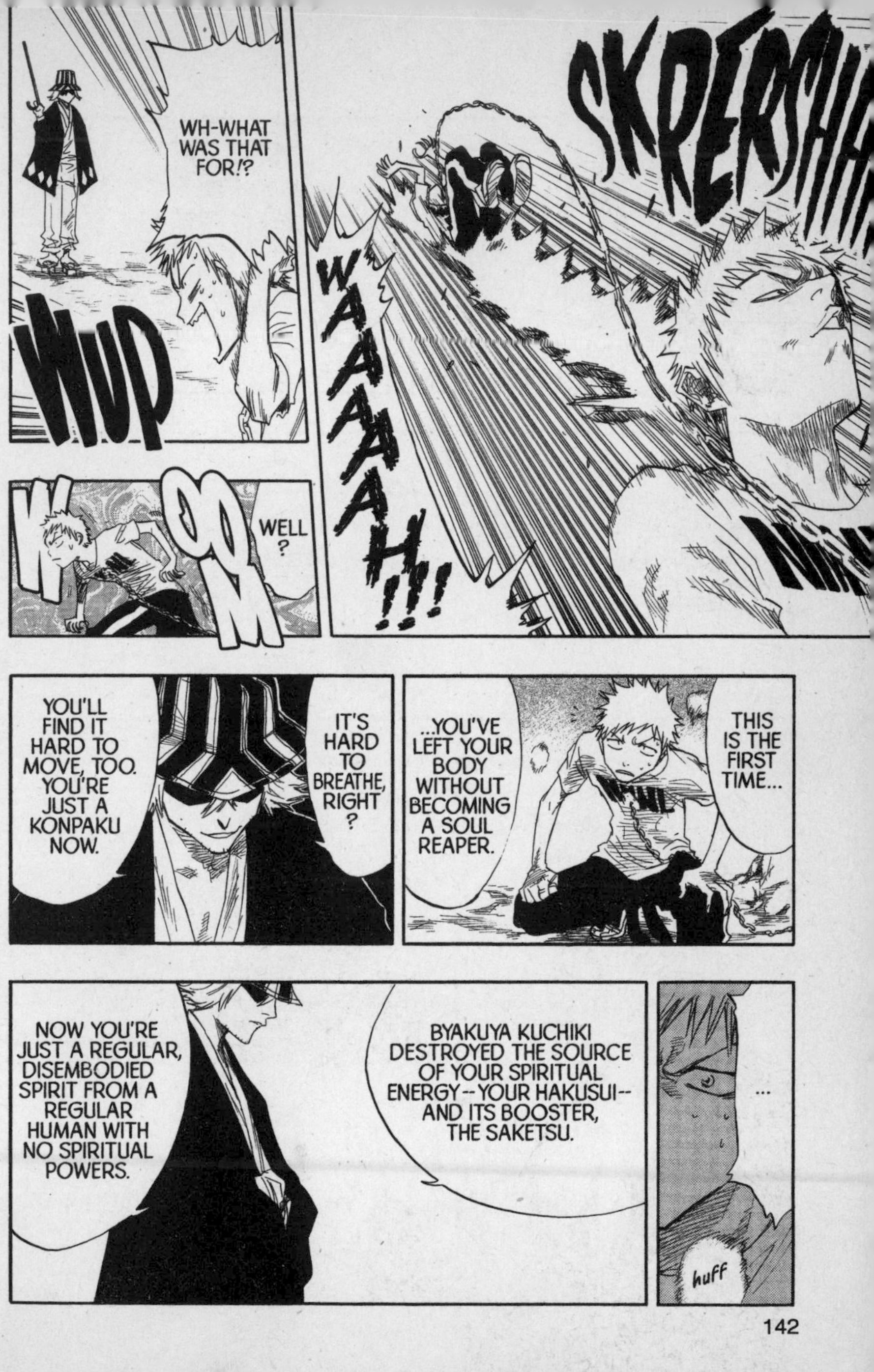
SKRERSHH
WAAAAAH!!!
WH-WHAT WAS THAT FOR!?
WUP
WOOM
WELL?
THIS IS THE FIRST TIME...
...YOU'VE LEFT YOUR BODY WITHOUT BECOMING A SOUL REAPER.
IT'S HARD TO BREATHE, RIGHT?
YOU'LL FIND IT HARD TO MOVE, TOO. YOU'RE JUST A KONPAKU NOW.
...
huff
BYAKUYA KUCHIKI DESTROYED THE SOURCE OF YOUR SPIRITUAL ENERGY--YOUR HAKUSUI--AND ITS BOOSTER, THE SAKETSU.
NOW YOU'RE JUST A REGULAR, DISEMBODIED SPIRIT FROM A REGULAR HUMAN WITH NO SPIRITUAL POWERS.

READ THIS WAY

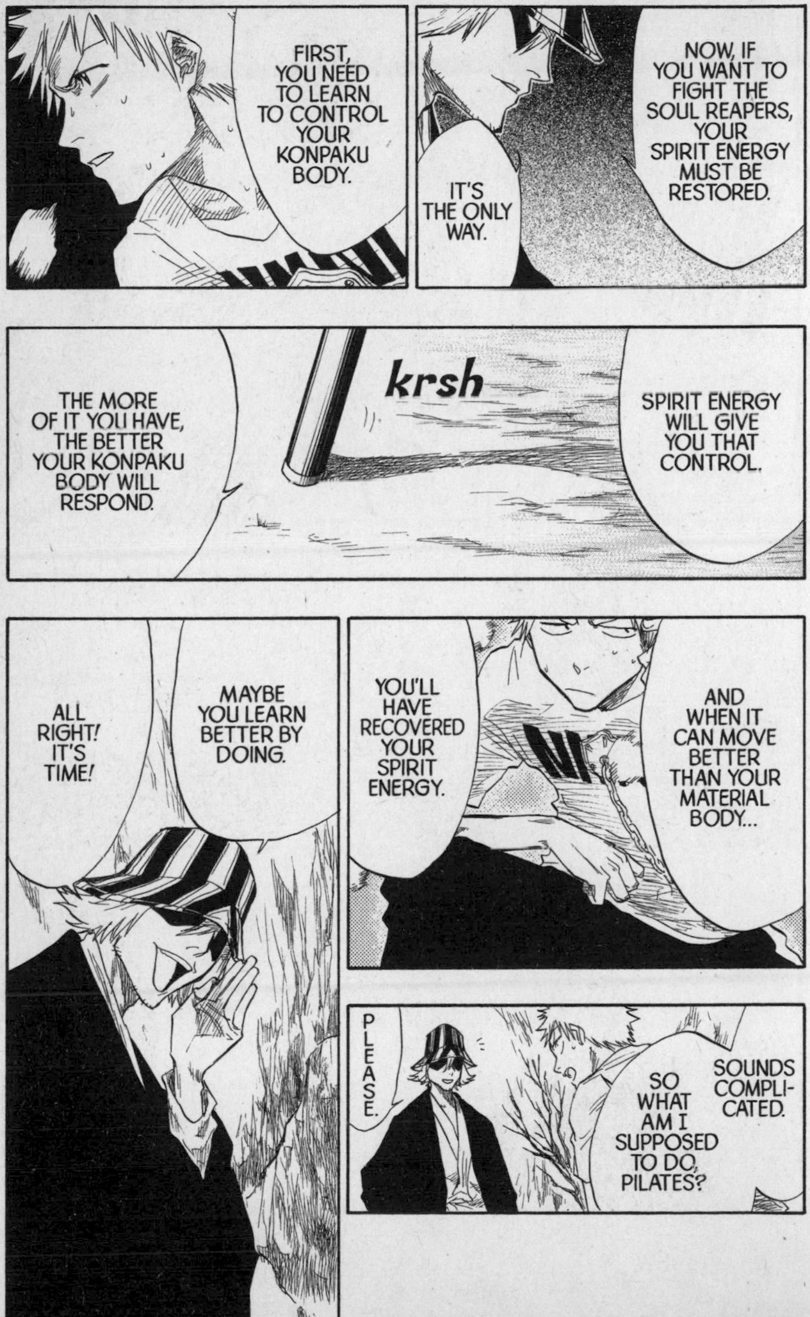
NOW, IF YOU WANT TO FIGHT THE SOUL REAPERS, YOUR SPIRIT ENERGY MUST BE RESTORED.
IT'S THE ONLY WAY.
FIRST, YOU NEED TO LEARN TO CONTROL YOUR KONPAKU BODY.
SPIRIT ENERGY WILL GIVE YOU THAT CONTROL.
krsh
THE MORE OF IT YOU HAVE, THE BETTER YOUR KONPAKU BODY WILL RESPOND.
AND WHEN IT CAN MOVE BETTER THAN YOUR MATERIAL BODY...
YOU'LL HAVE RECOVERED YOUR SPIRIT ENERGY.
SOUNDS COMPLI-CATED.
SO WHAT AM I SUPPOSED TO DO, PILATES?
PLEASE.
MAYBE YOU LEARN BETTER BY DOING.
ALL RIGHT! IT'S TIME!

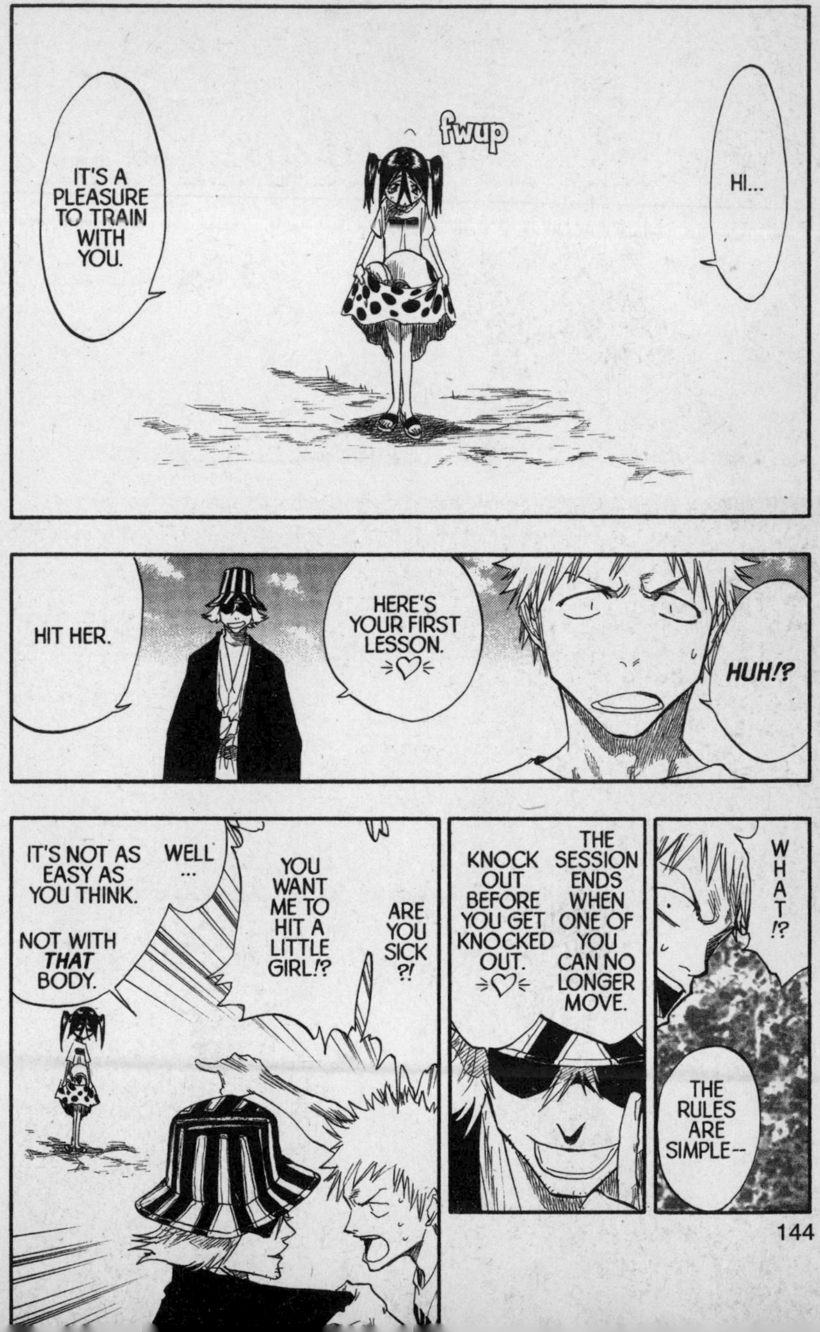

HI...
fwup
IT'S A PLEASURE TO TRAIN WITH YOU.
HUH!?
HERE'S YOUR FIRST LESSON. ♡
HIT HER.
WHAT!?
THE RULES ARE SIMPLE--
THE SESSION ENDS WHEN ONE OF YOU CAN NO LONGER MOVE.
KNOCK OUT BEFORE YOU GET KNOCKED OUT. ♡
YOU WANT ME TO HIT A LITTLE GIRL!?
ARE YOU SICK?!
WELL...
IT'S NOT AS EASY AS YOU THINK.
NOT WITH *THAT* BODY.

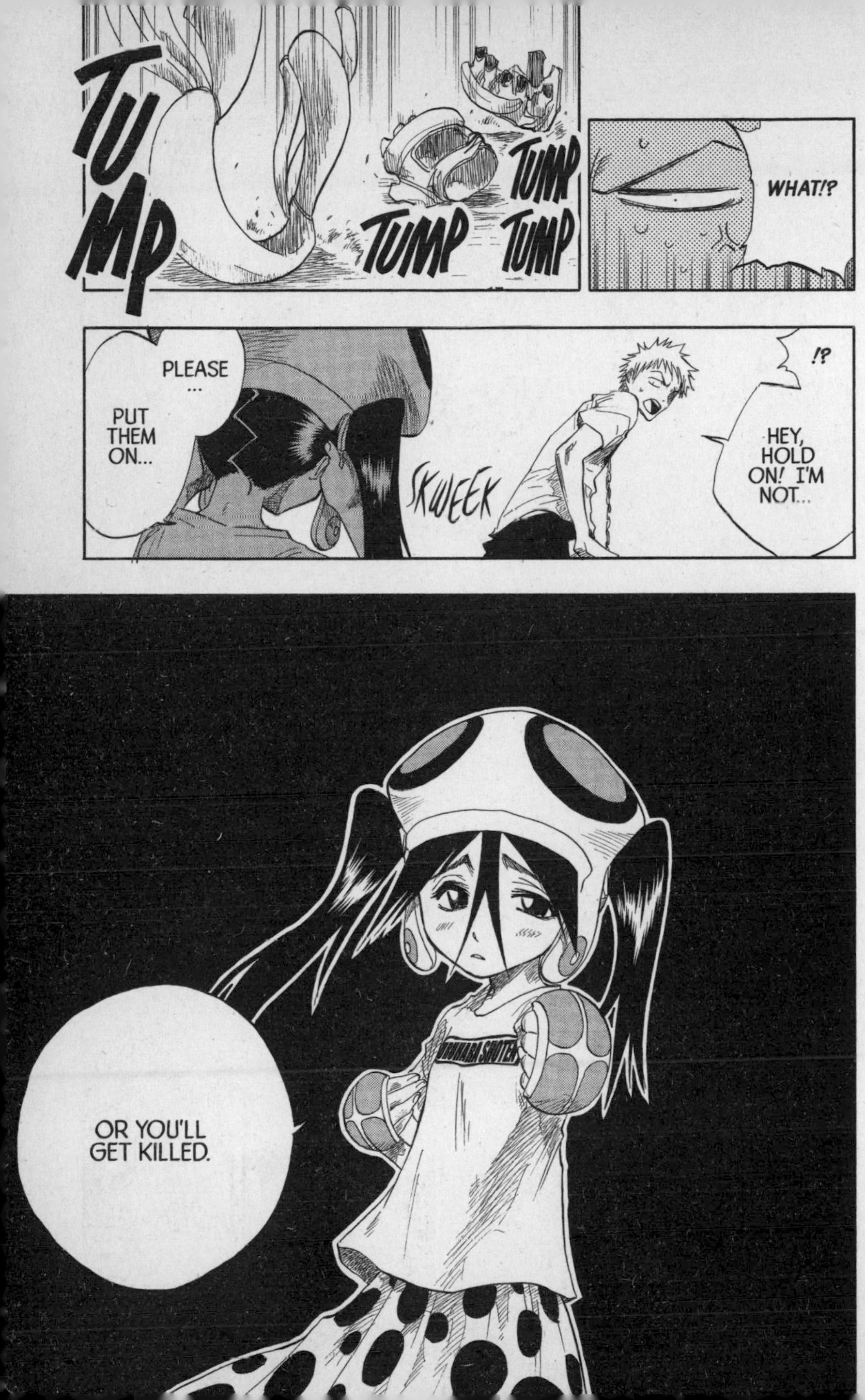
WHAT!?
TUMP TUMP
TUMP
TUMP
TUMP
!?
HEY, HOLD ON! I'M NOT...
SKWEEK
PLEASE ...
PUT THEM ON...
OR YOU'LL GET KILLED.

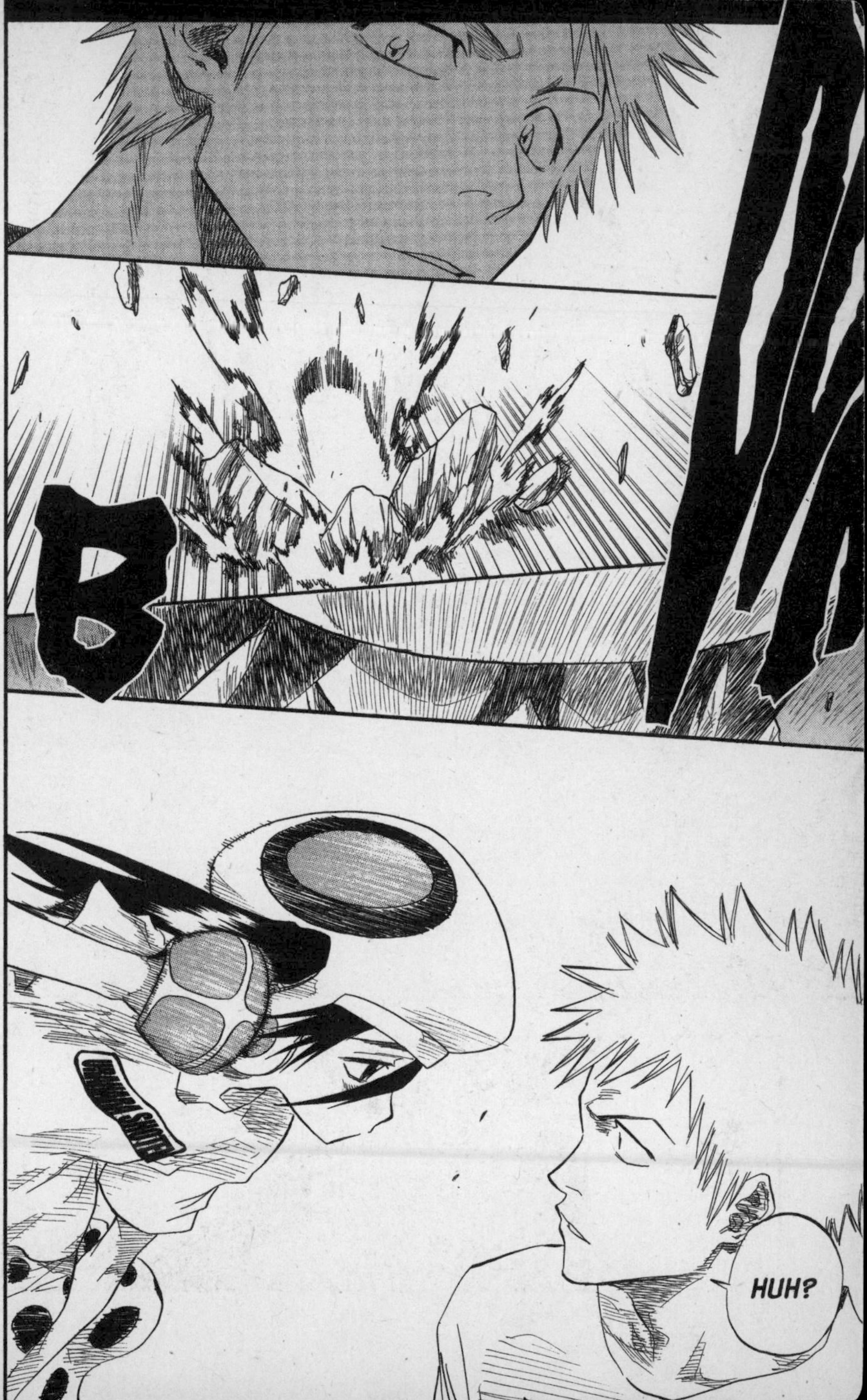
HUH?

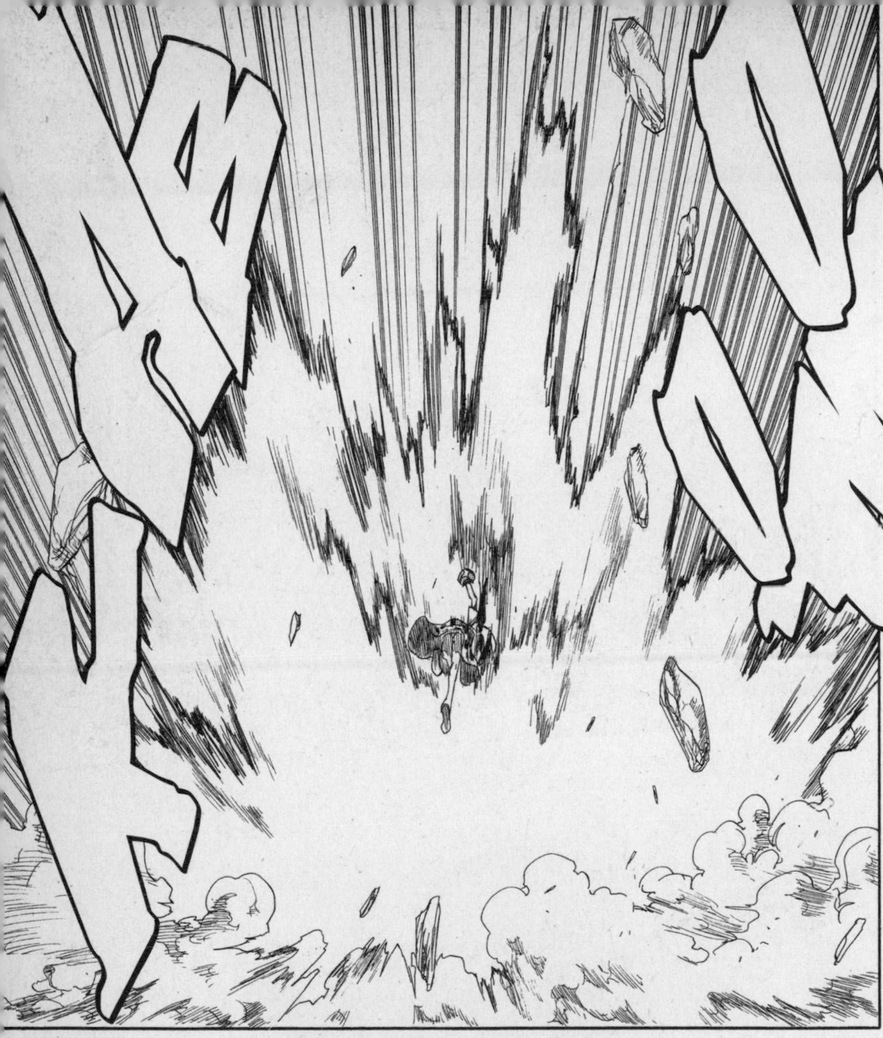

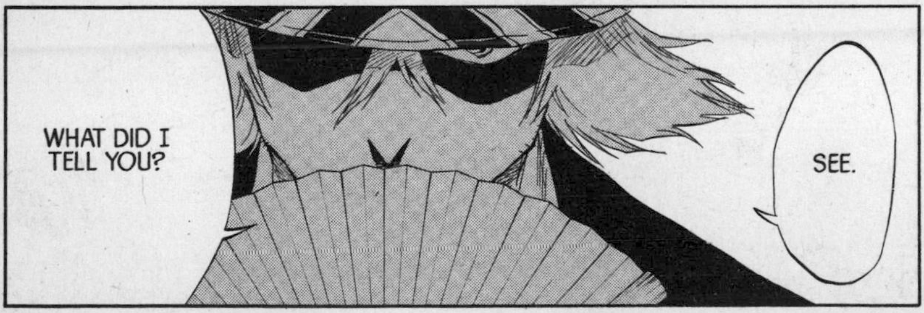
SEE.
WHAT DID I TELL YOU?

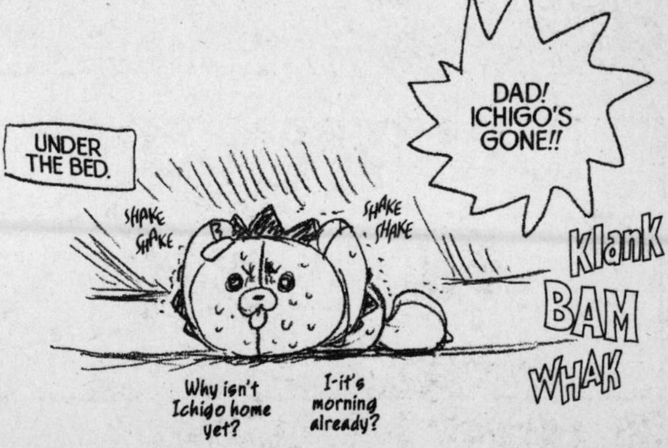
DAD! ICHIGO'S GONE!!
Klank
BAM
WHAK
UNDER THE BED.
SHAKE SHAKE
SHAKE SHAKE
I-it's morning already?
Why isn't Ichigo home yet?

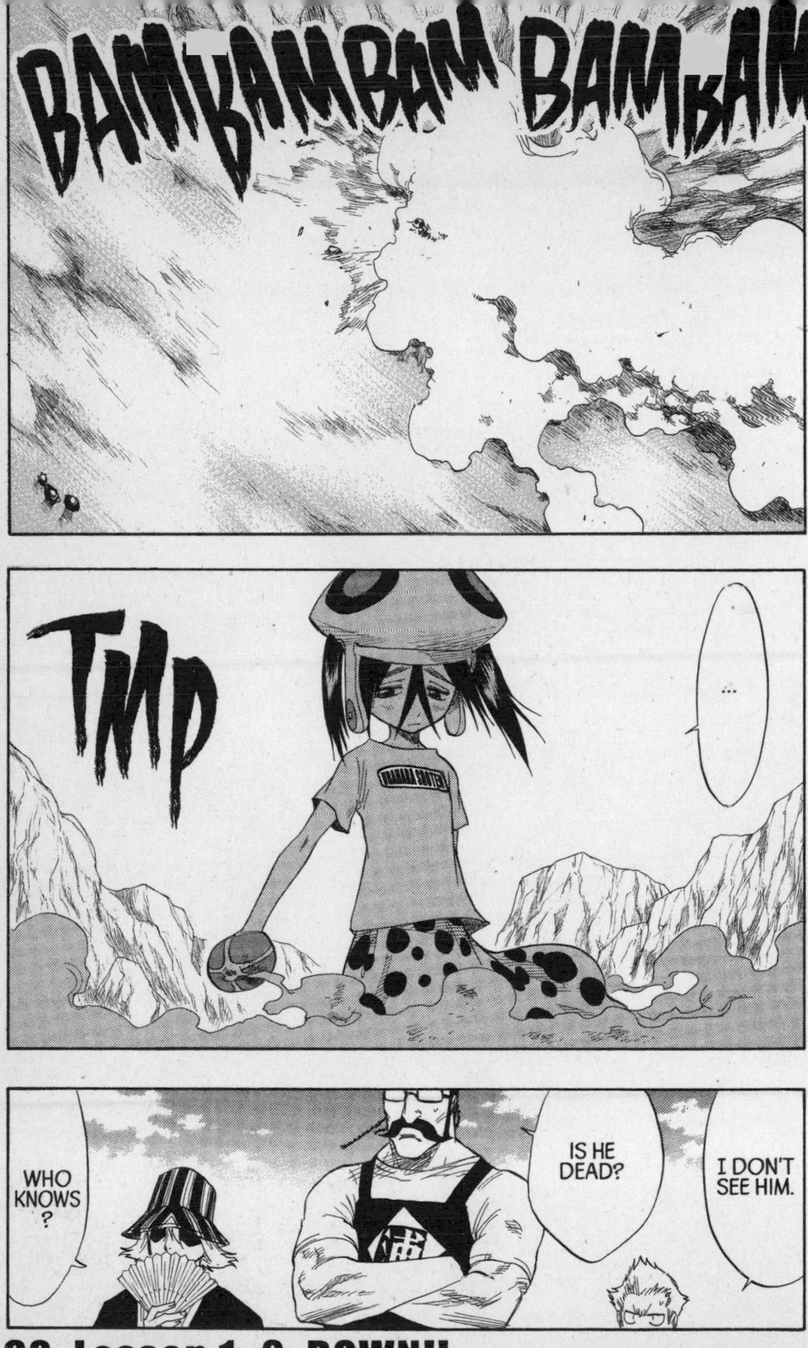
BAMBAMBAM BAMBAM
...
TMP
I DON'T SEE HIM.
IS HE DEAD?
WHO KNOWS?

60. Lesson 1–2: DOWN!!

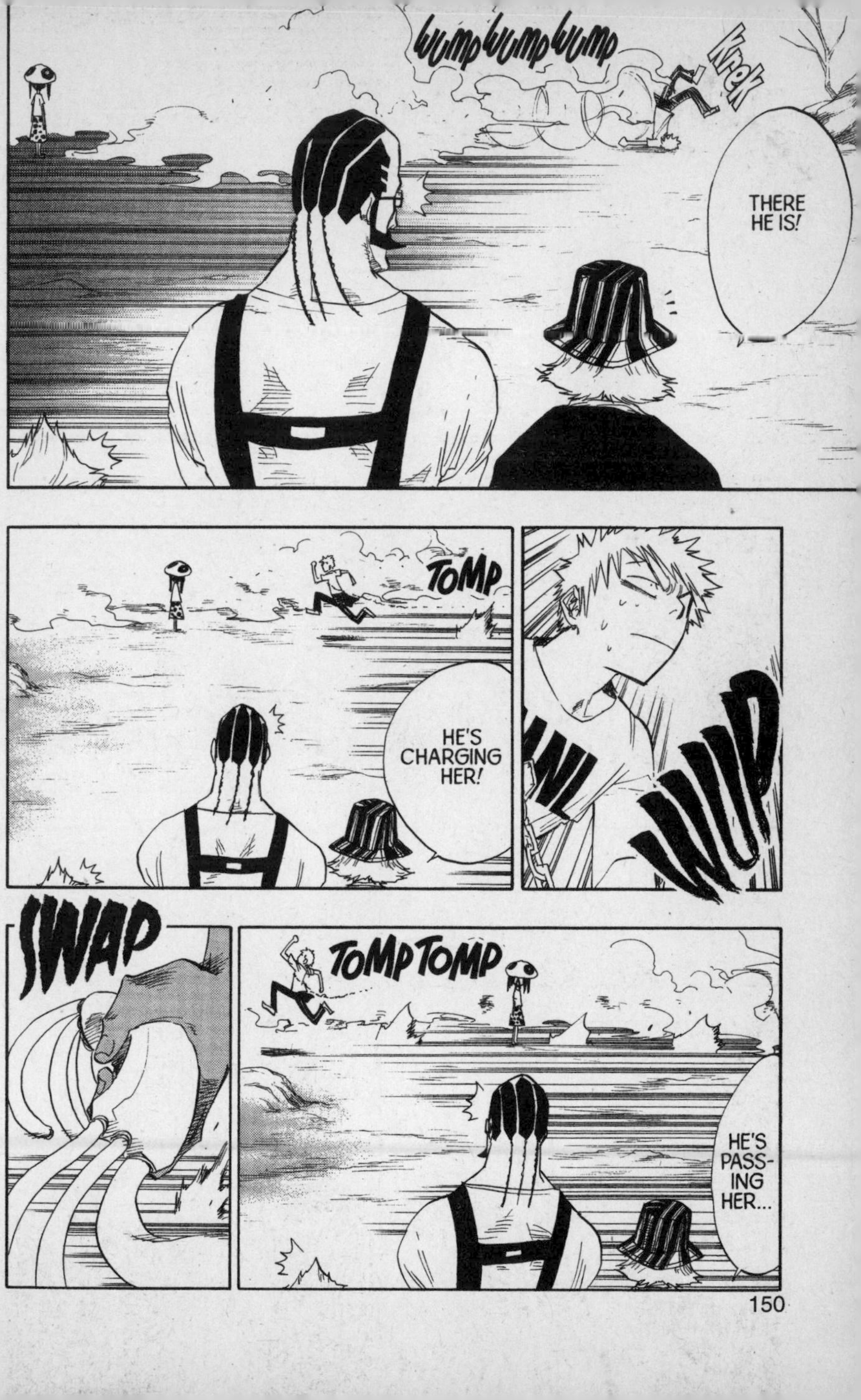

krek
wump wump wump
THERE HE IS!
WUP
TOMP
HE'S CHARGING HER!
TOMP TOMP
HE'S PASS-ING HER...
SWAP

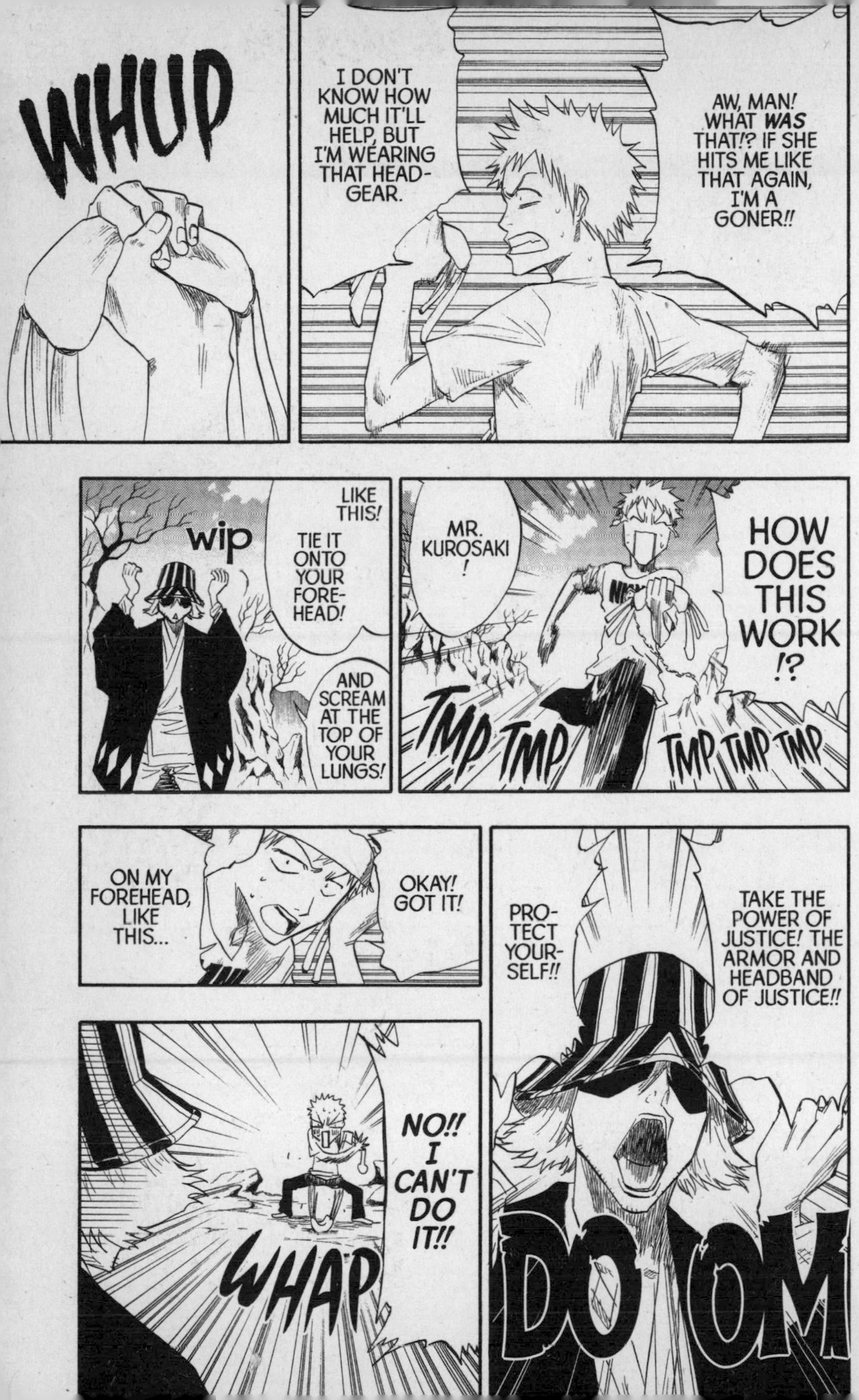

AW, MAN! WHAT *WAS* THAT!? IF SHE HITS ME LIKE THAT AGAIN, I'M A GONER!!
I DON'T KNOW HOW MUCH IT'LL HELP, BUT I'M WEARING THAT HEAD-GEAR.
WHUP
HOW DOES THIS WORK !?
MR. KUROSAKI !
TMP TMP TMP
TMP TMP
LIKE THIS!
TIE IT ONTO YOUR FORE-HEAD!
wip
AND SCREAM AT THE TOP OF YOUR LUNGS!
TAKE THE POWER OF JUSTICE! THE ARMOR AND HEADBAND OF JUSTICE!!
PRO-TECT YOUR-SELF!!
DO OM
OKAY! GOT IT!
ON MY FOREHEAD, LIKE THIS...
NO!! I CAN'T DO IT!!
WHAP

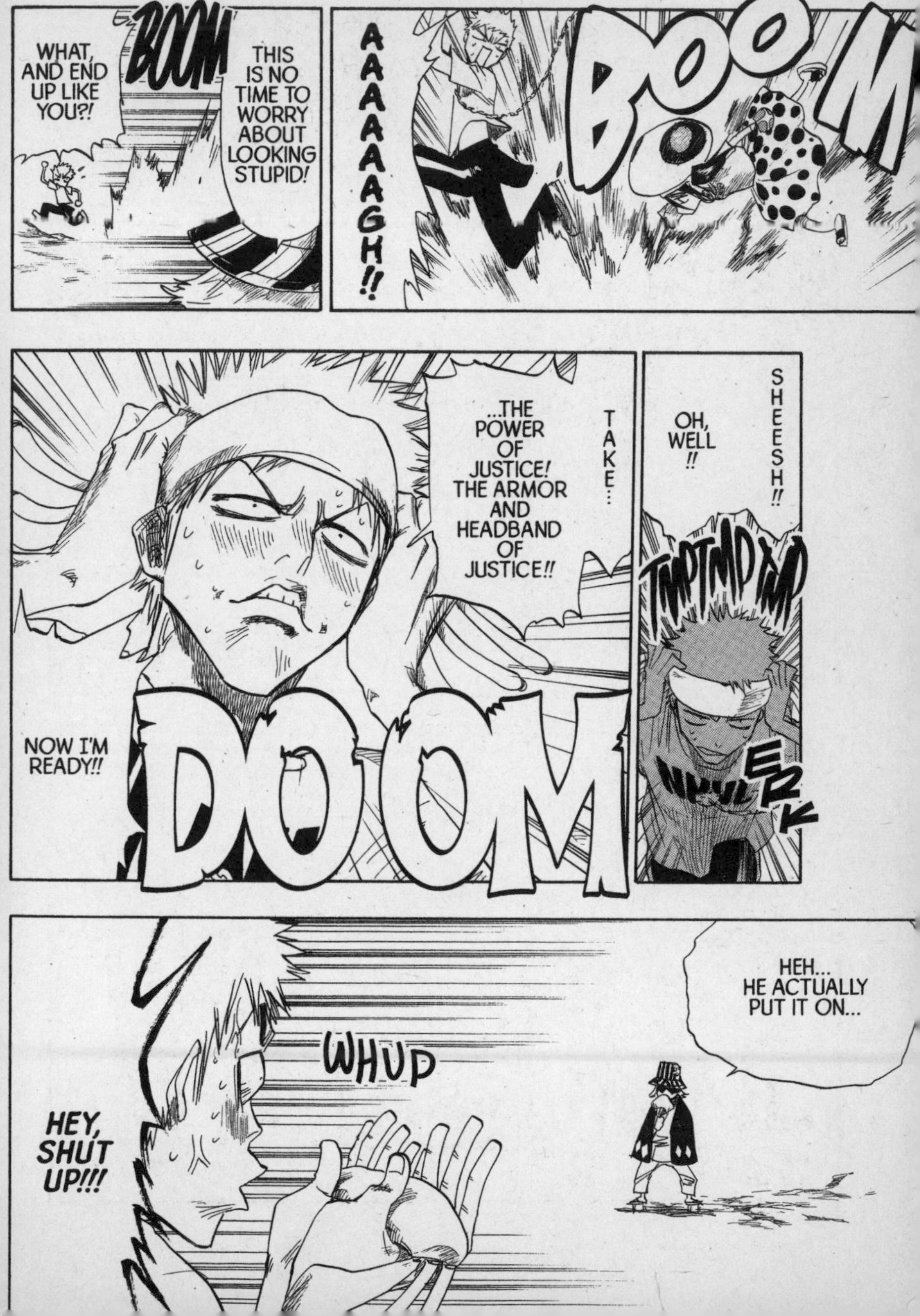
AAAAAAAAGH!!
BOOOM
THIS IS NO TIME TO WORRY ABOUT LOOKING STUPID!
BOOM
WHAT, AND END UP LIKE YOU?!
SHEESH!!
OH, WELL!!
TMPTMPTMP
ERK
TAKE...
...THE POWER OF JUSTICE! THE ARMOR AND HEADBAND OF JUSTICE!!
DOOM
NOW I'M READY!!
HEH... HE ACTUALLY PUT IT ON...
WHUP
HEY, SHUT UP!!!

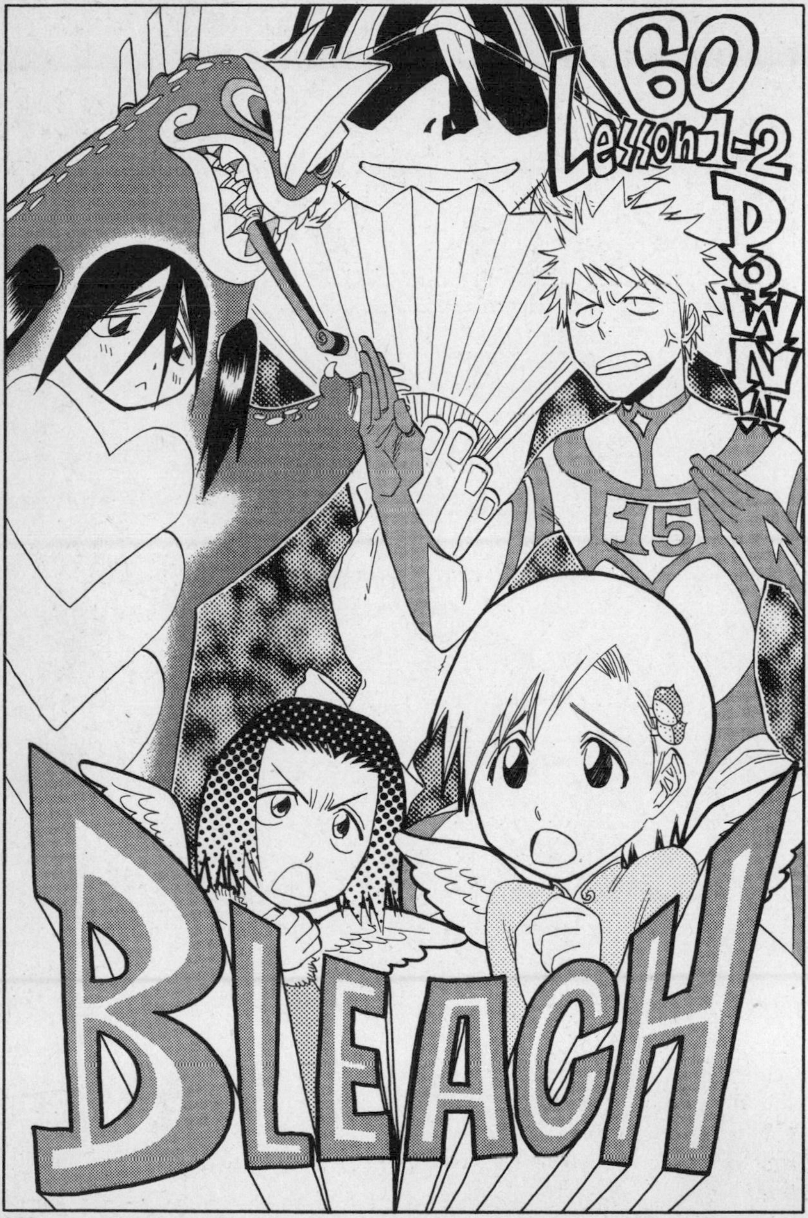
60
Lesson 1-2
DOWN!!
15
BLEACH

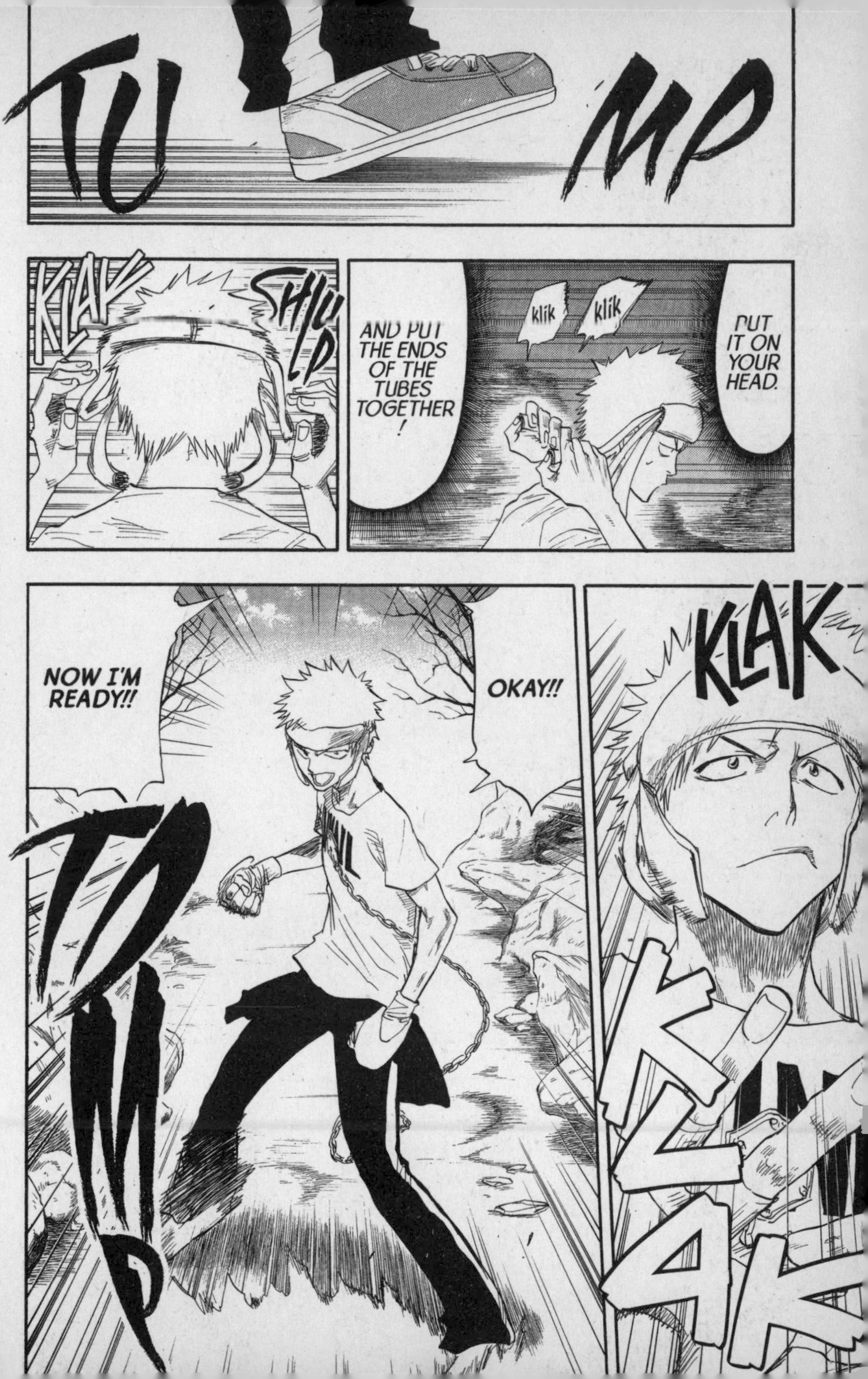
TUMP
PUT IT ON YOUR HEAD.
klik
klik
AND PUT THE ENDS OF THE TUBES TOGETHER!
KLAK
OKAY!!
NOW I'M READY!!

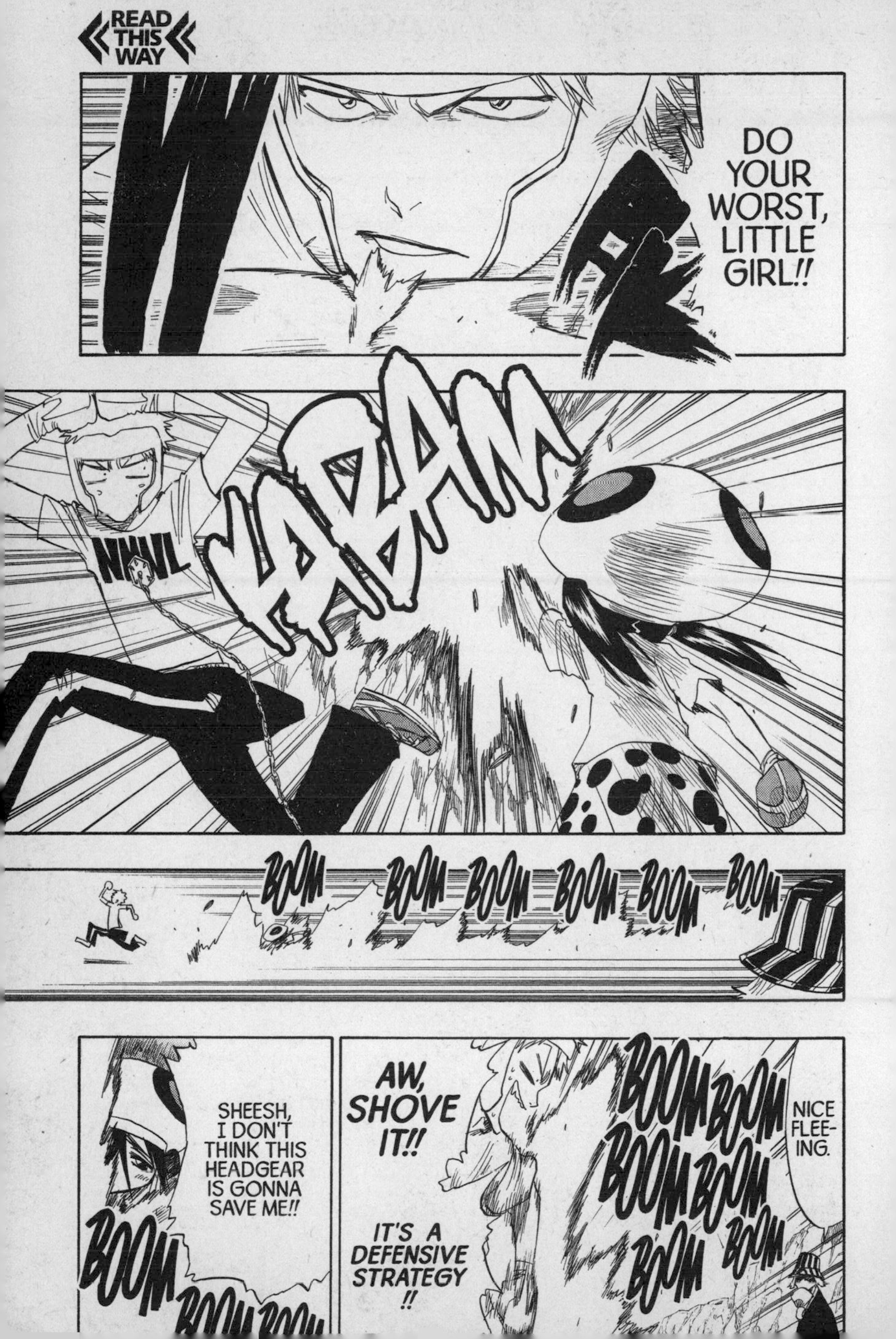
READ THIS WAY
DO YOUR WORST, LITTLE GIRL!!
KABAM
BOOM BOOM BOOM BOOM BOOM BOOM
NICE FLEE-ING.
BOOM BOOM BOOM BOOM BOOM BOOM BOOM BOOM
AW, SHOVE IT!!
IT'S A DEFENSIVE STRATEGY!!
SHEESH, I DON'T THINK THIS HEADGEAR IS GONNA SAVE ME!!
BOOM BOOM BOOM

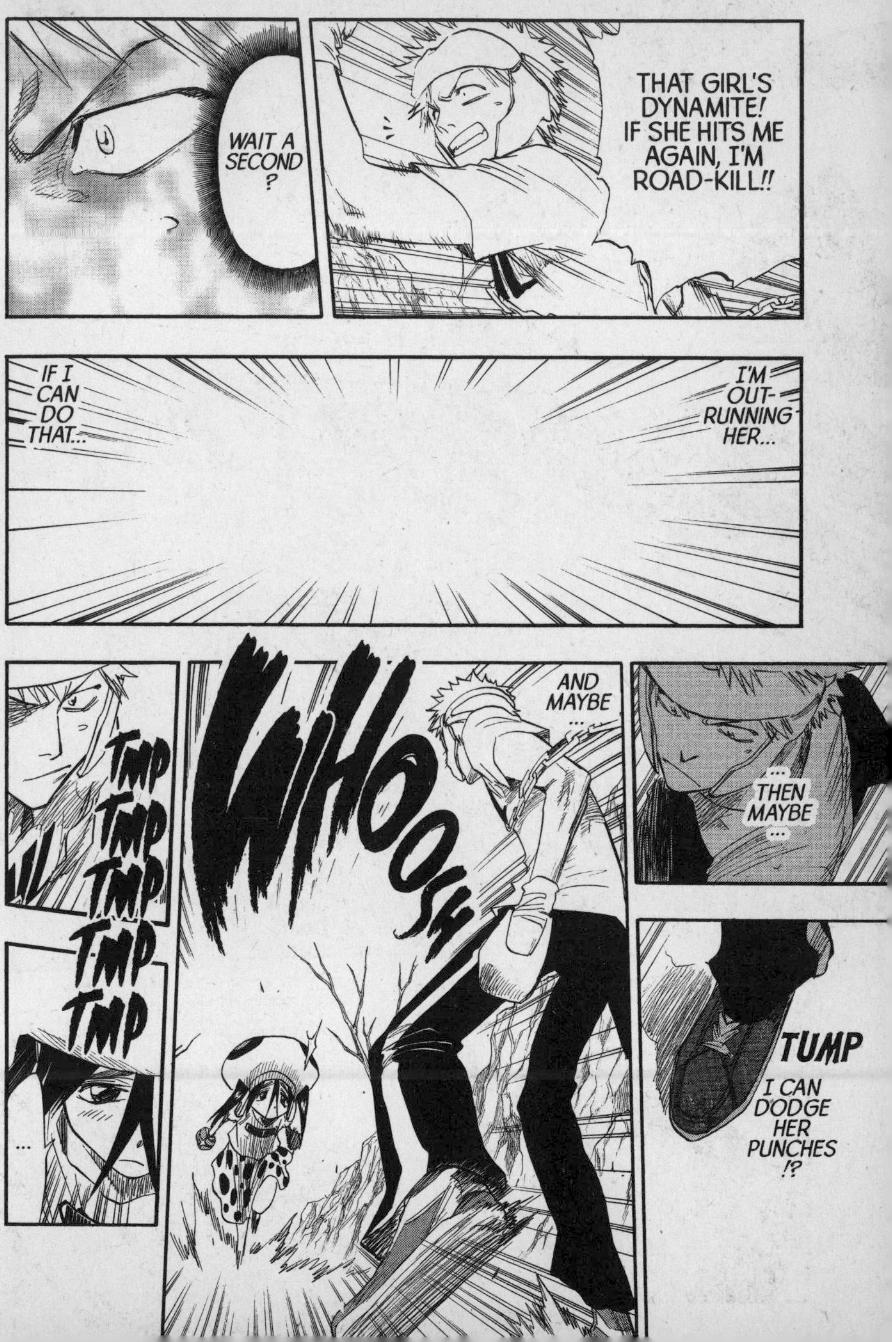
THAT GIRL'S DYNAMITE! IF SHE HITS ME AGAIN, I'M ROAD-KILL!!
WAIT A SECOND ?
I'M OUT-RUNNING HER...
IF I CAN DO THAT...
... THEN MAYBE ...
TUMP
I CAN DODGE HER PUNCHES !?
AND MAYBE ...
WHOOSH
TMP TMP TMP T-MP TMP
...

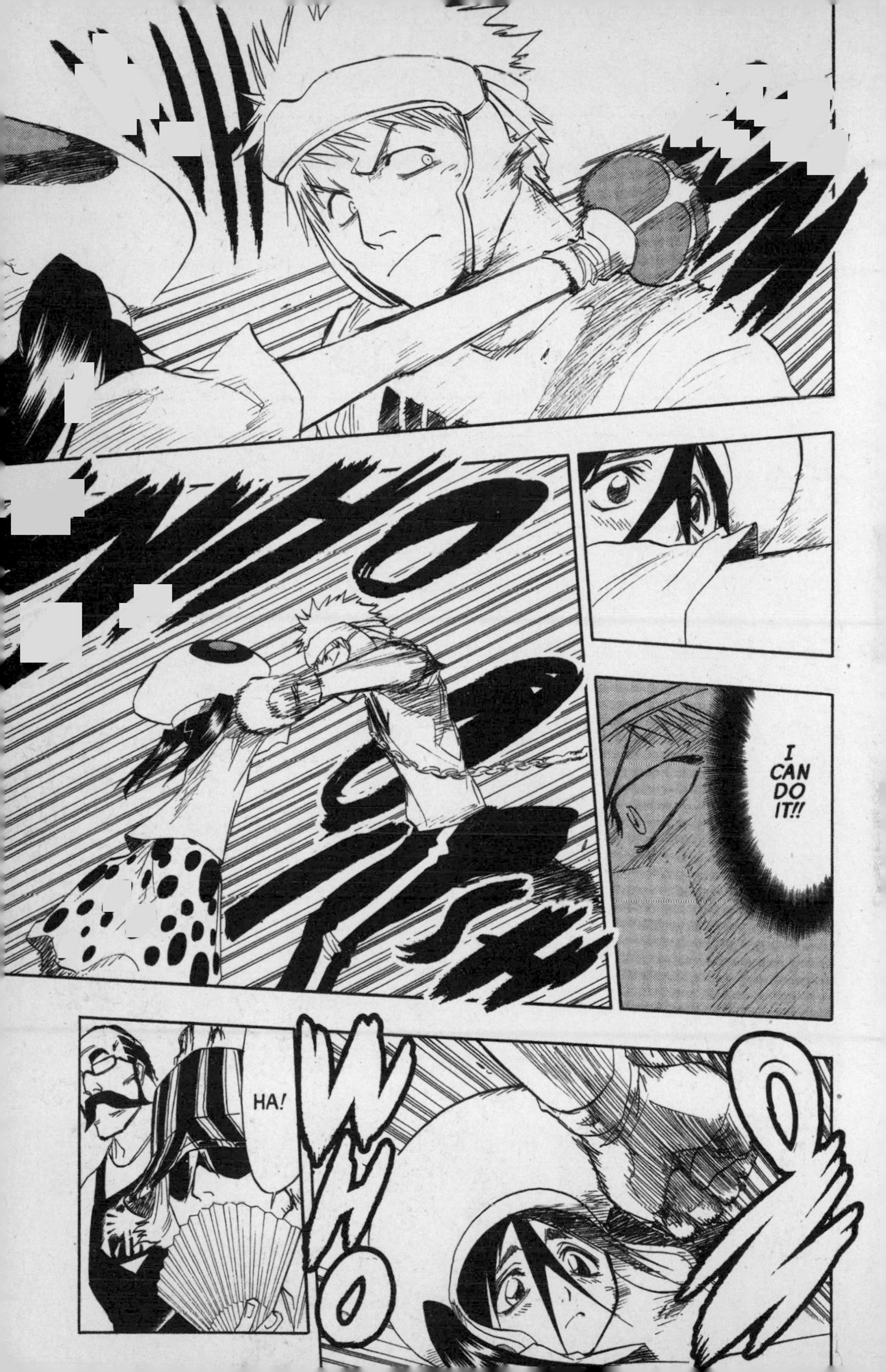
I CAN DO IT!!
HA!

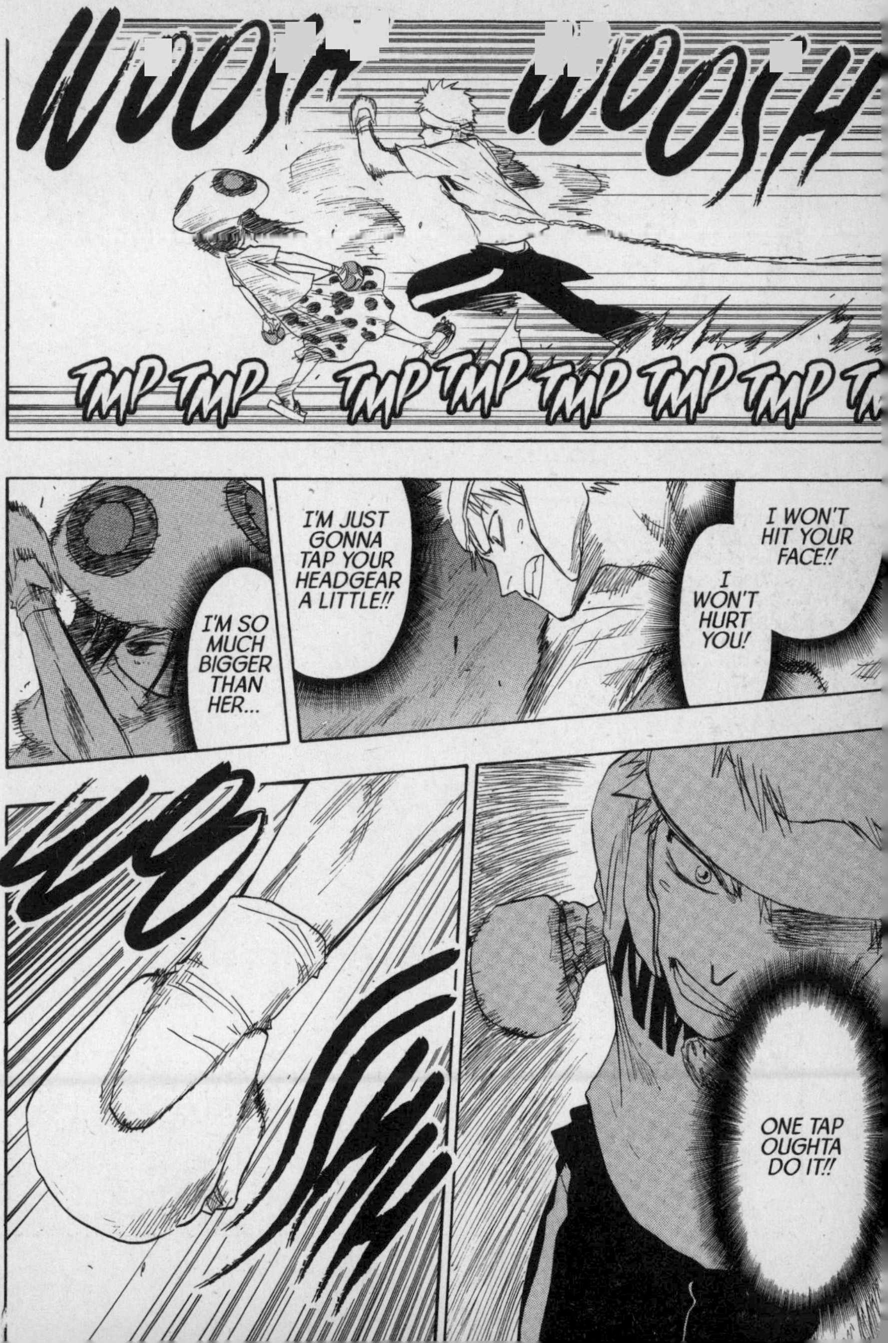
WOOSH
WOOSH
TMP TMP TMP TMP TMP TMP TMP TMP
I WON'T HIT YOUR FACE!!
I WON'T HURT YOU!
I'M JUST GONNA TAP YOUR HEADGEAR A LITTLE!!
I'M SO MUCH BIGGER THAN HER...
ONE TAP OUGHTA DO IT!!

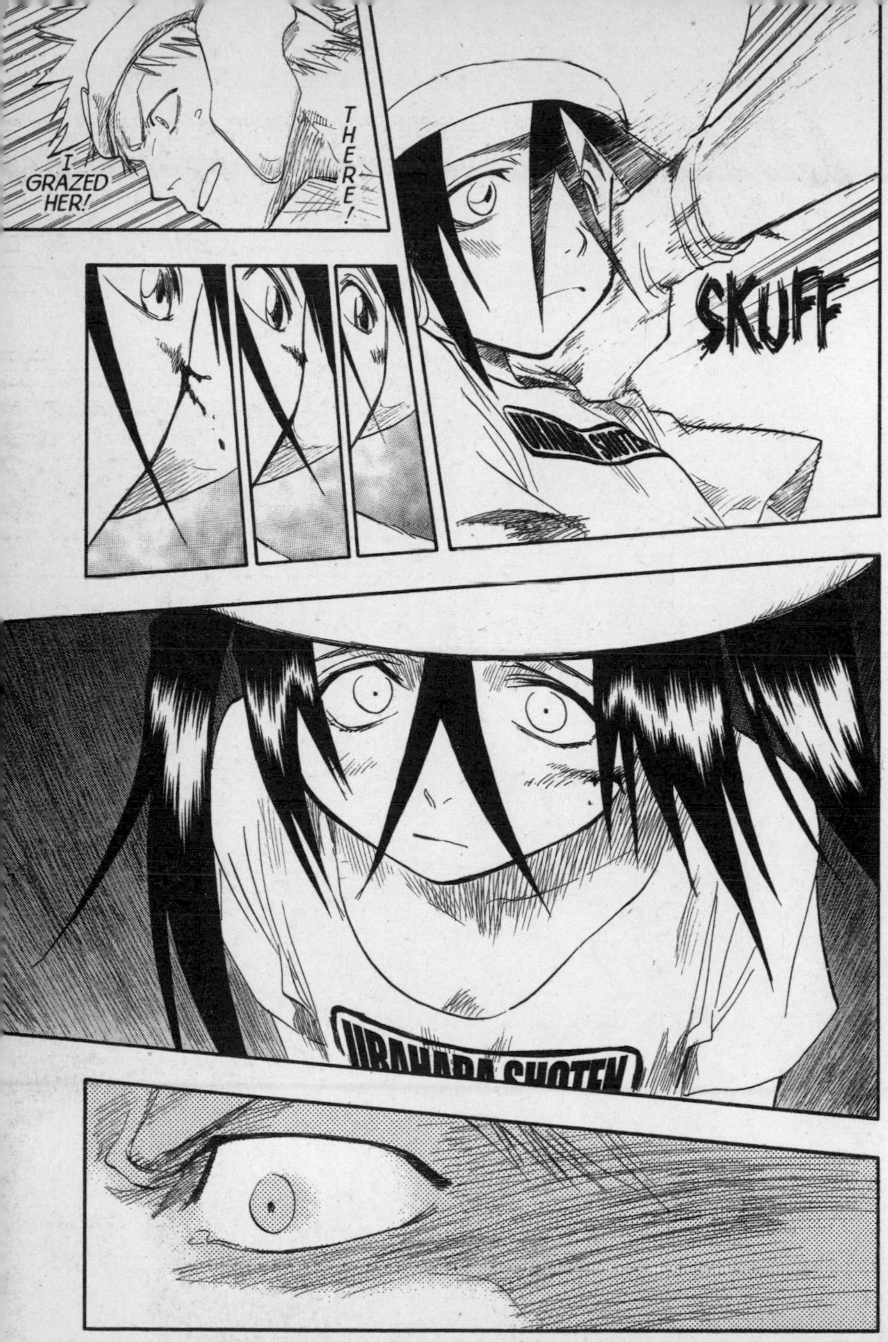
SKUFF
URAHARA SHOTEN
THERE!
I GRAZED HER!

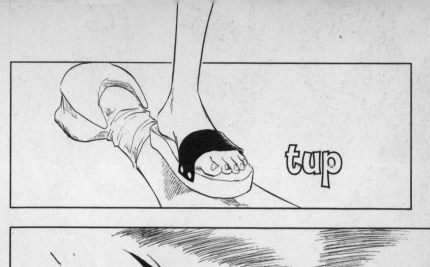

tup

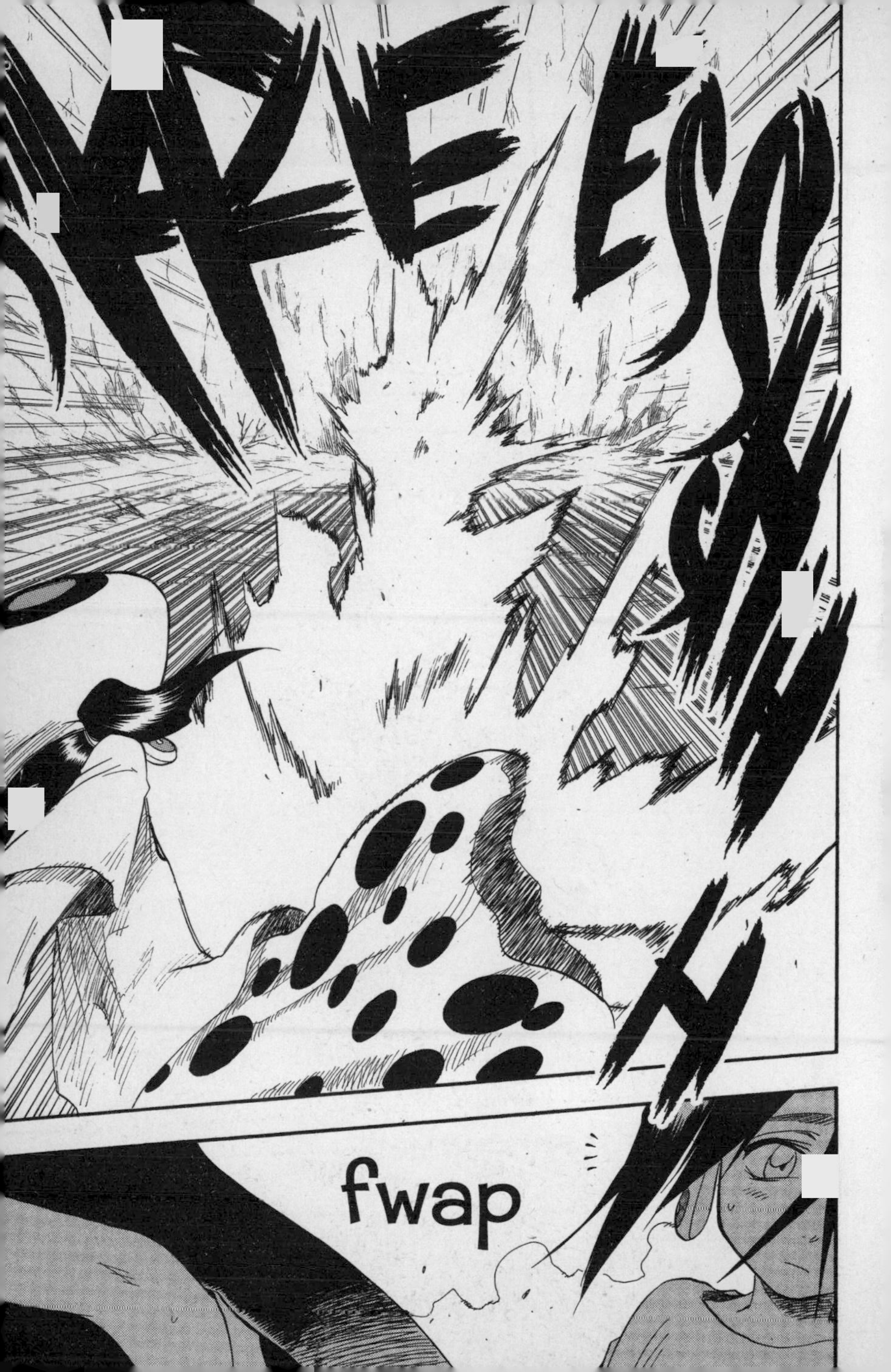
fwap

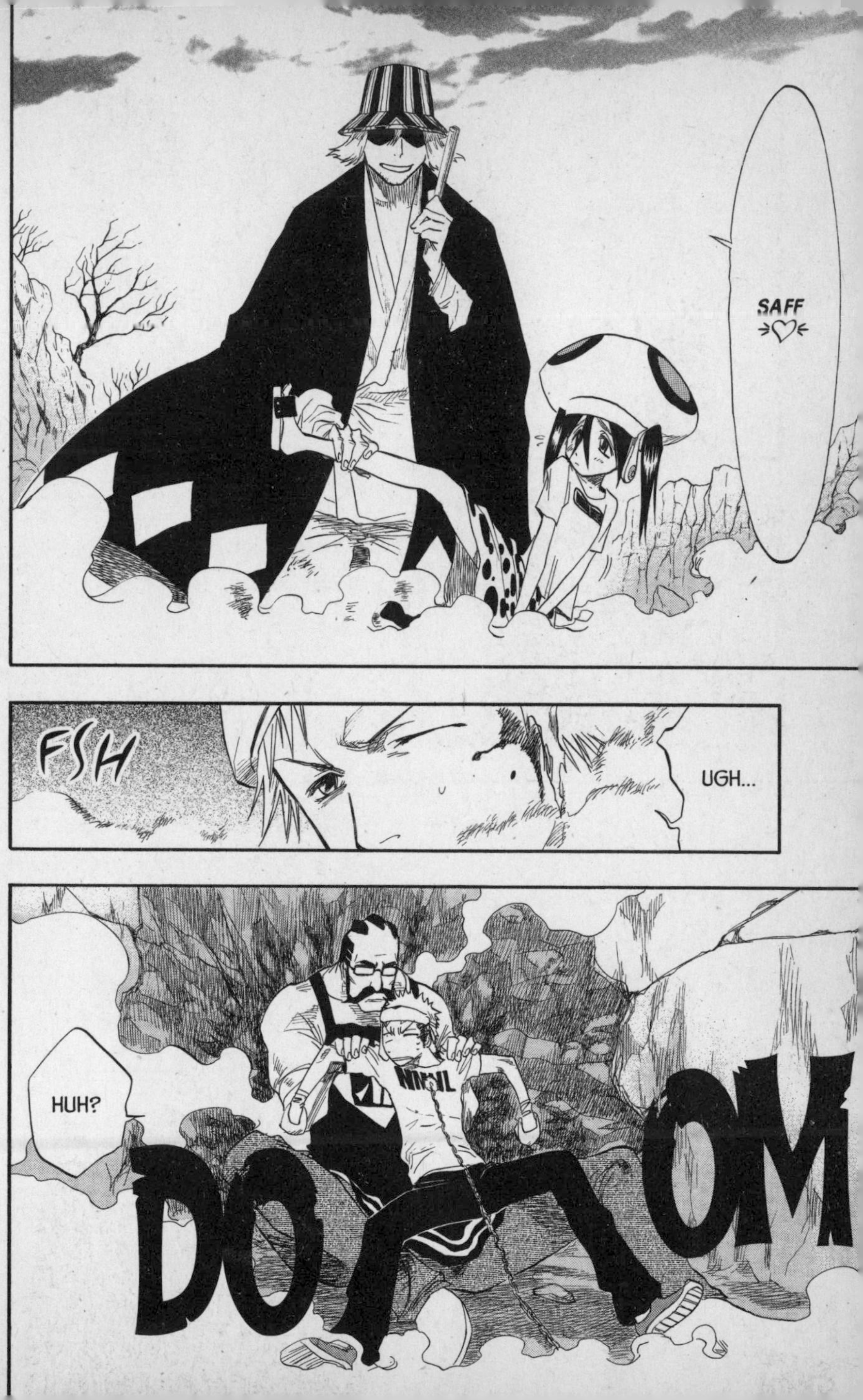
SAFF
UGH...
FSH
HUH?
DOOM

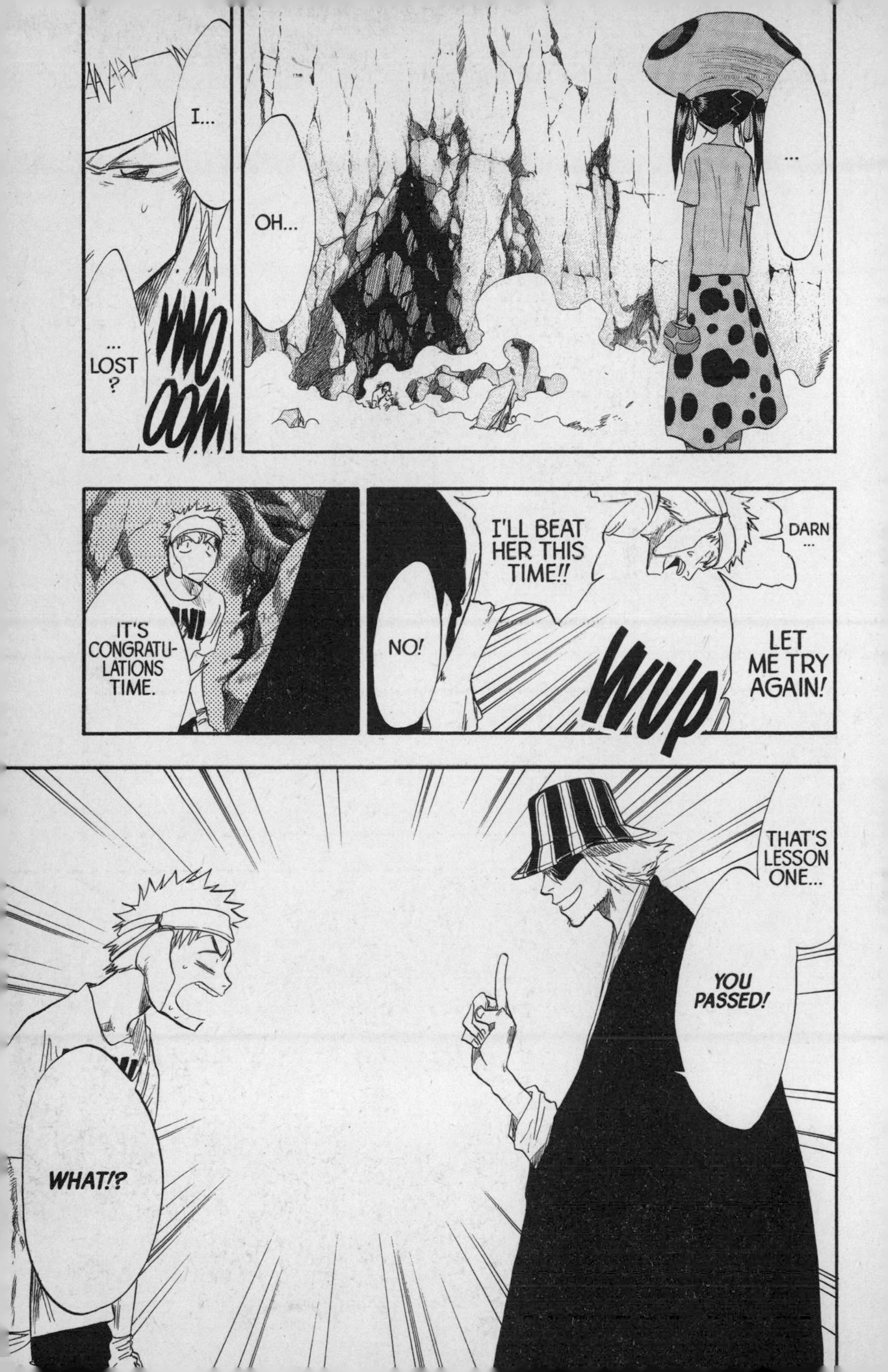
...
OH...
I...
... LOST ?
VWOOOM
DARN ...
I'LL BEAT HER THIS TIME!!
LET ME TRY AGAIN!
WUP
NO!
IT'S CONGRATULATIONS TIME.
THAT'S LESSON ONE...
YOU PASSED!
WHAT!?

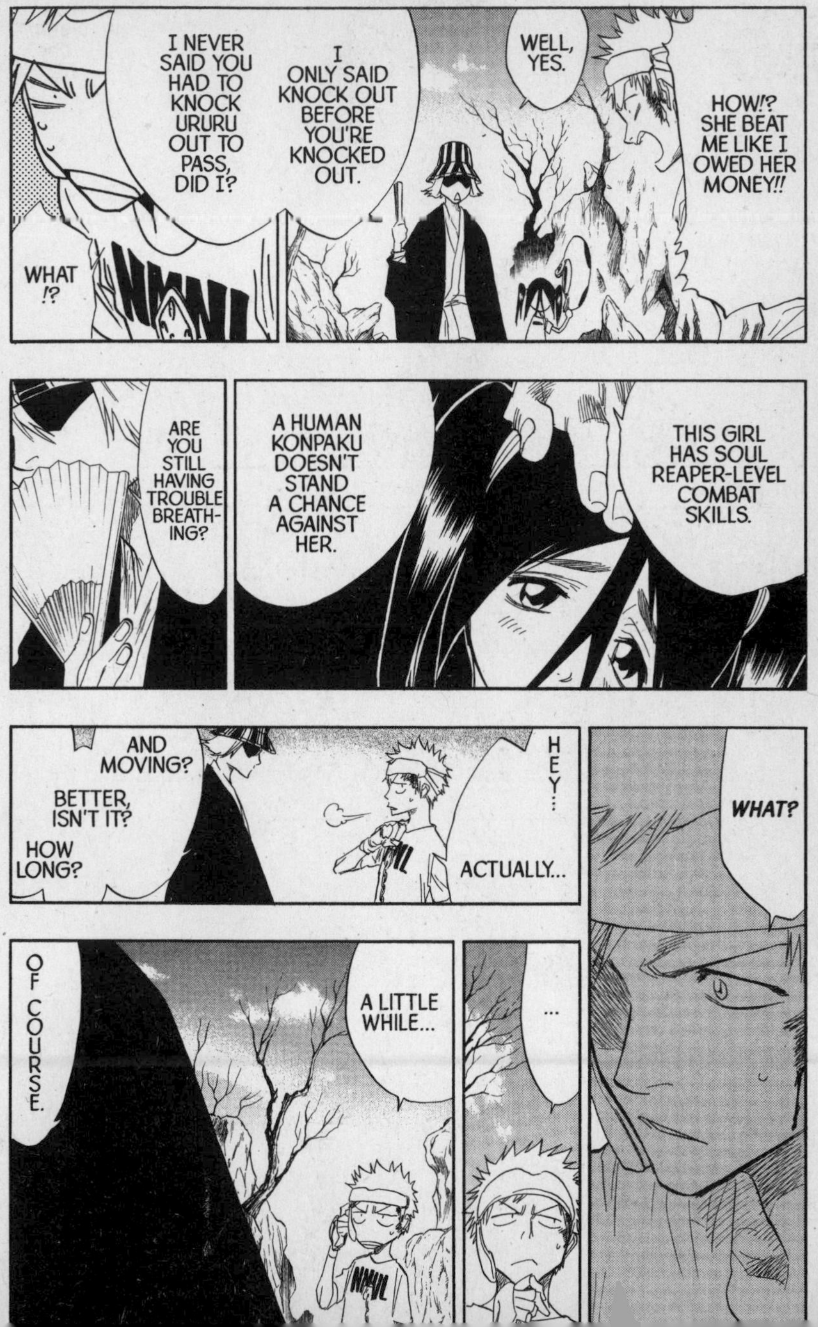
HOW!? SHE BEAT ME LIKE I OWED HER MONEY!!
WELL, YES.
I ONLY SAID KNOCK OUT BEFORE YOU'RE KNOCKED OUT.
I NEVER SAID YOU HAD TO KNOCK URURU OUT TO PASS, DID I?
WHAT!?
THIS GIRL HAS SOUL REAPER-LEVEL COMBAT SKILLS.
A HUMAN KONPAKU DOESN'T STAND A CHANCE AGAINST HER.
ARE YOU STILL HAVING TROUBLE BREATH-ING?
WHAT?
HEY...
ACTUALLY...
AND MOVING?
BETTER, ISN'T IT?
HOW LONG?
...
A LITTLE WHILE...
OF COURSE.

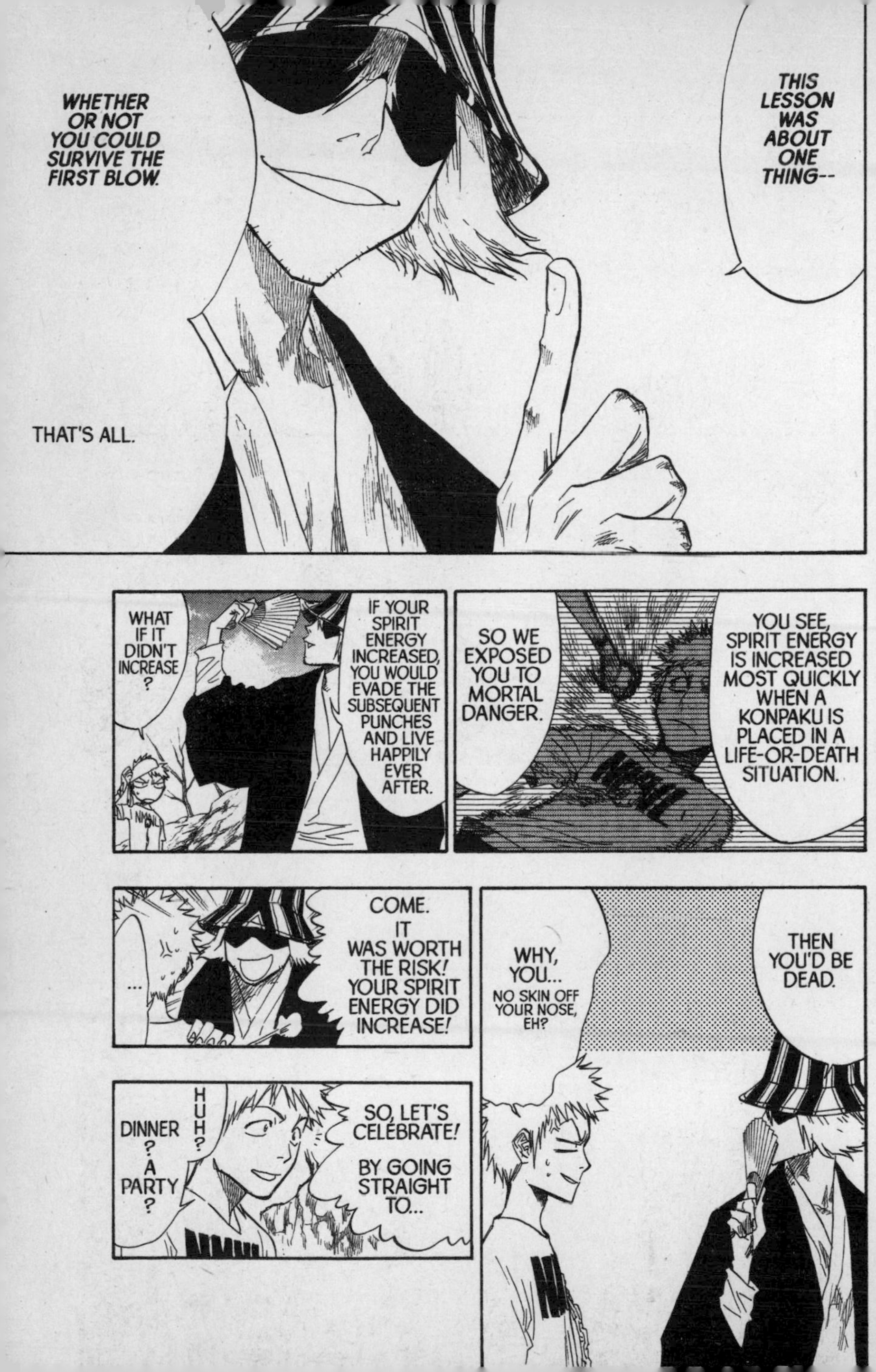
THIS LESSON WAS ABOUT ONE THING--
WHETHER OR NOT YOU COULD SURVIVE THE FIRST BLOW.
THAT'S ALL.
YOU SEE, SPIRIT ENERGY IS INCREASED MOST QUICKLY WHEN A KONPAKU IS PLACED IN A LIFE-OR-DEATH SITUATION.
SO WE EXPOSED YOU TO MORTAL DANGER.
IF YOUR SPIRIT ENERGY INCREASED, YOU WOULD EVADE THE SUBSEQUENT PUNCHES AND LIVE HAPPILY EVER AFTER.
WHAT IF IT DIDN'T INCREASE?
THEN YOU'D BE DEAD.
WHY, YOU...
NO SKIN OFF YOUR NOSE, EH?
COME. IT WAS WORTH THE RISK! YOUR SPIRIT ENERGY DID INCREASE!
...
SO, LET'S CELEBRATE!
BY GOING STRAIGHT TO...
HUH?
DINNER? A PARTY?

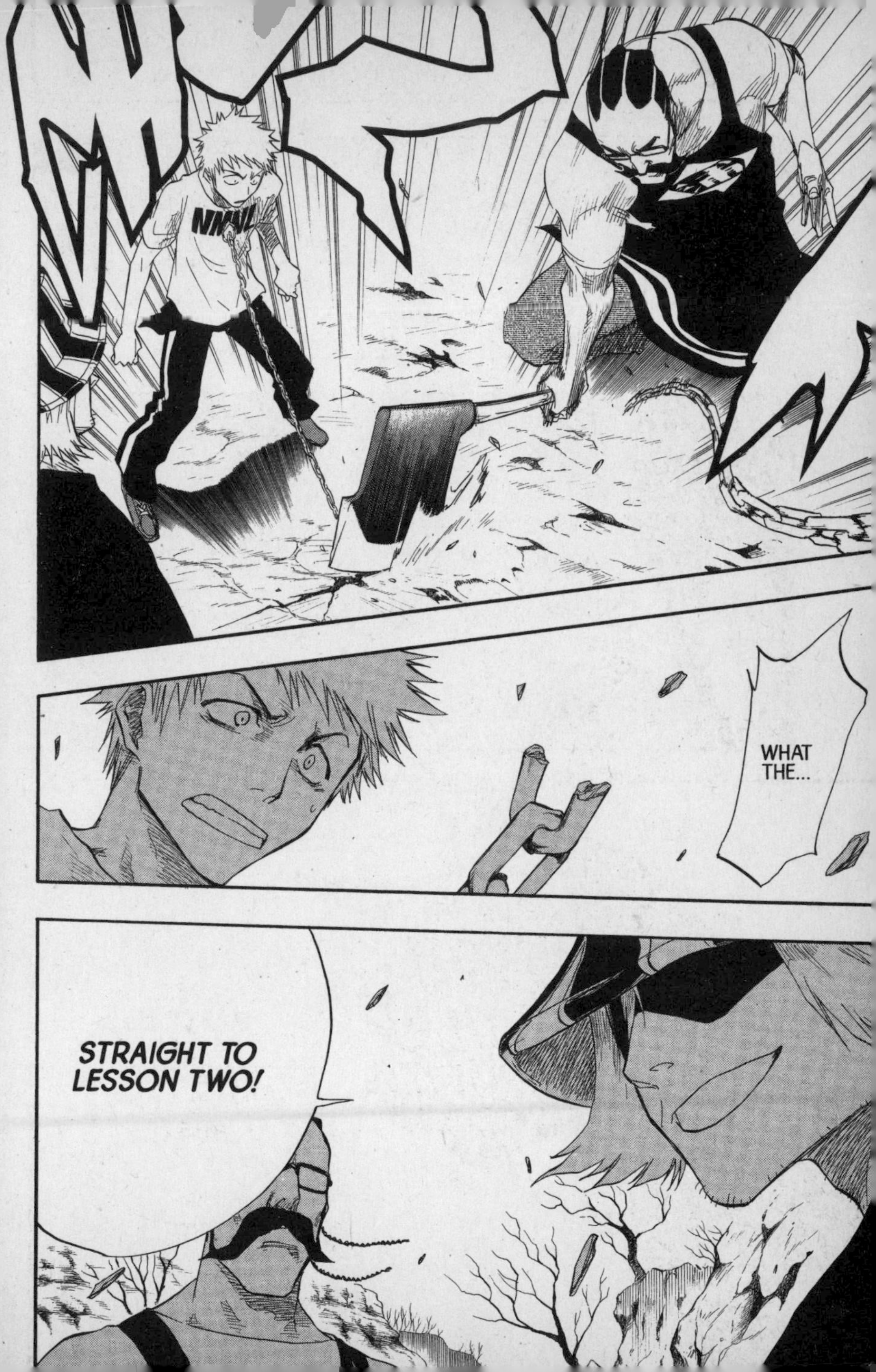
WHAT THE...
STRAIGHT TO LESSON TWO!

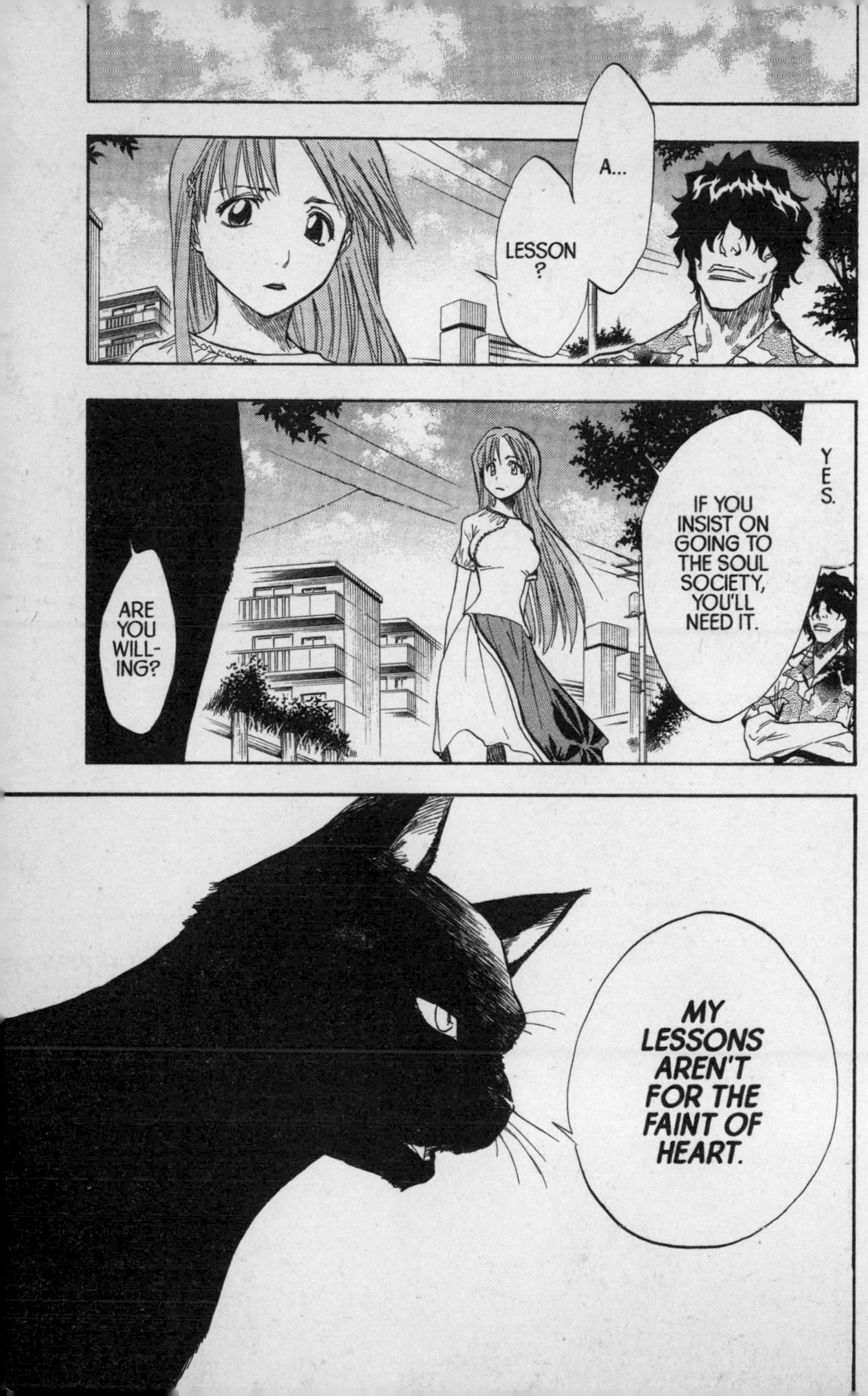
A...
LESSON?
YES.
IF YOU INSIST ON GOING TO THE SOUL SOCIETY, YOU'LL NEED IT.
ARE YOU WILL-ING?
MY LESSONS AREN'T FOR THE FAINT OF HEART.

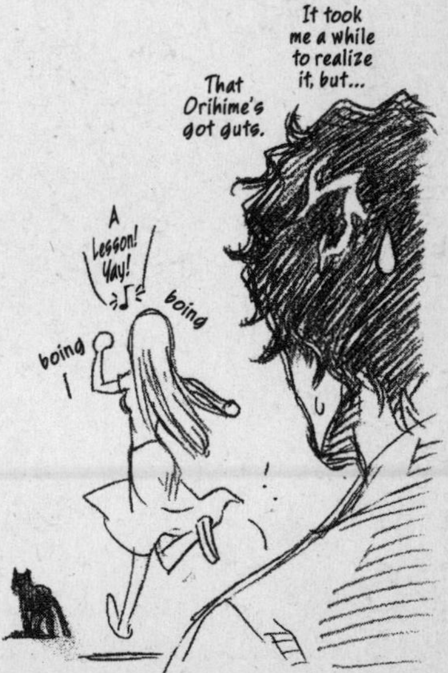
It took me a while to realize it, but...
That Orihime's got guts.
A Lesson! Yay!
boing
boing

61. Lesson 2: Shattered Shaft

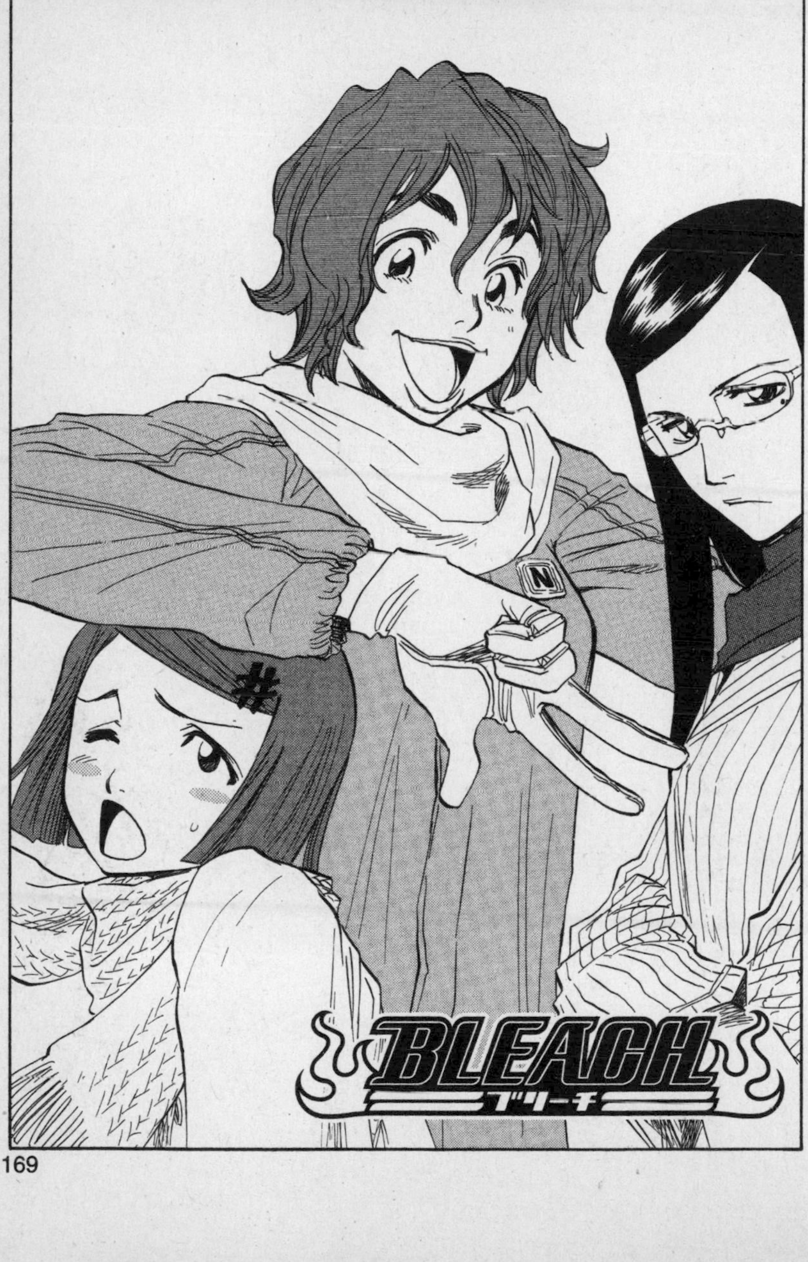
BLEACH
ブリーチ

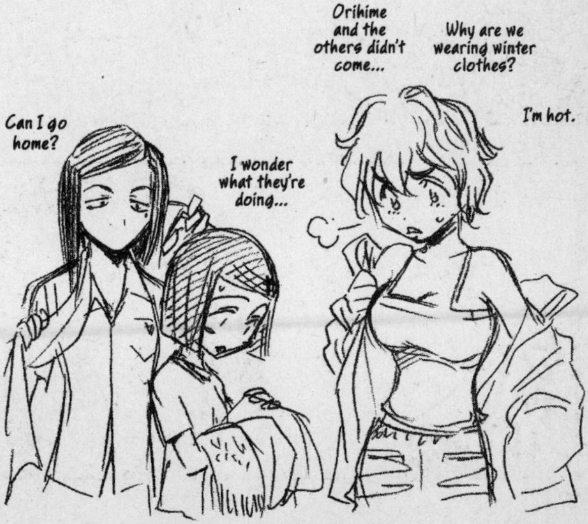
Why are we wearing winter clothes?
I'm hot.
Orihime and the others didn't come...
I wonder what they're doing...
Can I go home?

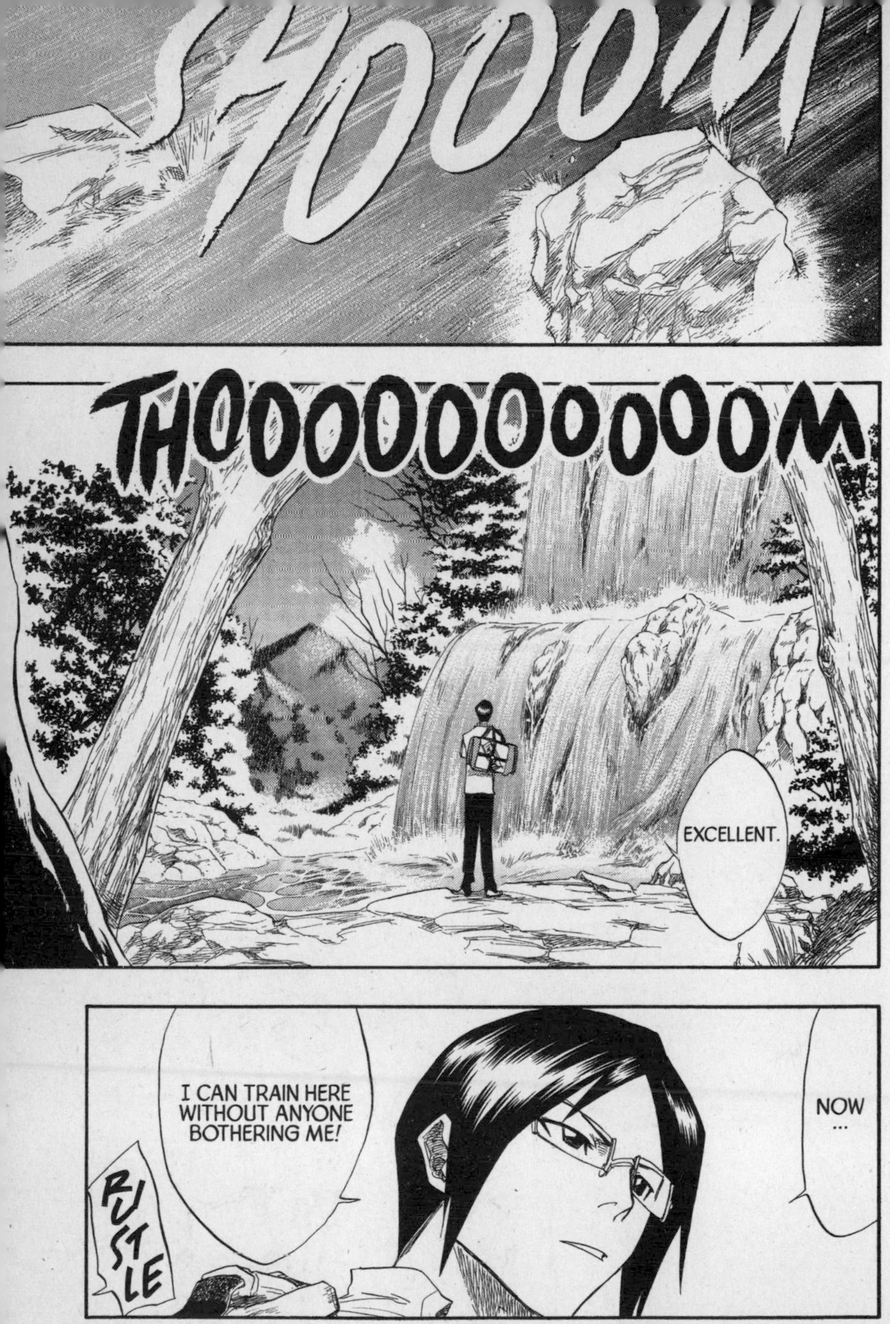
THOOOOOOOOOM
EXCELLENT.
NOW ...
I CAN TRAIN HERE WITHOUT ANYONE BOTHERING ME!
RUSTLE

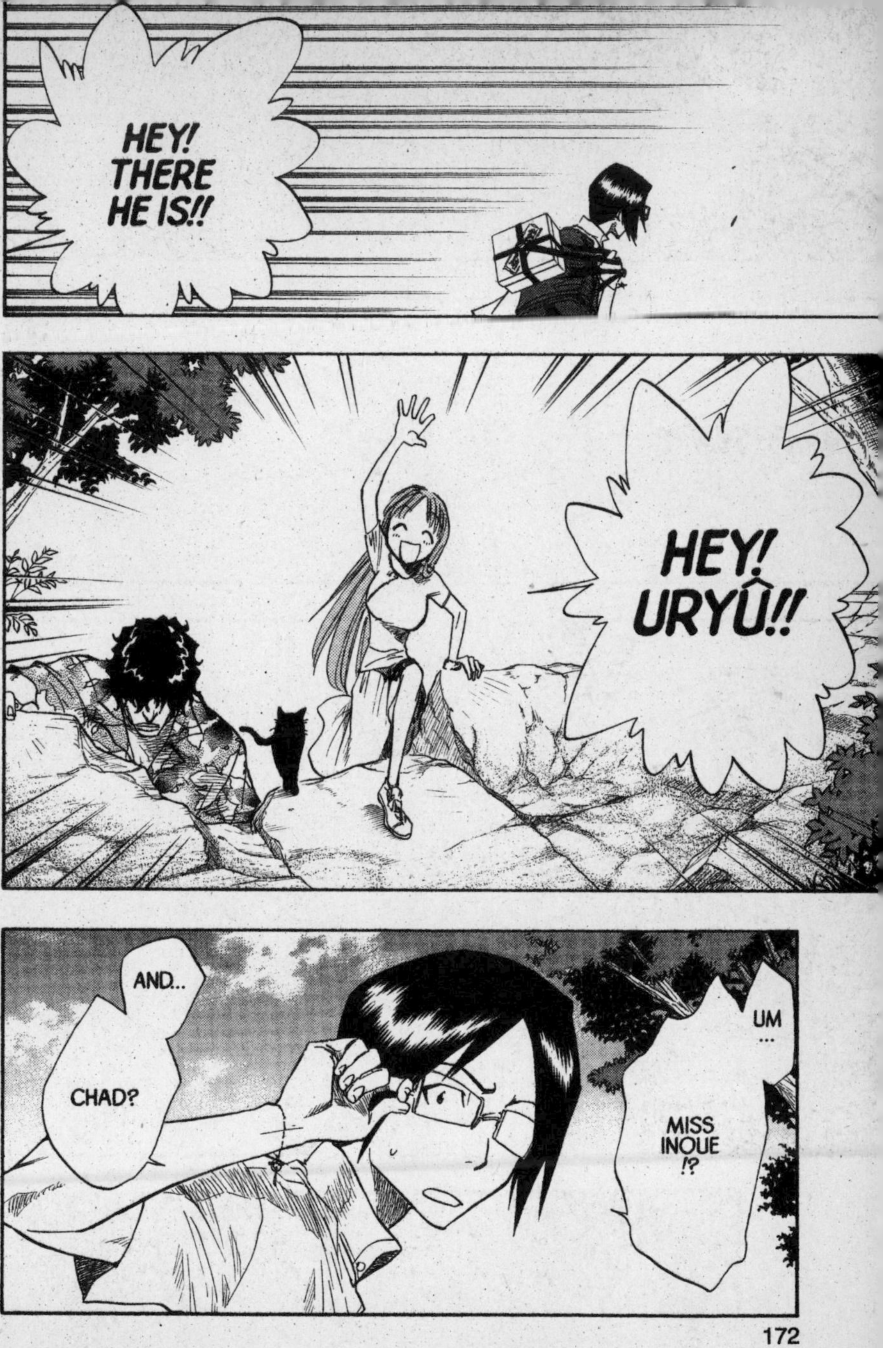
HEY! THERE HE IS!!
HEY! URYÛ!!
UM ... MISS INOUE !?
AND... CHAD?

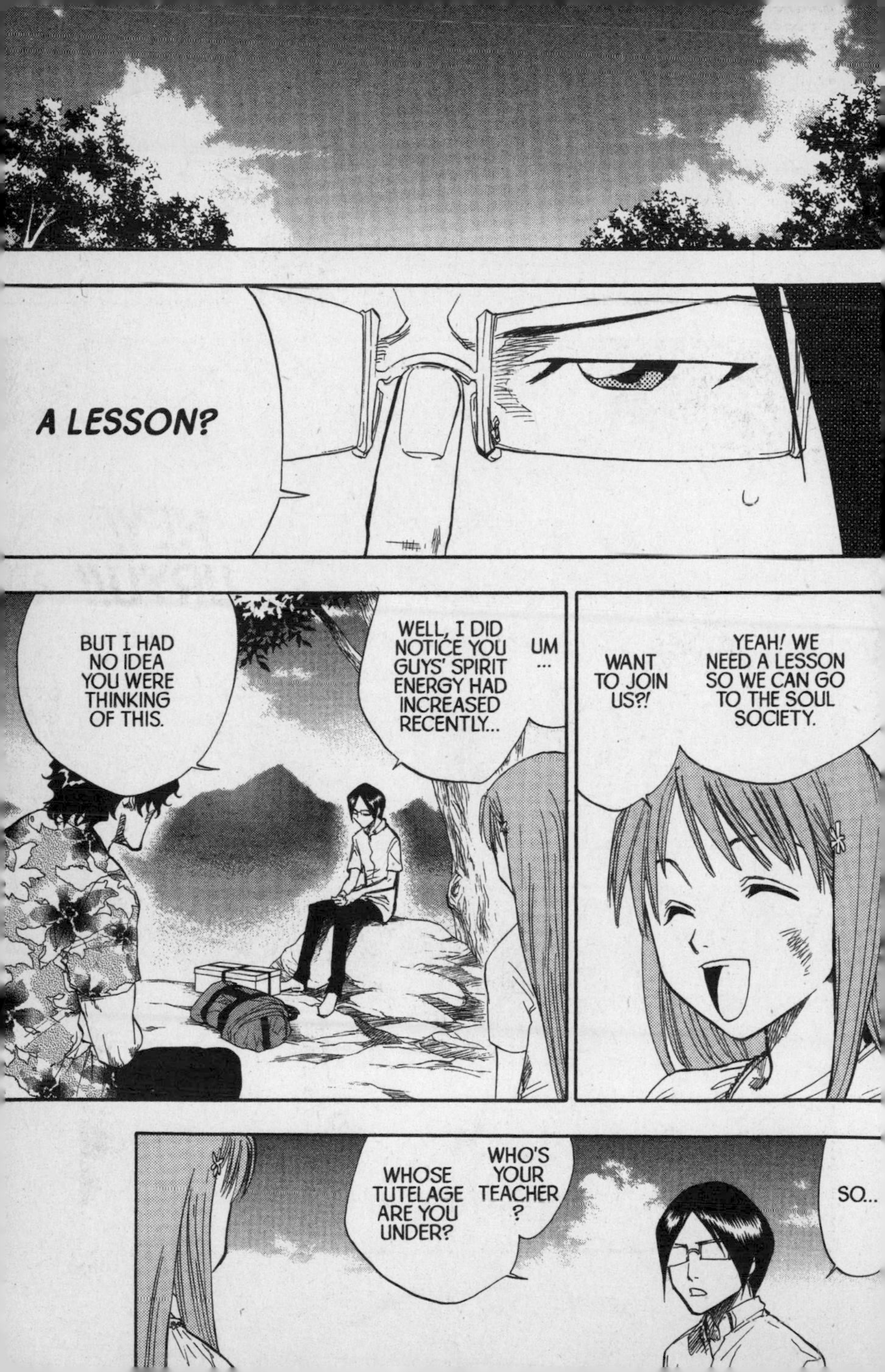
A LESSON?
YEAH! WE NEED A LESSON SO WE CAN GO TO THE SOUL SOCIETY.
WANT TO JOIN US?!
UM ...
WELL, I DID NOTICE YOU GUYS' SPIRIT ENERGY HAD INCREASED RECENTLY...
BUT I HAD NO IDEA YOU WERE THINKING OF THIS.
SO...
WHO'S YOUR TEACHER?
WHOSE TUTELAGE ARE YOU UNDER?

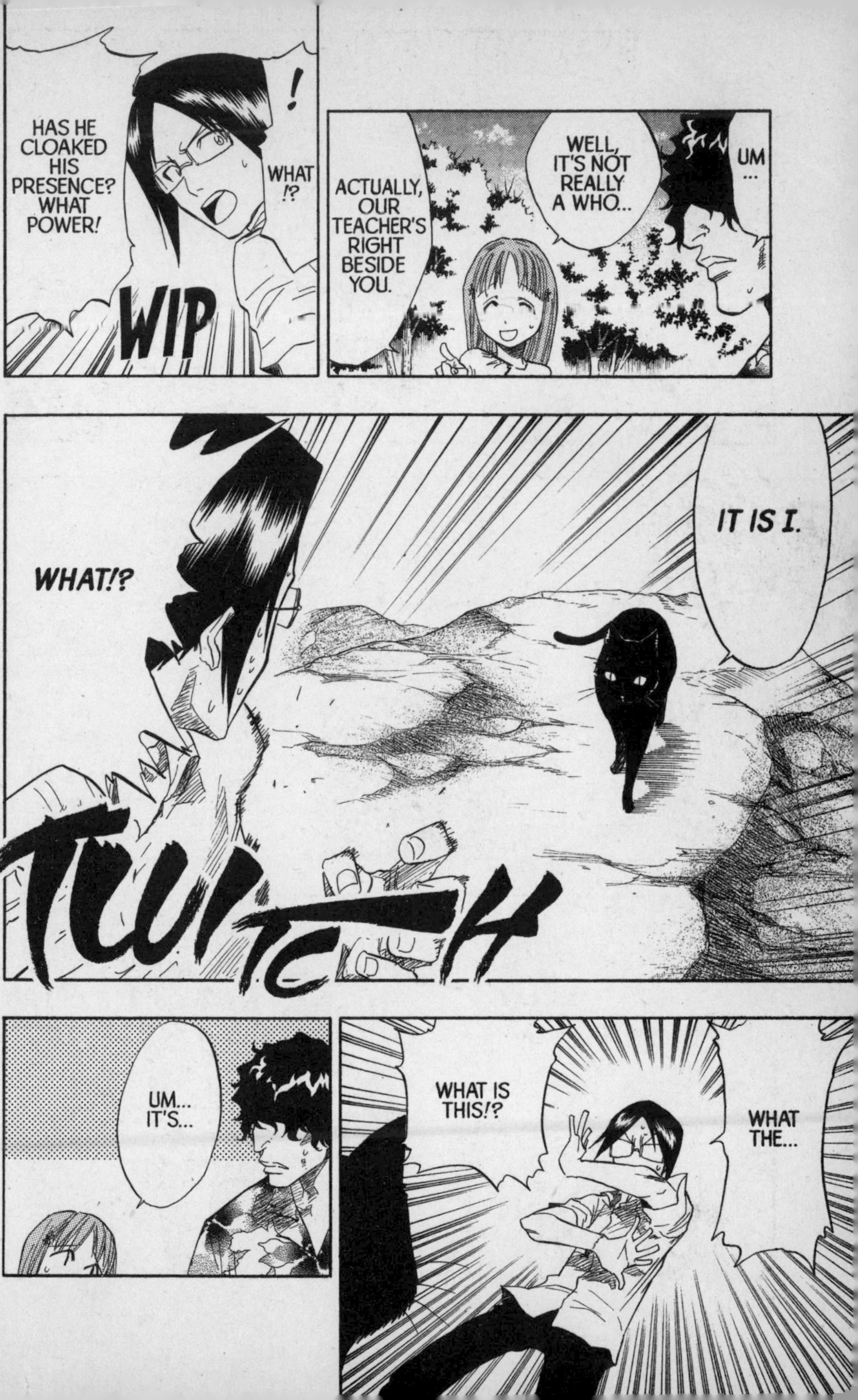
UM ...
WELL, IT'S NOT REALLY A WHO...
ACTUALLY, OUR TEACHER'S RIGHT BESIDE YOU.
!
WHAT !?
HAS HE CLOAKED HIS PRESENCE? WHAT POWER!
WIP
IT IS I.
WHAT!?
TWITCH
WHAT THE...
WHAT IS THIS!?
UM... IT'S...

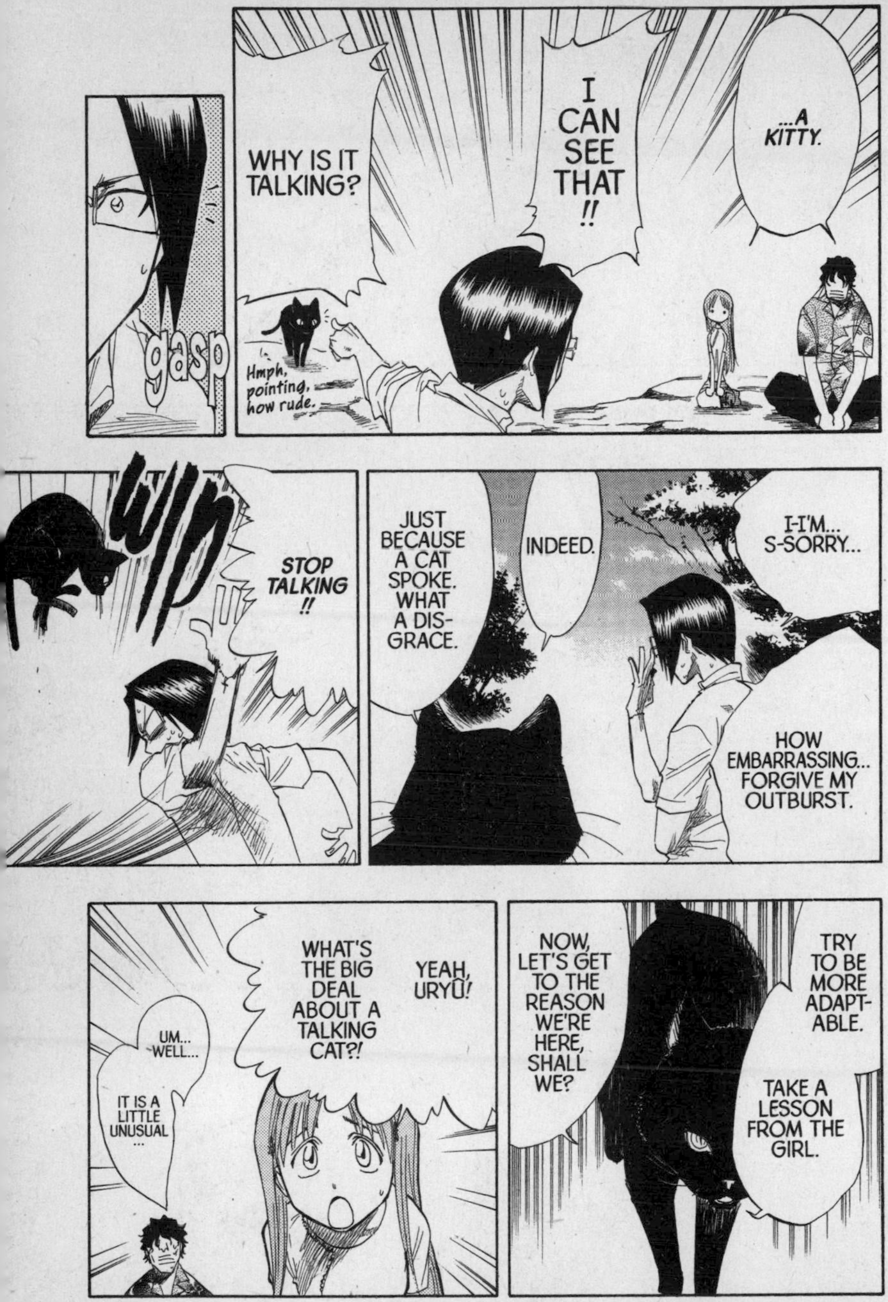
...A KITTY.
I CAN SEE THAT!!
WHY IS IT TALKING?
Hmph, pointing, how rude.
gasp
I-I'M... S-SORRY...
HOW EMBARRASSING... FORGIVE MY OUTBURST.
INDEED.
JUST BECAUSE A CAT SPOKE. WHAT A DISGRACE.
STOP TALKING!!
TRY TO BE MORE ADAPTABLE.
TAKE A LESSON FROM THE GIRL.
NOW, LET'S GET TO THE REASON WE'RE HERE, SHALL WE?
YEAH, URYŪ!
WHAT'S THE BIG DEAL ABOUT A TALKING CAT?!
UM... WELL...
IT IS A LITTLE UNUSUAL...

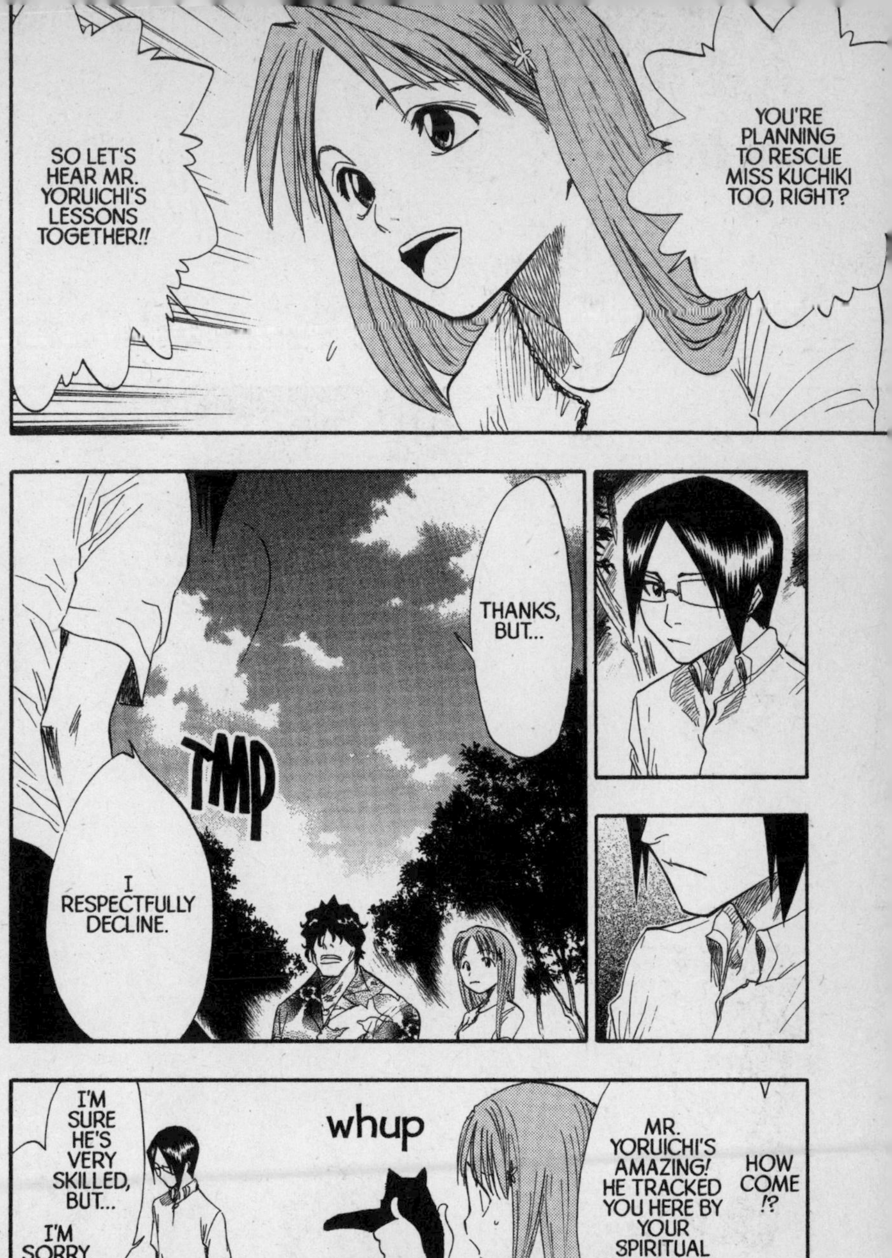
YOU'RE PLANNING TO RESCUE MISS KUCHIKI TOO, RIGHT?
SO LET'S HEAR MR. YORUICHI'S LESSONS TOGETHER!!
THANKS, BUT...
TMP
I RESPECTFULLY DECLINE.
HOW COME!?
MR. YORUICHI'S AMAZING! HE TRACKED YOU HERE BY YOUR SPIRITUAL PRESENCE!
whup
I'M SURE HE'S VERY SKILLED, BUT...
I'M SORRY.

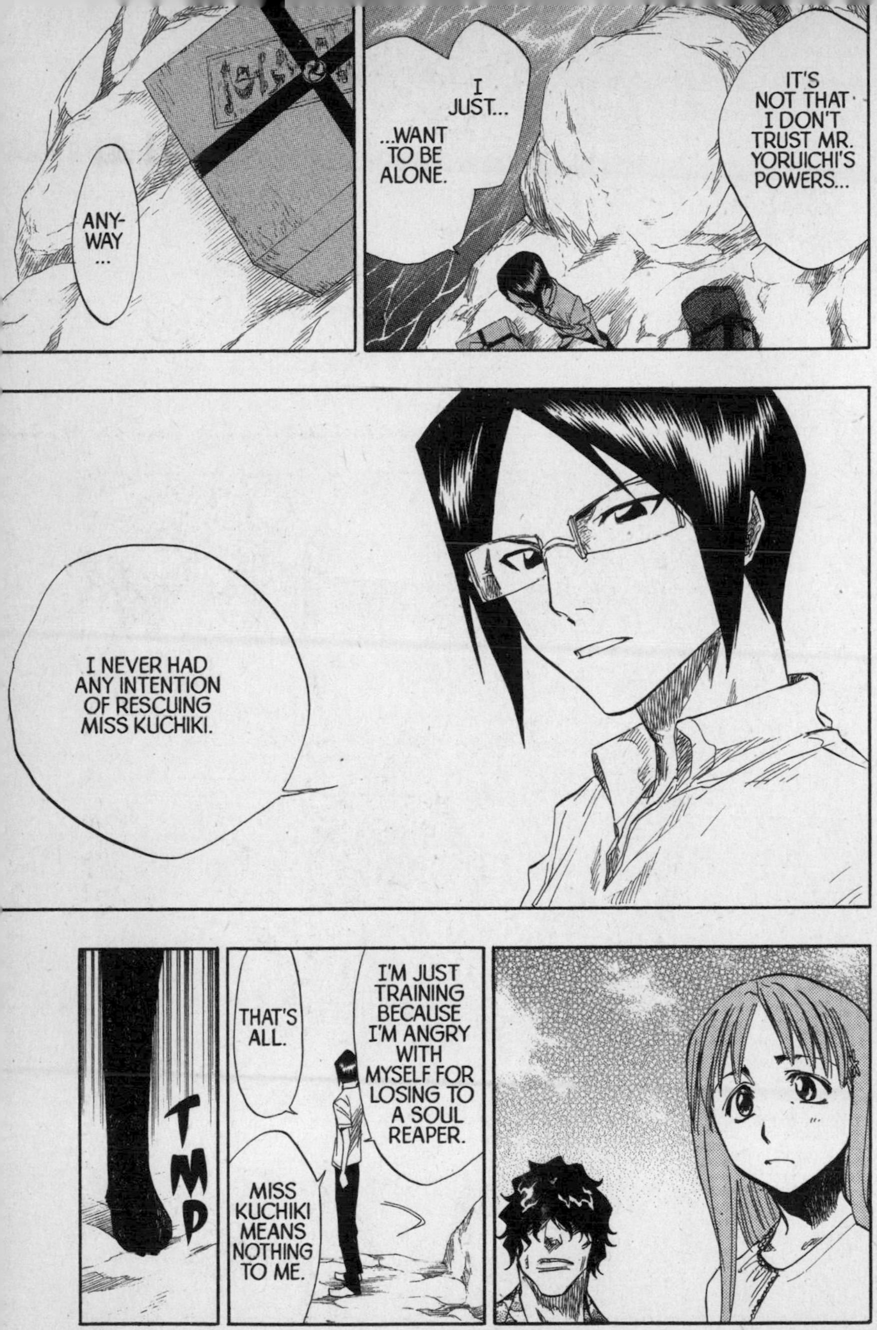
IT'S NOT THAT I DON'T TRUST MR. YORUICHI'S POWERS...
I JUST...
...WANT TO BE ALONE.
ANY-WAY...
I NEVER HAD ANY INTENTION OF RESCUING MISS KUCHIKI.
I'M JUST TRAINING BECAUSE I'M ANGRY WITH MYSELF FOR LOSING TO A SOUL REAPER.
THAT'S ALL.
MISS KUCHIKI MEANS NOTHING TO ME.
TMP

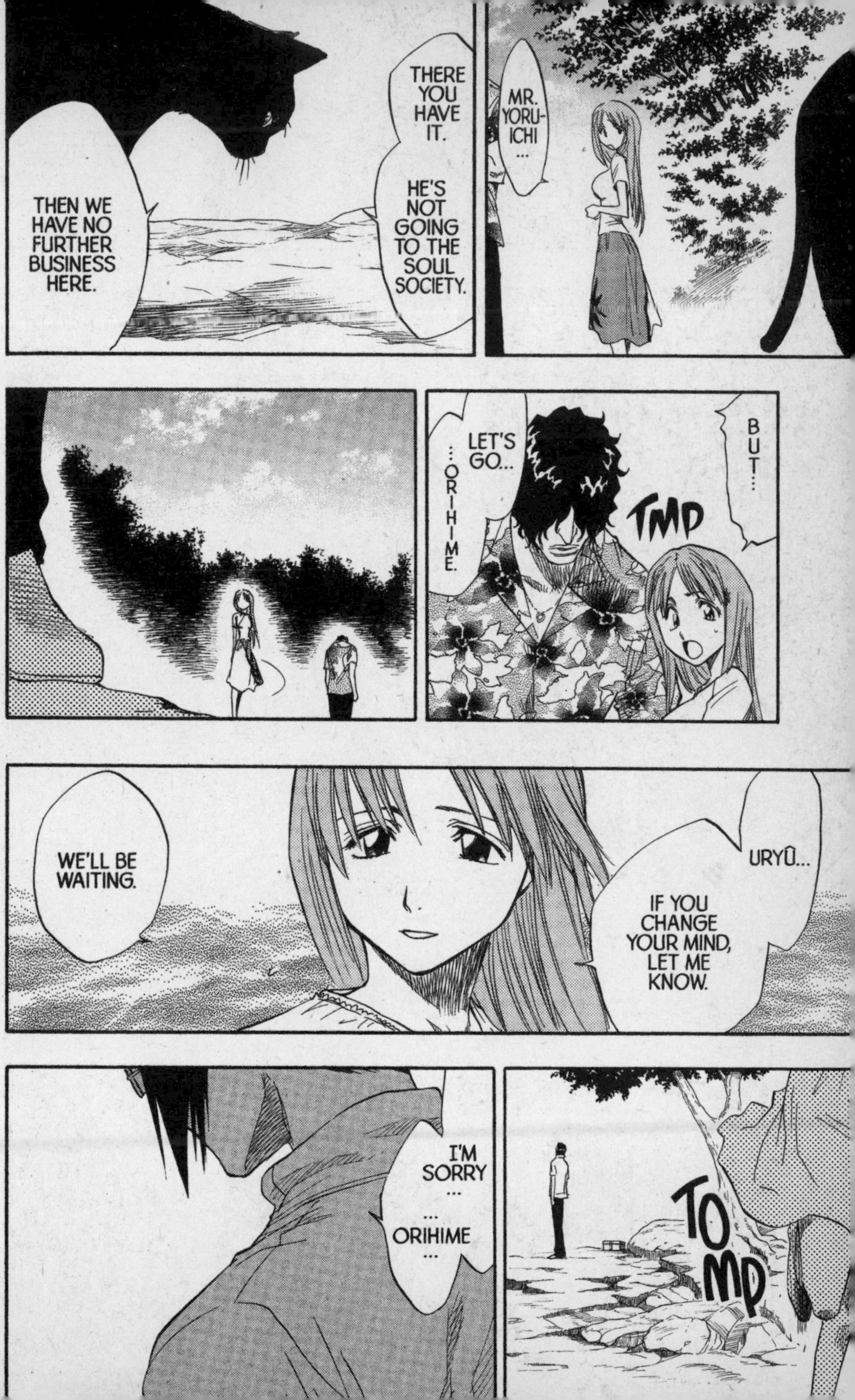
MR. YORUICHI...
THERE YOU HAVE IT.
HE'S NOT GOING TO THE SOUL SOCIETY.
THEN WE HAVE NO FURTHER BUSINESS HERE.
BUT...
LET'S GO...
...ORIHIME.
TMP
URYÛ...
IF YOU CHANGE YOUR MIND, LET ME KNOW.
WE'LL BE WAITING.
TOMP
I'M SORRY... ...ORIHIME...

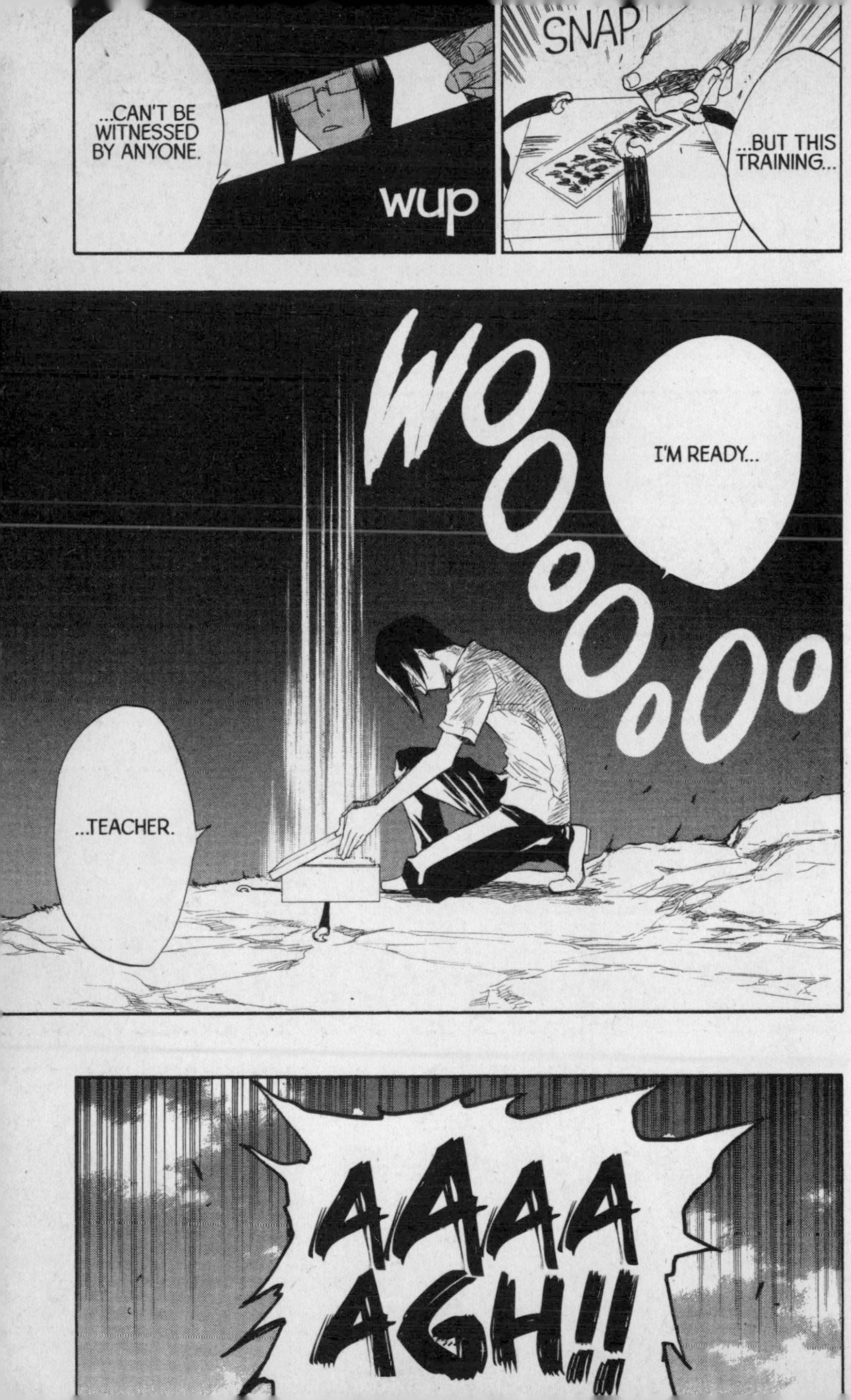
SNAP
...BUT THIS TRAINING...
...CAN'T BE WITNESSED BY ANYONE.
wup
WOOOOOOOO
I'M READY...
...TEACHER.
AAAA AGH!!

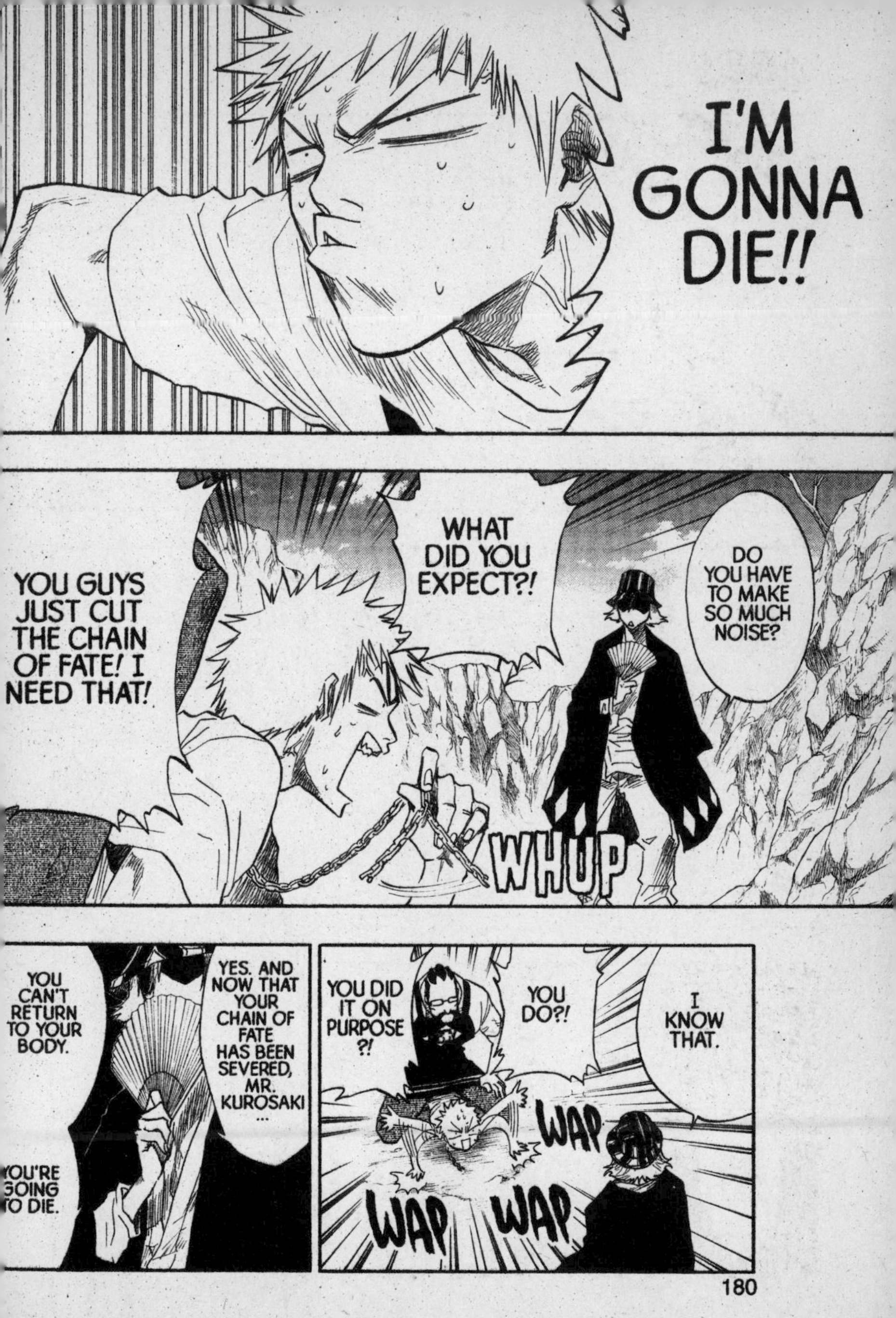
I'M GONNA DIE!!
DO YOU HAVE TO MAKE SO MUCH NOISE?
WHAT DID YOU EXPECT?!
YOU GUYS JUST CUT THE CHAIN OF FATE! I NEED THAT!
WHUP
I KNOW THAT.
YOU DO?!
YOU DID IT ON PURPOSE?!
WAP
WAP
WAP
YES. AND NOW THAT YOUR CHAIN OF FATE HAS BEEN SEVERED, MR. KUROSAKI ...
YOU CAN'T RETURN TO YOUR BODY.
YOU'RE GOING TO DIE.

READ THIS WAY

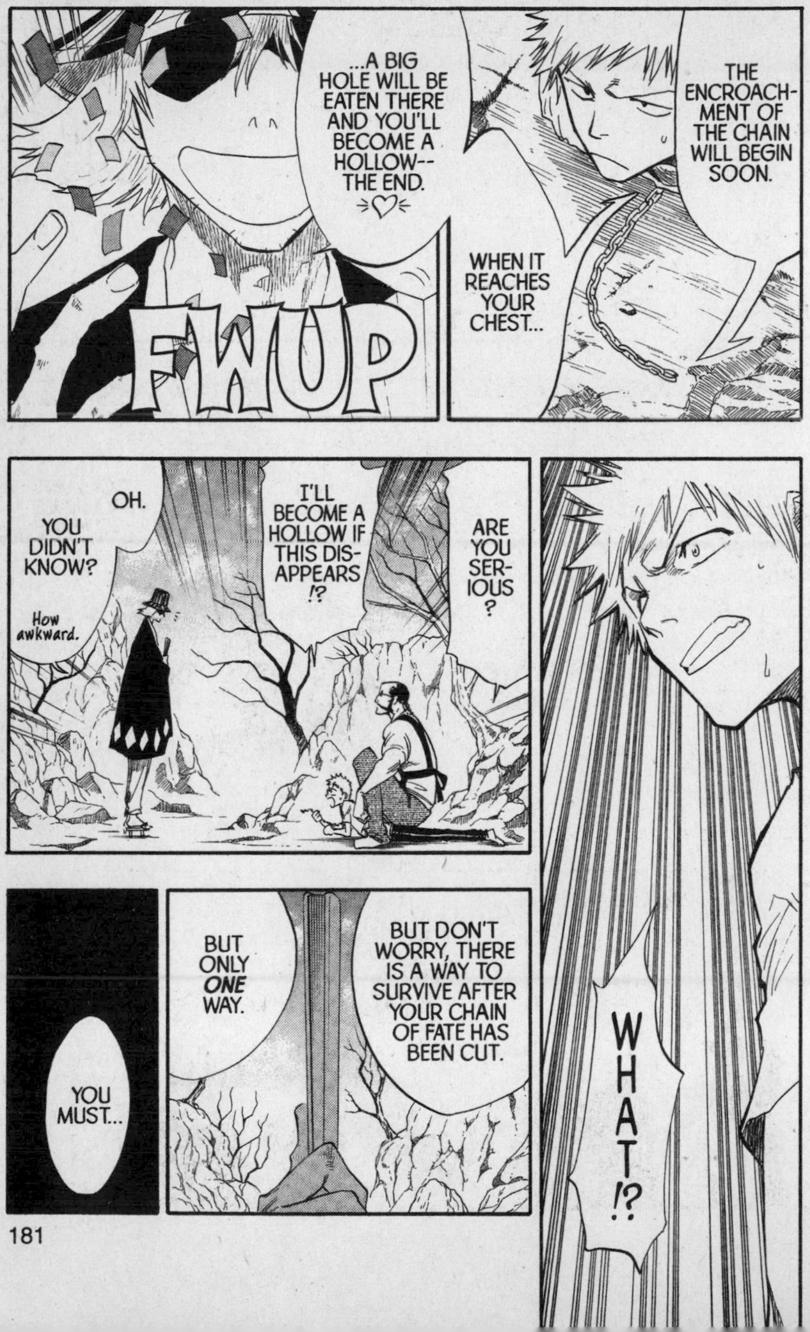
THE ENCROACHMENT OF THE CHAIN WILL BEGIN SOON.
WHEN IT REACHES YOUR CHEST...
...A BIG HOLE WILL BE EATEN THERE AND YOU'LL BECOME A HOLLOW-- THE END. ♡
FWUP
WHAT!?
ARE YOU SERIOUS?
I'LL BECOME A HOLLOW IF THIS DISAPPEARS!?
OH.
YOU DIDN'T KNOW?
How awkward.
BUT DON'T WORRY, THERE IS A WAY TO SURVIVE AFTER YOUR CHAIN OF FATE HAS BEEN CUT.
BUT ONLY *ONE* WAY.
YOU MUST...

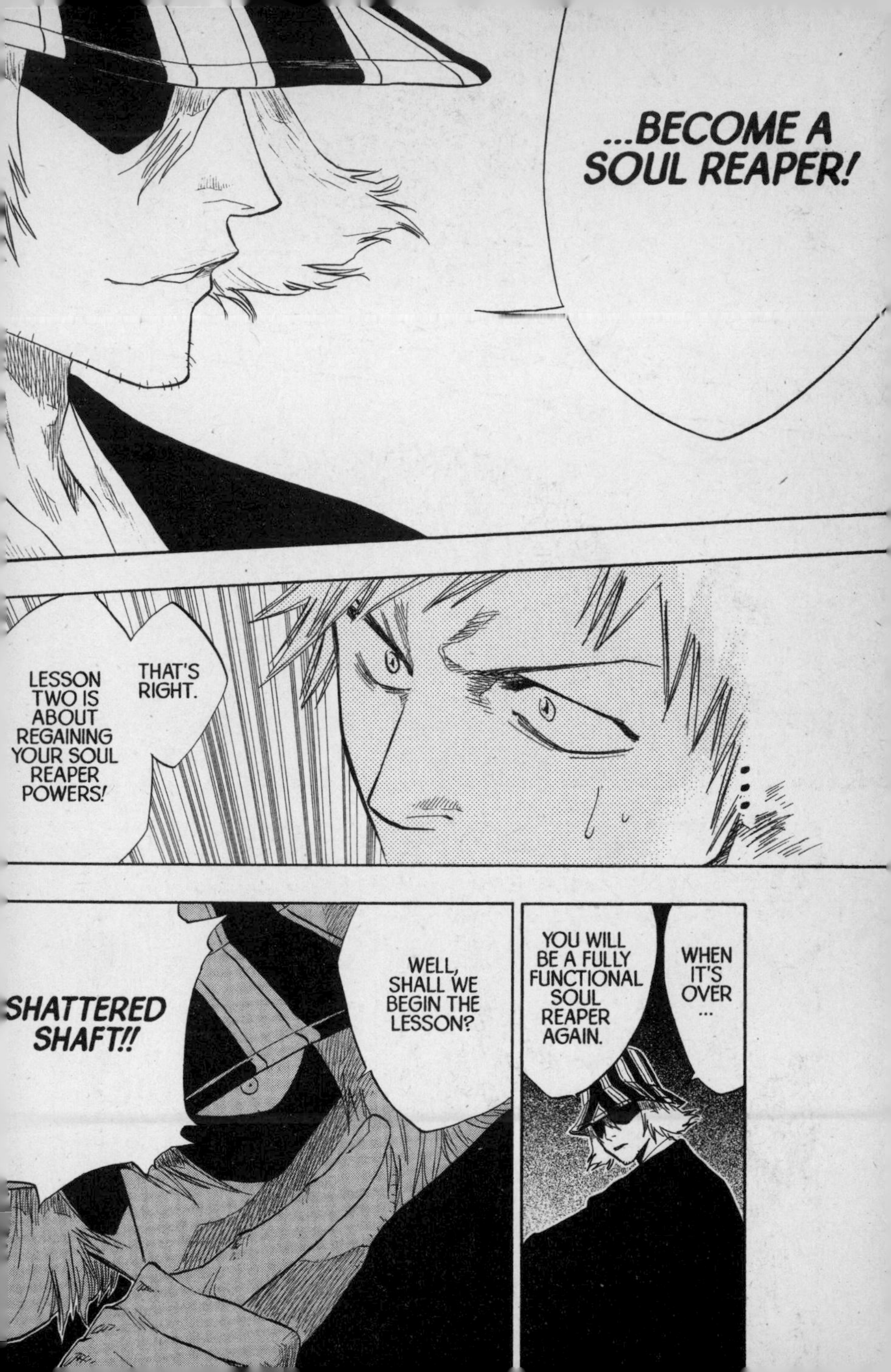
...BECOME A SOUL REAPER!
......
THAT'S RIGHT.
LESSON TWO IS ABOUT REGAINING YOUR SOUL REAPER POWERS!
WHEN IT'S OVER ...
YOU WILL BE A FULLY FUNCTIONAL SOUL REAPER AGAIN.
WELL, SHALL WE BEGIN THE LESSON?
SHATTERED SHAFT!!

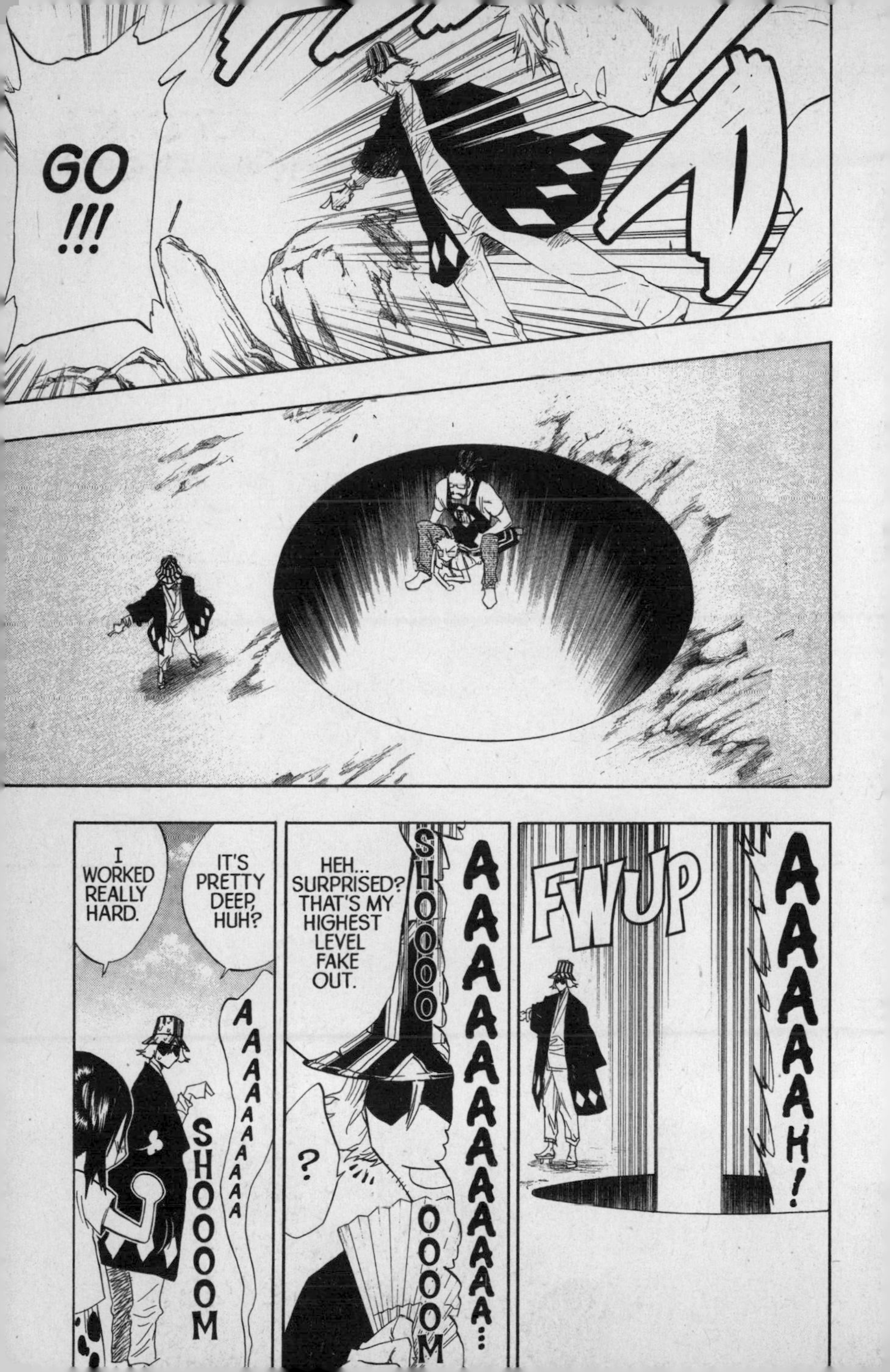
GO !!!
FWUP
AAAAAAAH!
AAAAAAAAAAAAA...
HEH... SURPRISED? THAT'S MY HIGHEST LEVEL FAKE OUT.
SHOOOO
?
OOOOM
IT'S PRETTY DEEP, HUH?
I WORKED REALLY HARD.
AAAAAAAAAAA
SHOOOOOM

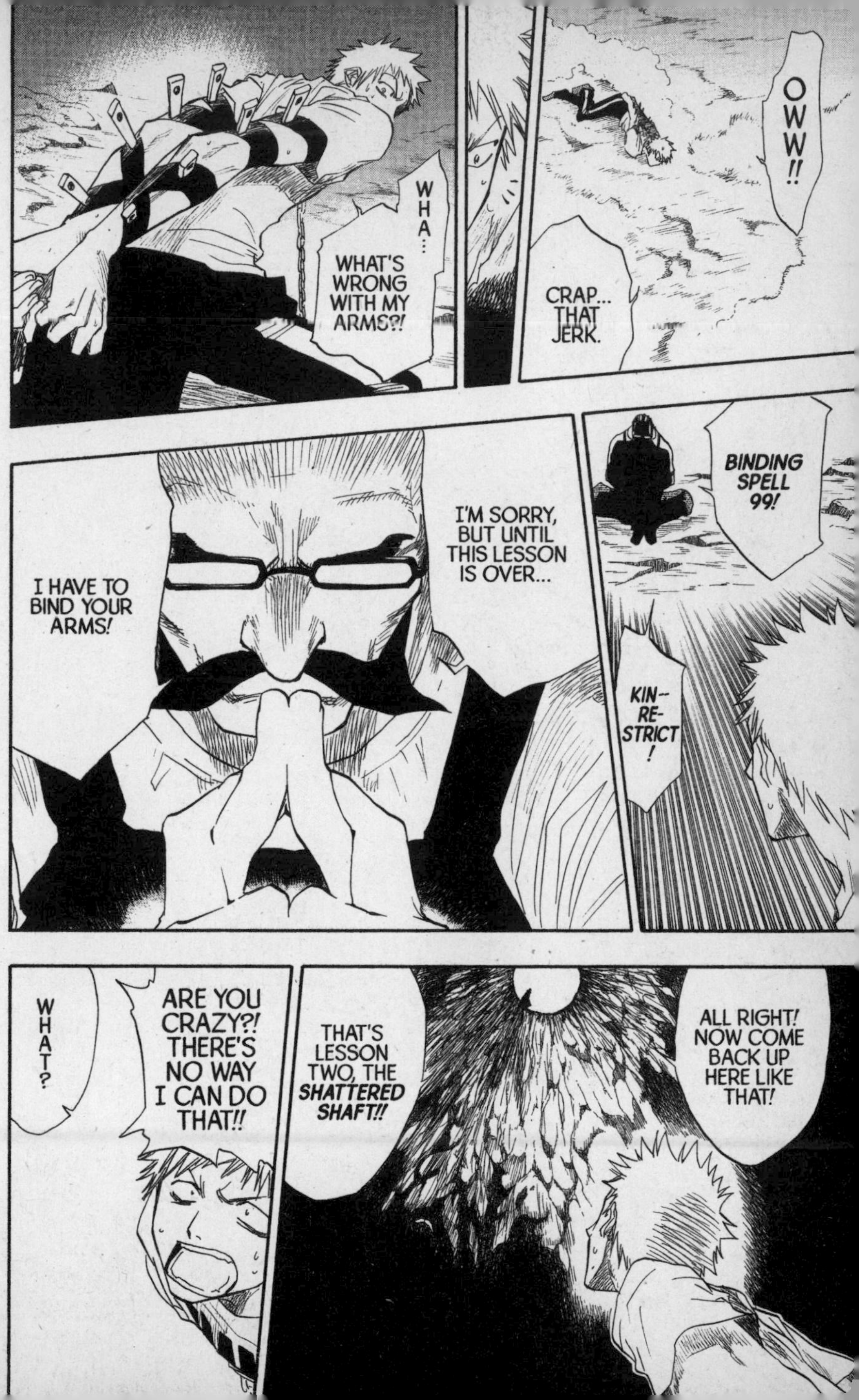
OWW!!
CRAP... THAT JERK.
WHA...
WHAT'S WRONG WITH MY ARMS?!
BINDING SPELL 99!
KIN-RE-STRICT!
I'M SORRY, BUT UNTIL THIS LESSON IS OVER...
I HAVE TO BIND YOUR ARMS!
ALL RIGHT! NOW COME BACK UP HERE LIKE THAT!
THAT'S LESSON TWO, THE SHATTERED SHAFT!!
WHAT?
ARE YOU CRAZY?! THERE'S NO WAY I CAN DO THAT!!

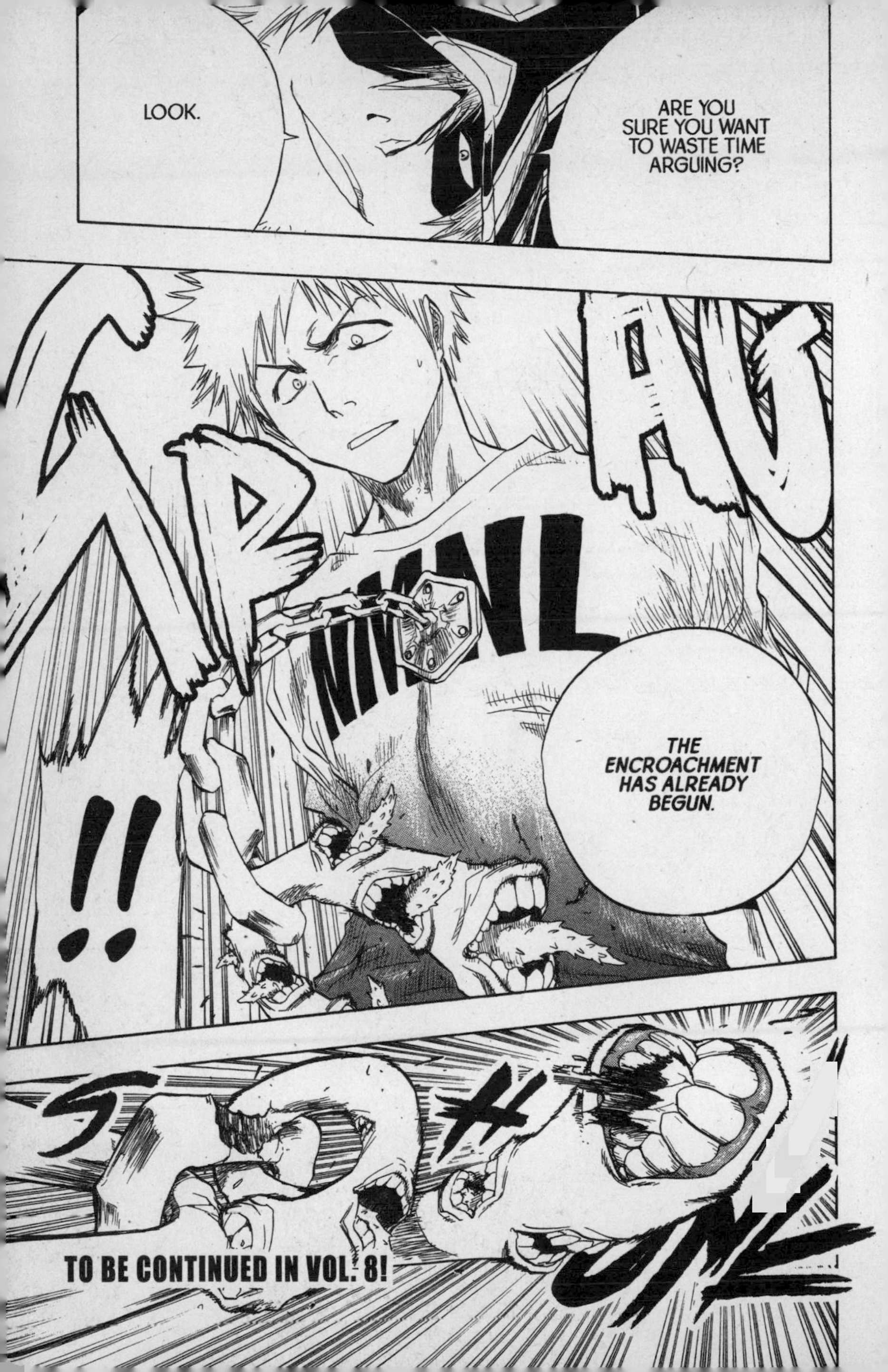
ARE YOU SURE YOU WANT TO WASTE TIME ARGUING?
LOOK.
THE ENCROACHMENT HAS ALREADY BEGUN.
!!
TO BE CONTINUED IN VOL. 8!

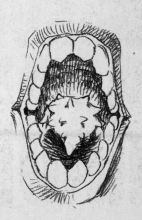

BLEACH EXTRA!!!
RADIO-KON

BLEACH EXTRA!!!
RADIO-KON2

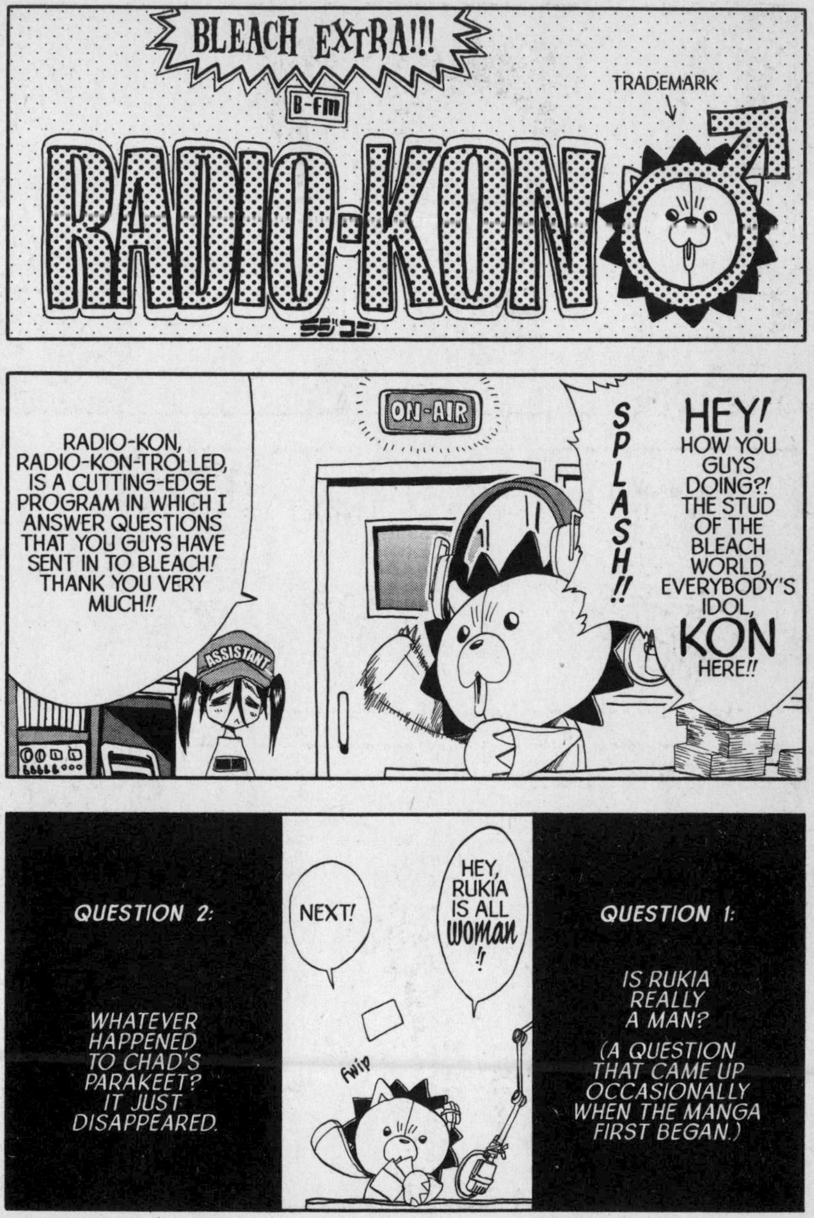
BLEACH EXTRA!!!
B-FM
RADIO-KON
ラジコン
TRADEMARK
ON-AIR
HEY! HOW YOU GUYS DOING?! THE STUD OF THE BLEACH WORLD, EVERYBODY'S IDOL, KON HERE!!
SPLASH!!
RADIO-KON, RADIO-KON-TROLLED, IS A CUTTING-EDGE PROGRAM IN WHICH I ANSWER QUESTIONS THAT YOU GUYS HAVE SENT IN TO BLEACH! THANK YOU VERY MUCH!!
ASSISTANT
QUESTION 1:
IS RUKIA REALLY A MAN?
(A QUESTION THAT CAME UP OCCASIONALLY WHEN THE MANGA FIRST BEGAN.)
HEY, RUKIA IS ALL WOMAN!!
NEXT!
FWIP
QUESTION 2:
WHATEVER HAPPENED TO CHAD'S PARAKEET? IT JUST DISAPPEARED.

READ THIS WAY

WHO'S CHAD?
Today's Topic Keanu Reeves's and Kevin Costner's similar auras.
Rustle rustle
SHIVER
I DON'T KNOW!!
DOOOM
SOUND OF TRAUMA
NEXT!!
AUTHOR'S ANSWER:
HE FLEW AWAY. THAT'S WHY CHAD IS SO GLUM. DON'T YOU FEEL SORRY FOR HIM? BY THE WAY, TO THE DAY HE FLEW THE COOP, HE NEVER LEARNED CHAD'S NAME.
QUESTION 3:
ARE YUZU AND KARIN TWINS?
YUZU?
Today's Topic Keanu Reeves's and Kevin Costner's similar auras.
Rustle rustle
ZING
↑ The throbbing of his old ear injury.

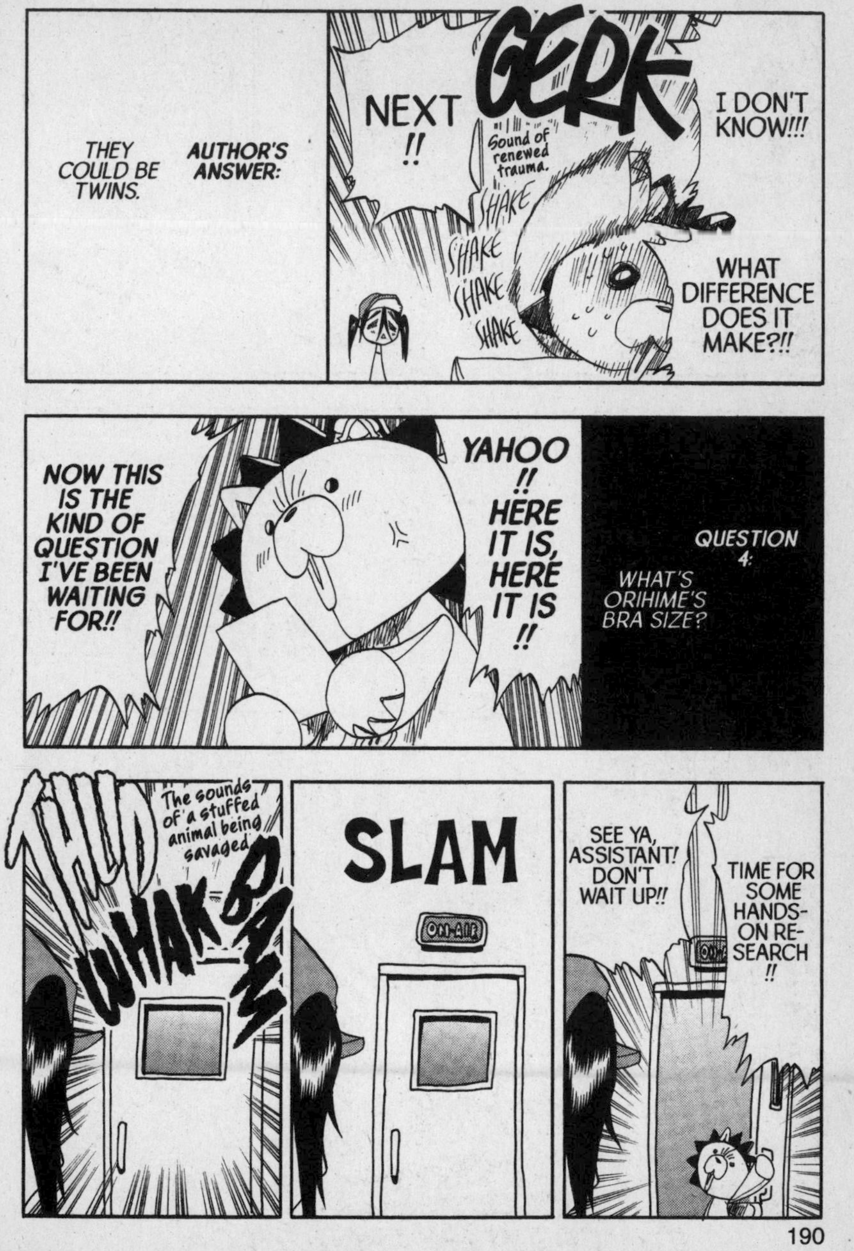
I DON'T KNOW!!!
WHAT DIFFERENCE DOES IT MAKE?!!
GERK
Sound of renewed trauma.
NEXT!!
SHAKE SHAKE SHAKE SHAKE
AUTHOR'S ANSWER:
THEY COULD BE TWINS.
QUESTION 4:
WHAT'S ORIHIME'S BRA SIZE?
YAHOO!! HERE IT IS, HERE IT IS!!
NOW THIS IS THE KIND OF QUESTION I'VE BEEN WAITING FOR!!
TIME FOR SOME HANDS-ON RE-SEARCH!!
SEE YA, ASSISTANT! DON'T WAIT UP!!
SLAM
ON-AIR
THUD
The sounds of a stuffed animal being savaged
WHAK
BAM

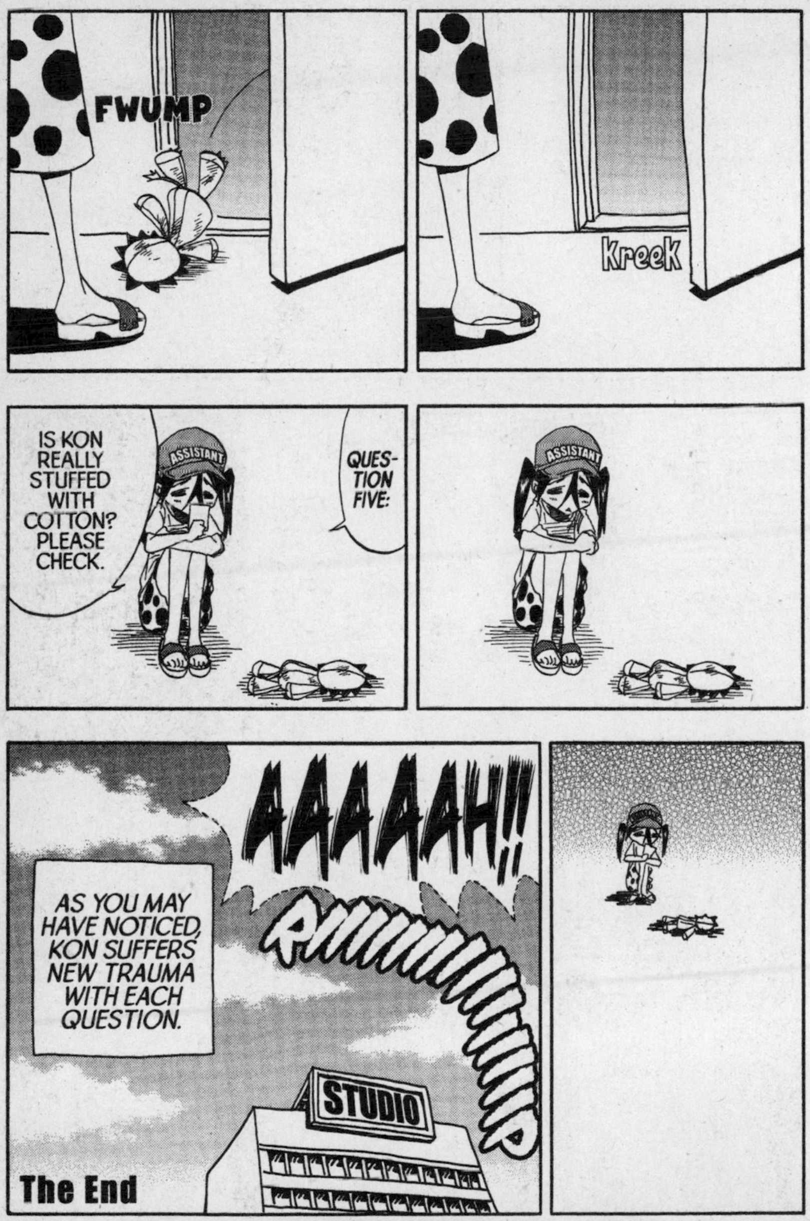
Kreek
FWUMP
QUES-TION FIVE:
IS KON REALLY STUFFED WITH COTTON? PLEASE CHECK.
AAAAAH!!
RIIIIIIIIIIIP
AS YOU MAY HAVE NOTICED, KON SUFFERS NEW TRAUMA WITH EACH QUESTION.
STUDIO
The End

BLEACH EXTRA!!! RADIO-KON

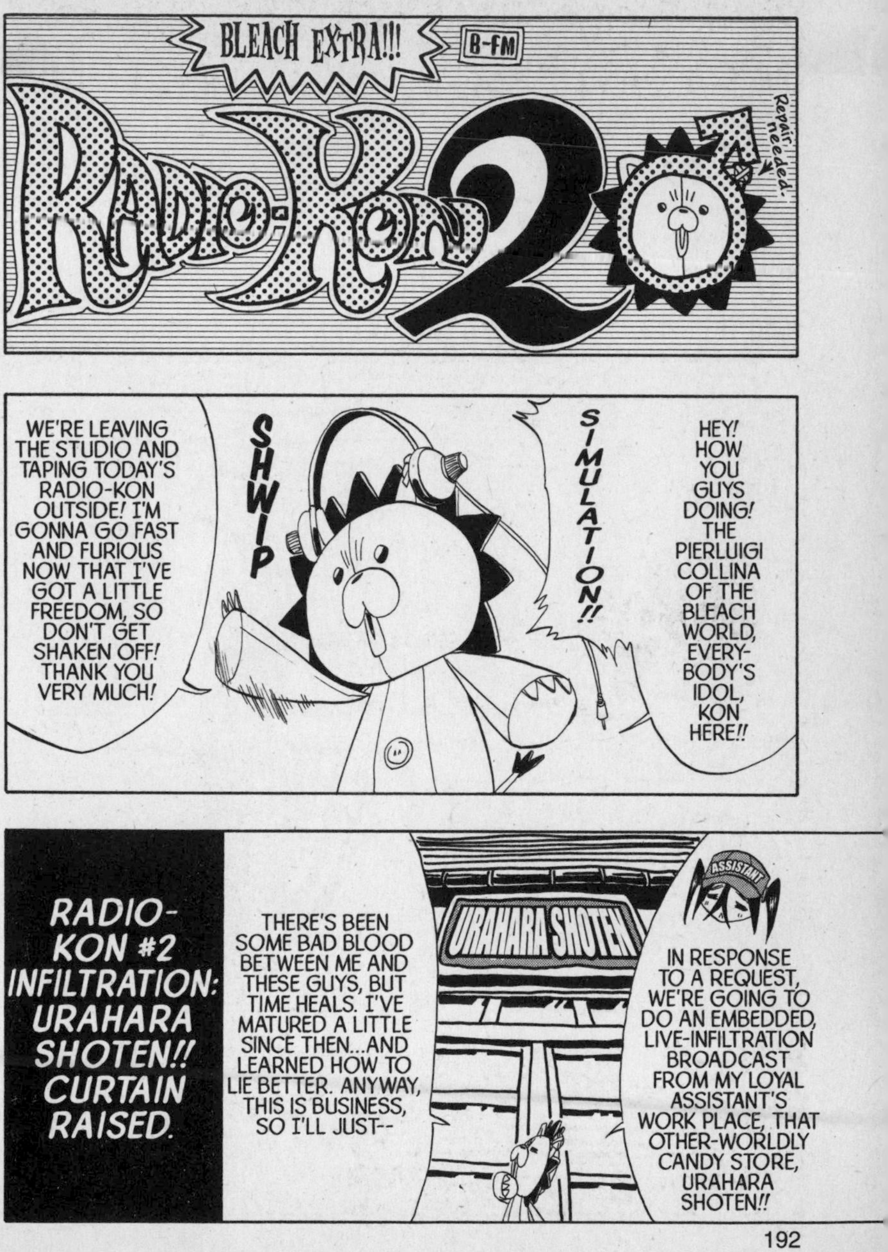
BLEACH EXTRA!!!
B-FM
RADIO-KON 2
Repair needed.
HEY! HOW YOU GUYS DOING! THE PIERLUIGI COLLINA OF THE BLEACH WORLD, EVERYBODY'S IDOL, KON HERE!!
SIMULATION!!
SHWIP
WE'RE LEAVING THE STUDIO AND TAPING TODAY'S RADIO-KON OUTSIDE! I'M GONNA GO FAST AND FURIOUS NOW THAT I'VE GOT A LITTLE FREEDOM, SO DON'T GET SHAKEN OFF! THANK YOU VERY MUCH!
ASSISTANT
IN RESPONSE TO A REQUEST, WE'RE GOING TO DO AN EMBEDDED, LIVE-INFILTRATION BROADCAST FROM MY LOYAL ASSISTANT'S WORK PLACE, THAT OTHER-WORLDLY CANDY STORE, URAHARA SHOTEN!!
URAHARA SHOTEN
THERE'S BEEN SOME BAD BLOOD BETWEEN ME AND THESE GUYS, BUT TIME HEALS. I'VE MATURED A LITTLE SINCE THEN...AND LEARNED HOW TO LIE BETTER. ANYWAY, THIS IS BUSINESS, SO I'LL JUST--
RADIO-KON #2 INFILTRATION: URAHARA SHOTEN!! CURTAIN RAISED.

Part 1: Tessai's Room

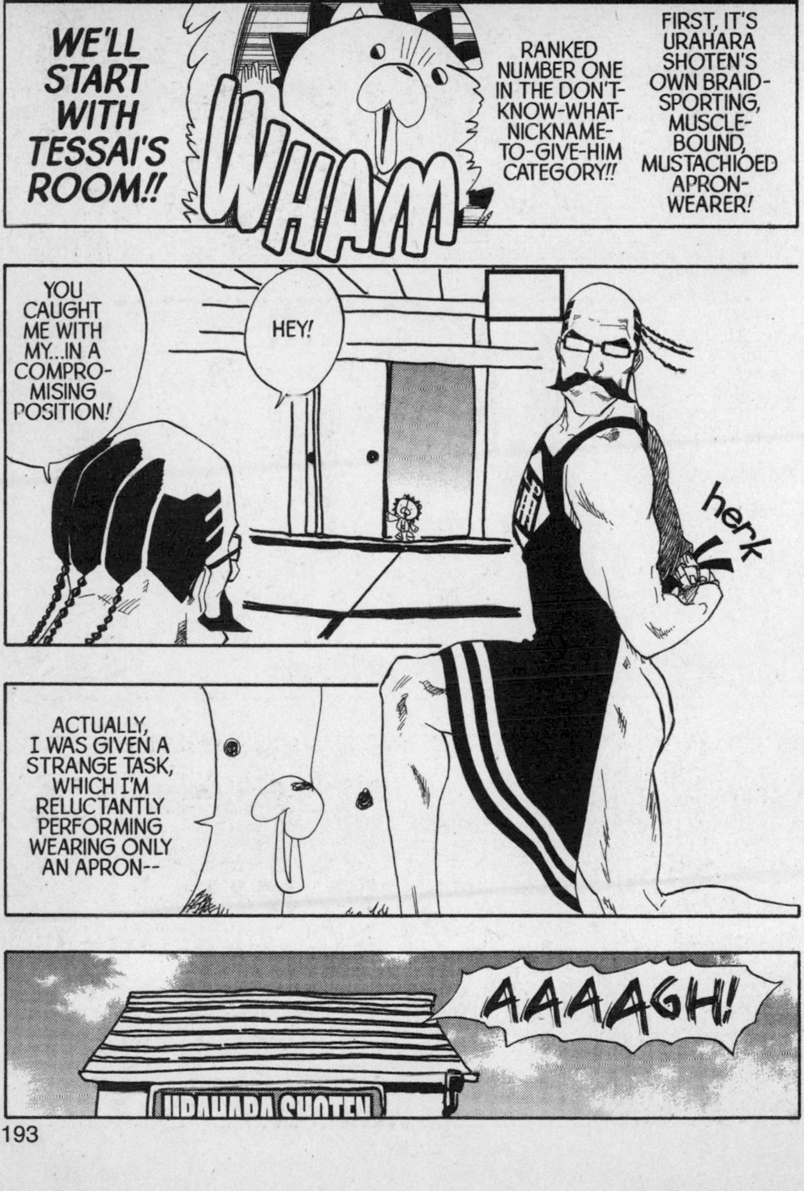
FIRST, IT'S URAHARA SHOTEN'S OWN BRAID-SPORTING, MUSCLE-BOUND, MUSTACHIOED APRON-WEARER!
RANKED NUMBER ONE IN THE DON'T-KNOW-WHAT-NICKNAME-TO-GIVE-HIM CATEGORY!!
WHAM
WE'LL START WITH TESSAI'S ROOM!!
HEY!
YOU CAUGHT ME WITH MY...IN A COMPROMISING POSITION!
herk
ACTUALLY, I WAS GIVEN A STRANGE TASK, WHICH I'M RELUCTANTLY PERFORMING WEARING ONLY AN APRON--
AAAAGH!

Part 2: Jinta and Ururu's Room

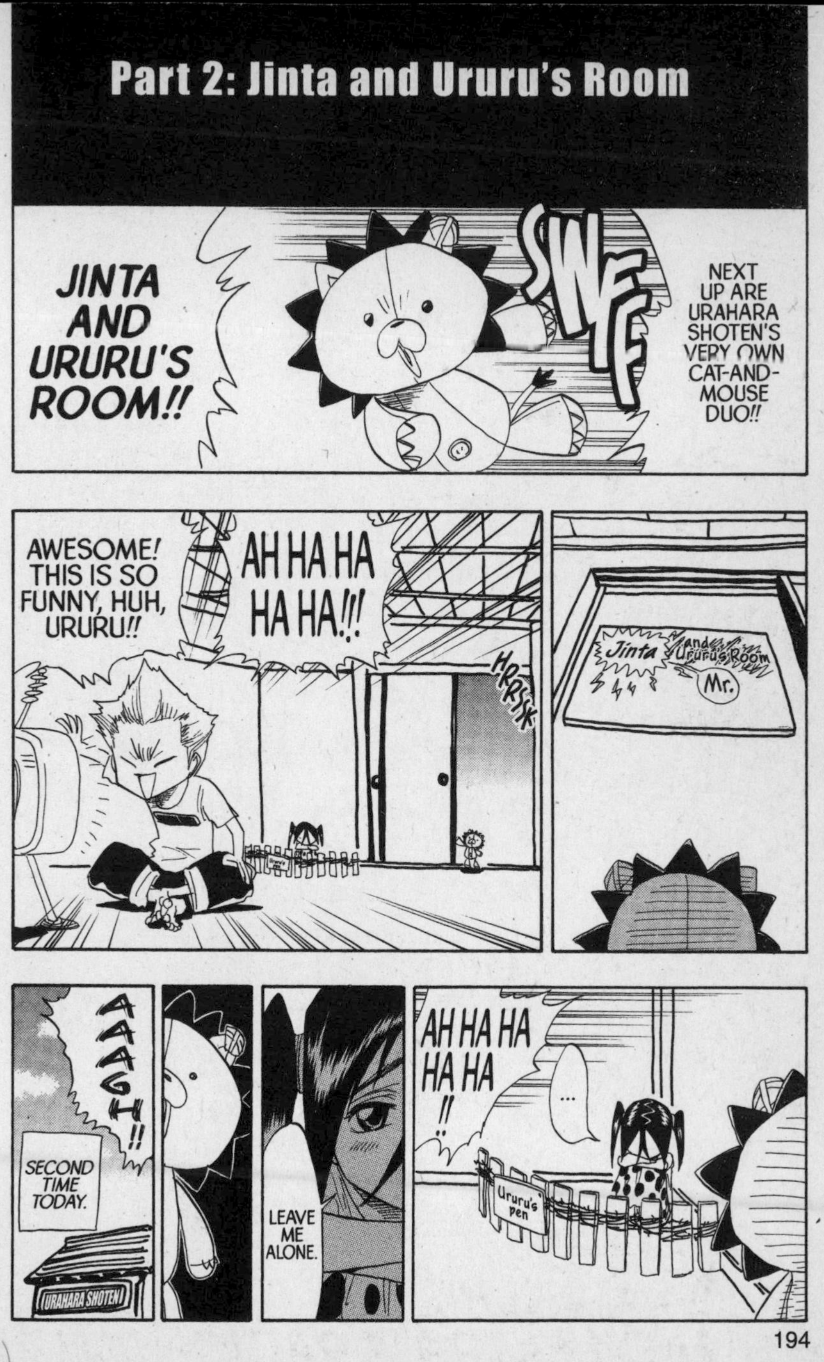
NEXT UP ARE URAHARA SHOTEN'S VERY OWN CAT-AND-MOUSE DUO!!
SNF
JINTA AND URURU'S ROOM!!
Jinta and Ururu's Room
Mr.
HRRSSK
AH HA HA HA HA!!!
AWESOME! THIS IS SO FUNNY, HUH, URURU!!
...
AH HA HA HA HA !!
Ururu's pen
LEAVE ME ALONE.
AAAAGH!!
SECOND TIME TODAY.
URAHARA SHOTEN

Part 3: Kisuke's Room

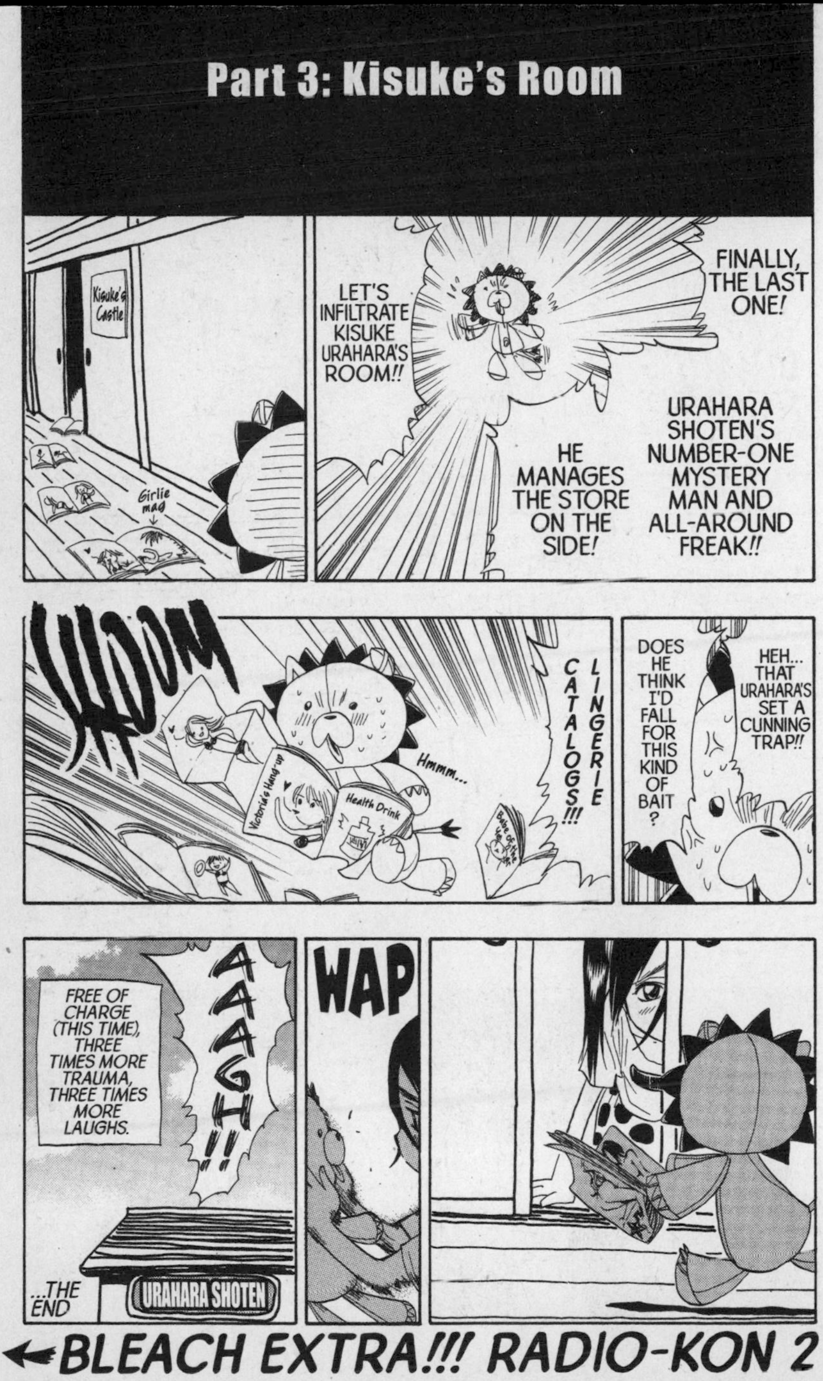
FINALLY, THE LAST ONE!
URAHARA SHOTEN'S NUMBER-ONE MYSTERY MAN AND ALL-AROUND FREAK!!
HE MANAGES THE STORE ON THE SIDE!
LET'S INFILTRATE KISUKE URAHARA'S ROOM!!
Kisuke's Castle
Girlie mag
HEH... THAT URAHARA'S SET A CUNNING TRAP!!
DOES HE THINK I'D FALL FOR THIS KIND OF BAIT?
LINGERIE CATALOGS!!!
Hmmm...
Health Drink
Victoria's Hang-up
WHOOM
WAP
AAAGH!!
FREE OF CHARGE (THIS TIME), THREE TIMES MORE TRAUMA, THREE TIMES MORE LAUGHS.
URAHARA SHOTEN
...THE END

← BLEACH EXTRA!!! RADIO-KON 2

ラジコンベイビー

RADIO-KON★BABY!!

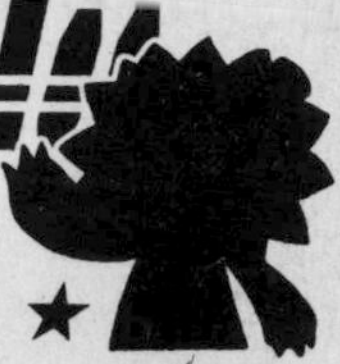

Opening theme:
"We are Radio-Kon Baby!!"

★7★

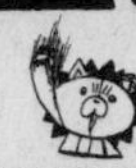

HEY! HOW YOU GUYS DOING? IT'S FINALLY HERE, A HEART-TO-HEART Q&A PROGRAM BETWEEN YOU GUYS AND ME! **RADIO-KON BABY!!** WE'VE BEEN DIGGING DEEP AND KEEPING IT UNREAL, SO CHECK IT OUT!!

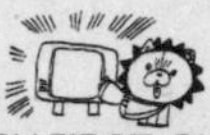

OUR VERY FIRST GUEST IS MY BEST GIRL RUKIA KUCHIKI!! DESPITE HER RECENT INCARCERATION, SHE'S STILL AGREED TO DO THE SHOW! WE'VE GOT A PRISON FEED DIRECT FROM THE SOUL SOCIETY'S SLAMMER!!

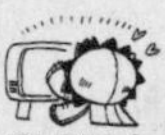

RUKIA! ♡ ♡

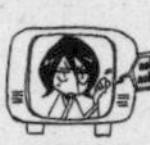

IS THIS FOR REAL?

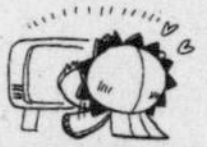

OF COURSE!! YOU LOOK RADIANT, AS ALWAYS, MY DEAR! ♡

WHAT IS THE SECRET TO YOUR BEAUTY!?

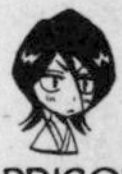

PRISON FOOD. THIS SHOW'S FOR READERS' QUESTIONS, RIGHT? LET'S GET ON WITH IT.

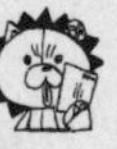

OF COURSE!! WELL THEN, NOW THAT THE MONITORS ARE SHOWING RUKIA, AND THE NEGATIVE IONS IN THE STUDIO HAVE DRASTICALLY INCREASED, LET ME READ THE MOST ASKED QUESTION OUT OF THE TONS OF LETTERS WE'VE RECEIVED!

Where does Rukia get her uniforms and civilian clothing? And while she's at the Kurosaki house, what does she do about bathing?

Naomi Kishino--Ishikawa, Japan

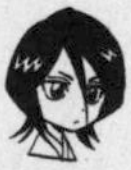

YOU REALLY WANT TO KNOW? FINE. FIRST OF ALL, THE UNIFORMS WERE ALL PROVIDED BY URAHARA. AS FOR MY CIVILIAN CLOTHING, AT FIRST I WAS BORROWING ICHIGO'S LITTLE SISTER YUZU'S, BUT ONE TIME...

...SHE CAUGHT ICHIGO GOING THROUGH HER DRESSER, AND...IT WAS AWKWARD. SINCE THEN, I'VE BEEN BORROWING OR BUYING FROM URAHARA ON CREDIT. AS FOR BATHS, AT FIRST I'D SNEAK ONE LATE AT NIGHT WHILE ICHIGO KEPT A LOOKOUT, BUT IT WAS TOO RISKY, SO AFTER ABOUT TWO WEEKS I STARTED GOING TO URAHARA'S TO BATHE.

THAT SEEMS EVEN RISKIER, TO ME, BUT...

Mr. Kubo, if you weren't a manga artist, what do you think you would be?

Ayaka Yokoyama--Chiba, Japan

WHO CARES?!!

HEY, THIS IS A QUESTION FOR TITE. WE CAN'T ANSWER IT. IF YOU HAVE A QUESTION FOR HIM, I'M SURE HE'LL BE INVITED AS A GUEST EVENTUALLY. SAVE IT UNTIL THEN.

NO WAY! I DON'T LIKE THAT GUY!! IF HE SHOWS UP, I'M OUTTA HERE! HE CAN DO THE SHOW BY HIMSELF!!

YOU'D BETTER WATCH IT. YOUR APPEARANCES MIGHT DECREASE IF YOU KEEP SAYING STUFF LIKE THAT...

Is Kon more of a Kyoko Fukada or Haruka Igawa fan?

Gunma--Everyday is Special

HARUKA IGAWA!!! BECAUSE HER SERVINGS ARE BIGGER!!

WHO? WHO ARE THESE PEOPLE?

I have a problem. I like someone, but we're in different classes so I just end up teasing her whenever I see her. What can I do so I won't tease her? Mr. Kon, please help me.

Hyogo--Baseball Player

HMMM... HERE IT IS. I THOUGHT NOBODY WOULD SEND A SERIOUS LOVE QUESTION TO A MANGA, BUT WE'VE GOT ONE.

ACTUALLY, THERE WERE A LOT OF OTHERS, BUT ALL OF THEM WERE SO SERIOUS AND HEAVY THAT I DIDN'T THINK RUKIA OR I COULD HANDLE THEM. IF ONLY I HAD A GUEST WHO WAS GOOD AT THIS KIND OF THING. OH, WELL. RUKIA! WHAT DO YOU THINK ABOUT THIS?

WELL, THERE WERE GUYS LIKE THAT WHEN I WAS IN SCHOOL, BOYS WHO'D PINCH ME OR SAY MEAN THINGS TO ME EVERY TIME I PASSED THEM IN THE HALL.

WHAT?! THE NERVE OF THOSE GUYS, TO TEASE MY RUKIA!!

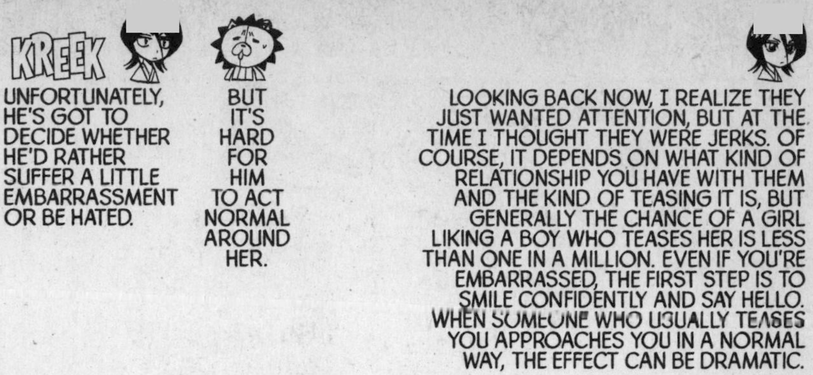

LOOKING BACK NOW, I REALIZE THEY JUST WANTED ATTENTION, BUT AT THE TIME I THOUGHT THEY WERE JERKS. OF COURSE, IT DEPENDS ON WHAT KIND OF RELATIONSHIP YOU HAVE WITH THEM AND THE KIND OF TEASING IT IS, BUT GENERALLY THE CHANCE OF A GIRL LIKING A BOY WHO TEASES HER IS LESS THAN ONE IN A MILLION. EVEN IF YOU'RE EMBARRASSED, THE FIRST STEP IS TO SMILE CONFIDENTLY AND SAY HELLO. WHEN SOMEONE WHO USUALLY TEASES YOU APPROACHES YOU IN A NORMAL WAY, THE EFFECT CAN BE DRAMATIC.
BUT IT'S HARD FOR HIM TO ACT NORMAL AROUND HER.
KREEK
UNFORTUNATELY, HE'S GOT TO DECIDE WHETHER HE'D RATHER SUFFER A LITTLE EMBARRASSMENT OR BE HATED.

RUKIA, I BROUGHT YOU SOME FOOD.
!!!
A CAMERA!? WHEN DID YOU SNEAK THAT THING IN HERE!?
WAIT! NO! IT'S NOT WHAT YOU THINK, RENJI!!
NOT WHAT I THINK?! I'LL BREAK THAT THING RIGHT NOW!!
RENJI, NO! STO--
R-RUKIA?! RUKIA!!
zap
Krash!!
krak
krak
krak

Accepting letters!! Any question is okay!!

We're accepting letters now!! And tell us which character you want the letters to be read by!! Our next guest will be Tatsuki Arisawa!! Include your question, name, address, age, and telephone number and send it all to the address below!

SHONEN JUMP c/o VIZ, LLC
P.O. Box 77010, San Francisco, CA 94107
ATTN: "Bleach" Radio-Kon Baby!!

Single: "Good night! Radio-Kon Baby!"

Ending theme music: SMAP "Lion Heart"

--Fade out...